This volume is published on behalf of the sponsors of a Conference on "Migration and Development" held in Paris in February 1987. The sponsors were:

OECD DEVELOPMENT CENTRE

COMMITTEE FOR INTERNATIONAL CO-OPERATION IN NATIONAL
RESEARCH IN DEMOGRAPHY

INTERGOVERNMENTAL COMMITTEE FOR MIGRATION

Also available

"Development Centre Studies"

TWO CRISES: LATIN AMERICA AND ASIA 1929-38 AND 1973-83 by Angus Maddison (1985)
(41 85 03 1) ISBN 92-64-12771-2   106 pages   £7.00   US$14.00   FF70.00   DM31.00

DEVELOPING COUNTRY DEBT: THE BUDGETARY AND TRANSFER PROBLEM by Helmut Reisen and Axel Van Trotsenburg (1988)
(41 88 01 1) ISBN 92-64-13053-5   196 pages   £14.00   US$26.40   FF120.00   DM52.00

"Development Centre Seminars"

DEVELOPMENT POLICIES AND THE CRISIS OF THE 1980s edited by L. Emmerij (1987)
(41 87 03 1) ISBN 92-64-12992-8   178 pages   £11.00   US$23.00   FF110.00   DM47.00

Prices charged at the OECD Bookshop

*THE OECD CATALOGUE OF PUBLICATIONS and supplements will be sent free of charge
on request addressed either to OECD Publications Service,
2, rue André-Pascal, 75775 PARIS CEDEX 16, or to the OECD Distributor in your country.*

TABLE OF CONTENTS

Part I

THEORY, MEASUREMENT AND POLICIES

Part II

TYPES OF MIGRATION

A. TEMPORARY

6

Part III

GENERAL AND OVERVIEWS

Temporay → Permanent

Trend Towards Temp Skilled

Labour

Acknowledgements

This project would not have been brought to completion without the strong and continuing support of many persons in CICRED, ICM and the OECD Development Centre. I am especially grateful to Christine Johnson of OECD who typed so accurately the final draft. The University of Western Australia has provided ongoing administrative and clerical support and special thanks are due to Caroline Baird, Jane Cozens and Sue Larcombe of the University's Department of Economics. Bill Highes of Westwools and George Schaffer of Calsil Ltd., provided generous financial support for the initiating meeting held in Perth during 1980. The final editing was done while I was Fellow-in-Residence at the Netherlands Institue for Advanced Study in the Humanities and Social Sciences.

R.A.   March 1988

PREFACE

This volume contains twenty-three papers contributed to a project sponsored jointly by the three international organisations undersigned -- the Committee for International Co-operation in National Research in Demography (CICRED), the Intergovernmental Committee for Migration (ICM) and the Development Centre of the Organisation for Economic Co-operation and Development (OECD). The general co-ordinatorship was assumed by Professor Reginald Appleyard of the University of Western Australia at Nedlands, Australia.

Three international research meetings led to the results of the project presented here. An initiating meeting was held in Perth, Australia, in 1980 following a decision taken by the CICRED Executive Council in 1977 to select international migration as the subject of one of four major co-operative research projects aimed at strengthening collaboration between demographic research centres the world over. The meeting emphasized the increasingly significant role being played by international migration in developing countries while at the same time noting a marked deficit in research in this field. It consequently supported the choice of "Impact of international migration upon developing countries" as the subject of an international research project. The following four topics were identified as priority areas for investigation: clandestine migration, transient professionals, transient workers, return migration.

A second meeting took place in 1984 at ICM Headquarters in Geneva. Its purpose was to discuss progress with research carried out by the participating demographic centres and international organisations and to decide how their findings could be best integrated into a publication. The meeting concluded with the adoption of a detailed research plan proposed by the project co-ordinator. This plan is reflected almost unchanged in the table of contents of the present volume although several new topics were added to the initial research plan approved in Perth, in particular theoretical issues, typology, aspects of measurement, policies, permanent migration and refugees. The proceedings of the meeting and the summaries of the research reports were published by ICM in 1985 as a booklet.

Early in 1987, a third project meeting took place at the OECD Development Centre in Paris. Its purpose was to discuss the papers contributed as a result of research carried out by the participating institutes and organisations and to formulate recommendations to authors in drafting the final text of their manuscripts.

The three sponsoring agencies are pleased that thanks to the joint efforts of CICRED, its affiliated demographic centres, ICM and the OECD

9

Development Centre, this compilation of research papers analysing the impact of migration upon developing countries has become available. Scholars from both developing and developed countries representing different scientific disciplines have contributed to the project. We hope that the project's results will stimulate further research on international migration in the developing countries. We also express the hope that decision-makers in governments and international organisations will bear in mind the manifold facets and effects of international migration in and upon developing countries discussed in this volume.

We sincerely thank all contributors to this volume for their research work. Our particular gratitude is of course for Professor Reginald Appleyard, the project's co-ordinator, for the innumerable efforts he undertook to bear during almost ten years the responsibility for this international and interdisciplinary project and for conducting it successfully to its final stage.

Mr. Louis Emmerij
President, OECD Development Centre

Mr. Jean Bourgeois-Pichat
President, Committee for International
Co-operation in National Research in
Demography (CICRED), Paris

Mr. James L. Carlin
Director General, Intergovernmental
Committee for Migration (ICM), Geneva

March 1988

INTRODUCTION

by

Reginald Appleyard

At the initiating meeting of the CICRED-sponsored project on inter-national migration held at Perth during 1980, participants identified two major difficulties that had hampered understanding of the impact of inter-national migration on developing countries: dearth of both information on stocks and flows and of an appropriate migration typology. Better data was unlikely to be obtained quickly or easily, for this would depend mainly upon governments, but there was no reason why the participants themselves could not construct an appropriate typology. Much of the debate at the Perth meet-ing was therefore directed towards constructing a framework that would facilitate explanation of the impact of specific types of international migration on developing countries.

A survey conducted prior to the Perth meeting among 320 demographic research centres affiliated with CICRED had also revealed a dearth of research on, and general interest in, international migration despite a United Nations report in 1975 having shown that more governments were interested in affecting trends in emigration and immigration than in affect-ing trends in fertility and population growth (Tabbarah, 1978). Of the 150 centres which responded to CICRED's survey, only 55 reported having done research or published papers on international migration. Furthermore, most of this research had been done outside formal population centres, particu-larly in universities where the facilities and personnel necessary to under-take multidisciplinary research were more readily available.

Having devised what they deemed was an appropriate typology for assessing impacts of migration on developing countries, participants at the Perth meeting then agreed that every effort should also be made to encourage issue-oriented research relating to the impacts of clandestine, contract labour, professional transient and return migration. One participant after another argued that these types of migration appeared to be very influential in determining processes of socio-economic change. A range of topics was therefore proposed by participants and later sent to CICRED's affiliated centres for comment and expressions of interest. Response was excellent; 42 centres indicated interest in, or willingness to conduct, research on the topics proposed. In October 1982 each centre was informed of the research interests of other centres and asked to make contact with those centres working on the same or kindred topics. Then in June 1984 CICRED and ICM jointly organised a meeting in Geneva of researchers and representatives of some UN specialised agencies to discuss progress and plans for the publication of findings. The final meeting was held in 1987 at the OECD Development Centre in Paris where the papers which comprise the present volume were delivered and discussed.

In his summary of proceedings at the 1984 Geneva meeting, Leon Tabah declared that participants had been well and truly reminded of the complexity of the determinants and consequences of international migration compared with other branches of demography. Furthermore, the classification sending or receiving country, which for decades had been a basic dichotomy used by migration scholars, was clearly inadequate to unravel the complexity of migration flows and types currently affecting developing countries. As the report of the Geneva meeting concluded,

> A developing country can be both a provider of semi-skilled workers (but not their dependents) to the Middle East and of permanent professional workers to the United States [the brain drain]; and a receiver of refugees on a "country of first asylum" basis, of professional transients to assist in the construction and operation of a factory owned by a multinational corporation, of former workers to the Middle East whose contracts had expired, and of professionally skilled nationals who had left a decade ago as part of the brain drain (Appleyard, 1985).

In addition to the demographic effects of such diverse flows on both sending and receiving countries, compositions cause socio-economic impacts through remittance payments, skill transfers, training of replacement workers, education of children during the migrant father's absence and family decision-making.

Papers comprising the present volume address the magnitude and complexity of these and other socio-economic impacts of international migration on developing countries. As already noted, contributors agreed from the outset that these impacts could be most effectively assessed in the first instance by isolating and attempting to measure the distinctive influences of each type of migration. However, participants also recognised that while the typology they had devised was appropriate for identifying impacts of specific types of migration, measurement of the aggregate impact of all types of migration during a specific period would require a great deal more analysis. The measurement of longer-term aggregative impacts, especially the specific and changing influences of different types of migration in the evolution of societies, posed even greater challenges for researchers.

Domenach touched on one of these aspects when he questioned whether the permanent deterioration of conditions necessary for social or family renewal, due in large measure to fluctuating job opportunities, explains why in some developing countries migration never ends; and why a strong trend towards "professional nomadism" has emerged in many developed countries. Federici, who for many years has been arguing that type and direction of international migration is linked to the evolution of a country's economic structure, addressed similar issues when she noted the remarkable changes in type, composition and direction of migration to and from Italy during the last one hundred, and especially in the last fifty, years. Although two world wars and the rise of fascism had created distortions in currents of migration, after

12

the 1950s flows were determined by a combination of political constraints imposed by receiving governments and by Italy's own economic growth which had led to the influx of foreign workers from developing countries with high rates of population growth and low rates of economic development. Despite high unemployment in Italy, she showed that present demand for migrant workers can be explained mainly by structural and technological change.

While few scholars would disagree with the proposition that the governments of receiving countries utilise immigration to facilitate their objectives for economic growth, there has been a tendency to ignore the influence of governments in determining volume and composition of emigration. A timely reminder of this neglect is given by Seccombe and Lawless in their review of the labour emigration policies of Arab countries. Arguing that migration scholars have tended to treat emigration policy almost as a postscript, they show that several Arab non-oil producing countries have taken active steps to increase the numbers of their nationals working abroad, especially in nearby Arab oil-producing countries. Such objectives had been facilitated during the early 1980s by Qatar and United Arab Emirates whose governments argued that Arab and Islamic identity was being threatened by the fact that two-thirds of their immigrant workers were Asians. Algeria also included emigration in its overall strategy of development; it became a "vital mechanism to reduce unemployment and underemployment" and emigrants were selected on the basis of Algeria's, not the receiving country's, perceived development needs. Jordan too has adopted a strategy of training manpower for emigration, having identified the explicit link between education and fulfilment of demand for skilled workers abroad.

Although attempts by governments of developing countries in other regions to control labour emigration have been less successful than those cited above, most governments exercise some control over the content and application of clauses in labour contracts between their nationals and employers in receiving countries. This point is made by Huguet in his paper on the ESCAP region. Recent changes in the skill composition of contract labour migrants have created many problems for sending countries. With the passing of the "construction phase" in the Middle East, skill composition of workers from Asian countries has moved towards professional and service occupations. Premature return of construction workers has therefore created an array of unforeseen difficulties relating to their reinsertion in the work-forces. His call for more research on socio-economic impacts of return migration, including the role of counselling services in reintegration and the utilisation of returnees' savings, is therefore timely. Seccombe and Lawless are also concerned that none of the Arab sending countries has drawn up contingency plans to cope with the impending return and reintegration of thousands of their workers abroad.

Recent increases in clandestine migration have, as Lohrman shows, become a major issue in both sending and receiving countries. It appears to occur more spontaneously in Africa and Latin America than in Asia where border controls are more effective. In Latin America it is the dominant form of migration; in Africa it is facilitated by both income differentials and "unrealistic borders" and in many cases is simply an extension of internal migration, although major expulsions of alien ethnic groups since the mid-1960s have highlighted volatile political situations created by previously unpoliced inflows. Lohrman predicts not only that illegal migration will remain an issue of growing controversy in developing countries but that pressure on developed countries to admit more migrants from developing countries will increase. Experts at a recent OECD conference on the Future of Migration identified illegal flows from developing countries as a potential "major socio-economic problem" (OECD, 1987).

The paper by Salt and Findlay emphasizes the important role being played by professional transients in developing countries. The modern global economy, they argue, functions through the movement of a highly-skilled elite which is responsible for the transfer of knowledge from one part of the system to another. Large transnational corporations with internal labour markets have created new patterns of international migration which, though difficult to incorporate into formal migration models based on real income differentials, nonetheless fit comfortably in the economic evolution approaches suggested by other contributors. Explanation of specific flows, argue Salt and Findlay, must be sought in the hierarchical structure of transnational corporations. Their description of the activities of corporations, especially their labour recruitment policies, not only raises fundamental issues concerning determinants of migration, but also shows that the corporate labour market has increasingly substituted business travel (a "type" of migration almost ignored by scholars) for longer-term migration.

Salt and Findlay's assessment of the contributions made by professional transients to the infrastructure and industrial development of many developing countries is judiciously balanced by judgement on the transients' roles as agents of socio-economic change. The stronger the cultural and political contrasts, they argue, the greater the tendency for transients to become a highly-segregated community. Modern transients do not represent a national ideology; they represent corporations "whose economic and political interests seldom coincide with any one state". The small numbers of transients relative to other types of migrants belies their economic, social and political importance, leading the authors to conclude that although great forces are at work very little is known of their strength and direction. The paper by Price on the number and activities of Australian transients emphasizes the importance of their contributions to economic and social change of developing countries in the Pacific region.

As would be expected, contributions concerning permanent migration to and from developing countries have focussed on the brain drain, one of the most polemic migration issues since World War II. Mundende is of the view that its net impact on developing countries has been negative, causing perpetual postponement of major development efforts and dependence on expatriates. He disagrees strongly with the view that its negative consequences have been compensated by remittances. The magnitude of brain drain from developing countries, as well as persistent attempts by sending countries to obtain compensation, is carefully tabulated in the paper by d'Oliveira e Sousa. Between 1971 and 1983 an estimated 700 000 scientists and other highly-skilled persons moved from Third World to First World countries. The "great challenge", he concludes, is still to find "appropriate solutions", especially regarding compensation, for sending countries.

Two of the three papers on refugees appropriately focus on Africa where reside over six million, or over half the world's refugees. The complex relationship between political, ecological and climatic factors, the special vulnerability of women and the fact that Africa's refugees are drawn from one of the poorest regions in the world and seek asylum in equally poor countries in the same region, has been carefully and sympathetically explored by Adepoju and Khasiani. Both refrain from offering simple solutions, although Adepoju's observation that assistance with sustained economic development would arrest the factors that generate refugees and increase the capacity of countries to absorb them, is as sound as Khasiani's claim that the problem of refugees is superimposed on other development problems.

As already noted, participants at the Perth meeting in 1980 believed that return migration was a type that posed many new and important problems for developing countries. Their judgement has been vindicated by the findings of papers in the final section of this volume. Though Huguet had already called for more research on socio-economic impacts of return to developing countries in Asia, and Seccombe and Lawless had warned that Arab sending countries should draw up contingency plans to cope with the return and re-integration of thousands of contract workers from Arab oil-producing countries, the papers in the section on return migration deal with specific situations.

For example, Perez-Itriago and Guendelman reported research on the integration of seasonal workers who travel back and forth between Mexico and the United States. In recent years, economic disparities and established networks have maintained migration flows that have increasingly involved women. The persistence of seasonal flows, they argue, suggest that, once initiated, migration streams take a life of their own, a proposition that is then carefully explored through a two-village, longitudinal study. Though the female migrants' reasons for going were primarily economic, their reasons for return were primarily homesickness and intention to build a house with savings accumulated in the United States. Changes in work environment induced marked changes in the way spouses related to each other. If they had emigrated and returned together, females experienced significant role shifts. For example, working together in the same vegetable field (in the United States) drew them closer together and bridged the traditional gender distance, but this re-lationship changed markedly on return to the village. "Rather than turning to each other, they sought same sex peers for support and validation". However, it was the women's powerful role models on return that led other village women to see migration as a way out of poverty.

The paper by Thomas-Hope and Nutter on return migration to the Caribbean emphasized the role of education in the long-term strategy of many migrants. Capital acquired and occupational change achieved through emigration certainly improved personal circumstances but it was rarely suf-ficient to improve class status. This was done through education acquired abroad. The authors report cases of children being taken abroad with their parents, or sent for later on, in order to acquire education which later became the medium for inter-generational advancement. Achievements of this kind strengthen the ideology of emigration for education and hence upward social mobility.

Condé's paper explores broader aspects of the return phenomenon: encouragement given by some European governments to migrants to return home. Some governments have offered attractive financial incentives; others have provided facilities for teaching migrant children in their own tongue so that they maintain a cultural link with the home country which assists their re-integration on return. Condé also notes that the high dependence of some sending countries on remittances from workers abroad makes them disinclined to co-operate in special resettlement projects unless adequately compensated. Other governments give priority to establishing industrial complexes in areas that have been affected by large-scale emigration, thus creating jobs for returnees.

The points noted in this Introduction simply illustrate the many diverse and important issues raised by contributors. Collectively, the papers confirm the magnitude and complexity of impacts already identified by other scholars, and offer new insights into the relationship between specific types of migration as well as the overall impact of international migration on processes of socio-economic change in developing countries.

BIBLIOGRAPHY

APPLEYARD, Reginald
Report of General Co-ordinator, CICRED and ICM, Inter-centre Cooperative Research, International Migration in the Third World, Paris and Geneva, 1985.

OECD
The Future of Migration, Paris, OECD, 1987.

TABBARAH, Riad
"International Migration: Issues and Policies", Migration Today -- an abbreviated version of a paper presented at the Ninth World Congress of Sociology, Uppsala, Sweden, August 1978.

Part I

THEORY, MEASUREMENT AND POLICIES

Chapter 1

INTERNATIONAL MIGRATION AND DEVELOPING COUNTRIES

by

Reginald Appleyard

There is a general consensus amongst scholars of international migration that their subject has not only been one of the most neglected in the field of population studies, but that recent changes in the flow and direction of international migration are so significant as to have made the subject a new field of inquiry. To many persons, the term "international migration" is synonymous with the flow of over 60 million Europeans to the New World during the 19th and early 20th centuries. And while the traditional receiving countries still admit several hundred thousand immigrants per year for permanent settlement, this is small relative to the total non-tourist flow of people between countries. The estimated 20 million contract workers living outside their homelands, the millions of refugees, the hundreds of thousands of transient professional workers and the unknown numbers (but clearly millions) of illegal workers, have added new dimensions and importance to the study of international migration.

One of these dimensions is the central and relatively recent involvement of persons from developing countries. Aside from the fact that they now comprise the majority of permanent immigrants to the traditional receiving countries, persons from developing countries also dominate the flows of other types of migration. Impacts of these movements (especially of remittances from hard-currency areas and the acquisition of skills and experience by contract workers) have clearly influenced economic growth and socio-economic change in many developing countries. By and large, the flows are of such recent origin that scholars have not had the time to study and measure their impacts. Thus the evidence and data presented in this chapter are both desultory and inadequate relative to the importance of the subject.

Definitions and Measurement

Assessment of the impact of "international migration" on "developing countries" first requires delineation and explanation of each concept. Official statistics of international migration are usually delineated on the basis of the mover's intention for either permanent or temporary stay. Legal permanent migration includes persons granted permission to settle in a country because of their characteristics, as well as refugees admitted under international or bilateral arrangements, including persons living in countries of asylum (e.g., Vietnamese refugees in Thailand selected for settlement by the United States Government). Very few developing countries nowadays accept large numbers of permanent immigrants. The main receiving countries are the United States, Canada, Australia and New Zealand. Legal temporary migration includes contract or guest-workers as well as professional transients who obtain employment or are sent by their employers to other countries or on private contracts. The contracts are usually for finite periods, at the end of which the temporary migrants are expected to return home or negotiate new finite contracts.

Official estimates of each type of legal migration indicate the number of movers at the times the moves are made. But being based on intention, accuracy ex post will be affected by "category jumpers", i.e., persons who later change their minds; for example, an intending settler who returns home soon after reaching his destination, or a contract worker who meets and marries a local girl and is granted residence status. Furthermore, many countries do not publish the statistics necessary to accurately assess stocks and flows of migrants; other countries do not accord as much attention to statistics on departures as they do to statistics on arrivals. While permanent and temporary immigrants are required to obtain formal entry permits, tourists, whose numbers run into tens of millions per annum, are not. Indeed, there has been a tendency in recent years for many countries to provide statistics only on net flows of persons across their borders.

Despite these difficulties, the major problems concerning accurate measurement of international migration relate to flows which governments have not been able to adequately control. These include clandestine migration -- persons who cross borders illegally or persons who were admitted for temporary stays (including tourists) but did not leave -- and refugees who cross neighbouring borders to avoid political oppression. As will be shown, these types of migration are nowadays not only counted in millions per annum but have occurred increasingly between developing countries.

Definition and identification of a developing country poses an equal if not greater array of problems, relating mainly to ranking on the basis of accepted criteria. GNP per capita has long been regarded as an appropriate index of development status. While generally accepted as useful for identifying relative status, especially of countries at each end of the table, the index is less useful for identifying the relative status of countries in the middle ranges. Indeed, without consideration of other key indices, relative classification could be meaningless, especially of countries experiencing high rates of economic growth and moving up the table. Nor is there any accepted barrier through which a country must break to achieve developed status.

International Migration and the Development Process in Developing Countries

A well-known phenomenon in the evolution of migratory flows is their constant transformation linked to the evolution of a country's economic structure. The migration policies of both sending and receiving countries, as well as the volume, direction and composition of flows, largely reflect a country's stage and rate of socio-economic development (Appleyard, 1984).

Although the development process depends upon a complex of socio-economic variables -- population density, resources, infrastructure, capital formation, trade, political stability, skill level, work ethic, etc. -- a country's immigration (and perhaps its emigration) policy will normally be determined by its stage and rate of economic development. Governments of countries at the lower end of the development ladder typically restrict entry for permanent settlement to a few dependents of residents, or persons possessing outstanding skills. They do not seek population through immigration. On the other hand, they generally do not prevent their professional and highly-skilled nationals from emigrating to countries at the upper end of the development spectrum (the so-called brain drain). Many developing countries which possess resources required by other countries (including ample supplies of relatively cheap labour) encourage foreign investors to utilise local labour to exploit resources or establish manufacturing and infrastructure, and also allow the investors to bring foreign professional and highly-skilled workers to supervise construction operations, although the basis of their stay is almost always short-term and finite.

If, as a result of these and other policies, economic growth is increased, as in the case of the so-called NICs (newly industrialising countries), to a stage where demand for professional and highly-skilled workers on a permanent basis is reached, the country may be able to attract home some of its nationals who left as brain drain emigrants during an earlier stage of economic development. Concurrently, the government may also make arrangements with governments of nearby countries at lower stages of economic development to provide contract labour on a short-term basis. Its provision may, in turn, stimulate the sending country's economic growth through remittance payments and, in due course, through the return home of workers with newly-acquired skills. A great deal of migration of these types is occurring between countries at different levels of economic development and rates of economic growth within a specific region, especially the ESCAP region. The more developed countries in this region provide professional transients and receive unskilled workers to fill "undesirable" jobs, in much the same way as they once received professional transients from, and provided unskilled workers to, other countries when they were at lower stages of development.

The proposition argued in this paper is that governments of developing countries utilise legal migration, both permanent and temporary, primarily to facilitate economic growth. The priorities accorded immigrants with particular ethnic characteristics, and judgements concerning the respective political advantages of alternative labour emigration agreements, are characteristically made within parameters set by economic policy. It is further argued that countries at the upper end of the development spectrum also utilise migration to facilitate economic growth. However, such countries are better able to absorb a proportion of immigrants for basically non-economic reasons (e.g., refugees). It should, however, be noted that this proposition does not relate to the decision-making processes of individual migrants. Economic motives may predominate, but decisions will almost certainly be influenced by a complex of social and psychological forces.

In recent years, international migration through legal processes has been supplemented by large flows of illegal migration. Though this too has been characteristically generated by economic forces -- significant income and opportunity differentials between neighbouring countries -- the salient difference is that receiving governments are unable, and perhaps unwilling, to prevent entry. Illegal migration may take the form of movement across borders, as in the case of migration from Mexico to the United States, or persons who initially were admitted legally but overstayed when their permits expired. Nor are economic determinants entirely absent from many so-called refugee migrations, even though international agencies tend to apply strict criteria to their classifications. Indeed, in recent years there has been much debate in receiving countries concerning the difficulties of drawing a clear line between economic and political refugees.

The Genesis of Modern Permanent Migration for Developing Countries

Although migration is a phenomenon as old as human history, volume, direction and composition of flows have changed enormously during the post-1945 period, reflecting to a large extent changing social, economic and political forces throughout the world. Nowhere has the influence of international migration been greater than on developing countries. The genesis of change was the widespread dethronement of colonialism after World War II. While it could be argued that decolonisation was simply the culmination of change which began with European dominance, achievement of independence was for many colonies a watershed following which they became masters of their own political destinies, including immigration policy. Immediately after independence many colonial expatriates returned home; others stayed on in advisory capacities or as representatives of companies with long-standing commercial interests in the country. However, their residence status was generally temporary. While the loss of many expatriates had demonstrable negative impacts during transition from colonial to independent status, many countries considered this a small price to pay. Thereafter, advisors with appropriate skills were obtained from many sources, some under aid programmes, but for only as long as they were needed.

Of far greater concern to many developing countries than the loss of expatriates was the loss of indigenous professionals through permanent emigration after the mid-1960s. About this time many developed countries, especially the traditional receivers, altered their permanent immigration policies to favour professional and highly-skilled persons irrespective of their country of origin. When the United States changed its quota system in 1965 to eliminate ethnic discrimination, and thereafter based entry on skill and sponsorship of close kin, the effect on sources of intake was quite dramatic (CICRED, 1981). By 1971, Europe had fallen to third place behind Latin America and Asia as areas of intake. By 1974, 45 per cent of immigrants to the United States were from the American continent and 32 per cent from Asia. Canada also made radical changes in its immigration policy. Invoking a policy based on current needs, the percentage of immigrants from Europe (the traditional source) fell from 84 per cent between 1946-50 to 50 per cent between 1968-73, and the percentage from Asia rose from one to 17 per cent. Australia also responded to the new forces by altering its longstanding preference for Europeans and admitting a small number of non-European skilled and professional immigrants. Though Australia's changes did not have as significant an impact on regional source as did the new policies of the United States and Canada, by the end of the 1960s a highly-qualified non-European, who could speak English and had been offered a job, would be admitted to Australia for permanent residence on the same basis as a European with similar qualifications.

The importance attached by governments and scholars to the consequences for developing countries of this so-called brain drain is reflected by the voluminous literature during the 1960s (Research Policy Program Lund, 1967). Zahlan (1977) showed that the migration of talent to the United States increased at an "exponential rate" during the late 1950s, and that by the mid-1960s "LDC professionals exceeded the European flow". Thus, by 1970, 60 per cent of the 60 000 foreign medical graduates working in the United States were from LDCs. Europe and Canada also admitted significant numbers of professionals from developing countries during this period. Indeed, many European countries also experienced a brain drain to the United States and Canada, which is quite consistent with the economic evolution thesis argued earlier in this chapter.

Literature on the migration of talent has tended to focus on deleterious impacts on developing countries, including the serious relative losses to countries with low levels of skills, and the extent to which such losses impeded fulfilment of plans for economic growth. Issues of morality also arose: whether or not developed countries should encourage or even admit professionals from developing countries; whether the professionals should stay home and contribute to their country's development; whether any government had the right to enforce such policies, and so on. Set against these issues was the view, heard frequently from residents of developed countries, that there was no brain drain at all; that LDCs overproduce various categories of professionals which developed countries have the capacity to absorb. In this regard, Pravin Visaria (1974) argued that where professionals in developing countries are underemployed or unemployed, their emigration could hardly have an adverse effect on the economy. Their departure, he concluded, should be viewed as an outflow rather than a brain drain. On the other hand, he also argued that insofar as emigration benefits both the migrants and the countries of immigration, and as the country of origin had paid a substantial part of the cost of training the migrant, a strong case could be made for levying a tax on the incomes of migrants living in developed countries. This proposal was further developed and strongly argued by Bhagwati, but to little avail; although on 6th November 1982 the Romanian Government announced that in future all Romanian citizens wishing to emigrate would first be required to repay the State (in foreign currency) the cost of their education from secondary to post-graduate levels (Australia, 1982).

The outflow from developing countries of professional and highly-skilled workers and their families after the early 1960s has not abated although numbers, direction and composition have been affected by changed economic conditions in the traditional receiving countries, especially after the so-called OPEC crisis in 1973. Sponsorship of close relatives by migrants who attained residence status has also contributed to outflows from developing countries. An event of major significance for traditional receivers, and several other developed countries, was the acceptance of refugees from Southeast Asia after the Vietnam conflict which, in turn, was also followed by further intakes under family reunion and orderly departure schemes. Although aggregate annual intakes of permanent immigrants (including refugees) by the traditional receivers are less than one million, the salient feature concerning origin has been the increasing proportion from developing countries. Tables 1.1 to 1.3 indicate both the magnitude and proportion of total intakes by traditional receivers of migrants from developing countries.

Table 1.1

IMMIGRATION TO THE UNITED STATES BY REGION OF BIRTH: 1960-84

(Per cent)

Region of birth	Number ('000)	All countries	Asia	North/Central America	Europe	South America	Africa	Oceania	Other countries
1960	265	100.0	7.8	32.1	52.6	4.9	0.9	0.4	1.3
1961	271	100.0	6.8	38.1	47.1	5.7	0.7	0.4	1.2
1962	284	100.0	6.7	42.7	42.2	6.2	0.7	0.4	1.1
1963	306	100.0	6.7	42.4	41.1	7.5	0.9	0.4	1.1
1964	292	100.0	6.2	38.7	42.1	10.6	1.0	0.5	1.0
1965	297	100.0	5.8	42.7	38.5	10.4	1.1	0.5	0.9
1966	323	100.0	11.1	39.4	38.7	8.0	1.0	0.6	1.3
1967	362	100.0	14.8	38.7	38.5	4.6	1.2	0.6	1.6
1968	454	100.0	11.2	50.2	30.7	4.8	1.1	0.6	1.4
1969	359	100.0	18.2	36.9	33.5	6.7	1.1	0.7	2.4
1970	373	100.0	22.4	34.6	31.6	5.9	2.2	0.9	2.5
1971	370	100.0	24.9	37.8	26.1	5.6	2.2	0.8	3.1
1972	385	100.0	28.1	37.5	23.4	5.0	1.7	0.9	3.3
1973	400	100.0	28.0	38.2	23.2	5.1	1.7	0.8	3.1
1974	395	100.0	29.6	38.4	20.6	5.7	1.6	0.8	3.5
1975	386	100.0	30.8	38.0	19.2	6.0	1.7	0.9	3.5
1976	399	100.0	33.5	35.7	18.2	5.7	1.9	0.9	4.1
1977	462	100.0	30.0	40.5	15.1	7.1	2.2	0.9	4.1
1978	601	100.0	38.6	36.7	12.2	6.9	1.9	0.7	2.9
1979	460	100.0	37.1	34.2	13.2	7.7	2.8	1.0	4.0
1980	531	100.0	41.0	31.1	13.6	7.5	2.6	0.7	3.5
1981	597	100.0	40.9	35.3	11.2	6.0	2.5	0.7	3.4
1982	594	100.0	49.5	26.6	11.6	6.0	2.4	0.6	3.3
1983	560	100.0	46.7	30.1	10.5	6.4	2.7	0.6	3.0
1984	544	100.0	44.1	30.6	11.8	6.9	2.9	0.7	3.0

Source: INS (1969, 1970: Table 14) and INS (1980, 1981: Table 13).

Calculated by J.T. Fawcett, et al., "Asian Immigration to the United States: Flows and Processes", East-West Population Institute, Honolulu, 1984 (mimeo.).

Updated from J.T. Fawcett, et al., "The New Immigration from Asia and the Pacific Islands", a chapter in Pacific Bridges, Centre of Migration Studies, Staten Island, New York, 1987.

Table 1.2

IMMIGRATION AND REFUGEE ADMISSIONS TO CANADA
(By region of last permanent residence)
(Per cent)

Year	Number (000s)	Asia	North/Central America	Europe	South America	Africa	Australasia/ Oceania
1946-73	3 842	7	13	75	2	2	2
1974	219	23	24	41	6	5	2
1975	188	25	21	39	7	5	3
1976	149	30	22	33	7	5	2
1977	155	27	23	35	7	6	2
1978	86	28	22	35	8	5	2
1979	125	50	13	28	4	3	2
1980	135	47	14	31	4	3	2

Source: Adapted with own calculations from Manpower and Immigration, 1975; Employment and Immigration to Canada, 1973-83 (annually); and Employment and Immigration Canada, Annual Report to Parliament, 1975-83.

Table 1.3

BIRTHPLACE OF SETTLER ARRIVALS, AUSTRALIA
(Per cent)

Year ended June 30	Number (000s)	Asia	United Kingdom and Ireland (Republic)	Other Europe	Middle East	Oceania	Other
1976	53	15.3	32.9	23.0	5.7	9.0	14.1
1977	71	15.1	27.1	16.9	20.0	9.5	11.5
1978	76	23.7	29.7	15.3	6.3	13.5	8.2
1979	81	30.8	20.6	14.2	4.1	18.4	12.0
1980	81	29.7	21.4	17.4	3.6	18.4	9.5
1981	111	23.7	29.2	18.4	2.9	17.8	8.0
1982	118	24.0	32.6	20.7	2.7	11.5	8.2
1983	93	28.0	29.6	21.4	2.6	8.8	9.7
1984	69	38.2	19.7	15.0	5.6	10.5	11.0
1985 (a)	78	39.6	15.8	12.7	6.6	13.7	11.5

a)   Preliminary.

Source: Department of Immigration and Ethnic Affairs, Australian Immigration Consolidated Statistics, 13, 1982 and unpublished statistics.

While further research is required to assess the skill-mix represented by these flows, there is no doubt that they include a large number of unskilled refugees and dependants of former immigrants and refugees. Other countries have also received large numbers of refugees as well as immigrants from former colonial territories. For example, immigration to the United Kingdom from former colonies during the 1950s was facilitated by loose Commonwealth migration laws and traditional links with the mother country. Though the Commonwealth Immigration Act of 1962 effectively imposed control over numbers and composition of intakes, by 1971 there were an estimated 322 000 Indian-born, and 140 000 Pakistan and Bangladesh-born persons residing in the United Kingdom. Some of these could be classified brain drain migrants, but the overwhelming majority were unskilled. Large numbers of Commonwealth-born immigrants from Africa and the Caribbean also settled in the United Kingdom during the 1950s and 1960s.

Refugees

Although refugees have comprised a significant proportion of immigrants to Western countries since the 1960s, by far the main refugee flows since World War II have been between developing countries. For example, an estimated 7 million Hindus moved from Pakistan to India and an approximately equal number of Moslems moved from India to Pakistan following Partition in 1947; 4 million Koreans moved from South to North Korea during the 1950s; 60 000 Tibetans moved to India; 100 000 Chinese were repatriated from Indonesia to the mainland; several million Afghanistan refugees fled to Pakistan and an estimated 130 000 left-over refugees from neighbouring countries still live in Thailand. In Africa, the refugee problem bears heavily upon receiving countries. Adepoju (forthcoming) argues that refugees constitute a dominant and increasingly disturbing aspect of international migration in Africa, especially in the Horn and the Sudan. Described as a sociologically heterogeneous group, they include political refugees, freedom fighters and a large residual group -- displaced persons -- with mixed characteristics: women and youths fleeing from war, conflicts and persecution, or escaping from famine and drought. He estimates that the refugee population in Africa presently exceeds 5 million, mostly in Sudan, Zaire, Ethiopia, Chad, Somalia and Cameroun. "In 1983", he concluded, "every second refugee and displaced person in the world was an African". In Latin America, intra-regional flows of refugees have not been large, but political upheavals have led many Paraguayans and Chileans to flee to Argentina; Nicaraguans to Honduras and Costa Rica; and Salvadoreans to Honduras and Guatemala. Jorge Balan (forthcoming) is of the view that the weakness or absence of regulations protecting the human rights of refugees is a problem of increasing concern.

The salient dilemmas for many refugees in developing countries, especially in Africa, are that the option of returning home has long since past and so they are considered quasi-permanent, though generally unwelcome, residents, and that they impose extended burdens on typically fragile economies lacking the resources necessary to resettle them. The latter problem is especially serious for fragile, drought-ridden terrains in the Horn of Africa. The United States Information Office (1983) predicts that group demands for refugee status and settlement, and individual appeals for asylum will, in the year 2000, still rank as major issues of domestic and international politics.

Contract Labour Migration

The temporary migration of workers between countries has become a significant phenomenon affecting, in various ways, socio-economic patterns in both sending and receiving countries. The first major post-war flow of labour migrants was from Southern to Northern Europe where labour scarcity was a constraint on economic growth. This flow can be largely explained by the economic evolution hypothesis articlulated earlier in this chapter: workers from countries with lower per capita incomes and rates of economic growth responded to opportunities for employment provided by labour-short countries at higher levels of economic development. Labour demand (total and composition) did not remain static. Indeed, by the 1970s, the major issues confronting receiving countries related to the status of original guest workers (and their receiving-country-born children) who opted not to return to the homeland at the expiration of their contracts. There is general consensus amongst scholars of international migration that administering a successful guest-worker programme is an elusive goal. In the case of Europe, receiving countries have tended to advocate entry only of unmarried workers in order to avoid familial immigration. Some countries view immigrants as strictly economic agents to the neglect of their social, cultural and political identity (Papademetriou, forthcoming).

In its recent survey of international migration policies and programmes, the Department of International Economic and Social Affairs of the United Nations (1982) concluded that although opportunities for permanent migration are very restricted, many countries show a clear and growing preference for temporary contract workers to meet their short-term labour requirements. Bohning (1983) estimated that there were probably 20 million migrant workers in the world at the beginning of the 1980s. Quoting a World Bank study, the UN survey noted that countries facing a demand for labour are increasingly buying man-hours, i.e., preferring to pay for a rolling stock of temporary labour whose demands on their social expenditures and whose integration with local populations would be minimal (Swami 1981). The tight controls now exercised by many labour-receiving countries concerning length of stay and refusal to admit dependants of workers, clearly reflects their determination to avoid the kind of difficulties presently being experienced by Northern European countries. For example, a genuine guest-worker programme became more firmly established in oil-rich countries in the Middle East than was possible in Western Europe during its labour-importing period. During the 1970s, the Middle East's characteristically small populations required labour supplies far beyond their capacities to provide from indigenous sources. Governments of oil-rich countries were especially severe in invoking conditions concerning composition (dependants are rarely admitted), skill-mix and enforcement of return at the expiration of contracts.

Because contract labour migration characteristically occurs between countries at different stages of economic evolution, the study of "impacts" has been directed mainly to developing countries. The assumed benefits from contract worker migration derived by sending countries include acquisition of scarce foreign exchange through remittances, relief of unemployment and underemployment, increase in national income per capita and a consequential increase in rates of savings and investment, as well as new skills acquired by workers which may be utilised upon their return for the development of an industrial base (Stahl, 1982). Achievement of these benefits clearly depends upon a complex of related variables. The economic benefits generally attributed to contract worker migration by receiving countries include reduced shortages in particular occupations, thus allowing better use of industrial capacity and hence profitability; that the increased supply of labour may prevent wage inflation and postpone costly structural transformation toward capital-intensive production; and that annual intakes can be quickly adjusted according to demand (Appleyard, 1984). Even though the extent of economic benefits accruing to the receiving country has been questioned, especially the value of employment multipliers deriving from this type of migration, Stahl (1982) for one has declared "with a high degree of certainty that whatever benefits are received far exceed those received by the labour-exporting countries".

Non-economic impacts of labour migration on sending countries include changes in social relations, in social roles, in cultural ideas and concepts, and in the level of personal stress experienced by migrants and those left behind. For example, wives may have to live with in-laws or other relatives, arrangements which result in friction and conflict. Research in Sri Lanka on the impact of emigration by wives showed that the husband was required to take active responsibility for the education and welfare of children. On the other hand, the emigration of husbands could lead to a range of impacts, from new opportunities and freedom for wives, to emotional strain known in Pakistan as the "Dubai syndrome". In rural areas, where agriculture was the primary activity, absence of a husband forced the wife into new social and economic relations (UN-ESCAP, 1985). Specific impacts clearly depend on a complex of social, economic and cultural conditions, and as most of the sending countries are undergoing rapid social change, it is not always clear that migration was the primary or only force in that change.

While the impact on sending countries of contract labour migration to the Middle East has received a great deal of attention in the literature, sight should not be lost of the fact that the numbers represent only a small proportion of the estimated 20 million migrant workers in the world at the beginning of the 1980s. For example, in Central Africa millions of workers characteristically move from nearby resource-poor to resource-rich countries, and in East Africa from over-populated and least-developed countries experiencing soil exhaustion and unemployment to nearby countries with relatively better conditions and opportunities. In Southern Africa, the Republic of South Africa has been a magnet for workers from nearby countries for many years, and because the Republic imposes tight restrictions on family reunion, workers may make many sojourns to and from their homelands during their working lives (Adepoju, forthcoming). Labour migration (both legal and illegal) has also been on the increase from countries comprising Latin America to the United States which has used legal systems of labour recruitment, such as the bracero programme, to attract Latin American workers. Venezuela and Argentina in South America, and to a lesser extent countries in Central America and the Caribbean (e.g., Dominican Republic), have also developed systems of temporary labour migration. However, these have been considerably less developed than the bracero programme and have involved relatively fewer people, with the important exception of Colombians to Venezuela (Balan, forthcoming). In the Pacific Islands, labour (and permanent) migration relative to population size has become so great as to have been identified as the most important process affecting the structures of Pacific Island populations and the growth and distribution of their work-forces (SPC/ILO, 1982). Indeed, the keynote speaker at a conference in Noumea in 1982 argued that there are few areas in the world where migration behaviour has had such an important bearing on the causes and consequences of population trends as the Pacific.

Even though the sum impact of contract labour emigration on socio-economic change in sending countries is difficult, if not impossible, to calculate, evidence on some specific impacts shows that migration has become a significant force. Take, for example, the impact of remittances. Table 1.4, on selected Asian countries indicates the magnitude of remittances in the balance of payments of several labour-sending countries in Asia. While some economists have argued that larger proportions should have been invested by remittees in capital-generating activities (Bohning, 1983), the contemporary wisdom in this regard is that more attention should be given to assessing the impact of total remittances on economic growth, to whether expenditure is made on foreign or locally produced goods, and especially on the capacity of national banking systems to effectively utilise funds remitted from abroad (UN-ESCAP, 1985a). Some countries in the ESCAP region have adopted incentive measures designed to channel remittances into official funds for use on projects of high national priority. Others have offered higher interest rates on bank deposits and issued special bonds to mobilise remittances into more productive uses (UN-ESCAP, 1985b). Whether or not remittances are being utilised in the most effective manner, there is no doubt that in most countries they have a major impact on development strategies. For example, the estimated $2.8 billion received by Pakistan in 1983 represented 97 per cent of merchandise exports, and remittances of $610 million to Bangladesh in 1983 made this item the second largest foreign exchange item after earnings from the export of jute.

In the absence of adequate research, it is not possible to verify or refute the proposition that emigration has contributed to inflation in sending countries. The most positive conclusion reached in this regard concerning Pakistan, India and Bangladesh is based on research which suggests that remittances were partly responsible for high inflation in the real estate sector (Appleyard, forthcoming). One can be a little more conclusive concerning the role of emigration as a safety valve against high unemployment. The Pakistan study suggested that because emigrants were better skilled and more enterprising than non-migrants, and because only 10 per cent of emigrants had been unemployed prior to departure, their absence "eased the job market". On the other hand, because skilled and enterprising workers are not easily replaced, the filling of their jobs by relatively untrained and inexperienced replacement workers may have caused a decline in productivity and output.

The social consequences of labour migration are both manifold and varied, touching all aspects of the worker's family and community life, and varying between countries (and regions within countries) on the basis of ethnicity, religion, family size and structure, class, skills and earnings. Although the impacts cited in this paper are selective, they indicate significance in certain situations. Research by anthropologists in some Pacific islands indicates that increased income through remittances has raised consumption levels and therefore improved levels of health and productivity. On the other hand, the same remittances have led to a breakdown in communal obligations and a disinterest in agricultural production and village enterprises (Appleyard, forthcoming). Research in Latin America indicates that selective emigration has become a crucial element in early family formation and on the structure of family relations (Balan, forthcoming). The departure of workers from Lesotho for South Africa has also exerted considerable

Table 1.4

REMITTANCES FROM MIGRANT WORKERS IN RELATION TO MERCHANDISE EXPORTS, IMPORTS,
GROSS NATIONAL PRODUCT AND FOREIGN AID FOR SELECTED ASIAN COUNTRIES,
1980-85

Country		Remittances				
		Total ($ million)	Percentage of merchandise exports	Percentage of merchandise imports	Percentage of gross national product	Percentage of foreign aid
Bangladesh	1980	257	33.9	9.9	2.7	12.0
	1981	280	35.5	10.3	2.8	16.9
	1982	515	66.8	21.0	5.2	29.4
	1983	610	84.2	28.2	5.6	42.2
India	1980	1 600	19.3	11.5	1.3	56.7
Pakistan	1981	1 900	69.6	33.6	7.7	159.8
	1983	2 810	97.7	50.3	10.9	209.4
	1984	2 405	91.4	37.3	8.6	n.a.
	1985 (Jan.-Sept.)	1 800	n.a.	n.a.	n.a.	n.a.
Philippines	1980	774	13.4	10.0	2.8	171.9
	1981	798	13.9	10.0	2.5	168.0
	1982	810	16.1	10.6	2.4	163.5
	1983	955	19.1	12.8	3.6	178.2
	1984	625	11.6	10.3	2.2	n.a.
	1985 (Jan.-May)	296	n.a.	n.a.	n.a.	n.a.
South Korea	1980	1 102	6.3	4.9	2.0	343.7
	1981	1 359	6.4	5.2	2.2	344.7
	1982	1 538	7.0	6.3	2.3	2 050.7
Sri Lanka	1980	137	12.9	7.4	4.7	19.9
	1981	229	21.0	12.0	5.2	30.7
	1982	237	23.4	13.2	5.6	47.0
	1983	294	27.7	17.0	5.8	62.9
	1984	301	20.6	15.6	5.1	n.a.
Thailand (from Middle East)	1980	240	3.7	2.9	0.9	48.6
	1981	480	7.0	5.4	1.6	86.6
	1982	446	6.5	5.9	1.3	71.0
	1983	676	10.7	7.4	1.8	109.4
	1984 (Jan.-Sept.)	441	8.0	6.3	1.6	n.a.

n.a. = not available.

Sources: Arnold and Shah (1984), Korale (1986), Stahl (1985), International Monetary Fund (1985), Kim (1986), Abella (1984), Asian Development Bank (1985), unpublished data for Habib Bank, Pakistan.

Reproduced from Stahl and Arnold, "Overseas Workers' Remittances in Asian Development", mimeo., revised 10th October 1986.

influence on family structure and marriage patterns which may have affected both reproductive behaviour and population growth (Adepoju, forthcoming). And in India, some returning contract workers are accorded higher status as marriage partners (Appleyard, forthcoming).

There is no doubt that the absence of male breadwinners over long periods has placed new pressures on both spouses and dependants left behind. In Latin America, nuclear families (typical of the region) have been merged into extended family networks, and there have also been important impacts on the sexual division of labour. Where women have emigrated, their loss to the rural sector (where they typically produce most of the food grown) has adversely affected rural production. Balan is very critical of the many "crude simplifications" which have been made concerning the impacts of emigration on families, and has argued for the need to consider a whole set of impacts arising from temporary absence within the household as a system. Adepoju has also emphasized the complexity of these impacts in the African situation. In countries which provide workers for mines in South Africa, women have not only been saddled with additional responsibilities, but family bonds and solidarity have been eroded.

Transient Professional Workers

These are characteristically highly-skilled or professional workers sent by their employers, or by governments under aid programmes, to work on assignments in overseas countries: e.g., an engineer sent by his government to supervise construction of a road system, or an accountant exchanged by companies tied together by a joint-venture agreement. While statistics available on this type of migration are quite inadequate to assess both composition and magnitude, there is no doubt that transient professionals have had a major impact on improving both skill levels and rates of economic growth in some developing countries.

The transient professional is not a newcomer to international migration. During the inter-war years, he was the foreign engineer or accountant who worked in the company's overseas office, plantation or mine, generally as overseer of construction or production, or perhaps as supervisor of the training of local workers. Following independence of colonial territories, new immigration policies concerning number and type of transients were made on the basis of new objectives for economic growth. Today, transients are the conveyors of technology, and while their skills and experiences are directed primarily towards maximising returns for the investors, they are also instrumental in raising the general level of skills in the recipient country (Appleyard, 1984). Economic changes facilitated by this type of migration inevitably affect social cohesion in the recipient country, especially if migration quickens the process of urbanisation and internal migration, thus exposing people to a wider spectrum of ideas and relationships. Although transients may remain in developing countries for only short periods, their influence as agents of socio-economic change has been considerable, perhaps matching the influence of contract labour returnees who had been exposed to many new experiences in the receiving countries.

Illegal and Undocumented Migration

As already noted, illegal migration is most likely to occur between countries with significantly different GNPs per capita and/or rates of economic growth. Propensity for illegal migration is high in situations where the two countries share a common border, although legal migrants may become illegal if, having entered a country on, say, a tourist visa they overstay and take employment. Illegal migrants are therefore more likely to leave developing than developed countries. A recent UN Report (1982) argued that illegal migration is a rational process, a continuation of traditional migration in the context of new nation states or new international borders; a substitute for a foreign worker programme, or a flow sanctioned or ignored by the receiving country. In instances where it circumvents strict barriers, and involves great personal risk and/or severe penalties, the motivation may be quite different and the system of rationality may be put to its extreme test.

It has been the readiness of people to move into areas where they can obtain higher wages that has led the world population to, as Balan (forthcoming) argues, "become integrated into a common set of values". Where countries have been prepared to condone the entry of illegal workers so long as they do not compete with local workers, clandestine migration has become a significant component of work-forces. Perhaps the most celebrated example of contemporary illegal migration is to the United States from neighbouring Mexico where economic conditions and opportunities are greatly inferior. Estimates of the illegal population vary considerably, which is understandable. The United States Government has also found repatriation difficult to enforce.

Illegal migration occurs not only between developed and developing countries, but also between developing countries with relatively narrow income differentials. According to Adepoju, undocumented migration is a pervasive phenomenon in Africa. While strict labour recruitment laws in South Africa restrict the intake of illegal workers, it occurs "routinely" in West Africa because of different political, economic and social factors, and in East Africa because of unreal borders imposed by European colonisers. In Latin America, Venezuela has become a major receiver of illegal temporary workers. The major sending country is less-developed Colombia, although Jamaica, the Dominican Republic and other countries contribute to this flow (Balan, forthcoming). In Asia, the major and most persistent flow of illegal migration has been between the People's Republic of China and Hong Kong. Between 1976 and 1980 an estimated 400 000 illegal migrants entered the colony, but when economic conditions deteriorated, diplomatic pressures were applied on the Republic to curb the flow. Other known flows of illegal migration in the region have been to labour-short, high-growth ASEAN countries. Singapore has attracted a large number (estimated at 120 000 in 1981), and approximately one million Indonesians work in mainly rural and construction jobs in Malaysia (Appleyard, forthcoming).

The impacts of illegal migration on sending countries are clearly conditioned by the absence of agreed conditions such as those set down in formal labour contracts. For example, Koreans who sign formal contracts for employment in Middle East countries are required to remit a large proportion of their earnings through official channels. Illegal workers, on the other hand, are not only absolved from such arrangements but, bereft of legal protection in the receiving country, are vulnerable to exploitation (especially regarding income) and to deportation when the conditions which allowed their illegal entry no longer apply. Because the funds they remit are likely to be much lower than those remitted by contract workers in similar occupations, so economic impacts on their home country are different; although where illegal populations are large, the total value of money and goods brought back to the home country could be considerable. Non-economic impacts for families at home are, of course, exacerbated by the uncertainties, and dangers, surrounding the lifestyle of the breadwinner in the receiving country.

CONCLUSION

The proposition presented here is that the governments of most developing countries attempt to utilise legal migration to facilitate economic growth. Under agreements made with labour-short countries, contract workers emigrate under fairly strict conditions imposed by receivers. By and large, developing countries have been unable, and largely unwilling, to prevent the emigration of their professional and skilled workers to developed countries on a permanent basis. And in view of the characteristic pressure of population on resources, most developing countries are not willing to admit immigrants for permanent residence although they readily accept transient professionals for short periods. Explanation of migration patterns which have evolved in recent years can be readily related to the well-known phenomenon that these are linked to the evolution of each country's economic structure.

Derived impacts of international migration for developing countries vary according to an array of social, economic and cultural differentials. In the case of contract labour emigration, the acquisition of scarce foreign exchange through remittances, and the new skills acquired by workers while abroad, have been identified as important gains. On the other hand, many developing countries are unable to adequately exploit the skills acquired abroad by contract workers, and the loss in the first place of skilled and enterprising workers may have caused declines in productivity and output. Among social impacts, pressures on spouses and dependants left behind clearly test family structures and relations.

A general conclusion drawn from this brief survey is that a great deal more research needs to be undertaken on the magnitude of migration from developing to developed countries, and between developing countries. Only then will it be possible to assess the very complex impacts, only some of which have been touched upon in this chapter. The direction and composition of future flows will change, but the impacts on developing (and in a directly derived sense, developed) countries will require a great deal more sophisticated research to unravel.

BIBLIOGRAPHY

ADEPOJU, A. (forthcoming)
A chapter in International Migration Today: Trends and Prospects, Paris, UNESCO.

APPLEYARD, R.T.
"International Migration in the ESCAP Region", a chapter in United Nations, Third Asian and Pacific Population Conference, Selected Papers, New York, 1984

APPLEYARD, R.T. (forthcoming)
A chapter in International Migration Today: Trends and Prospects, Paris, UNESCO.

ARNOLD, F. and SHAH, N.M.
"Asian Labour Migration to the Middle East", International Migration Review, Summer, Vol. 18, No. 2, 1984..

AUSTRALIA, Department of Foreign Affairs
Backgrounder, No. 360, Canberra, 24th November 1982.

BALAN, J. (forthcoming)
A chapter in International Migration Today: Trends and Prospects, Paris, UNESCO.

BOHNING, W.R.
"International Migration: Implications for Development and Policies", mimeo., paper prepared for the Expert Group on Population Distribution, Migration and Development, held at Hammamet, Tunisia, March 1983.

CICRED
International Migration in the Third World, initiating meeting, Nedlands, Australia, Paris, CICRED, 1981.

DEMERY, L.
"Asian Labour Migration to the Middle East: An Empirical Assessment", paper prepared for the Conference on Asian labour migration to the Middle East, Honolulu, 19th-23rd September 1983.

ECONOMIC AND SOCIAL COMMISSION FOR ASIA AND THE PACIFIC (ESCAP)
Report of Policy Workshop on International Migration in Asia and the Pacific, Bangkok, 15th-21st October 1985, New York, United Nations, 1985a.

Report of the Expert Group Meeting on Remittances from International Labour Migration, mimeo., Bangkok, 2nd-4th September 1985b.

HALL, S. (forthcoming)
A chapter in International Migration Today: Trends and Prospects, Paris, UNESCO.

PAPADEMETRIOU, D. (forthcoming)
A chapter in International Migration Today: Trends and Prospects, Paris, UNESCO.

RESEARCH POLICY PROGRAMME
Brain Drain and Brain Gain, a bibliography on migration of scientists, engineers, doctors and students, Lund, Sweden, 1967.

SOUTH PACIFIC COMMISSION AND ILO
Report of Meeting, Regional Conference on Migration, Employment and Development in the South Pacific, mimeo., Noumea, 22nd-26th February 1982.

STAHL, C.W.
"International Labour Migration and International Development", a working paper in the series, International Migration for Employment, Geneva, ILO, 1982.

"Contract Labour Migration and Economic Development with Special Reference to Indonesia, Malaysia, the Philippines and Thailand", paper prepared for the Conference on Asian Labour Migration to the Middle East, Honolulu, 19th-23rd September 1983.

SWAMI, G.
International Migrant Workers' Remittances: Issues and Prospects, World Bank Staff Working Paper No. 481, 1981.

UNITED NATIONS, Department of International Economic and Social Affairs
International Migration Policies and Programmes, Population Studies, No. 80, New York, 1982.

UNITED NATIONS -- ESCAP, 1985
Expert Group Meeting on International Migration in Asia and the Pacific, Manila, Bangkok, November 1984.

UNITED STATES INFORMATION OFFICE
Official Text, Canberra, 20th September 1983.

VISARIA, P.
"The Determinants of 'Brain Drain'". A chapter in G. Tapinos, ed., International Migration. Proceedings of a Seminar on Demographic Research in Relation to International Migration, Buenos Aires, Paris, CICRED, 1974.

ZAHLAN, A.B.
"The Brain Drain Controversy", International Population Conference, Mexico, IUSSP, Vol. 2, 1977.

Chapter 2

TYPOLOGIES AND THE LIKELIHOOD OF REVERSIBLE MIGRATION

by

H. Domenach and M. Picouet

INTRODUCTION

Until recent times, any analysis of migration was based upon where individuals originated. Most individuals were born, lived, and died in the same place, although there were a number who, because of war, business, or education spent time elsewhere. But by and large a typology of movement was very simple and the number of "types" very limited. With few exceptions, all new places of settlement were considered permanent. Indeed, some current studies still rest on the premise that migration is "movement of persons crossing certain boundaries in order to establish a new place of permanent residence" (Population Reference Bureau, 1980). This criterion of permanent residence is then related to all the consequences of the move -- territorial, financial, socio-economic.

Although current forms of human mobility are very different in both time and space (Courgeau, 1980), they are often classified according to the permanent/non-permanent typology. In such cases, researchers take only one facet of migration into account. Attempts to conceptualise diversity and translate reality into quantitative terms come up against limits imposed by existing methods of measurement and analysis (Findley, 1983).

Classification Criteria

First, there is the problem of taking into account all types of movement that does not necessarily involve a change of residence. Multiple places of residence are a social fact, especially in Western countries; nor can we ignore the multiple places in which professional, social and family activities occur (Collomb, 1985). Furthermore, place of origin usually refers to place of birth, with the presupposition of return that may not be relevant in every case. In fact it may no longer be possible to systematically equate the socio-cultural aspects implied in "origin" with the actual place of birth which may have only a transitory character. It is therefore important that

37

analysis of the migration process determine the exact character of the origin of the individual. Even the process and new forms of mobility (e.g., illegal, refugee, and temporary workers) can vary considerably from one situation to the next which means decisions must be made on an appropriate measurement criteria. Be it seasonal or illegal migration, group or individual migration, it is clear that the available statistical tools to measure such movements are inadequate (Chaire Quelelet, 1985).

Second, there is the problem of assessing the impact of migration. What consequences does it have on fertility, family structure, morbidity? What are its effects on urbanisation, infrastructure, planning? While some studies have established correlations between migration and other variables, many are descriptive or narrative accounts which do not pinpoint overall trends.

Faced with such diverse of forms of mobility, any attempt to devise a universal typology is risky. Some recent studies (Central America -- Teller, 1982; Bolivia -- Blanes, 1984; Caribbean -- Domenach and Guengant, 1984; Burkina Faso -- Boutillier, Quesnal and Vaugelade, 1975; Togo -- Dupont, Quesnel and Vimard, 1984; Venezuela -- Picouet, Pellegrino and Papail, 1984) provide examples of new mobility patterns and show, in fact, that one can create a classification, or at least an ordering of multiple forms according to different criteria. These may include length and frequency of residence in each place, well-being, income, work, training, means of travel, distance, short- and long-term events, etc.

Finally, different sets of typologies can be established according to the dependent or independent variables chosen. Here we treat various forms of migration according to their relatively permanent or non-permanent character, with a view to assessing possible reversibility, which is a critical determinant.

One-way flow

By its definition, a permanent move implies a single residence. However, change of residence by an individual, family or social group may be made without ever using the old residence again. It may be abandoned and plays no further part in the life of those who moved. Such moves may be caused either by natural catastrophes or ecological pressures, or be imposed through expulsion or a voluntary break with the social life of the place of origin.

The principal migratory flows result from natural catastrophes that can be sudden and violent (e.g., earthquakes, cyclones) or progressive (e.g., drought, desertification). Other moves come in response to such human conflict as wars, religious persecution, or oppressive political regimes (Caribbean Basin, Latin America, Southeast Asia, etc.) and/or severe economic crises.

In such instances, people find themselves forced into exile: groups migrate under difficult conditions and without being able to chose their destination. Destinations for such moves arise for the most part from political agreements, chains of support at the international level, or through diverse socio-economic channels. From a statistical point of view, these migrants represent a defined movement, even if the receiving country does not

always become the permanent place of residence. In contrast, the
may be in a situation of illegality -- following the most spont
often the only accessible paths -- and go unapprehended. Delicate
procedures are generally required to determine their numbers.

The great international migrations of the 19th and early part of the
20th Century which contributed so much to the rapid settlement of the Americas
were one-way flows. Today, movements of that magnitude are prevented by lack
of virgin land and the relative stability of national boundaries following
World War II. Likewise, the flow of rural inhabitants to cities takes on the
same characteristics of irreversibility. In Western countries, notably since
the post-industrial era, some rural regions have been largely abandoned, a
pattern that can be seen occurring in developing countries at the present
time. Rapid urbanisation has brought about the same type of phenomenon,
stimulated by a simple draining-away effect, the loss of ancestral land, and
hence progressive depopulation. However, in the total set of movements found
in these countries, rupture with the milieu of origin is an exception often
linked to political, religious, or even ecological factors.

Reversible Flow Following Long Stays

This type refers to movement of population involving family and social
survival in regions experiencing population/resource imbalance; e.g., traditional workers, organised by the social body itself, who assign a share of
the human resources to migration, while a sedentary share of the population
stays and cultivates the native land. This type of migration is often characterised by a distinctive culture or religion, such as the movement in the
South Maghreb by the Jerbians, Mozabites, Ghomrassis, etc. Only a little
different are those insulated peoples situated in small economies such as the
Lesser Antilles, Micronesia, Polynesia, or persons coming from highland
plateaux such as the Andes and Central Asia. In general, the movement takes
place at the beginning of active economic life or after several years of work
training in the region of origin, depending on the social organisation of the
societies. These migrations consist mainly of young persons, seeking as soon
as possible to establish a family, if this has not already been accomplished
before the move. They remain in close contact with the community left behind
and maintain close ties with the community of fellow migrants. In cases where
ties extend to the receiving society, the progressive weakening of links with
the society of origin can lead to irreversibility of migration.

The reversible character of these flows is part of a migratory process
oriented from the beginning towards return. Maintenance of family and social
solidarity; investment implanted into the region of origin; financial remittances even if irregular, are customary steps that organise and make possible
the eventual return of the migrant, which occurs at the end of his working
life or when he has succeeded.

A complete family cycle marks in general the duration of the expatriation, which can have only a regional character, in the course of which
the relationship with the society of origin has more or less survived. The
distance, cost and transport difficulties can limit frequency and periodicity
of visits to the place of origin. In the Alps, for example, migration often
took place only from one valley to another, but it was sufficient to keep some
migrants separated from their places of origin for several decades. Today,

ith higher incomes, paid holidays and spare time, the nature and frequency of these contacts have continued to evolve. Reduction in duration has, without doubt, been an important factor weakening the transmission of cultural values.

The situation of return concerns especially the migrant himself and to a lesser extent his decendants who may be fully integrated into the receiving society and therefore yield to irreversibility. The evolution of the family structure, in the sense of weakened lines of authority and increased cultural overlap, have less importance where the family moves back to the place of origin and may be a reason why more persons see the place or places of previous residence as discriminating factors against reversibility.

Flow with Renewed Reversibility

Taking into account current concepts and available statistics, one is attracted by the notion of a "residence-base", a place from which departures are made of variable duration and uncertain periodicity. However, such a concept presents two difficulties. First, it is necessary to specify the initial place in which to apply the principle of reversibility, i.e., to define the nature of the place of departure which constitutes the "residence-base" and its identification as a city or town, region or country or cultural area. Second, it is important to specify the different destinations in order to eventually clarify the notion of a residence which can be one or more places according to their mode of utilisation (extent of space of daily activities, work, leisure, etc.).

Statistical observations have proved to be particularly insensitive to the nuances and scales of these types of movements. Usually only entries and exits from the country are recorded, and even the best data delineate motives as either business or pleasure. It is therefore important to try and standardise more specifically the types of movers. E.g., migration for work across borders, which affects numerous countries, can have mutliple forms: daily (e.g., Swiss); seasonal (e.g., Haitians to cut cane in Santo Domingo) or contract (Colombians in the oil basin of Maracaibo in Venezuela). A common characteristic of these different categories is constancy of the journey taken. It is therefore the frequency of trips that appears to be the most fitting criterion.

Teller (1982) provides one of the rare quantitative examples of these different types of movements with repeated reversibility, drawing on research conducted between 1973 and 1979 in six Latino and Indian villages in Guatemala. It appears that socio-economic and cultural "determinism" presides over the choice of place or places; thereafter individual characteristics intervene -- financial, family, psychological, etc. -- on which depend the distribution of absences over time.

Repeated reversibility, which is expressed in data as a succession of absences and for the individual by reporting of "present" to "absent", has been applied in studies on the Mossi in Burkina Faso, to determine outmigrant workers (Boutillier, Quesnel and Vaugelade, 1975). Such an approach rarely provides insight into whether the move was permanent or reversible after a long duration. Although specific data on this question are not available, it is likely that as the means and speed of transport improves, the frequency of return moves will increase, without necessarily varying the total duration of time spent in each of the places frequented.

Sporadic Flow

Throughout history workers have been assembled for great works of construction and land development -- building pyramids, temples, fortifications, dams, railroads -- just as today workers from many places are involved in major development projects. In all cases, some characteristics were very precisely determined by the duration and scale of work and the numbers of skilled and unskilled workers required. Migration simply represents the imbalance between capacity of the local force, often unskilled, and the occasional character of the strong growth of demand for manpower. The dismantling of the migrant work-force comes at the end of the project, even though some workers may remain on the site.

Numerous types of movers participate in this modern mobility. They differ, however, from former types in two basic ways:

i) They are marked by a degree of uncertainty, depending not on a specific structure but instead upon occasional situations. They are also influenced by the intensity of the financial flows and may also occur simply by the process of urbanisation;

ii) The movements are also marked by strong instability. Durations of stay can vary for individuals and, equally, for the same individual in the course of several moves. In fact, the situation often involves choice between several opportunities, resulting in an individual acting ambivalently in different places. Micro-societies (e.g., rural, islands) furnish numerous examples. The uniformity of urbanisation across continents shows the development of similar migratory processes in spite of constraints (quotas, entry permits, etc.) that have been imposed by governments. Furthermore, the receiving places have been chosen because of job opportunities, from the perspective of better gain or other financial and professional reasons.

The reversibility of these movements increases as a result of contacts with the residence-base which denote the traditional aspect of movement and organisation of the moves with exploitation by the receiving places and new demands for emigration outlets. The economic circumstances of these movements improve capacity to move (demographic, family, occupational potential of communities or origin) through the capacity of external employment markets (labour, commercial, financial markets) and an enlargement of traditional migration space. Maghrebian migration is largely of this type. Also, the Djeballas of South Tunisia have adapted their migrations to current socioeconomic conditions with an extension of receiving places. To some extent, these movements are made in an area of activity (cultural, geographic, or economic) that is fairly well delimited and in which the receiving places are ordered according to criteria defined by the society of origin as a function of their economic, social and family interests. There is an ordering of places and even the determination of the first "areas of activity". Changes in direction and volume of Colombian migration following devaluation of the Venezuelan currency, the exchange of population between Puerto Rico and the

United States, migrations between Mexico and the United States, Filipinos to the Middle East and Haitians in the Caribbean region are other examples. The capacity of modern transport permits extension of areas of activity, even from continent to continent.

Flows of Itinerants

Reference to an established residence-base is a common characteristic of the movements described above. The point of departure of moves remains the same, only their destinations change -- one or several places according to the pre-established itinerary. The basis is return to the region of origin. The pattern of these moves thus resembles a closed loop. It is quite different when successive movements are uncertain, where the point of departure for the moves is defined by the last residence and the successive places of destination are unpredictable. Return to the original milieu is then improbable, or if it is realised accidentally, the loop remains open.

Lack of reference to a residence-base reveals a break, willingly or forced, with the milieu of the place of origin -- an expression of uprooting or social marginality, a certain propensity to follow opportunities that arise (work mobility). Permanent deterioration of conditions necessary for social and family renewal, due in large measure to fluctuating conditions in job opportunities, may explain why in certain developing countries migration never ends. One observes in this case the development of a new professional nomadism in developed countries, providing survival for a number of societies. In Venezuela, for example, some internal migration occurs because of economic changes, where some constraint appeared in receiving places that made them less attractive than others. In Colombia, the interaction between internal and external migration flows led the sphere of activity to include the Caribbean, North America and Europe.

This type of movement, which we have labelled non-reversible to illustrate non-return to the region of origin and itinerant to characterise the succession of places of living, generally applies to both sexes, young families at the time of separation with the milieu of origin, or at middle age when it is a question of professional nomadism or results from societal marginality. An exception occurs in family formation, where with increasing age of children, settlement at one of the points bends the line some years to reduce the uncertain character of moves and alters their nature, perhaps leading to semi-permanent settlement that is equivalent to a residence-base.

CONCLUSION

In considering the likelihood of reversibility of migration, we have underlined new characteristics of actual mobility, in particular the use of several residences, the extension of life spaces and the introduction of sequences of unpredictable duration in routes taken. The dichotomy used until now, between permanent and temporary moves, did not adequately reveal the diversity of migratory patterns and particularly the transition from one type of migration to another in the evolution of societies. In dealing with the concept of reversibility one sees emerging modes of movement not found in the classical typologies. Indeed, in seeking a continuity classification, irreversible and reversible moves of long duration are identified when once they were deemed permanent movement. Reversible movements that are repeated or problematic are not limited solely to temporary moves, but integrate equally with some permanent moves of the itinerant (according to some ordering of places) or sporadic (nomadism, professional or of survival) type.

BIBLIOGRAPHY

BLANES, J.
"Movilidad especial en Bolivia. Reflectiones sobre su caracter temporal", Ponencia seminario Migraciones Temporarias en America Latina, Quito, CENEP-CIUDAD, PISPAL, 1984.

BOUTILLIER, J., A. QUESNEL and J. VAUGELADE
Les migrations de travail Mossi, Ouagadougou, ORSTOM, fasc. 2, 1975.

CHAIRE QUELELET
Migrations internes. Collecte des donnés et méthodes d'analyse, Département de Démographie, Université Catholique de Louvain, Louvain-la-Neuve, 1985.

COLLOMB, P.
"Pour une approche fine des liaisons entre activités, mobilités et peuplement local, application au cas du peuplement agricole", Séminaire Migration interne et développement économique régional, Montreal, 1985.

COURGEAU, D.
Analyse quantitative des migrations humaines, Collection d'Anthropologie physique, Paris, Masson, 1980.

DOMENACH, H. and J.P. GUENGANT.
Dossiers Antilles Guyane, Nos. 2, 7 and 8, INSEE-Sirag, 1979-1983.

DUPONT, V.
"Dynamique des villes secondaires et processus migratoires en Afrique de l'Ouest -- Le cas de trois centres urbains en région de plantation, au Togo: Atakpamé, Kpalime, Badou", Thèse de 3ème cycle, Paris, Institut d'Etudes Politiques de Paris, 1984.

FINDLEY, Sally
"Migration Survey Methodologies: A Review of Design Issues", Liege, IUSSP Papers No. 20, 1983.

PICOUET, M., A. PELLEGRINO and J. PAPAIL
"L'immigration au Venezuela", Revue Européenne des migrations internationales, No. 4, 1986.

POPULATION REFERENCE BUREAU
New York, 1980.

QUESNEL, A. and P. VIMARD
"Migration et economie de plantation, plateau de Dates au Togo", forthcoming.

TELLER, C.H.
    "Impermanent and Seasonal Migration in Central America: Conceptual
    Methodological Approach Utilized in its Measurement", <u>IARUS</u> 13th
    Meeting, Székesfehérvar, 1982.

UNITED NATIONS
    "World Population Prospects: Estimates and Projections as Assessed in
    1984", Population Studies, No. 98, New York, 1986.

Chapter 3

CAUSES OF INTERNATIONAL MIGRATION

by

N. Federici

The migration of human beings is as old as humanity itself. Prehistoric hunters and food gatherers migrated in search of new areas that
contained richer edible plant and animal life and were therefore generally
more suitable for survival. Whole continents were populated mainly by migrations during prehistoric eras, as archeological finds demonstrate. Then,
in the periods of recorded history, mass migration became an important component of the evolution of populations. For centuries, the main reason why
people emigrated was to find better land and climate that would bring, once
farming began, better harvests.

The consolidation of large populations stimulated desire for expansion
through the conquest of new territories that would make possible added wealth
through the appropriation of natural resources and the exploitation of slave
labour. The political-military conquests of antiquity and of medieval times
further provoked and encouraged large population shifts, both from the
motherland towards the conquered territories and from the latter towards the
land of the conquerors, with different motivations: spontaneous moves for
political-military and economic reasons, and forced moves.

With the modern age came several changes in the general conditions for
political and economic development but although reasons for population shifts
became more differentiated and complex, basic causes remained the same. Great
geographical explorations opened up new political and economic prospects.
Whole new continents were discovered, and the growing European powers looked
upon colonisation as a way of adding to their wealth and expanding their
power. Thus, colonial empires were formed and the settling of conquered lands
was promoted. The pioneers who populated new territories certainly had, along
with economic motivation, the spirit of adventure which made them ready to
face the dangers of the unknown with courage and enthusiasm. But early experience in agricultural exploitation of vast new territories brought with it
forms of forced migration, including the use of slaves transferred against
their will from Africa to the New World. Colonial domination led to a particular kind of migratory flow from the motherland to the colonies: political, military and technical cadres for whom the move was not always

47

completely voluntary, or not tied to the individual's perceptions but rather to the organising needs of the colonising country.

Beginning in the 18th Century, after demographic ups and downs of previous centuries had been punctuated by epidemics that varied in their severity, a large increase in the population of Europe occurred (1). This induced some economists to foresee fearful imbalances between population increase and economic growth, and even to predict an incurable and growing discrepancy between population and resources. In Malthus's essay the necessity of a check to fertility is declared (though in rather different forms from those that were to become widespread) in order to mitigate the consequences of this imbalance (2).

The availability of rich natural resources in the new territories discovered or explored on very sparsely populated continents, together with existing divergencies between population growth and economic development in Europe, caused differential population pressures. The expression "population pressure" refers, in its static meaning, to the relationship between population and economic resources (the "subsistence level" of classic economic theories); and in its dynamic sense, the relationship between rate of population increase and rate of economic development. Two different territories with diverse numerical values in this relationship will present an imbalance which may be considered the cause of a population transfer from the zone under higher demographic pressure towards the one with lower demographic pressure.

According to this formulation, in the hypothetical case of a territory in which the demographic pressure indicates a relationship of balance, migration should not take place, or net migration should be approximately zero (3). In such cases any migration that occurs would be in the nature of an interchange of population and, as such, could be defined as "normal". In the case of a proportion greater than unity there should be (and generally is) a net emigration that tends to increase with the increase in numerical value of the ratio. In the case of proportions less than unity there should be a net immigration that increases with the decrease in the numerical value of the ratio. These are the two cases in which migration takes on what may be called a "pathological" nature. Obviously, in the first case, the places of destination would be those with low population pressures; in the second case, the places of origin would be those with high population pressures. Transfers could also occur within the boundaries of a single country, between regions that have diverse levels of demographic pressure (4).

For several reasons this pattern corresponds only approximately to what actually happens. First, in accepting this formulation, it must be kept in mind that the transfer can occur independently of the numerical value of the proportion in the country of origin A and the country of destination B. It would be enough for these two values to differ from each other. In other words, it is possible to have a migratory flow from A to B even though there exists a ratio of more than one-to-one both in A and in B, or below one-to-one in both. What causes the flux is the fact that the ratio is higher in A than in B. Second, the stimulus to emigrate depends also on individual possibilities of access to a certain level of income. This depends, in turn, on the characteristics of the distribution of income in the country of destination, among other things, as Tapinos has clearly stated (5). Third, other motivations besides economic ones contribute to migration. We return to this last point later. Here, we would like to clarify further the mechanism of

48

exchange of population between territories with diverse population pressure. The case of Italy serves as a good illustration of how the mechanism functions.

Italy, which became a united nation much later than other European countries (1861), was almost exclusively an agricultural country at the commencement of its nationhood. Twenty years later, according to the 1881 census, agricultural activities still surpassed non-agricultural activities in virtually all regions. At the national level about 60 per cent of the active population worked in agriculture. Until World War II, economic growth was slow although industrialisation (albeit slow) occurred in regions of northern Italy. Non-agricultural sectors elsewhere remained in a state of prolonged economic crisis. Development of non-agricultural activities occurred between the 1920s and the 1930s in north and central Italy and in the south and the islands of Sicily and Sardinia after 1950. Non-agricultural activities had overtaken agriculture in the north by 1930, in the central area at the end of World War II, on the islands around 1951, and in the continental south a few years later (see Figure 3.1) (6).

During this period Italy experienced rapid population expansion. The death rate began a rapid decline after 1880 but the decline in the birth rate was more than a decade behind and occurred very slowly until 1915 (see Figure 3.2).

It is therefore easy to understand why under these circumstances emigration became an important phenomenon. At first it was mainly temporary in nature and directed towards neighbouring countries that were more industrialised, particularly France, where an early decline in the birth rate had greatly reduced population pressure. This flow came, for the most part, from northern Italy because of its geographical and historical-cultural affinity with France. Outflow from the southern regions, which had been more hindered than helped by the country's unification (practically isolating them economically and politically), was towards the Americas, to lands that seemed to offer good possibilities of permanent residence as well as promise of rapid integration in the society.

Over 4 million Italians emigrated during the last quarter of the 19th Century, and a further 5 million during the first fifteen years of the 20th Century. At first, they headed mainly towards other European countries (especially France) but towards the turn of the century the flow to the Americas became as numerically important. Average initial annual departures rose from 100 000 to 500 000-600 000 on the eve of World War I. In Europe, Germany and Switzerland were the main destinations. The transatlantic flow, which at first had been mainly towards Argentina and thereafter Brazil, shifted to the United States. By the beginning of the 20th Century, the number of migrants bound for the United States was exceptionally high; and in the first fifteen years of the 20th Century more than 3 million Italians arrived there (see Table 3.1).

Changes in numbers and direction of flows were the result of several concurrent factors. Italian emigration progressively increased because difficulties arising from the nation's unification exacerbated, rather than attenuated, the demographic-economic imbalances that existed within the country and between Italy and the more advanced foreign countries. The early

FIGURE 3.1: RATES OF AGRICULTURAL AND NON-AGRICULTURAL EMPLOYMENT (BOTH SEXES)

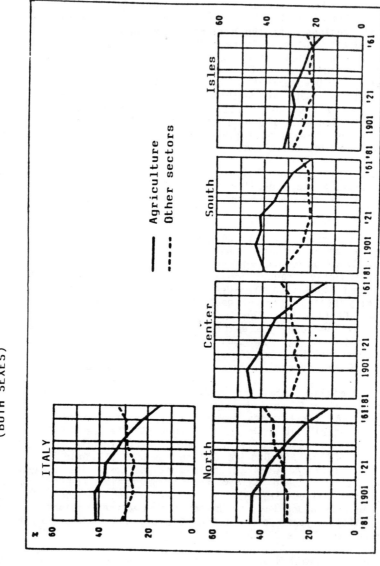

Source: O. Vitali, Aspetti dello sviluppo economico italiano alla luce della ricostruzione della popolazione attiva.

50

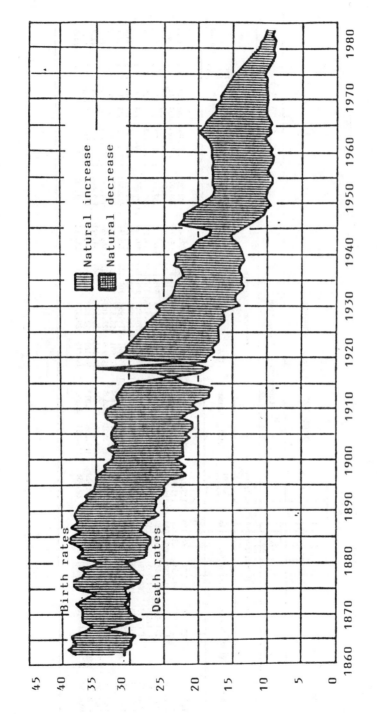

FIGURE 3.2: VITAL STATISTICS: RATES PER 1000 POPULATION –
ITALY 1862–1975

Source: N. Federici, Istituzioni di Demografia.

51

Table 3.1

EMIGRATION FROM ITALY (1876-1940)

Countries of destination

Years	Europe and Mediterranean countries						American countries						All countries			
	Belgium	France	Germany	Switzerland	Other countries	Total	Canada	USA	Argentina	Brazil	Other countries,	Total	Numbers	Annual average	Per '000 pop.	% Europe
1876-80		184.279	36.574	66.410	123.741	411.004		13.368	43.039	18.612	57.961	132.980	543.984	108.797	3.9	24.4
1881-85		212.501	34.634	35.161	193.436	475.732	1.059	74.398	132.660	41.857	44.999	294.973	770.705	154.141	5.3	38.3
1886-90		151.570	51.758	36.014	214.127	453.469	5.213	170.472	258.843	173.695	46.804	655.027	1 108.496	221.699	7.4	59.1
1891-95		134.484	76.228	60.829	273.794	545.335	2.344	206.596	155.583	329.904	42.791	737.218	1 282.553	256.511	8.3	57.5
1896-00		124.839	154.703	128.233	334.891	742.666	3.571	397.731	211.637	250.320	36.248	809.507	1 552.173	310.435	9.3	52.2
1901-05		271.493	280.045	269.141	403.561	1 224.040	19.654	998.352	278.511	100.103	49.592	1 546.212	2 770.252	554.050	16.8	55.8
1906-10		301.123	310.999	386.527	289.319	1 287.968	45.451	1 331.099	456.086	103.258	32.576	1 968.470	3 256.438	651.288	19.3	60.4
1911-15		325.317	280.906	350.977	253.477	1 217.677	71.134	1 054.701	259.957	107.422	32.168	1 525.382	2 743.059	548.612	15.5	55.6
1916-20		339.170	4.167	75.525	59.909	478.771	12.494	512.081	55.558	18.462	7.640	606.235	1 085.006	217.001	6.9	55.9
1921-25		659.472	7.235	51.253	143.861	861.801	20.655	225.969	322.483	48.526	36.885	654.518	1 516.319	303.264	7.9	43.2
1926-30	29.761	431.597	4.294	90.656	58.061	614.359	11.918	162.644	210.817	27.066	34.421	446.866	1 061.225	212.245	5.3	42.1
1931-35	5.972	175.767	3.138	64.438	67.920	317.235	2.077	66.220	50.823	7.455	14.331	140.906	458.141	91.628	2.2	30.8
1936-40	1.526	38.016	54.965	21.421	29.936	145.864	1.392	48.416	29.950	5.041	13.866	98.645	244.509	48.902	1.1	24.5

thrust of immigration towards France was certainly due to the population pressure differential between the two bordering nations. Its economic expansion required a growing work-force and the younger generations in regions of northern Italy faced great difficulties in their efforts to find work on a labour market that was slow to modernise, due to lagging industrialisation and a backward agricultural sector. In fact, the largest migrations were from the Veneto which was still almost completely agricultural and had a high birth rate. Emigration from two other northern regions that were not as economically depressed (Piedmont and Lombardy) was temporary, or seasonal, especially toward Switzerland. The exceptional economic expansion of Switzerland attracted increasing numbers of immigrants who created political problems not easily solved.

Meanwhile, towards the end of the 19th Century, other Western European countries, besides France, had begun their demographic transition. From the beginning of this century until the eve of World War I, annual emigration of Italians was more than half a million, of whom 40 to 50 per cent went to Western European countries and the remainder to the Americas, particularly the United States, where population remained small relative to demand for labour, a situation that offered excellent opportunities for newcomers.

It is not easy to verify in quantitative terms the relationship between intensity of migratory flow and differential population pressure between the territories of origin and destination. One reason is lack of adequate data. It is necessary to have at one's disposal information from which could be calculated the variations of population pressure differential between Italy and the countries of destination. While it is possible to reconstruct a good approximation of a time series of population increase both for Italy and the destination countries, it is much more difficult to calculate parallel and comparable time series on indicators of economic expansion (7). Another difficulty is that in Italy's migration history, certain internal (inter-regional) migratory flows can be considered "pathological" and linked to differential population pressures, a factor which considerably distorts attempts to quantify the relationship (8). A third reason is that the flux also depends on other concurrent circumstances which, in certain periods, can become prevalent. Among these, three factors in particular should be mentioned.

First, forces of inertia tend to keep choices of destination the same even when conditions there have changed. This occurs because of the network of relations between the country of origin and communities of immigrants in countries of destination, and also because information about new opportunities is usually sparse and late in arriving. This factor is especially important when the choice of migration is an individual one and not organised through governmental agencies. Second, other motivations that act as a stimulus for deciding destination include geographical proximity, similarity of climate and cultural affinity (language and customs). Among reasons for emigrating, factors of an ideological-political and/or sociological nature often come into play. Some population transfers are forms of voluntary exile, others take place because of a desire to experience ways of life that are different from one's own and seem to be (rightly or wrongly) more attractive. Third, aside from spontaneous personal choices, there are also juridical-political factors that may either hinder or facilitate transfers, and thus create greater or less possibility of access to the labour market of the host country as well as length of stay in it.

53

Non-economic considerations are clearly important. For instance northern Italians view France as a favourite destination (even aside from job opportunities) both for its proximity and the characteristics of its society. Moreover, French policy has facilitated permanent residence there, a situation that was different in Switzerland, and thus affected the nature of Italian migration to that country.

Another example concerns early currents of Italian overseas migration. At first Latin America was preferred, especially Argentina, whose society had considerable affinity with Italy's. It was only later that job opportunities in the United States attracted great numbers of workers from Italy and from Austria, Hungary, Poland and Russia, where the first signs of a reduction in the birth rate were late in coming compared to the Eastern European countries in which a drop in birth rates had already begun.

Although no attempt will be made to give a quantitative verification of the relationship between population pressure and currents of Italian emigration in the various countries of destination from the time of the unification of Italy until World War II, we will provide a series of statistics (Tables 3.1, 3.2 and 3.3, and Figures 3.3 and 3.4). The demographic and economic trends in these series are in accord, we feel, with the hypothesis. Moreover, the non-matching phases in the demographic transitions of various countries, and the diversity in their economic development seem consistent, by and large, with this hypothesis.

World War I, the years between the two wars (with the international political upheavals brought on by the Russian revolution and then by the establishment of totalitarian regimes -- Italian fascism, German naziism and Spanish Francoism), and World War II, all created distortions in currents of migration. It was not until the 1950s that these flows were re-formed, though on new bases. The economic transformations and, even more importantly perhaps, the political upheavals had left indelible marks. Migratory streams had lost their spontaneous nature; their directions were determined mainly by either bilateral agreements between governments or by other forms of migration policy. Population transfers that had occurred at the end of the 19th Century and during the first fifteen years of the 20th Century caused political and economic problems in places of destination which led host countries to adopt restrictive measures on the entry of new immigrants (9). On the one hand, this resulted in a deviation of flows; on the other it caused an increase in illegal entries.

At present, political factors take on greater importance than economic ones with regard to the destination of emigrants. While demographic-economic factors still prevail, in many instances political-ideological motivations are also important.

Profound transformations in Italian migration since the end of World War II deserve mention. Between 1946 and the 1960s, emigration was considerable but thereafter it fell dramatically (Table 3.4). As for places of destination, the European countries (particularly Germany and Switzerland) progressively overtook non-European ones. With reduction in emigration, moreover, went increasing return, with the result that during the 1970s net migration balance became zero or slightly positive (10).

Table 3.2

NATURAL INCREASE PER THOUSAND OF THE POPULATION — SELECTED EUROPEAN COUNTRIES

Years	France	Germany	England and Wales	Belgium	Switzerland	Italy
1861-65	3.7	10.8	12.6	8.9		8.8
1866-70	1.6	9.8	12.9	8.2		6.6
1871-75	0.6	10.6	13.5	9.1	6.4	6.4
1876-80	2.9	13.3	14.6	10.2	8.2	7.5
1881-85	2.5	11.2	14.1	10.2	6.2	10.7
1886-90	1.1	12.1	12.6	9.2	7.1	10.3
1991-95	0	13.1	11.9	8.9	7.9	10.6
1896-1900	1.3	15.5	11.7	10.8	10.3	10.9
1901-05	1.7	14.4	12.1	10.5	10.3	10.9
1906-10	0.7	14.1	11.4	8.9	10.0	11.5
1911-15	-1.1	8.7	9.7	6.4	8.4	11.7
1916-20	-5.5	-1.0	7.4	-0.9	4.3	-1.4
1921-25	2.1	8.9	9.1	7.2	7.0	12.4
1926-30	1.4	6.7	6.0	6.4	5.4	10.8
1931-35	0.8	5.4	3.2	4.2	4.6	9.8
1936-40	-1.2	7.6	2.2	1.9	3.6	9.4
1941-45	-1.3		3.0	-0.9	7.6	5.1
1946-50	7.9		6.3	4.5	8.2	10.5

Source: B.R. Mitchell, European Historical Statistics, 1750-1970.

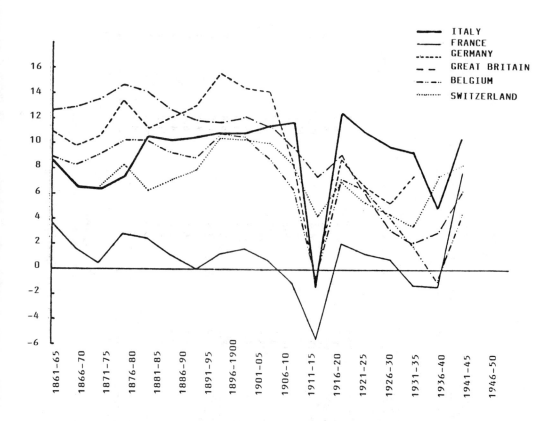

FIGURE 3.3: NATURAL INCREASE PER 1000 POPULATION 1861-1950

ITALY
FRANCE
GERMANY
GREAT BRITAIN
BELGIUM
SWITZERLAND

FIGURES 3.4 a + b

GROWTH OF OUTPUT PER
HEAD OF POPULATION

EMIGRATION FROM ITALY
(Annual average thousands)

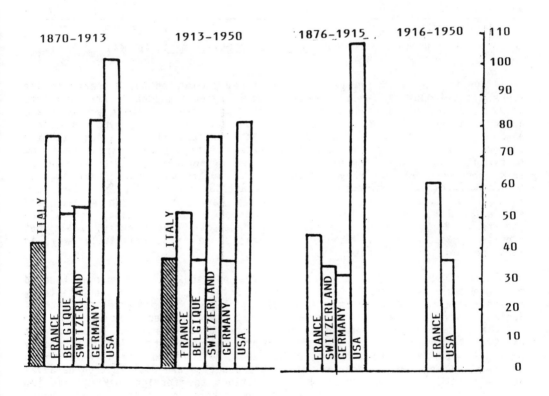

Table 3.3

ECONOMIC DEVELOPMENT AND EMIGRATION FROM ITALY TO VARIOUS COUNTRIES

Countries	Growth of output per head of population (Annual average compound growth rates GDP at constant prices)		Emigration from Italy to different countries (Annual average) (In thousands)	
	1870-1913	1913-50	1876-1915	1916-50
Italy	0.8	0.7		
France	1.5	1.0	43.733	61.204
Switzerland	1.2	1.5	34.187	2.057
Germany	1.6	0.7	31.432	2.967
United States	2.0	1.6	106.582	36.047

Source: A. Maddison, Phases of Capitalistic Development, (p. 44).

During the last ten years, a major new phenomenon has appeared on the scene: the influx of foreign workers. Many entered illegally and therefore do not appear in official statistics, although signs of their presence are apparent to a certain extent (11). In confirmation of the hypothesis that high population pressure determines a sharp increase in migration, today's workers come from countries with high rates of population increase and low rates of economic development. But the really surprising characteristic of this phenomenon is that they are entering a country with one of the highest official rates of unemployment in the industrialised world (12). They come mainly from countries in the Mediterranean basin, both North African and Middle Eastern, and also from Asia (Philippines and Thailand) and Africa (Eritrea and Cape Verde Islands). The rate of illegal entry, while not precisely measured, is certainly very high, since it is relatively easy, in fact, for foreigners to enter Italy.

At first glance, it may appear incongruous that high unemployment could be compatible with large immigration. Actually, no real inconsistency exists. Italian unemployment is partially linked to processes of techno-logical and structural transformation that have caused upheavals in the official labour market. These processes have created another labour market parallel to the official one. This complex transformation has made poorly paid jobs and/or unpleasant work undesirable, while simultaneously fostering an "underground" semi-hidden structure of production and distribution parallel to the traditional one. Under these conditions the foreign worker finds job opportunities in types of work that Italian workers refuse (unskilled labour, domestic service) or in temporary jobs without any kind of legal contract or coverage.

Furthermore, there is also an influx of foreigners who come for politi-cal as well as economic reasons. Many are students who attend institutes of learning and/or political exiles who have either exiled themselves or are true refugees. Often they migrate because they have found it less difficult to get

Table 3.4

ITALIAN MIGRATION WITH EUROPEAN AND NON-EUROPEAN COUNTRIES

Periods	Expatriations			Repatriations			Net migration		
	Europe	Extra-Europe	Total	Europe	Extra-Europe	Total	Europe	Extra-Europe	Total
1946-50	638.492	489.228	1 127.720	297.126	82.882	380.008	-341.366	-406.346	-747.722
1951-55	662.956	680.058	1 343.014	359.582	158.043	517.625	-303.374	-522.015	-825.389
1956-60	1 104.160	490.232	1 594.392	644.822	161.142	805.964	-459.338	-329.090	-788.428
1961-65	1 329.445	242.025	1 571.470	961.905	85.073	1 046.978	-367.540	-156.952	-524.492
1966-70	798.766	276.758	1 075.524	749.279	72.363	821.642	-49.487	-204.395	-253.881
1971-75	503.095	134.798	637.893	519.662	111.806	631.468	+16.567	-22.992	-6.425
1976-80	332.304	111.975	444.279	379.416	110.619	490.035	+47.112	-1.356	+45.756
1981-83	209.205	63.395	272.600	205.680	63.433	269.113	-3.525	+38.000	-3.487

into Italy than other countries. Finally, there are the "mobile" foreigners who do not come spontaneously but are sent in by nationalistic organisations or international political groups and, in some cases, come for purposes of terrorism.

The image of mass migration today is extremely complex. Its diverse components are quite difficult to estimate either quantitatively or qualitatively (13). The process of transformation with economic evolution is differentiated from country to country, including technicians and experts from the highly advanced countries to the less developed areas. Flows such as these are in origin-destination directions that are the opposite of mass transfers and therefore unconnected with the relationship demographic development/economic expansion that characterises mass flows. If anything, they manifest a reverse relationship. Italy contributes to these streams and because of their geographic mobility and temporary nature, they give rise to a considerable flux of repatriations. In fact, it would be more precise to say that in Italy today it is not so much that expatriation has disappeared but that negative net migration has disappeared (14).

Italy has taken on the characteristics of both an immigration and an emigration country. It receives workers from the overpopulated areas of Africa and Asia; for the most part non-skilled illegals, but also political exiles and persons from the fringes of the upper-middle categories of less developed countries who seek either refuge or the opportunity for socio-cultural betterment. It sends out temporary emigrants, including the self-employed, often with Italian capital or in conjunction with work projects carried out by Italian companies. This diverse nature of present-day Italian migration represents the new (and in some measure, contradictory) position of Italy in today's world demographic-economic context.

NOTES AND REFERENCES

1. The characteristics of the evolution of European peoples are clearly outlined and documented in the fundamental work: M. Reinhard, A. Armengaud, J.J. Dupaquier, _Histoire générale de la population mondiale,_ Paris, Montchrestien, 1968.

2. T.R. Malthus, _An Essay on the Principle of Population,_ second edition, 18. The first edition came out anonymously, as is well-known, in 1798.

3. This formulation was first expressed in 1955 and later developed further. Cf. N. Federici, Lezioni di Demographia, Rome, De Santis, 1955-56, pp. 403-5; N. Federici, _Instituzioni di Demografia,_ Rome, Elia, 1979, pp. 591-7.

4. Cf. N. Federici, A. Golini, _Les Migrations entre les régions à l'intérieur des six Pays,_ in "La population des Pays du Marché Commun : problèmes économiques et sociaux", IDEAD, Turcoing, 1972, reprinted in "Genus", Vol. XXVIII, No. 1-4, 1972.

5. According to Tapinos, the decision to emigrate is determined by a necessary condition (even if not sufficient), expressed by the following relationship:

$$\frac{V_i}{P_i} \, q < \frac{V_i}{P_j} \, r$$

in which V_i = income of the country of origin, V_j = income of the country of destination, P_i = population of the country of origin, P_j = population of the country of destination, q = probability of the individual of producing a given income in $\underline{i}$, r = probability of producing a certain income in $\underline{j}$. Cf. G. Tapinos, _L'économie des migrations internationales,_ p. 61, Paris, Colin, 1974.

6. A reconstruction of the result of various censuses in order to get a comparable picture of the evolution of the active population in different economic sectors is to be found in: O. Vitali, _Aspetti della sviluppo economico italiano alla luce della ricostruzione della populazione attiva,_ Rome, Instituto di Demografia dell'Università, 1970.

7. Attempts by some countries in that direction are not lacking (Cf. B.R. Mitchell, European Historical Statistics 1750-1970, Macmillan Columbia University Press, 1978; A. Maddison, Phases of Capitalist Development, Oxford University Press, 1982) but for various reasons are not fully usable for our purposes.

8. In this regard, see the study cited in note (4).

9. There were, in particular, tight restrictions imposed by legislation in the United States beginning in the 1920s ("Quota Act", 1921) which quickly caused the inflow from Italy to drop by half. The figures continued to diminish until Italian immigration to the United States fell to very small figures at the outbreak of World War II.

10. Regarding the dynamics of Italian migration in the post-war period see: E. Reyneri, La Catena Migratoria, Bologna, Il Mulino publishers, 1979; F. Pittau, L'altra Italia -- il pianeta emigrazione, Padova, Edizioni Messaggero, 1986; F. Calvanese, Emigrazione e politica migratoria negli anni '70: l'esperienza ed europea, Salerno, La Veglia publishers.

11. On the basis of the 1981 population census foreigners residing in Italy numbered 210 037 and the foreigners present temporarily were 109 841. Statistics furnished by the Ministry of Internal Affairs on the number of residence permits show 383 765 at 31st December 1983 and 403 983 at 31st December 1984.

12. According to figures from the sample survey done by ISTAT on the labour force, the number of unemployed persons (the total of persons in search of work) has increased during the past ten years from 1 230 000 in 1975 to 2 472 000 in 1985, and reaching the percentage of 10.6 per cent.

13. See the works cited in note (10) and Atti della Giornata di studio su "l'immigrazione straniera in Italia", (Rome, CNR, 22 March 1983) in "Studi Emigrazione -- Etudes migrations", Rome, CSER, September 1983; var. auth., La presenza straniera in Italia -- Nuovi contributi conoscitivi, in "Studi Emigrazione -- Etudes Migrations", Rome, CSER, June 1986.

14. On the size and structure of recent Italian migration, see: A.M. Birindelli, Il consolidarsi della nuove caratteristiche migratorie dell'Italia, paper presented at the Giornata di studio su: "Migrazioni internazionali, nuove tendenze, prospettive e problemi interpretativi", Rome.

Chapter 4

PROBLEMS OF MEASUREMENT

by

Chantal Blayo

Counting the Events

In order to analyse the demographic impact of international migration on the development of a developing country, it is necessary to measure its influence on the resident population. Annual statistics on the departure of residents for more developed countries and statistics on their return are therefore essential. Statistics should also be available on the arrival of foreigners. Availability of these data presupposes a registration system of all entries and departures. Unfortunately, this is seldom available in developing countries. If reliance has to be placed on data available in receiving countries it is necessary to obtain it for all the countries to which migrants went. These countries would have to possess complete registration systems. Lack of adequate statistics on departure from many countries poses a considerable difficulty in this regard.

It is therefore necessary to turn our attention to direct methods. If in a census in a country of origin, an individual is asked whether he/she was present in the country at the previous census, whether he/she had migrated at least once (and if so the year of the last departure and the year of last return), it is possible, after correction for deaths and after estimating the omission rate in censuses, to calculate the number of returns, provided that these are not too frequent. However, such a system would cover only departures since the previous census. Departures that occurred before the previous census and were not followed by a return cannot be detected (1).

Some researchers have proposed including questions in censuses which seek information on whether the respondent's brothers and sisters or their children are living abroad. The method has already been tried in several countries (IUSSP, 1981). This method makes it possible to estimate the number of emigrants who have not returned and also to obtain data on the year of departure.

The census schedule in receiving countries might include questions on whether each individual was present or absent in the country at the previous census, together with questions on natality, place of birth, and year of last arrival in the country. After appropriate corrections had been made, it would be possible to estimate the number of immigrants who did not return according to year of arrival. Immigrants who arrived before the previous census and who left the country between the previous and the present censuses would be counted globally. However, immigrants who arrived and returned before the previous census or between the last two censuses could not be detected. Such data would be useful for the country of origin only if the country in which the data are obtained is a receiver of significant numbers of immigrants from that country.

It is also possible to combine data obtained from several sources. In a paper presented at the Geneva meeting of the CICRED/ICM workshop, J. Papail explained how it was possible to estimate the net migration of people from Colombia in Venezuela between 1971 to 1981 by a judicious combination of heterogeneous data usually gathered on foreigners in a receiving country. After correction for omission, census data on the population born abroad, irrespective of the place of birth, the total size of the foreign population was calculated. Then, by using data on the issuing of visas for residents, naturalisation and on regularisation of the position of foreigners born abroad but not in Colombia, it was possible to estimate the total foreign population born outside Colombia. By differences one obtained the foreign population born in Colombia. In order to test these results, the foreign population born in Colombia was estimated by another method making use of data on death by age, sex and natality and by making an hypothesis on the level of mortality in these populations born in Colombia. Along the same lines, comparison of census data combined with data on entries, births and deaths of foreigners and data on naturalisation and losses of nationality permit estimates of the total number of departures from a receiving country between two censuses (Zamora, 1986).

Measuring the Phenomenon

Just as a count of the number of births and deaths is not sufficient for studying fertility and mortality, so a count of migratory events is not enough to study migration. Analysis of a demographic phenomenon requires grouping people in various cohorts, each composed of individuals who had encountered an event at the same time which is previous to the one which constituted the subject of the analysis. This requires observing the timing of the studied event according to the duration between the initial event and the studied event. Emigration should therefore be studied in each birth cohort on the basis of age at departure; in the same way, return migration should be studied through emigration cohorts, according to duration of stay abroad.

It would be necessary, however, to obtain statistics on departures classified by year of birth and statistics of return migration by year of departure. A systematic count of national in-moves and out-moves is also required but not sufficient. Information would also be required on each out-migrant concerning his year of birth and for each return migrant on the year he left the country. One also requires annual distribution by age of the national population.

If information is not available, retrospective observation is required. To reach the above objective, retrospective observation has to include: (i) people who have never left the country; (ii) people who left and returned; and (iii) people who left but have not returned. At the time of observation, the first two groups would be within the national borders whereas the third group would be scattered in various receiving countries.

A survey based on a representative sample carried out simultaneously in the sending country and the various receiving countries and covering all the three groups would be highly informative. Nevertheless, such a survey is not easy to implement because of the numerous places of survey, incomplete sampling frames or their absence in the receiving countries and administrative and technical problems raised by the required simultaneity of all operations in various national contexts. One solution would be to carry out a survey only in the receiving country. This would cover the first two groups but not the third. Information on the third group could be obtained by questioning relatives who have remained. Although mothers and fathers are the best source of information on emigrants who have not returned, it is better to question siblings whose survival rate at the time of survey would be higher.

If in-depth information has to be obtained on the migration and demographic stories of the three groups, it is not sufficient to simply include some additional questions on the census form. An ad hoc survey specifically designed for this purpose would be necessary and would allow comparisons of migrants and non-migrants and of return migrants and non-return migrants. Moreover, it would pave the way for identifying the various effects of migration on the demography and economic development of the sending country. In particular, such a survey would allow us to measure the intensity of migration and to assess differential propensity to emigrate (and to return) according to various characteristics (age, sex, education, etc.). This survey would also address variations of demographic behaviour (fertility, nuptiality ...) according to migration status.

Let us now consider practical problems. Group (iii) includes not only emigrants who had not returned but also their children who were born abroad. Second, if a non-return migrant does not have a sister or brother currently residing in the country, it is necessary to question instead his parents or other relatives. The problem is that we cannot obtain information on those in group (iii) who do not have any relatives residing in the country. However, on the basis of information collected in the survey, or from other sources (vital statistics, census, other surveys ...), one could design several probabilities concerning frequencies of one-child families, migration and mortality. Combination of these probabilities would lead to estimates concerning the population not covered by the survey.

Another problem regarding group (iii) is that most individuals in this group have more than one relative within the country (e.g., several siblings, two parents ...) and data collected on them is therefore often overweighted. Correction could be made by multiplying data on an emigrant by the reciprocal of the number of people in the country who may provide information on him. The survey would be made by simple random sampling, the fraction being determined by the presumed number of departures and of returns during the last thirty or forty years. As the surveyed people have to be statistically significant after break-down by birth cohort and other characteristics, the sample size depends on the type of breakdown envisaged. On the other hand, the sampling fraction may be low if migrations have been numerically important.

Finally, to carry out the survey, a sampling frame is needed; for example, a census or an equivalent enumeration which is recent or updated. For each surveyed individual, a white questionnaire could be used for detailing his/her demographic and migratory history and coloured questionnaires used for each of his/her relatives abroad. The questionnaire would provide information on migratory history of the individual if he/she had spent at least six months abroad and demographic history, including year of birth, country of birth, countries of birth of his/her mother and father.

Additional information could also be collected for the study of differential migration according to some demographic criteria, and the study of differential demography according to attitudes concerning migration (year of birth and country of birth for children, economic activity at year of migration, residence at migration, residence at return ...). This information should be collected for the three groups under study: persons who never left the country of origin, those who migrated and returned, and those who left and never returned. As the former group could not be directly reached and as someone has to substitute for them, it would be preferable to avoid difficult questions in order to ensure that the information will be uniform. One of the important objectives of characterising a cohort of migrants who returned is to compare them with migrants of the same cohort who did not return.

With a view to determining the number of persons presented by the spokesperson and of weighting responses, the questionnaire asked of dwellers to obtain information on the size of the _fratrie_, the possible presence of brothers and sisters at the country of origin, their possible out-migration, their year of death (if applicable) and the presence in the country of origin of other family members when all children live in a foreign country. As many colour sheets as the dweller has brothers and sisters who have migrated should be completed. Although an inquiry of this kind appears to be the best way of obtaining data for measuring the impact of emigration and, more important, the impact of return to the country of origin, we should realise that the implementation of the inquiry presents difficulties.

It requires a good sample base. Quality and competence of field investigators are of utmost importance, including an aptitude for helping respondents recall the timing of events concerning brothers and sisters. The quality of the inquiry will depend as much on the capacity of the interviewees to provide information on their brothers and sisters, as on the interviewers to help them.

Although the inquiry would exclude persons who have no spokesperson in the country of origin, the bias would be difficult to correct. It is therefore important to emphasize that inquiries of this kind will be difficult in countries where _fratries_ are small. If these problems could be overcome, the information obtained would make up for the absence of recording entries and exits and permit the migratory history during a half-century, would obtain the correct measure of departures and returns, and would assist in the understanding of determinants and consequences of migrations and returns. An inquiry of this kind is presently in progress in Portugal, organised by the Centre for Demographic Studies of the National Institute of Statistics with the co-operation of INED. A questionnaire of the type already described has been tested in a pilot survey of 300 households. Field investigators, well-trained in helping interviewees recall dates of events, have obtained answers of astonishing quality. Non-response to questions has been very rare.

NOTES AND REFERENCES

1.   The cost of such a procedure would be low. Only four questions need to be added to the census schedules.

BIBLIOGRAPHY

IUSSP
J. Somoza, "A Proposal for Estimating the Emigrant Population by Sex and Age from Special Census Questions"; K. Hill, "A Proposal for the Use of Information on Residence of Siblings to Estimate Migration by Age"; and J. Somoza, "Indirect Estimates of Emigration: Applications of Two Procedures Using Information on Residence of Children and Siblings" in Indirect Procedures for Estimating Emigration, IUSSP Papers No. 18, 1981.

ZAMORA, F.
"Mesure du nombre de départs d'étrangers entre deux recensements : l'exemple de la France entre 1975 et 1982". Paper presented at the Second International Seminar of AIDELF on International Migration, September 1986.

Chapter 5

STATE INTERVENTION AND THE INTERNATIONAL LABOUR MARKET:
A REVIEW OF LABOUR EMIGRATION POLICIES IN THE ARAB WORLD

by

I.J. Seccombe and R.I. Lawless

INTRODUCTION

Although there have been numerous studies of immigration policy, systematic discussion of its counterpart, emigration policy, has been seriously
neglected despite a world-wide increase in international migration during the
last thirty years. This neglect is attributed by Adler (1980) to the implicit
assumption that, since the international labour market is effectively controlled by labour-receiving countries, the question of policy should be
approached from their perspectives. While the level of labour emigration is
primarily demand-determined (Böhning, 1978), many countries are faced with an
(often post facto) important policy decision concerning the extent of state
intervention. Richards and Martin (1983) argue that within the Arab world,
migration for employment occurs virtually unimpeded in a fundamentally
laissez-faire environment. However, while foreign workers, a large proportion
of them from other Arab states, poured into Saudi Arabia, Libya and the Arab
Gulf States between 1973 and 1982 as rising oil revenues stimulated unprecedented investment in industrial and infrastructural development, the idea
that this occurred in an entirely laissez-faire environment is an over-
simplification.

In practice, countries of labour emigration do have discernible and
differing policies towards labour exports. These policies range from outright
prohibition of labour emigration (in Algeria and the People's Democratic
Republic of Yemen, hereafter PDRY), through selective control (Egypt and
Syria) and laissez-faire (Lebanon, Morocco and the Yemen Arab Republic, hereafter YAR), to positive encouragement (Jordan and Tunisia). Indeed most
countries have pursued a range of different policies throughout their migration histories and differing policies have been applied concomitantly to
different segments of the labour market.

Richards and Martin (1983) also infer that a laissez-faire approach
towards labour emigration implies an explicit absence of policy directives.

This ignores the fact that a _laissez-faire_ approach may involve the removal of pre-existing barriers to emigration (as in Egypt) and as such must involve an explicit policy decision. There is a tendency in migration literature to treat emigration policy almost as a postscript in which recommendations are propounded in a political and historical vacuum, ignorant of extant strategy (and the constraints imposed upon it) and its formulation and iteration.

Although emigration policies are often determined by _ad hoc_ and short-term considerations (Höpfner and Huber, 1978), they are nevertheless influenced by, and in the longer term are an influence on, the broader development strategy adopted by the state. The evaluation of emigration policies must therefore be examined in the context of an evolving development strategy. From the development standpoint emigration policies have two primary functions:

i)   To safeguard national development interests; and

ii) To maximize returns from migration to the benefit of these development interests.

Both areas of concern are represented in the two sub-divisions of emigration policy which can be defined as management and structural.

Management policies can be defined in relatively narrow terms as those which are primarily concerned with the short-term organisation and functioning of the migration process. These include the classic concerns of emigration policy, namely protecting the legal status, rights and conditions of nationals working and living abroad, together with intervention in the recruitment and selection process to prevent the abuse of individuals by recruiting agents or to control the withdrawal of specific skills. A related set of management issues include policies to influence the level, use and distribution of emigrant workers' remittance earnings through, for example, multiple exchange rates, foreign currency account provision, tax advantages, and investment opportunities.

In contrast, structural policies are more broadly based and concerned with a range of medium- and long-term measures that can be adopted by a labour-supplying country to regulate external migration in a manner consonant with national development goals. These concern the overall level, composition and determinates of emigration as well as its effects on social and economic conditions in the country (or region) of migrant origin (and return). Structural policies therefore impinge rather more closely on the government's wider development strategy. In the long term such policies may aim to stabilize the flow of labour and remittances to enable the formulation of long-term resource policies. The attainment of these objectives may involve the negotiation of bilateral or multilateral manpower agreements. Most frequently structural emigration policies have a relief function; to reduce the pressures imposed by international labour migration on, for example, domestic production, patterns of investment or the costs and availability of labour. Such policies are largely ameliorative in nature, for example in tackling skill shortages through the promotion of vocational training and the manipulation of participation rates. They may involve measures designed to encourage or discourage the emigration of specific groups, or emigration from particular areas.

The differences between management and structural emigration policies are illustrated in Figure 5.1. The major, but not exclusive concern in this chapter will be with "structural" emigration policies. The main purpose is to present a broad review of policy choices made by labour-exporting countries of the Arab world and to illustrate the gap between policy articulation and policy implementation. The second half of the chapter presents detailed and contrasting case studies of labour emigration policy: Algeria and Jordan.

From Prohibition to Encouragement: A Review of International Labour Emigration Policies in the Arab World

Three countries in the Arab world, namely Algeria, Oman and the PDRY have, at different times and for varying reasons, adopted prohibitive emigration policies in the recent past. Of these, only the Algerian ban (September 1973) on emigration has been successful.

South Yemen (PDRY) imposed a ban on emigration for employment in 1973 following a long history of emigration, particularly to Indonesia and more recently to the neighbouring oil-rich states of Saudi Arabia and Kuwait. British military withdrawal from Aden and the termination of budgetary support following transfer of power from Britain and the Sultans to the National Front in November 1967, together with the closure of the Suez Canal, precipitated economic decline and labour emigration from the PDRY. The departure of professional, skilled and technical manpower was given further impetus in the early 1970s by repeated reductions in public sector salaries following the accession to power of the radical wing of the National Front in June 1969. Restrictions on foreign travel by technical and university educated cadres were introduced following further salary cuts in August 1972 and, in the face of growing skilled labour shortages, the government imposed a comprehensive ban on emigration in December 1973.

Although imposed for primarily economic reasons, the ban on emigration was defended in political terms as part of the revolutionary struggle. In a pronouncement on the state of the revolution in 1977 the Secretary General of the Central Committee (Abdel Fattah Isma'il) stated:

> The idea prevails in imperialist circles that the revolution in Democratic Yemen has been hostile to specialists and technicians because of its policies and has thus led them to emigrate in search of work. Our position is that our revolution has always regarded people with scientific training as potential cadres on whom the people will depend for the revolutionary renaissance and to create a new life, because of the education and experience they possess.

> Contrary to imperialist ideas, it has been demonstrated that the counter-revolutionary forces at home and abroad had followed a policy of enticing numerous technically skilled cadres to leave the country to work in industrial centres abroad ... aiming thereby to deprive Democratic Yemen of their skills in the process of its social and economic development.

The examples of the PDRY (and Algeria) contrast with the Sultanate of Oman which removed a ban on emigration during the 1970s. During the 1950s conflict

FIGURE 5.1: INFLUENCES ON, AND ASPECTS OF, LABOUR EMIGRATION POLICY

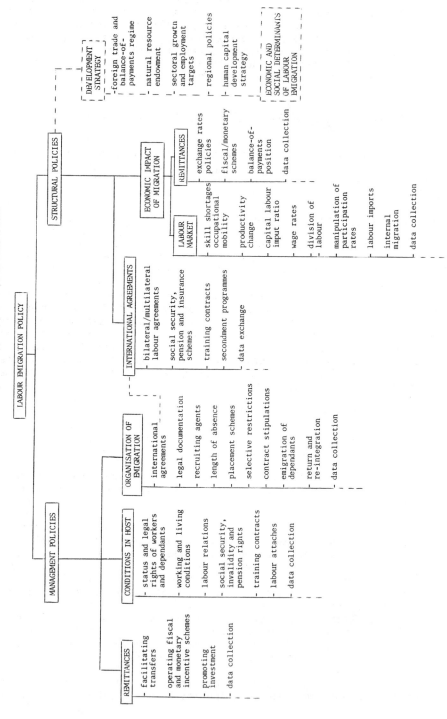

between the Sultanate, based in Muscat, and the Imamate in the interior, led to the substantial outflow of refugees from the interior to Saudi Arabia. With the final assertion of Sultanate power over the interior in 1955-56 the Imam and his supporters fled to Saudi Arabia. The Sultan, Sa'id bin Taimur, imposed a ban on foreign travel which aimed to prevent the return of the Imam and his political followers. All who left Oman without one of the rarely-granted permits, were automatically exiled for life and were subject to arrest and detention if they returned (Birks and Sinclair, 1978).

Despite this prohibition the emigration of opponents to the Sultan's regime continued. In the 1960s these political émigrés were joined by wage labourers who risked the penalities of clandestine emigration to find employment in the expanding oil economies of Abu Dhabi and Saudi Arabia. Such movements were made at considerable risk; the clandestine status of emigration made the migrants vulnerable to exploitation by agents organising the border crossings and by customs and other government officials who had to be bribed. In July 1970 however Sultan Sa'id bin Taimur was overthrown in a British-backed coup d'état and replaced by his son, Qaboos. The ban on foreign travel was lifted shortly afterwards and an amnesty granted to all returning exiles.

In practice, the effectiveness of such prohibition orders has been undermined by their limited implementation and by the considerable demand for manpower in neighbouring states, in this case Saudi Arabia. Indeed, it is estimated that the number of South Yemenis abroad increased at a greater rate (3.5 per cent per annum) between 1975 and 1980 than in neighbouring YAR (3.0 per cent per annum) where there was no such ban on emigration (Birks and Sinclair, 1982). The limited impact of the ban was made clear during a speech by the PDRY President (Salem Robaya Ali) in November 1976 in which he deplored the continuing high rate of emigration which was "contrary to our national interests". Nevertheless, earnings from emigrant workers provide PDRY with a major source of foreign exchange consistently greater than external assistance and comparable with the level of export earnings. Workers' remittances to PDRY increased from only $33 million in 1973 to $311 million in 1979 and $450 million in 1982. Customs regulations on goods brought in by emigrant workers were liberalised in 1978 (Shirreff, 1979), an indication of the government's policy of taking the opportunities provided by emigration while at the same time maintaining its political integrity by retaining the official ban on emigration. Further indication of a move away from the initial position came with the establishment in May 1985 of a committee to protect the interests of nationals working abroad.

Restrictive regulations

A number of Arab countries have sought to limit, rather than prohibit emigration for employment. For example, the emigration policies of Egypt have passed through several phases, including a period of prohibition in the mid-1950s and regulation in the 1960s and early 1970s. In the mid-1960s, some members of the Egyptian Government promoted emigration as a solution to Egypt's growing population problem although others feared that unless restrictions were retained, a growing "brain drain" would undermine the principles of socialist development and self-reliance. The government allowed, and indeed encouraged, emigration (primarily to North America and Australia) while in practice administrative constraints (such as the mandatory work assignment of university graduates) prevented the departure of those most acceptable to immigration countries. Between 1962 and 1968 only 6 046 emigrants (and 7 067 dependants) left Egypt to settle abroad (Dessouki, 1982).

The government's approach to emigration changed after 1967. In 1969 it established a committee on emigration and employment abroad to encourage temporary emigration, channel job opportunities abroad and negotiate bilateral agreements with potential labour-receiving states. In the wake of economic stagnation after the 1967 Arab-Israeli war, increasing numbers of Egyptians sought employment abroad (Ayubi, 1983). The number of work permits issued rose from 5 245 in 1966 to 9 169 in 1968; in 1969 more than 28 000 applications were received. Although welcoming the revenue generated by Egyptians working abroad, the government, prompted in particular by the Ministry of Health and by the Ministry of Industry which had continued to defend a policy of restricting the mobility of doctors and engineers, suspended permission to emigrate pending further review.

A new policy introduced in 1970 encouraged labour emigration but imposed quota restrictions on persons with skills required for national development: architecture; dentistry; engineering; pharmacology; nursing; medicine; veterinary sciences and statisticians. For example, the 1970 quota made provision for an emigration quota of only 20 pharmacists and 5 statisticians. While applications from persons with post-graduate degrees were subject to individual review by the ministerial committee for manpower, the government's increasing commitment to temporary emigration is apparent from the enormous growth in the secondment of personnel to other Arab countries; in 1973 over 19 400 Egyptians worked abroad on secondment and by 1975-76 the number of school teachers alone exceeded 20 000 (Messiha, 1980).

The increase in official secondments reflects the emergence of a liberal emigration policy in association with Sadat's economic policy of infitah (the open door). Article 52 of the new (1971) constitution made both temporary and permanent emigration a constitutional right; many restrictions on emigration were relaxed and bureaucratic procedures were simplified. By 1973 emigration was seen in terms of the export of "surplus" labour rather than of the "brain drain". Indeed, by 1975 there were an estimated 447 550 Egyptian migrant workers in the Arab region, some 24.5 per cent of all expatriate workers in the Arab world (Birks and Sinclair, 1980). The broad policy of exporting labour was matched by measures designed to ease the problems faced by emigrants. For example, legislation passed in 1971 gave emigrants from the public sector the right to be reinstated in their former jobs within one year of their resignation if they experienced unexpected difficulties abroad and had to return to Egypt. In 1975 Egypt ratified the inter-Arab agreement on manpower movements and subsequently negotiated bilateral agreements with a number of labour-receiving states.

Despite the adoption of a liberal emigration policy and the existence of several agencies responsible for processing the emigration of Egyptians, there is still no comprehensive policy for planning, monitoring or co-ordinating labour emigration. Restrictions which remain do not address Egypt's real needs, while the procedures and documents required from potential emigrants are excessive. Moreover, there is still a lack of consensus among government officials concerning the virtue of a liberal emigration policy. As Dessouki (1982) concludes, the "liberalisation" of emigration policy was primarily a political decision related to the events of 1971-72, in particular the alliance between Egypt, Saudi Arabia and the Gulf States, together with the change in development strategy away from a socialist, centrally-planned economy to a more open, free market economy.

In contrast to Egypt, Syria, which also falls into the "regulatory" policy camp, has maintained a restrictive policy despite its clear lack of success. In the mid-1970s the Syrian Government, concerned by the large number of skilled manual, technical and professional workers leaving the country, imposed restrictions on issuance of passports and visas to certain categories of citizens. Despite this, an estimated 16 000 Syrians holding degrees of higher education and technical qualifications left the country between 1975-79 without official permission (Dib, 1982). While the emigration of professional and civil servants has now been brought under greater control, skilled and semi-skilled manual workers remain much less amenable to government restrictions which can be evaded simply by providing the authorities with an inaccurate account of personal skills and experience in order to obtain a passport. Syrians were also able to evade restrictions by first moving to Jordan (where they were exempted from residence and work permit requirements until the post-1979 deterioration in relations) and subsequently seeking employment in Saudi Arabia or the Gulf States through recruiting agents operating in Jordan. Syria's concern over the level of clandestine emigration is illustrated by the government's promulgation, in March 1980, of a legislative decree granting amnesty to all who had left without permission if they returned to Syria within six months. Failing this they would be liable to heavy fines or imprisonment if apprehended on return.

Laissez-faire policies

Laissez-faire policies, in which the barriers to labour emigration are minimal or non-existent, have been pursued by a number of labour-sending countries in the region. In the case of Lebanon, laissez-faire policy has occurred largely by default. Despite high levels of emigration since the late 19th Century, the government's involvement in emigration has been minimal. In 1983 a National Council for External Economic Relations was created to establish links with major Lebanese emigrant communities. A prime function of the 20 offices established abroad for this purpose was to boost remittance earnings (which had provided up to 35 per cent of GNP) and foreign trade, rather than promote or control temporary emigration for employment. While considerable concern has been voiced in the Lebanese press over the loss of skilled labour, particularly since the 1975-76 civil war and the Israeli invasion in 1982, no official action has been taken to restrict or control the outflow. In many respects this reflects the state's overriding free-enterprise and market-oriented economic strategy. Furthermore, effective disintegration of the Lebanese polity since the mid-1970s and the increasing cantonisation of the state preclude the adoption of an alternative migration policy.

The YAR has also been a major supplier of manpower to oil-exporting states of the Gulf Co-operation Council (GCC) since the mid-1970s. It has been estimated that more than 20 per cent (336 000 in 1980) of the total Yemeni work-force is employed abroad. As a result, labour and skill shortages are pervasive while remittance earnings have dominated the balance of payments since 1973-74; in 1982, for example, workers' remittances totalled Yemeni Rials (YR) 4 160 million compared to commodity export earnings of only YR 22 million. Despite its critical importance and adverse effects on the economy (Fergany, 1980), volume of emigration for employment has been virtually uninfluenced by state intervention. In practical terms, the government has little if any room for manoeuvre. The YAR's long and largely undefined border with Saudi Arabia cannot be effectively controlled to prevent emigration. Moreover, YAR remains a fragmented state; tribes in the northern highlands, from which a high proportion of migrants originate (Steffen, 1979), effectively maintain independence from the central government. As in the case of Lebanon, weak central control combined with strong external demand has undermined the state's ability to implement effective migration policies relating to both qualitative control and restrictive practices.

Among the North African labour-exporting countries, Morocco has also adopted a largely laissez-faire approach to labour emigration. While its policy statements clearly favour a labour-export strategy, the Moroccan authorities have done little, beyond negotiating bilateral labour agreements, to actively promote emigration for employment. By the early 1960s emigration had become firmly orientated towards European labour markets. International agreements concerning labour transfer were signed with France and West Germany in 1963 and with the Netherlands in 1968. By the late 1960s Morocco's planning policy stressed emigration to Europe as one solution for underemployment and unemployment. The 1968-72 Moroccan Development Plan aimed to achieve a significant increase in number of Moroccans working abroad. Emigration was seen as an outlet for surplus labour, a source of revenue to finance investments within Morocco and as a means by which Moroccans could gain professional qualifications. The plan also recommended the reorganisation and strengthening of the Service central de l'émigration in order to ensure more effective co-ordination between ministerial departments involved in emigration procedures.

Positive encouragement

The final group of countries in this brief overview of labour emigration policies in the Arab world are those which have actively promoted emigration for employment. Although none of the Arab states comes close to the kind of collective contract migration strategy (in which migrant workers are employed abroad by a company from their country of origin) practised by the Republic of Korea (Kim, 1982) or the Philippines (Lazo et al., 1982), several Arab labour exporters have taken active steps to increase the number of their nationals working abroad.

Unlike Algeria and Morocco, Tunisia had no tradition of labour migration to Europe, although free circulation between Tunisia and France was established in 1936. Indeed, during the colonial period, Tunisia was a country of immigration rather than emigration. Decolonisation and the departure of foreign communities following independence in 1956 stimulated a rapid increase in emigration to Europe, mainly to France. At first both the Tunisian Government and the Neo-Destour party did not encourage emigration, fearing the loss of skilled workers and professionals. Later, the gravity of the unemployment problem led to a more favourable attitude towards emigration, and in 1963 the Tunisian Government signed a labour agreement with France. The agreement, which was not implemented until 1969 because of strained relations between the two countries following Tunisia's nationalisation of European estates in 1964, determined different types of employment contracts, and the procedure for placement of Tunisian workers in France, and their rights to social welfare provisions. Faced with a growing deficit between job creation and the number of new demands for employment, the Tunisian Government in 1970 began to actively promote emigration. The official Tunisian press declared "Il est necessaire, pour le pays, de conquérir le marché international du travail. La main-d'oeuvre est considérée, par les spécialistes, comme une exportation, et doit être traitée comme elle" (Simon, 1978). At the same time efforts were made by the Tunisian authorities to bring emigration more firmly under official control. The Office de la Formation Professionnelle et de l'Emploi (OFPE), created in 1967, was renamed the Office des Travailleurs Tunisiens à l'Etranger, de l'Emploi et de la Formation Professionnelle (OTTEEFP) in 1973 and became responsible for finding new overseas markets for Tunisian manpower, for selecting candidates and preventing the departure of those skilled workers who were required for the development of the national economy. Regional offices were opened in each governorate and local offices in each delegation. Whereas in 1967 only 15 per cent of departures were controlled by the OFPE, by 1972 77 per cent of departures passed through official channels.

Bilateral and multilateral agreements

In addition to national policies on emigration, bilateral and multilateral agreements have also been pursued with varying degrees of effectiveness.

During the 1960s and early 1970s emigration from North Africa to Europe was closely regulated and controlled through a series of bilateral labour agreements. In the case of Tunisia, for example, the accord signed with France in 1963 defined the administrative procedures governing the migration of Tunisian workers to France and the role of the organisations set up to control recruitment, entry and employment. Under the terms of the accord a permanent mission of the French Office National de l'Immigration was established in Tunisia in 1969 to recruit workers from applicants registered with the regional offices of the Tunisian Office de la Formation Professionelle et de l'Emploi, to supervise medical examinations and to arrange transport to France.

Before the closure of West European labour markets to North African workers in the mid-1970s only Tunisia had succeeded in diversifying the destination for migrants to include Libya. A bilateral agreement on technical manpower was signed by Tunisia and Libya in 1971 but Tunisian emigration to Libya proved extremely vulnerable to fluctuating political relations between the two countries. A Moroccan-Libyan labour agreement signed in 1965 ended abruptly in 1969 with the Libyan revolution. Strained political relations between the two states acted as a major constraint on labour transfer until the dramatic improvement in relations in the early 1980s, culminating in the Oujda Accord in August 1984. It has been suggested that one of the main advantages of this treaty for Morocco would be an increase in the number of its workers admitted to Libya from an estimated 14 000 in 1985 to 100 000 (Parker, 1985).

Since the closure of West European labour markets, the capital-poor economies of Tunisia and Morocco have encouraged emigration to the oil-rich Gulf Emirates and Saudi Arabia (Lawless and Seccombe, 1984). Morocco signed an agreement with Saudi Arabia in 1976 for the transfer of 50-100 000 Moroccan workers, while bilateral co-operation programmes were established in 1982 between Tunisia and Saudi Arabia. Since 1975 Tunisia has also entered into a number of technical co-operation agreements with Kuwait. In the lower Gulf, Qatar signed labour agreements with both Morocco and Tunisia in 1981 and the UAE with Tunisia in 1981 and Morocco in 1982. In the early 1980s both Qatar and the UAE expressed concern about their dependence on traditional labour markets in the Indian sub-continent and Southeast Asia on the grounds that their Arab and Islamic identity was threatened by the fact that some two-thirds of the immigrant workers were Asians, mainly Indians and Pakistanis. Their aim was to recruit workers from Arab countries. In addition to agreements with Tunisia and Morocco, they signed labour agreements with Egypt, Sudan and Somalia. Egypt had already concluded an agreement with Qatar (September 1974) and an agreement with Libya (April 1971). Jordan, as both exporter and importer of labour, had concluded agreements with Saudi Arabia, the UAE and Tunisia (1982), Morocco (1982) and Egypt (1985). Neighbouring Iraq, suffering from acute manpower shortages as a result of the massive mobilisation of Iraqi nationals for the war with Iran, signed a labour agreement with Egypt in November 1985. In September 1985 it had offered employment in the oil, transport and communication sectors to 2 460 Tunisians expelled from Libya.

In contrast to agreements made between the North African labour exporters and the West European countries during the 1960s, bilateral agreements made between Arab importers and exporters in the 1970s and early 1980s have remained little more than statements of intent. There is no evidence, for example, that the 1976 labour agreement between Morocco and Saudi Arabia was ever implemented. Regional co-operation on labour movements has also proved elusive. The Arab Labour Organisation was created in 1965 to encourage co-operation between member states of the Arab League on labour problems. An agreement in 1967 aimed to facilitate manpower transfers between Arab countries and to give priority to recruitment of Arab workers over those of other nationalities. Although Jordan, Iraq, Egypt and Syria ratified the agreement, with the exception of Iraq, no major labour importing country ratified it, thus rendering it ineffective.

Case Studies of Emigration Policies in the Arab World

Algeria, a centrally-planned socialist economy, was the major Arab labour supplier to Western Europe prior to the recession of the mid-1970s. In contrast, Jordan, a liberal free market economy, has been one of the principal sources of expatriate manpower for Saudi Arabia and the other Arab oil-exporting states since the economic boom which followed the oil price increases of 1973-74. The experiences of these countries will demonstrate how difficult it is to develop an autonomous response to processes that are largely determined abroad.

Algeria

Prior to its independence in 1962, Algeria's emigration policy was determined by France (the colonial power) on the basis of requirements of the French labour market. Until World War I, employment of Algerians in France was severely restricted by a decree of the Governor-General requiring all travellers to hold permits. These strict formalities placed an effective check on emigration. The restrictions were relaxed in 1913 and 1914, when Algerian labour was recruited directly by the French Government for work in munitions factories, army service workshops, transport and the mines. While the majority of Algerian workers were repatriated at the end of the war, an economic boom in the 1920s led to a new influx of Algerians to France. Pressure from European settlers in Algeria opposed to the departure of their supply of cheap labour led to new restrictive measures, including in 1924 a decree that each prospective emigrant must obtain a work contract, medical certificate and identity card. This decree was replaced in 1928 by even stricter regulations concerning emigration.

A period of economic expansion after 1936 led to demands in Algeria by the Muslim community for an easing of restrictions on emigration. In July 1936 the French Government permitted free circulation between Algeria and France on condition that each migrant obtain an identity card. Emigration was suspended during World War II but after liberation the French Government sought migrant labour to service economic recovery and reconstruction. In spite of attempts by the colonial authorities to regulate the outflow, Algerians secured the right to work in France under the 1947 "Organic Law" which declared that Muslim Algerians were to be considered French citizens.

Prior to the outbreak of the War of Independence, the policy of Algerian colonial authorities to restrict emigration proved successful only when economic conditions in France required a reduction in immigration. However, growing unrest in Algeria after 1954 led colonial authorities to encourage emigration on the grounds that it was a safety valve for pent-up nationalist feeling. In contrast, the French Ministry of the Interior sought to restrict emigration on the grounds that political activities were easier to suppress in Algeria than in France. As a result, migration policy neither satisfied the needs of the French labour market nor the exigencies of counter-revolution in Algeria (Adler, 1977).

The Evian Accords (1962), which set out in detail the nature of relations between France and the independent Algerian Republic, provided for continued access of Algerians to the French labour market. But the freedom of circulation guaranteed by these accords soon came under attack from French officials who felt that a renewed influx of Algerians seeking work in France would strain the absorptive capacity of the French economy. In Algeria, continuing reliance on the export of labour as a solution to the country's unemployment problems was denounced by left wing forces within the Front de Liberation Nationale (FLN). Their leading spokesman, Mohamed Harbi, declared that "the only valid solution is the stabilization of employment at home and the immediate halt to emigration" (Adler, 1977). The Algerian Government of Ben Bella, though regarding the interruption of emigration as unrealistic, nonetheless agreed to bring it more firmly under government control. In November 1962 it set up the Office National Algérien de Main d'Oeuvre (ONAMO), to apply selective criteria to prospective emigrants and check the outflow.

Then in 1964 Algeria and France signed the Nekkache and Grandval Accord on emigration. Almost at once it was criticised in Algeria not only because it gave France the right to determine unilaterally the number of Algerian immigrant workers, but also because the annual quota imposed (12 000), was considered insufficient.

After the military coup in 1965, major changes occurred in the Algerian Government's attitude towards emigration. The new government, led by Boumedienne, chose to modernise the economy through a programme of high technology which would create relatively few jobs in its early stages and, therefore, hardly touch the agricultural sector where some two-thirds of the population gained their livelihood. As ability to export surplus labour was deemed a vital safety valve for relief of social pressures due to unemployment and underemployment, the Nekkache-Grandval Accord was considered an obstacle to the new industrialisation strategy. Economic planners sought substantial outflows of labour from rural areas so that resources could be devoted to the industrialisation programme rather than be sidetracked into what they regarded as less productive rural investment. Their objective in the next round of negotiations with France was to achieve agreement concerning annual emigration. In the Accord, which was eventually signed in October 1968, 35 000 workers were authorised to enter France each year for a period of three years. In 1971 a target of 25 000 per year was negotiated for the following two years. In September 1973, only a few months before new negotiations were due, the Algerian Government unilaterally terminated all emigration to France and announced that this represented the first step in a programme to reintegrate the migrant community back into the Algerian economy (Lawless and Findlay, 1982).

The laissez-faire approach to emigration adopted by the Evian Accords (1962) had been replaced by a system of fixed quotas in 1964, 1968 and 1971. The French sought to apply greater restrictions and regulations to Algerian workers, while the Algerians (after 1965 and until the termination of all new emigration in 1973) sought to organise emigration in accordance with their overall strategy of development. The development policy of the Boumedienne Government included nationalisation of foreign economic interests, state control of all key economic sectors and the creation of a modern industrial sector based on hydrocarbons and heavy industries. The traditional agricultural sector, where 60 per cent of the Algerian population gained its livelihood, was neglected and few jobs were to be created in the modern sector. Consequently, emigration was seen as a vital mechanism to reduce unemployment and underemployment. In 1968, Algerian negotiators sought a larger emigration quota guaranteed for several years in advance. Emigrants were selected by ONAMO: choice of age, education and skill was made on the basis of Algeria's rather than France's perceived development needs.

Having secured a more advantageous fixed multi-annual agreement, the Algerian Government attempted to diversify the sources from which emigrants were drawn so as to ensure a more even distribution of revenues and other benefits from migration. New criteria for the distribution of emigrants by wilaya of origin gave a weighting coefficient of three for the wilaya's population, two for the number of residents already absent and one for the actual number of persons wishing to emigrate. As areas which traditionally had the highest rates of emigration (i.e., the wilayas of Tizi Ouzou, Setif and Constantine) were not those with the largest populations, they were disadvantaged under the new criteria. The policy of regional diversification was also supplemented with a series of "special programmes" to create employment in areas which traditionally had experienced high rates of underemployment, notably the wilayas of Tizi Ouzou and Setif and parts of the Aurès. In Tizi Ouzou, selected for the first special programme in 1968, employment expanded so rapidly in the building and construction sector that the wilaya actually refused its share of the national emigration quota in 1973.

Attempts by the Algerian Government to regulate the quality of emigrants were less successful. Because of high demand for skilled manpower in the newly created modern sector, the authorities sought to restrict the departure of qualified workers. At the same time they wanted migrant workers to benefit from training programmes in France and for that the workers had to be literate. The government therefore adopted a policy of keeping skilled workers at home and encouraging more literate workers to emigrate. Whereas in 1964 and 1965 over 13 per cent of all departures were skilled workers, by the early 1970s the proportion had fallen to 2 per cent. Unfortunately, most unskilled workers were also illiterate, thus reducing their chances of acquiring skills abroad. Algeria's two aims in this area therefore proved to be contradictory.

In order to ensure that the "benefits" of emigration were distributed as widely as possible, other criteria for selecting candidates favoured those most in need. Although in theory no one who could be found a job in Algeria was eligible for emigration, in practice Algerians who might have found work at home were given permission to leave. In an attempt to tighten procedures, the Minister of Labour issued a circular in January 1972 requiring ONAMO to accept applications only from unemployed married workers with at least one child and unmarried unemployed workers over 24 years of age. Applications from other persons were refused.

Algeria's unilateral termination of all new emigration to France came almost a year before the French Government's own decision, in the face of worsening economic recession, to suspend further labour immigration. Adler suggests that the Algerian decision was essentially political. Dependence on France to employ a large proportion of its workers was a source of embarrassment to Algeria which considered itself as a leader of the non-aligned world. According to Adler, the termination of emigration was intended "to bring lustre to its anti-imperialist armour and prove that Algeria was not the cat's paw of world capitalism". Officially, however, Algeria claimed that that the decision was made possible by the creation of new employment opportunities through planned industrialisation and land reform.

Despite strong evidence of continuing high levels of domestic under-employment, the Charte Nationale adopted in 1976 reaffirmed Algeria's commitment to the return and reintegration of emigrants as a major objective of the socialist revolution:

> Because of the development of the country workers no longer need to emigrate to find a job. Moreover by the different actions which it has undertaken to transform the society and to build socialism, the Revolution has created for each Algerian the obligation to making his contribution to the common task of national reconstruction ... the necessary efforts will be accomplished to facilitate the reinsertion of our migrant workers into the national community.

Jordan

Emigration for employment has been an increasingly dominant feature of the Jordanian economy since the early 1950s when high rates of unemployment and underemployment, coupled with low levels of capital investment, encouraged a steady outflow of labour. During the British mandate (1921-46) Trans-jordanian labour was involved in seasonal migration to Palestine, especially in years of drought during the 1930s. The flood of refugees into the independent and enlarged Kingdom of Jordan during and immediately after the 1948 Palestine war generated a new scale and pattern of migration. Increasing numbers of Palestinians (and later, Jordanians) found employment in the nascent oil economies of Saudi Arabia and the Gulf (Seccombe and Lawless, forthcoming). Much of that emigration was from the West Bank sub-districts, where overt political motives joined the economic imperative for emigration (Seccombe, 1984). The multiple crises of 1967-71, beginning with the Israeli occupation of the West Bank and culminating in the 1970-71 civil war, promoted sector-wide economic collapse and considerable labour outflows. In 1972 unemployment in Jordan was officially estimated at over 14 per cent while the number of emigrant workers increased to over 80 000. With this emigration tradition, and a relatively skilled labour force, Jordan was well placed to meet the growing regional demand for manpower which followed oil price increases in 1973-74. By 1975 almost 140 000 migrant workers from the East Bank were employed abroad, and in the late 1970s annual net labour outflows were in excess of 10 000. The outflow of labour during the 1976-80 Five-Year Plan period represented a loss of more than 35 per cent of the expected growth in domestic labour supply.

Prior to the mid-1970s, emigration for employment from Jordan can be characterised as a response to a succession of political and economic crises. Increases in the rate of labour emigration were regarded by successive Jordanian administrations as a means of reducing labour surpluses. What was originally an individual response to political and economic crises had, by the early 1970s, become an accepted plank of economic policy. By including within its manpower supply/demand projections for 1976-80 an estimated outflow of 30-40 per cent of available supply, the National Planning Council not only implicitly accepted Jordan's role as a supplier of regional labour but also indicated willingness to plan, at least superficially, for emigration (Seccombe, 1985). Significantly, the outflow of sub-professional/technical manpower was projected at 55.6 per cent of available supply.

While maintaining an unrestricted emigration policy, Jordan has also sought to maximise the returns from emigration. A principle feature of its pro-emigration policy has been the commitment of successive governments to increasing the supply of technical and skilled manpower available for both the domestic and international labour markets. This focus was first articulated in the 1973-75 Three-Year Development Plan which called for considerable investment in vocational education so that Jordan could benefit from the higher earnings potential of its work-force abroad. Emphasis on vocational and technical education continued through the 1976-80 and 1981-85 Five-Year Development Plans. The link between education and emigration policies is quite explicit in the 1981-85 Plan:

> The base of qualified and training manpower in the vocational
> and technical categories will be expanded in a manner consonant
> with the requirements of the development process in Jordan and
> the level of growth and development of sister Arab countries.

In the absence of restrictions on emigration this clearly amounts to a strategy of training manpower for migration.

Important innovations occurred in Jordan's vocational education and training system during the 1970s; e.g., an increased emphasis on vocational education within the formal education structure and the development of a centralised training organisation (the Vocational Training Corporation) to co-ordinate and promote trade training activities within industry. Since the early 1970s there has been a remarkable increase in both vocational education facilities and student numbers. Between 1973 and 1982 the number of students in vocational education rose from 6 500 to 20 550, representing over 18 per cent of secondary cycle enrolments. In addition, the Ministry of Education's trade training centres (two-year vocational courses for preparatory school leavers), first opened in 1971, now enrol more than 2 000 students.

There has also been a dramatic growth (at 29 per cent per annum 1971/2-1980/1) in enrolments in post-secondary vocational institutes, particularly the new polytechnics and in the number of private institutions offering post-secondary level training in a variety of occupational skills. In 1973 there were only 7 community colleges; by 1982 the number had grown to 44, of which 20 were privately run. These private colleges account for more than 18 000 of the 28 200 students enrolled in 1982 (compared with total enrolments in 1973 of under 3 000).

As a result of this massive investment in education and training, Jordan's emigrant workers have the highest skills profile of any emigrant Arab nationality. Even though the number of Jordanians going to Saudi Arabia declined after 1979, the share and number of professional, technical and skilled workers in the outflow increased from 15 per cent in 1978 to 32 per cent in 1982, in Kuwait the proportion rose from 38 per cent to 65 per cent over the same period (Seccombe, 1985).

Any illusions which Jordanian authorities may have had regarding the benefits of a positive emigration policy had unquestionably paled by the mid-1970s with the growing problems of skill scarcity, wage inflation and the apparent incongruity of large inflows of non-Jordanian "replacement" labour (Seccombe, forthcoming). A more stoical view of labour emigration was reflected in the speech given by Crown Prince Hassan bin Talal to the International Labour Conference at Geneva in June 1977. In that address the Crown Prince called for the creation of an "International Labour Compensatory Facility" to compensate Jordan (and other labour exporters) for the negative effects of large scale labour outflows. While this view has been reiterated by other Jordanian officials (see for example Anani and Jaber, 1980), the administration has nevertheless maintained its commitment to a positive emigration policy.

In 1976-77 the Jordanian authorities attempted to bring emigration for employment under closer control. Such new measures as a ban on newspaper advertisements for job vacancies abroad, the imposition of restrictions on the mobility of specific industrial skills and the requirement that public sector employees obtain prior permission before taking up employment abroad, were largely unsuccessful. Selective restrictions, mainly on oil refinery technicians and other specialists were easily circumvented. The government has been more successful in channelling the emigration of public sector employees through an increasing number of secondment schemes negotiated mainly for school teachers (the number on secondment from the Ministry of Education increased from 271 in 1979 to over 2 330 in 1983) and medical and security service personnel. In addition, Jordan has negotiated bilateral labour agreements for the supply of skilled labour with Saudi Arabia and the United Arab Emirates (UAE). Advisers have also been posted to Jordanian embassies in

Kuwait, Qatar, Saudi Arabia and the UAE to promote the employment of Jordanians abroad and to protect the interests of those already employed.

Jordan's response towards labour emigration has been conditioned by several interrelated factors. First, the significance of workers' remittances to the Jordanian economy. The volume of recorded remittances increased from Jordanian Dinars (JD) 7.4 million in 1972 to over JD 330 million in 1983, a level substantially higher than domestic exports and accounting for between 25 per cent and 33 per cent of both imports and gross national product. This growth reflects financial and political stability as well as the banking sector's relative success in attracting remittances. In several years remittances were not only higher than external budgetary support and aid, but have become increasingly important as more signatories of the Baghdad agreement renege on aid payments as a result of the continuing Iraq-Iran war and the Gulf recession. A dramatic fall in Jordan's remittance receipts would transform the positive balance of invisible earnings, leading to a substantial balance-of-payments deficit and debt-servicing problems.

Second, a decision by the Jordanian Government to restrict labour outflows could have had a negative impact on the level of external budgetary support which Jordan receives from the labour-importing, oil-rich, states. Although this aid is provided for a host of reasons, a close relationship between foreign aid receipts and the supply of labour has been identified on several occasions in official reports. The 1981-85 Five-year Development Plan noted that:

> Jordan is inextricably linked with the other Arab countries. Relations have been cemented on the one hand by the positive role played by the trained Jordanian labour force in the Arab oil-producing states and on the other hand by the financial assistance extended by the Arab countries to strengthen Jordan's steadfastness.

Third, although selected sectors of the Jordanian economy have experienced manpower shortages partly as a result of out-migration, it is apparent that domestic labour market expansion alone could not absorb the increasing labour force. The collapse of agricultural employment, which accounts for less than 10 per cent of the work-force, has been a notable feature of the last ten years. Moreover, with the increasing educational attainment of women, there are likely to be a growing number of labour market entrants. The rapid increase in output from general secondary education may lead to further pressure on the government to expand public sector employment (already at more than 40 per cent of the labour force) beyond the level that can be afforded or is necessary. A fall in external budgetary support, remittances or labour outflows would have severe implications for the level of employment in general and for the two major employers, the construction and public sectors, in particular.

Fourth, a restrictive emigration policy would be difficult to police and politically naive to institute. Jordan would undoubtedly be condemned for preventing Palestinians, who comprise a substantial proportion of the East Bank population, from leaving the country. Moreover, such a policy would run counter to the consistent _laissez-faire_ economic philosophy adopted by successive Jordanian Governments during the last thirty years. This view was expressed in the final report (1977) of the ad hoc Committee on Labour Emigration:

> No matter how adverse the labour situation may become we must not resort to the use of police restrictions. Such measures do not conform to the private free enterprise system to which we adhere.

CONCLUSION

This chapter has shown the range of emigration policies adopted, and some of the constraints on policy choice and implementation, in the Arab labour-supplying countries. Emigration policies can be successful only when they meet the requirements of, or are backed by, the countries of immigration. This is illustrated by the contrasting failure of the PDRY's prohibition on emigration for employment and the successful ban imposed by Algeria and backed by subsequent action in France.

One national group for whom external policies have been the major factor in determining migration patterns is the Palestinians. Without a state of their own, Palestinians have not been in a position to formulate or implement national emigration policies. The establishment of the State of Israel in 1948 led some three-quarters of a million Palestinians to seek refuge in neighbouring Arab countries, an event which triggered the first phase of migration for employment in the nascent oil economies of the Gulf States and Saudi Arabia. The Israeli occupation of the West Bank and Gaza in 1967 provoked a new exodus of Palestinian refugees and introduced a period of profound economic stagnation in the local economy of occupied territories. Consequently educated persons on the West Bank are forced to emigrate in search of employment to other parts of the Arab world and to the United States while peasants and destitute refugees of Gaza have become increasingly incorporated into the Israeli labour market as a source of cheap unskilled and semi-skilled labour (Graham-Brown, 1979). In 1970 only 12 per cent of the territories' labour force was employed in Israel; by 1983 the percentage had risen to 38.

The importance of external factors in determining the extent of labour flows and the potential instability of the international labour market have been amply demonstrated by recent events in North Africa. In August and September 1985 Libya pursued a policy of forced expulsions of thousands of expatriate workers from Egypt, Mali, Mauritania, Niger, Senegal and Tunisia. The deportations were directed at nationals of countries with whom Libya has poor international relations, particularly Tunisia. More than 29 000 Tunisians were expelled. Although the wave of deportations had political overtones similar to previous expulsions in 1976 and 1980, they were also symptomatic of a wider decline in regional demand for foreign labour which accompanied the reduction of world oil prices and reduced capital expenditure in Arab oil-exporting countries. Rates of return migration from these states are likely to grow over the next five years. Saudi Arabia, the region's largest labour importer, has already announced its intention of reducing expatriate employment by 22.6 per cent (600 000 workers) between 1985 and 1990. Similar proposals have been adopted by the Kuwait Government which aims to balance national and non-national components of its population by the year 2000. Such a balance can be achieved only by a reduction in the size of its foreign labour force.

Declining demand for foreign labour in oil-exporting economies presents the labour-sending states with a dual challenge. Remittance earnings, which are the major source of foreign revenue in Egypt, Jordan and the Yemens, are likely to fall significantly with the return of unskilled and semi-skilled migrants, thus forcing further cuts in government expenditure and undermining private sector business confidence. At the same time there is likely to be a dramatic increase in unemployment. The likelihood of rapidly rising unemployment at a time of economic austerity must give cause for considerable concern. So far, none of the Arab labour-sending countries has drawn up contingency plans to cope with the return and reintegration of migrant workers. Thus policy formulation and implementation in the labour-sending countries may once again lag behind reality.

BIBLIOGRAPHY

ADLER, S.
International Migration and Dependence, Westmead, Farnborough, England, Saxon House, 1977.

ADLER, S.
Swallow's Children -- Emigration and Development in Algeria, Geneva, ILO, 1980.

ANANI, J. and T. JABER
"Jordan's Experience and Policies in the Field of Reverse Transfer of Technology", Amman, Ministry of Labour, mimeo, 1980.

AYUBI, N.
"The Egyptian Brain Drain: A Multi-dimentional Problem", International Journal of Middle Eastern Studies, Vol. 15, No. 4, 1983.

BIRKS, J. and C. SINCLAIR
The Sultanate of Oman: Economic Development, the Domestic Labour Market and International Migration, Geneva, ILO, 1978.

Arab Manpower: The Crisis of Development, London, Croom Helm, 1980.

"The Socio-economic Determinants of Intra-regional Migration" in ECWA, International Migration in the Arab World, Beirut, ECWA, 1982.

BOHNING, R.
Elements of a Theory of International Migration and Compensation, Geneva, ILO, 1978.

DESSOUKI, A.
"The Shift in Egypt's Migration Policy: 1952-78", Middle Eastern Studies, Vol. 18, No. 1, 1982.

DIB, G.
"Laws and Decrees and Their Application: Their Influence on Migration in the Arab World -- Towards a Regional Charter", in ECWA, International Migration in the Arab World, Beirut, ECWA, 1982.

FERGANY, N.
The Affluent Years Are Over: Emigration and Development in the Yemen Arab Republic, Geneva, ILO, 1980.

GRAHAM-BROWN, S.
"The West Bank and Gaza -- the Structural Impact of Israeli Colonization", MERIP Reports, No. 74, 1979.

87

HOPFNER, K. and M. HUBER
Regulating International Migration in the Interests of the Developing Countries: With Particular Reference to the Mediterranean Countries, Geneva, ILO, 1978.

KIM, S.
Contract Migration in the Republic of Korea, Geneva, ILO, 1982.

LAWLESS, R. and A. FINDLAY
"Algerian Emigration to France and the Franco-Algerian Accords of 1980", Orient, Vol. 23, No. 3, 1982.

LAWLESS, R. and I. SECCOMBE
"North African Labour Migration: The Search for Alternatives", Immigrants and Minorities, Vol. 3, No. 2, 1984.

LAZO, L. et al.
Contract Migration Policies in the Philippines, Geneva, ILO, 1982.

MESSIHA, S.
The Export of Egyptian Teachers, Cairo, American University of Cairo, Cairo Papers in Social Sciences 3, No. 4, 1980.

PARKER, R.
"L'accord d'Oujda -- quinze mois après", Jeune Afrique, 1297, 1985.

RICHARDS, A. and P. MARTIN
"The Laissez-faire Approach to International Labour Migration: The Case of the Middle East", Economic Development and Cultural Change, Vol. 31, No. 3, 1983.

SECCOMBE, I.
International Labour Migration and Skill Scarcity: The Hashemite Kingdom of Jordan, Geneva, ILO, 1984.

"Labour Emigration Policies and Economic Development in Jordan: From Unemployment to Labour Shortage" in B. Khader, ed., The Economic Development of Jordan, Louvain-la-Neuve, CERMAC, 1985.

"Immigration Workers in an Emigrant Economy: An Examination of Replacement Migration in the Middle East", International Migration, No. 24, March 1986.

SECCOMBE, I. and R. LAWLESS
"Migrant Labour and the Early Oil Industry in the Arabian Gulf, 1930-50", Maghreb-Machrek, January 1986.

SHIRREFF, D.
"Expatriate Remittances Open New Vistas for South Yemen", Middle East Economic Digest, Vol. 23, No. 29, 1979.

SIMON, G.
L'espace des travailleurs tunisiens en France, Poitiers, Université de Poitiers, 1978.

STEFFEN, H.

Population Geography of the Yemen Arab Republic. The Major Findings of the Population and Housing Census of February 1975 and of Supplementary Demographic and Cartographic Surveys, Wiesbaden, Ludwig Reichert, 1979.

Part II

TYPES OF MIGRATION

A. TEMPORARY

Chapter 6

INTERNATIONAL LABOUR MIGRATION FROM THE ESCAP REGION

by

J.W. Huguet

The most numerically significant types of international migration in Asia and the Pacific are permanent, temporary labour and refugee. Permanent emigration from Asia and the Pacific increased rapidly during the last two decades mainly because the major receiving countries (Australia, Canada, New Zealand and the United States of America) enacted immigration legislation that removed many restrictions on Asian migrants. The 264 000 Asian immigrants to the United States in 1983 represented 47 per cent of all immigrants to that country. Over the past few years an average 34 000 migrants from Asia and the Pacific islands have entered Canada and 25 000 have entered Australia. In both cases, these intakes comprised over one-third of the total. There are also significant flows of international migrants across the Nepal-India border and from Bangladesh into the Indian State of Assam. Refugee flows have traditionally comprised a large proportion of international migration in Asia. At the end of 1985 there were 130 000 refugees and displaced persons from the Indochina States in Thailand, about 1.8 million from Afghanistan in the Islamic Republic of Iran and 2.3 million from Afghanistan being assisted by the United Nations High Commissioner for Refugees in Pakistan.

Because permanent migration and refugee flows are addressed in other sections of the publication, this chapter will focus on temporary labour migration, primarily to destinations outside South and East Asia. Although approximately 80 per cent of labour migration from Asia and the Pacific goes to the Middle East, important movements within the region of the Economic and Social Commission for Asia and the Pacific (ESCAP) include 100 000-120 000 Malaysians working in Singapore and the (unofficial) estimated 300 000-700 000 Indonesians working in Malaysia (Lin, 1984). Sizeable numbers of domestic servants also migrate within the region, particularly from Sri Lanka to Singapore and from the Philippines to Hong Kong. While significant numbers of women from the Philippines and Thailand work in the entertainment industry in Japan, the number cannot be estimated because nearly all of them have an irregular migration status. International migration within and from the Pacific region is small in numbers but often extremely large as a proportion of the populations of the countries of origin. The major movements are from

Pacific island countries to Australia, New Zealand and the United States. The large proportion of circular mobility and return migration in this region prevents accurate classification according to type of migration.

The present chapter is based primarily on the results of a project on international migration policy carried out in 1984 and 1985 by the Population Division of ESCAP with financial support from the United Nations Fund for Population Activities (UNFPA). The project was initiated by the Expert Group Meeting on International Migration in Asia and the Pacific organised jointly by ESCAP and the Population Centre Foundation (PCF) of the Philippines at Manila in November 1984. Following a review of international migration in the ESCAP region the Expert Group Meeting recommended that seven small-scale research projects be conducted on aspects of return migration. Reports of the projects implemented between January and August 1985 formed the basis for discussion at the Policy Workshop on International Migration in Asia and the Pacific held at Bangkok in October 1985.

Dimensions of International Labour Migration

Asia

The great majority of workers from the ESCAP region migrate to the Middle East under labour contracts of one, two and occasionally three years' duration. Although international statistical guidelines recommend that a duration of one year distinguish short-term and long-term migration, for the purposes of this paper, all labour migration will be considered temporary. Because they migrate under contract, nearly all workers return to their home country; very few settle in the host country.

The rapidity with which labour migration from the ESCAP region to the Middle East expanded after the late 1970s is demonstrated in Table 6.1, which shows that the number of persons registering for overseas employment doubled in several countries during a two-year period. Other estimates which, unlike Table 6.1, include non-registered workers, suggest that the total number of workers from the ESCAP region in the Middle East had reached 3.5 million in 1983 (ESCAP, 1985b). This included approximately 1 million workers from India and 1.2 to 2.0 million Pakistanis (1984), although data on Pakistanis should be interpreted with caution. For example, Table 6.1 indicates that 760 000 Pakistanis went overseas to work between 1975 and 1981 and an estimated 800 000 were still abroad in 1981. These figures are obviously inconsistent even before allowance is made for return migration. Nor was the issue re-solved by the 1981 National Census of Pakistan estimate of 1.7 million Pakistanis abroad in all countries (Gilani, 1983).

An estimated half million Filipino labour migrants were in the Middle East in 1983. The Philippines Overseas Employment Administration (POEA) recently estimated that 166 884 workers deployed were rehires, or nearly 48 per cent of the total and a majority of land-based migrant workers, indicating that a high proportion of returning workers find re-employment overseas (The Philippines, 1985).

The Republic of Korea, Sri Lanka, Thailand and perhaps Bangladesh each had approximately 200 000 workers in the Middle East in 1982 or 1983. Over 98 per cent of Korean workers in the Middle East in 1980 were employed by

Table 6.1

LABOUR MIGRANTS FROM SELECTED ASIAN COUNTRIES, 1975-84

Year	Labour migrants to the Middle East				
	India	Republic of Korea	Philippines	Sri Lanka	Thailand
1975	n.a.	6 466	1 552	n.a.	984
1976	4 200	21 269	7 812	526	1 287
1977	22 900	52 247	25 721	633	3 870
1978	69 000	81 987	34 441	8 082	14 215
1979	171 000	99 141	73 210	20 980	8 329
1980	236 200	127 323	132 044	24 053	20 475
1981	276 000	153 699	183 582	47 800	23 848
1982	239 545	159 950	210 972	55 000	105 143
1983	225 000	--	323 298	55 000	64 527
Stock					
1981	800 000	171 040	342 300	90-115 000	159 000
1982	--	213 000	--	--	--
1983	930 000	--	500 000	185-215 000	230 000

Year	All foreign labour migrants				
	Bangladesh	Indonesia	Republic of Korea	Pakistan	Philippines
1975	n.a.	--	20 986	23 077	12 501
1976	6 087	1 923	37 192	41 690	19 221
1977	15 725	2 994	69 623	140 522	36 676
1978	22 809	8 213	101 998	130 525	50 961
1979	24 485	10 367	120 990	125 507	92 519
1980	30 573	7 967	146 436	129 847	157 394
1981	55 787	12 675	175 114	168 403	210 936
1982	62 805	--	196 885	142 945	353 894
1983	59 216	--	184 277	128 206	--
1984	56 754	--	152 673	--	350 982
Stock					
1981	178 500	--	202 500	800 200	--
1984	--	--	196 100	--	--

Sources: Lionel Demery, "Asian Labour Migration to the Middle East: An Empirical Assessment", paper prepared for Conference on Asian Labour Migration to the Middle East, Honolulu, 19th-23rd September 1983; Fred Arnold and Nasra M. Shah, "Asian Labour Migration to the Middle East", Working Paper No. 32 (Honolulu, East-West Population Institute, March 1984); Seok Hyun-ho and Yang Jong-hoe, "A Decade of Korean Labour Migration to the Middle East: An Overview", Korean Social Science Journal, Vol. 11, 1984, pp. 117-142; papers and statements presented at Expert Group Meeting on International Migration in Asia and the Pacific, Manila, 6th-12th November 1984, and at Expert Group Meeting on Remittances from International Labour Migration, Bangkok, 24th September 1985.

Korean companies. Of these, 10 per cent (mostly professional and managerial workers) were regular employees of the companies and 90 per cent were temporary employees (Seok and Yang, 1984). The 50 000 Sri Lankans who migrated to the Middle East for employment in 1982, 1983 and probably in 1984 comprised 85-90 per cent of all overseas Sri Lankan workers. Numbers shown in Table 6.1 for Sri Lanka relate only to workers registered by the Ministry of Labour; it is well-known that many workers find jobs themselves or through unlicensed recruitment agencies and are not registered. A unique feature of Sri Lankan labour migration is that since 1980 the number of females (employed mainly as housemaids) has exceeded the number of males. Estimates in Table 6.1 of Thai workers in the Middle East also relate to persons registered by the Department of Labour and are believed to seriously underrepresent actual numbers. The decline shown in Table 6.1 between 1982 and 1983 is not corroborated by data on workers' remittances, which increased steadily during 1983.

It appears that labour migration from the ESCAP region to the Middle East reached a peak by 1983. For example, the number of registered workers from India reached 276 000 in 1981 and declined to 225 000 in 1983 (Table 6.1). A similar pattern, but involving smaller numbers, may also be observed for overseas workers to all destinations from Pakistan and the Republic of Korea. In both cases, decline in registered workers exceeded 20 per cent over the two most recent years for which data are available (Table 6.1). There is certainly a common perception in the Philippines, Sri Lanka and Thailand that the number of persons taking overseas employment will continue to decline. Initial declines have been attributed to the completion of infrastructure construction projects in the Middle East and the effects of a sharp drop in the price of petroleum during late 1985. Many sending countries expect that the number of returning migrants will soon exceed the number of new contract workers.

During the peak period of labour emigration the vast majority of the workers were employed in construction, many as unskilled labourers. For example, of Pakistani workers employed in the Middle East, an estimated 1.6 per cent are professionals, 4.5 per cent are clerical workers, 14.9 per cent are service workers and 79 per cent are mainly construction workers, half of whom are classed as unskilled (Aftab, 1984).

As infrastructure construction projects were completed, a shift occurred in the skill composition of migrant workers from construction to professional and service occupations. For example, of land-based contract workers processed in the Philippines in 1984, 17.6 per cent were professionals, 20.9 per cent were service workers, 56 per cent were production (mostly construction) workers, and 5.5 per cent were in other occupational groups. These represent a shift in skill composition towards higher skill categories since 1983; the number of professional workers having increased by 24 per cent and the number of service workers by 33 per cent (The Philippines, 1985).

The decline in construction in the Middle East also resulted in a shift in the occupations of overseas workers from Sri Lanka toward unskilled service jobs, including domestic service. The proportion of professional and technical workers decreased from 10.9 per cent in 1979 to 8.2 per cent in 1981, and the proportion of skilled workers decreased from 24.7 to 17.3 per cent while that of unskilled workers increased from 54.8 to 59.9 per cent. These figures probably understate the shift to unskilled workers because they omit about 12 000 workers who could not be classified by country of destination but who are believed to have been mainly unskilled workers going to the Middle East (Korale, 1985).

The Pacific

(This section is an abstract of a paper by Hayes (1985) reprinted by ESCAP (1985a).

The South Pacific region (excluding Australia and New Zealand) is a heterogeneous area with countries and territories ranging in population from 3.1 million in Papua New Guinea to fewer than 100 people in Pitcairn Island. The estimated total population of the region was 5.1 million in mid-1982. Three main international migration flows affect populations in the South Pacific: movement from Pacific islands to the Pacific rim countries of Australia, New Zealand and the United States of America; movement from one Pacific island country to another; and movement from the Philippines to Papua New Guinea and Western Micronesia, primarily Guam and the Northern Mariana Islands.

Emigration from the Pacific islands to the Pacific rim countries is primarily a Polynesian phenomenon, the major sending countries being American Samoa, Cook Islands, Niue, Samoa, Tokelau and Tonga. During the period 1962-82, the net inflow of Pacific islanders to New Zealand, measured by ethnicity, was about 36 000, which is small relative to the outward gross movement of about 400 000. The 1980 United States census recorded 46 255 Pacific islands-born persons (excluding Guam), the vast majority of whom (63 per cent) originated in Polynesia. The 1981 Australian census recorded an increase of almost 26 000 in the number of Pacific-born persons (270 per cent) since 1976, due mainly to the inflow of Europeans from Papua New Guinea following independence in 1975.

While intra-Pacific migration is small compared with other international migration flows, in some countries its demographic, social and economic impacts are considerable. Probably the largest migratory stream is between Samoa and American Samoa. The largest Asian immigration streams entering the Pacific islands are from the Philippines to Guam and the Northern Mariana Islands. In 1980, 16 per cent of Guam's population of 106 000 had been born in the Philippines and 5 per cent in other Asian countries, principally Japan and the Republic of Korea. About 9 per cent of the population of the Northern Mariana Islands in 1980 had been born in the Philippines and altogether 10 per cent of the population had been born in Asia. The majority of Asian immigrants were contract labourers.

The direction of international migration in the South Pacific is from countries with low wages to those with both high wages and an effective demand for labour. As composition favours persons aged 15-40 years, dependency ratios, especially in remote atolls, have tended to increase with emigration until offset by reductions in fertility, which have also occurred. The flows also comprise many skilled or semi-skilled workers whose remittances in the form of cash and goods have become an important component of several Pacific island economies, raising consumption levels and the level of material welfare. Dependence on agriculture and erratic commodity markets has consequently declined, contributing to declining agricultural production and increased food imports.

Measurement Issues

A major obstacle to formulation of international migration policy is absence of comprehensive and reliable data. Such basic information as numbers of annual migrants, stocks already overseas and rates of return are frequently not known or are mere approximations. In an attempt to estimate the number of persons returning to Sri Lanka from overseas employment during a one-year period, a sample survey of passengers arriving at Colombo airport was carried out by the Sri Lanka Ministry of Plan Implementation and reported by Korale, Gunapala and others (1985). A stratified random sample of returning migrants was made of all Sri Lanka citizens visiting Sri Lanka on 28 randomly selected days spread equally over the four quarters of 1984. An amended disembarkation (and embarkation) card had been introduced in 1983 with the object of monitoring foreign employment. The new card contained questions on marital status, occupation, education, address and duration of stay abroad, purpose for leaving Sri Lanka and, for those who where employed overseas, occupation and country of employment. The survey collected a total of 14 447 landing cards, including 6 188 from persons who stated that they had worked overseas. The survey indicated that two-thirds of the labour migrants were aged 25-39 years, 57 per cent of those who stated their occupation were unskilled or housemaids and 48 per cent of the returning workers were females, of whom at least 84 per cent had worked as housemaids. It was also found that returning migrants had a higher average level of education than the Sri Lankan population in general and that 39.5 per cent were from the District of Colombo.

While a disembarkation card survey, if implemented on a continuing basis, provides valuable data on levels and trends in overseas employment, it should be employed in conjunction with other sources of information, such as reliable departure data and surveys on the use of remittances, skills acquired overseas and problems relating to re-employment. Technical problems of measuring return migration include definition of "return". An overseas worker returning for a vacation should not be counted as a returning migrant, but there is a case for including returning workers who intend securing another contract overseas. Distinction should also be made between returning contract workers and returning emigrants who intend to remain overseas. The Sri Lanka survey found that the proportion of persons not completing some items on disembarkation cards was quite high due perhaps to ambiguity in definition (such as "purpose of return") and complexity of language used on the card, especially for unskilled workers or housemaids.

Economic Impact of Labour Migration

In theory, labour emigration should reduce rates of unemployment and underemployment and create skill shortages in certain occupations or sectors which lead to wage increases. In fact, most labour-supplying countries in Asia have substantial levels of unemployment on which labour migration has had little measurable impact. As most labour migrants were employed prior to emigration, unemployment would be reduced if the migrants were replaced by unemployed persons. However, the majority of labour migrants come from rural areas, where underemployment is pervasive, so their departure does not greatly affect rates of employment (Smart, 1984).

However, one study estimated that emigration from the Republic of Korea in 1978-81 had reduced unemployment from 6.8 to 5.5 per cent (Kim, 1983). As yet no comprehensive study has been undertaken on the indirect effects of labour migration on employment in recruitment agencies, airlines, government services, banking and training institutions. While labour migration has had limited impact on aggregate levels of unemployment, because most of the migrants have worked in the construction sector, some skill shortages in that sector have been reported. In Bangladesh, e.g., barriers to labour mobility imposed by government have created skill shortages despite unemployment among vocational school graduates. While a general lowering of quality of skilled work has been noted in Pakistan, the Governments of the Republic of Korea and Sri Lanka, foreseeing that foreign demand for labour might constitute an obstacle to the success of ambitious domestic construction programmes, took steps to increase the numbers of persons trained in skilled occupations (Smart, 1984). Wages in the construction sector in the Republic of Korea increased rapidly between 1975 and 1980 and those in Pakistan, the Philippines and Thailand increased at higher rates than for other industries. In each of these countries, however, it is difficult to determine the degree to which the increases were caused by labour migration or by the demands of domestic construction (Smart, 1984).

Governments in the ESCAP region recognise the contribution that labour migration can make in relieving unemployment, and thus actively work to promote the foreign employment of their nationals (Philippines, 1985; Roongshivin, 1985). Korale (1985) noted the importance of the emigration of 60 000 workers a year from Sri Lanka at a time when the rate of unemployment was 15 per cent and the labour force was growing by about 140 000 persons a year. Migration to the Middle East from Sri Lanka led to a loss of construction and engineering skills and resulted in a lowering of output and a lengthening of project implementation schedules. Korale also reported that a "significant increase in employment mobility in the occupations affected by labour migration was noticeable. This increased labour mobility was at the expense of the small firms who lost their skilled and semi-skilled workers to the larger employers, thus transferring training costs to the lowest level". The loss of instructors through emigration or larger companies also hampered technical and vocational training, although these expanded greatly in Sri Lanka after the late 1970s. Korale also noted that since the mid-1970s, wages in occupations affected by migration to the Middle East have risen at a faster rate than wages in other sectors, and cites heavy equipment operators, motor vehicle drivers, English stenographers, engineering technicians and engineering maintanance workers as examples.

While it is difficult to measure impacts attributable to labour emigration because of the characteristically large size of the domestic labour force in the labour-sending countries, Smart (1984) has noted a number of positive changes that have occurred:

> A significant consequence of M.E. circulation is the flexibility introduced into domestic labour markets. The incentive of high wages and domestic employment opportunities created through worker departure have generally expanded labour participation and mobility. Females are extending their

activity both socially and economically. Governments are supporting the development of more extensive and up-to-date vocational training. In general a much more responsive labour
supply system is being created and such changes could prove an
important stimulus/support in future development.

The impact of remitted earnings on sending economies is probably
greater than the impact of changes in the labour force. As Appleyard has
shown (Chapter 1), remittances have become a major source of foreign exchange
earnings for countries of origin. Though remittances comprised about 3 per
cent of gross national product (GNP) in several countries in the ESCAP region
during the early 1980s, amounts have declined sharply during the last two
years as a result of a decline in the number of migrant workers and generally
lower wages for all occupations in the Middle East.

A major debate in the area of labour migration has centred on the use
of remittances and their contribution to national economic development. Many
scholars have argued that remittances are spent primarily on consumer goods
and services rather than investments, and thus make little contribution to
development. To the extent that consumer goods are imported, the value of
remittances is lost to the country. The purchase of land and construction of
houses leads to inflation without necessarily increasing productivity. Other
experts contend that spending on domestic consumption increases GNP and generates employment through multiplier effects. The debate is inconclusive partly
because of the absence of adequate research on the indirect economic effects
of remittances. A number of small-scale surveys in Asia have investigated
expenditure patterns of migrants or their families. For example, a survey in
Bangladesh showed that expenditure patterns vary according to level of income
and place of residence (Ali, et. al., 1981). Families in the lowest income
bracket used most of their remittances to repay debt and buy food; middle
income recipients spent more on housing.

In a survey of return migrants in urban Manila, Go (1985) found that
they either sent or brought back 80 per cent of their average earnings of
$4 632 in the year prior to their return. The study also found that nearly
all the migrants spent remittance money on basic necessities and that 47.5 per
cent spent some on the education of members of the household. About one-third
used remittances to repay debts and 23.7 per cent for housing. Only two out
of the 59 respondents reported making productive investments.

A study by Korale (1985) for Sri Lanka, while not dealing specifically
with the use of remittances, revealed considerable variation in propensity to
remit on the basis of occupation. Professional and managerial persons remitted 44 per cent of average monthly earnings; technical, clerical and related
workers 38 per cent; skilled workers 56 per cent and unskilled workers 69 per
cent. Female domestic aides remitted over 92 per cent.

In a survey of 113 return migrants in a rural area in northeastern
Thailand, Roongshivin (1985) found that returnees had remitted or brought back
an average of $3 300. Eighteen per cent of the returnees spent remittance
money to repay debts, 15.8 per cent on consumption and recreation, 15.8 per
cent on electrical appliances, 12.7 per cent on housing, 9.3 per cent on education and only 4.9 per cent on the purchase of agricultural land. With a
decline in the wages of foreign workers in the Middle East, the use of smaller
remittances can be expected to shift toward paying for basic necessities (such

as food, clothing and medicine), debt repayment and a limited number of consumer durables. Perhaps the most encouraging finding from the surveys in the Philippines and Thailand is that education has been accorded a relatively high priority for the use of remittances.

It is clear from these surveys, conducted in small geographical areas, that the impacts of labour migration vary greatly at the individual level. Some workers accumulate debts greater than those they had accumulated before migrating; others manage to save considerable sums which they use to build a new house, buy land, educate their children or start a small business. While differences may be partly the result of chance (e.g., whether or not the worker was recruited by a reputable agent for an honest employer) they also depend to a great extent on the individual's training, occupation, income and prior financial situation.

While studies in Pakistan and Thailand have shown that migrant workers come primarily from rural areas, the majority of country studies note that high proportions also come from urban areas. This may be attributed to the fact that institutions involved in labour migration are generally located in cities; for example, recruitment offices, government offices that provide passports and test skills and vocational training institutes. The most educated and qualified workers are also more likely to be living in cities (Seccombe and Findlay, Chapter 7). A survey in Sri Lanka in 1981 found that two-thirds of persons going overseas for employment were from Colombo or the adjoining districts of Gampaha and Kalutara (Korale, 1985). Chain migration also contributes to initial impacts being concentrated in the areas of origin of original migrants who provided their relatives and acquaintances with information necessary for selection by recruiting agencies. These and other social and economic factors create areas with high rates of out-migration, both to cities and overseas. A poor economic base has made the Al-Kura subdistrict of northwest Jordan, the Ilocos provinces in the Philippines and the northeast region of Thailand regular suppliers of labour migrants. Villages that have traditionally produced skilled construction workers, such as carpenters or masons, have also furnished a high proportion of overseas migrants.

Concentration of the impacts of migration is also shown by data on the incidence of repeat migration. A survey of 59 skilled migrant returnees to the Philippines found that they had worked overseas an average 2.4 times and that 56 respondents were planning to return overseas (Go, 1985). Wong (1986) also observed that between 1982 and 1984, the Philippines provided 3 600 person-years of temporary workers to Canada per year. Filipinos also had the longest mean length of stay of any group of temporary workers.

Social Impact of Labour Migration

The absence of a male breadwinner in the Middle East for a period of one or two years placed abnormal pressures on his family and community. Individuals' roles change and family stability is affected, although many social problems derive from, and are exacerbated by, the family's social and economic situation before migration. Indeed, the motive to seek employment in the Middle East is generally low level of earnings at home. Strong family traditions in Asia help prevent or moderate many problems that could be exacerbated by labour migration. The extended family frequently shares in assuming the role of the absent member (Arnold, 1984, p. 20).

A study in the Republic of Korea (Ro, 1985) showed that the father's absence abroad had a negative impact on children's education because of a decrease in discipline or motivation. In the Philippines and Thailand, in contrast, the fact that education is one of the major objects of expenditure of remittances may imply that labour migration has a net positive effect on children's education. Other studies have suggested that the sons of unskilled migrants, having seen that lack of education did not prevent their father from earning satisfactory wages overseas, tried to discontinue their formal education, or choose vocational school over higher education. On the other hand, many persons who probably would have received very little education are motivated to complete vocational or technical school courses.

Worker migration also poses psycho-social problems for families. Studies in South Asia suggest that the wife of a migrant workers often suffers depression as a result of his absence and by being required to live in the same household as his relatives. In Southeast Asia, social problems among children which are attributed to the absence of fathers include truancy from school, use of drugs and association with youth gangs, although incidence is generally low and not necessarily higher among migrant than non-migrant families.

International labour migration is also contributing to change in the status of women, although degree and type of change varies between countries. In Pakistan, where migrant families live with the extended family, a male relative usually becomes the major decision-maker and the wife's status may actually be diminished (Gilani, 1983). On the other hand, research in India and Sri Lanka has found that the wife usually manages the family and household during her husband's absence, including financial transactions. A survey of the wives of migrant workers in the Philippines found that during the husband's absence wives felt more independent (64 per cent), developed new interests (58 per cent), had greater self-confidence (68 per cent), were stronger as persons (74 per cent) and discovered new potential (77 per cent), (Go, et. al., 1983).

Some researchers have reported that measures taken by families to cope with the absence of a labour migrant have strengthened family ties. Korale (1985) noted that in a small survey of migrant families in Sri Lanka, 40 per cent had moved to the residence of a relative during the migrant's absence but 30 per cent had arranged for a relative to move into their household. About 20 per cent felt a greater obligation to relatives as a result of assistance received, and an equal proportion reported spending a significant amount of their savings on relatives other than immediate family members.

Available evidence does not suggest a high prevalence of family problems related to temporary labour migration. The most serious problems relate to the economic condition of the migrant and with household finances. Although labour migration provides families with significant increases in income and assets, many fall prey to the fraudulent practices of middlemen. In nearly every labour-exporting country, numerous cases have been reported of workers paying large fees to agents in order to obtain employment abroad, only to have the agent disappear, with the money collected. In other instances, workers have arrived in the Middle East only to discover that no employment had been arranged and that they were reponsible for their return travel. Even when a promised job materialises, wages and/or working conditions may be inferior to what had been promised. Many prospective workers sell property or borrow money to pay the agent's fee, so when no employment is gained, or when the wages are less than promised, he and his family face great economic hardship. Even when fraud is not involved, high agent's fees may create problems. Although most labour-exporting countries have laws limiting or banning such fees, they remain common practice. A skilled worker would have to work several months simply to repay from wages an agent's fee of $1 000 or more.

The risk of being defrauded and the high cost of obtaining an overseas contract have discouraged some workers from emigrating. In the survey of returned migrants in Thailand, which included questions on why they had not returned to the Middle East, fewer than 10 per cent gave reasons related to dissatisfaction with their employment there, but 17.7 per cent said that they were afraid of being cheated or of being stranded overseas, and another 24.8 per cent said that their main reasons were the combination of high costs and low wages associated with overseas employment or that they did not have enough money to finance the costs of obtaining another job overseas (Roongshivin, 1985).

The Thailand study also revealed that 81 per cent of respondents had debts averaging $1 200 prior to going overseas. Of those in debt, 95 per cent said that it had been incurred through financing the costs of obtaining the overseas job. Half of the workers in debt had obtained loans from money lenders at rates of interest ranging from 5-10 per cent a month (Roongshivin, 1985). The recruitment procedure itself was time-consuming and involved considerable cost for low-income workers. Applications had to be completed and a passport, visa, medical examination, birth certificate, education record and certification of skills obtained. Since most recruiting agencies are located in the capital city, many prospective employees from rural areas or other towns had to leave their home and employment in order to apply for overseas work and then remain in the city until a position became available. A study in the Republic of Korea found that workers spent an average of one month in applying for overseas employment (Seok and Yang, 1984). The recruitment procedure is probably longer in most other countries. A study in the Philippines showed that for 57 per cent of overseas workers the period between first applying and actual departure was three months or less, but for 27 per cent the period was 4-6 months and for 13 per cent it was 7-12 months (Arnold, 1984). Many workers accumulated debts during this period and suffered considerable hardship if they did not ultimately obtain foreign employment.

When workers return at the end of their contracts, many face a new set of problems. While readjustment to their family or community does not appear to be a major problem, several surveys have shown that returnees experience difficulties in handling financial matters. For example, a survey of returned skilled construction workers in the Philippines revealed that one-third reported difficulties associated with the high cost of living and low wages, while 14 per cent reported difficulties in finding either local or overseas employment. A survey of returned professional workers in the Philippines showed that one-third of repondents cited unavailability of jobs and 17 per cent financial problems, including high prices and low wages at home, as major problems associated with resettlement (Paganoni and de los Reyes, 1985).

A survey of returnees in Thailand showed that only about half of those with debts prior to departure had become debt-free at the time of the survey. Furthermore, while the number of migrants who owned some land was the same before departure and after return, the average size of landholding had declined from 22.9 _rais_ to 12.2 _rais_. Many workers had sold or mortgaged their land in order to acquire an overseas job (Roongshivin, 1985).

Perhaps the most critical aspect of the reintegration was participation in the labour force. While research so far has not been sufficient to describe major patterns, a survey in Pakistan showed that two-thirds of return migrants had no problems of readjustment and another 26 per cent reported only minor problems (Gilani, 1983). Other studies indicate that problems of reintegration may be emerging because of unrealistic expectations held by workers when they return. The Pakistan study found that 63 per cent of returnees had expected to start a small business upon return but that only 6 per cent had in fact done so. A survey in the Philippines revealed that 77 per cent of migrant workers wanted to start a business (Arnold, 1984), and a survey of return migrants in Sri Lanka indicated that only 12.5 per cent were self-employed (Balasooriya, _et. al._, 1985, Table 29).

Following employment in the Middle East for wages several times higher than they had earned at home, many workers seem reluctant to take employment in the same occupation that they had held before migrating. Returning Korean workers took an average of three months to obtain employment (Seok and Yang, 1984), and a survey by the Sri Lanka Ministry of Labour indicated that 19.5 per cent of returnees were unemployed and another 56.2 per cent were described as living on their savings. Forty-four per cent had no savings and another 41 per cent reported savings of less than $1 000 (Balasooriya, _et. al._, 1985). Furthermore, when return migrants find employment, they are likely to be dissatisfied with it. Paganoni and de los Reyes (1985) found that returned professional workers rated their job satisfication at home only half as high as their overseas employment.

One reason for low rates of labour force participation is that returnees prefer to return to the Middle East and so they spend their time seeking a new contract rather than employment at home. The Sri Lanka survey reported that 61 per cent of returnees were expecting to return to the Middle East (Balasooriya, _et. al._, 1985), and a Philippines survey showed that 56 of 59 skilled returnees were looking, or planned to look, for employment abroad (Go, 1985). Among returned professionals, 96 per cent stated that they would like to return overseas (Paganoni and de los Reyes, 1985). Although fear of being cheated and the high costs of obtaining a job overseas discouraged many Thai workers from returning abroad, 13.3 per cent of those surveyed stated that they were in the process of getting another job overseas and another 17.7 per cent replied that they were not going abroad again because their contract had not been renewed, implying that they would go if they had a contract (Roongshivin, 1985).

The extremely limited data currently available suggest that the migration experience is on balance positive for most families. This is not to deny that many individual families experience serious problems including being defrauded, deterioration in mental and physical health, disruption of marriage, lack of parental guidance for children, etc. Because labour-exporting countries greatly benefit from the remittances earned by workers overseas, much more attention has been given to assessing the broader socio-economic aspects of labour migration. Although the impact of labour emigration on sending communities has not been well-researched, numerous studies have identified some effects. These include impact on the community of construction of new houses by families of migrant workers and expenditure of remittances on consumer goods. While the expenditure of remittances should benefit a village, cases have been cited of return migrants investing in small businesses (such as a taxi service or grocery store) which competed with existing businesses and led to the closure of one of them. Some studies have suggested that labour migration promotes a more egalitarian income distribution, while others have shown that it has had the opposite effect (Arnold, 1984).

CONCLUSION

Decline in petroleum prices since December 1985 has reduced demand for construction workers in the Middle East with consequential impacts on the economies of sending countries in the ESCAP region. While many governments have tried to prevent fraudulent practices associated with recruitment, it is expected that some of the more serious problems will be resolved by more effective future control and regulation. In addition, the large cadre of professional and technical workers with several years work experience in the Middle East is now less dependent on employment agencies to obtain further contracts. Decreased demand for foreign workers in the Middle East, changes in skill composition and reduced wages may well lead to a net return of workers to sending countries which will cause serious social and economic problems.

In the past, government assistance or advice to labour migrants during preparation for departure, while overseas and upon return, has been minimal. Paganoni and de los Reyes (1985) showed that only 4 of 144 returned professional workers in their survey reported having received any help from any agency or organisation while planning their return or during their reintegration. Individual counselling of the tens of thousands of workers emigrating every year is not possible in the less developed countries of origin in Asia, although both the government and employers in the Republic of Korea have large-scale counselling programmes for workers' families. It would be feasible, however, for all governments to sponsor mass media campaigns informing citizens how to make use of banking systems and to handle family finance. Drama programmes could also stress the important roles which family and community can play in assisting labour migrants. These could include sharing of family roles during periods of stress.

Most governments in the ESCAP region were relatively slow to react to the sudden increase in demand for labour in the Middle East. They may be similarly unprepared for the massive return migration looming in the near future.

BIBLIOGRAPHY

AFTAB, Mohammad
"The Pipeline Runs Dry", Far Eastern Economic Review, 13th September 1984.

ALI, Syed Ashraf et. al.
"Labour Migration from Bangladesh to the Middle East", World Bank Staff Working Paper No. 454, Washintgon, D.C., World Bank, 1981.

ARNOLD, Fred
"The Social Situation of Asian Migrant Workers and Their Families", paper prepared for the United Nations Centre for Social Development and Humanitarian Affairs, Vienna, 1984.

BALASOORIYA, Hemachandra, Vinne KANKANAMGE and Jayampathi HEENDENIYA, revised by Dilesh JAYANNTHA
Sri Lanka's Migrant Workers, Colombo, Ministry of Labour, 1985.

ECONOMIC AND SOCIAL COMMISSION FOR ASIA AND THE PACIFIC (ESCAP)
International Migration in the Pacific, Sri Lanka and Thailand, ST/ESCAP/376, Bangkok, 1985a.

Report of the Policy Workshop on International Migration in Asia and the Pacific, Bangkok, 15th-21st October 1985, New York, United Nations, 1985b.

GILANI, I.S.
"Overseas Pakistanis", paper presented at the Conference on Asian Labour Migration to the Middle East, Honolulu, 19th-23rd September 1983.

GO, Stella P.
"Returning Filipino Overseas Contract Workers: The Case of Barangay Vergara, Metro Manila", paper presented at Policy Workshop on International Migration in Asia and the Pacific, Bangkok, 15th-21st October 1985.

GO, Stella P., Leticia T. POSTRADO and Pilar RAMOS-JIMENEZ
The Effects of International Contract Labour, Vol. 1, Manila, Integrated Research Centre, De La Salle University, 1983.

HAYES, Geoffrey R.
"International Migration in the Pacific Islands: A Brief History and a Review of Recent Patterns", International Migration in the Pacific, Sri Lanka and Thailand, ST/ESCAP/376, Bangkok, 1985.

KIM, Sooyong
"The Labour Migration from Korea to the Middle East: Its Trends and Impacts on the Korean Economy", paper presented at the Conference on Asian Labour Migration to the Middle East, Honolulu, 1983.

KORALE, R.B.M.
"Middle East Migration: The Sri Lankan Experience", International Migration in the Pacific, Sri Lanka and Thailand, ST/ESCAP/376, Bangkok, 1985.

KORALE, R.B.M., G.D.C. GUNAPALA et al.
"Dimensions of Return Migration in Sri Lanka", paper presented at the Policy Workshop on International Migration in Asia and the Pacific, Bangkok, 15th-21st October 1985.

LIN, Lim Lean
"The Consequences of International Migration for Social Change: The Case of Malaysia", paper presented at the Workshop on the Consequences of International Migration (International Union for the Scientific Study of Population), Canberra, 16th-19th July 1984.

PAGANONI, Anthony and Angelo DE LOS REYES
"Return Migrants: An Exploratory Study into Their Decision-making Process and Value Orientation", paper presented at the Policy Workshop on International Migration in Asia and the Pacific, Bangkok, 15th-21st October 1985.

THE PHILIPPINES, Ministry of Labour and Employment, Philippines Overseas Employment Administration
1984 Annual Report, Manila, 1985.

RO, Kong-Kyun
"Workers of the Republic of Korea Returning from the Middle East and Their Families: Socio-economic Conditions and Their Problems", paper presented at the Policy Workshop on International Migration in Asia and the Pacific, Bangkok, 15th-21st October 1985.

ROONGSHIVIN, Peerathep
"Survey of the Situation of Thai Returned Migrant Workers for Develop-ment of a Re-integration Policy for the Sixth Five-year Plan, 1987-1991: A Case Study in Khon Kaen", paper presented at the Policy Workshop on International Migration in Asia and the Pacific, Bangkok, 15th-21st October 1985.

SEOK, Hyun-ho and Jong-hoe YANG
"A Decade of Korean Labour Migration to the Middle East: An Overview", Korean Social Science Journal, Vol. 11, 1984.

SMART, John E.
"Worker Circulation Between Asia and the Middle East: The Structural Intersection of Labour Markets", paper presented at the Workshop on the Consequences of International Migration, International Union for the Scientific Study of Population, Canberra, 16th-19th July 1984.

WONG, Lloyd L.
    "Temporary Workers in Canada: Some Recent Trends", Calgary, York
    University, mimeo., 1986.

Chapter 7

THE CONSEQUENCES OF TEMPORARY EMIGRATION AND REMITTANCE EXPENDITURE
FROM RURAL AND URBAN SETTLEMENTS: EVIDENCE FROM JORDAN

by

I.J. Seccombe and A.M. Findlay

One of the most marked consequences of international migration in the
Arab world has been its influence in modifying settlement hierarchies in both
the regions of emigration and immigration (Findlay, 1985). Labour exporting
countries have also experienced a concentration of remittance investments in
housing projects and in household consumer goods.   In some countries, such as
Jordan, the effects of this have been most evident in the rapid expansion of
large cities, while in other countries, such as Morocco, remittances have
fostered the growth of small towns in the peripheral regions of labour emigration (Lepeltier, 1984;   Findlay et al, forthcoming).

Temporary emigration has also had a varied impact on villages of
migrant origin.   In some cases, such as interior Oman, labour emigration has
reinforced the decline of the rural economy and increased rural depopulation
(Birks and Letts, 1977).   In other areas, for example parts of North Yemen and
Egypt, temporary worker outflows have provided new income sources to subsidise
and maintain the village economy (Swanson, 1979;   Taylor, 1984).   On the other
hand, host societies have had to provide accommodation for foreign workers
whose employment has usually been in major cities.   It is in these urban locations that the oil-rich states have tended to encounter labour shortages and
have required immigrant workers to fill both the technically-skilled jobs
lying beyond the professional qualifications and experience of the local population, and also the less-skilled and unskilled jobs created during phases of
rapid infrastructural development.

International migration therefore promotes a variety of changes in
forms of settlement in both host and sender societies.   The purpose of this
paper is to investigate the characteristics of temporary emigration for
employment and the nature of remittance expenditure within one country of
labour emigration in the Arab world.   The paper seeks to assess the extent to
which temporary labour emigration promotes new regional disparities and new
patterns of population redistribution.   This is done by comparing two independent household surveys conducted at opposite ends of the settlement continuum,

one in the village of Sammu' in northwest Jordan and the other in Marka, a suburb of the Jordanian capital, Amman.

Jordanian Emigration for Employment: An Historical Perspective

Emigration for employment has been an important element in the social and economic life of Jordan since its creation under the British mandate for Palestine and Transjordan in July 1922. Documentary evidence demonstrates that the period 1922-36 saw the increasing incorporation, on a temporary basis, of manpower from northwest and central Transjordan into the Palestinian labour market. The considerable infrastructural investment that characterised the early mandate years in Palestine created an enormous demand for labour at a time when Transjordan was suffering a cycle of poor harvests and almost continuous drought conditions (Seccombe, 1985a). The creation of the State of Israel in May 1948 led to a reversal of this pattern of migration and by the 1950s emigration for employment was dominated by the West Bank sub-districts which, in 1948-49, had received the bulk of Palestinian refugees. Here overtly political motives joined the economic imperative of high unemployment and low capital investment to encourage a growing labour outflow (Plascov, 1981). Indeed some 80 per cent of the 63 000 "Jordanians" recorded as "temporarily resident abroad" in the 1961 census had departed from the West Bank sub-districts (Figure 7.1). New patterns of long-distance emigration for employment emerged as Palestinians (and later Jordanians) increasingly found work in the expanding oil-economies of Kuwait and Saudi Arabia (Seccombe, 1983, 1986) which, by 1961, already accounted for more than 57 per cent of recorded emigrants.

Labour outflows continued to increase steadily throughout the 1960s, with annual net departures from Jordan averaging 26 000 in the three years prior to 1967. The demographic upheavals, economic chaos and political uncertainty of the 1967-71 period, which began with the Israeli occupation of the West Bank and culminated in the Syrian invasion of northern Jordan, and the Jordanian conflict with the Palestinian fedayeen, served to increase emigration. In 1972 unemployment in Jordan was estimated at over 14 per cent (World Bank, 1976), while the number of Jordanians working abroad had increased to over 80 000 with 41 000 in Kuwait alone (Seccombe, 1984). With this tradition of emigration for employment and a relatively skilled labour force, Jordan was well placed to meet the growing regional demand for manpower which followed oil price increases in 1973/74.

By 1980 the earnings of an estimated 300 000 Jordanians (including Palestinians) abroad accounted for some 20 per cent of Jordan's gross national product. In addition, the Jordanian economy received substantial income from Arab aid programmes following the Baghdad Arab summit of 1978 at which all the Arab oil producers except Libya and Algeria agreed to provide Jordan with substantial grants to fund capital development projects. As a result, foreign aid has been as large as, and frequently greater than, domestic revenues, accounting for over one-third of GDP. Thus, by 1980, the Jordanian economy had become highly dependent on external sources of revenue. Despite the recognition that high rates of labour out-migration were having detrimental effects on the domestic labour market, the Jordanian Government was reluctant to restrict labour outflows (Seccombe, 1985b).

FIGURE 7.1: JORDAN AND THE WEST BANK

a. Rates of emigration from Jordan by sub-district, 1961

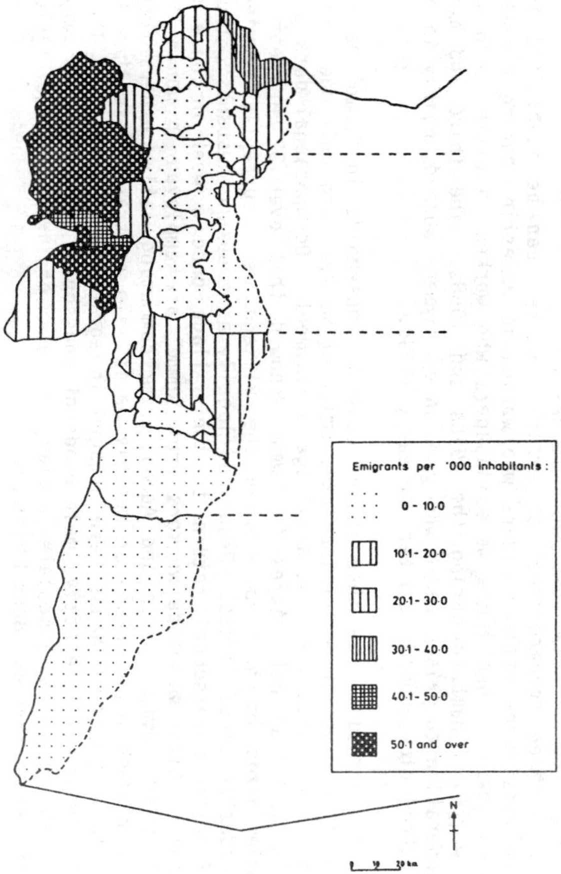

b. Administrative sub-districts of Jordan, 1961

Survey Methodology

The data on which this paper is based are drawn from two independent research projects and represent only a small part of much larger surveys carried out in Amman (Findlay and Samha, 1985) and northwest Jordan (Seccombe, 1985a). Selected data have been used to explore some of the consequences of international migration for two very different geographical environments. Unlike the general and larger systematic surveys carried out by the authors, neither the Sammu' nor the Marka samples include many Palestinian families whose remittance expenditure patterns may differ significantly from those of East Bank Jordanians. However, both Sammu' and Marka had been profoundly involved in labour emigration during the 1970s and early 1980s and reflect respectively the rural and urban dimension of the process in which the authors were interested.

The village of Sammu', in the Al-Kura sub-district of northwest Jordan, lies on a narrow watershed between two deeply incised tributaries of the river Jordan: Wadi At-Taibeh to the north and Wadi Ziqlab to the south. Its problems typify those faced by many of Al-Kura's highland villages. Population growth has been rapid, increasing from 942 in November 1961 to 2 529 in 1979 and 2 875 in 1983 and placing pressure on the meagre land resources of the village (less than 5 000 dunums). Together with poor land management, it has contributed to a serious ecological degradation of the two drainage basins first described by Atkinson and Beaumont (1967). As elsewhere in the Al-Kura, land shortages and diminishing real agricultural incomes have been a major cause of out-of-village employment since the early 1930s. Emigration has been a consistent factor in this long history of extra-village employment. Basson (1984) suggests that the folklore associated with emigration from this part of Jordan is "... so pervasive that leaving for work is often a step in life planning".

Three "generations" of emigrant worker can be identified in Sammu'. The first were village elders who worked in Palestine during the middle mandate years. Then there were villagers who worked in cities such as Beirut, Kuwait and Hamburg during the 1950s and 1960s. The third and most recent generation comprises those who took up employment abroad, mainly in neighbouring oil-rich economies after the early 1970s.

Although more than 10 per cent of households in Sammu' have at least one family member working abroad, emigrant workers are only one element in an extensive pattern of extra-village employment. Occupational data provided by the municipal authorities in Sammu' showed that over 32 per cent of active male heads of households from the village were currently serving in the Jordanian armed forces. Described locally as "weekend husbands", the majority of service personnel return to the village once a week or once every two weeks. Other absentee workers from Sammu' are employed in non-military jobs in Irbid, Amman, Zarqa and Aqaba, some commuting daily, others returning to the village on a weekly or monthly basis. In contrast, less than 9 per cent of male household heads were engaged in agricultural pursuits. Thus, at any one time, half the active male heads of households were employed away from the village and its immediate region, a rate of extra-village residence not unusual in the East Bank highlands.

Marka is an eastern surburb of Amman city lying on the south side of Wadi Ain Ghazal, in the less prosperous part of the Amman conurbation.

Settlements which developed during the 1970s along Wadi Ain Ghazal between Amman and Zarqa are home to both the workers of Jordan's most industrialised valley and to many in-migrants who came to Amman from the surrounding rural districts in search of employment. Marka itself was located, until the early 1980s, next to Jordan's international airport. The transfer of the airport functions to the Queen Alid airport south of Amman led to the transformation of the Marka airstrip into a military and training base. Marka's links with the military are reinforced by the presence of a large military hospital, as well as a medical school. To the north of the established settlement are many much poorer quarters into which internal migrants moved during the 1950s and 1970s. It was in these poorer quarters of north Marka that the sample survey was conducted. Only 6 per cent of the sample were native to Marka, 21 per cent had moved there from another part of Amman city, 45 per cent from the Amman region and 20 per cent from other parts of the East Bank. Only a small proportion of the sample had come to Marka directly from the West Bank (2.5 per cent) although 20 per cent had been born in Palestine. Choosing a study area with a relatively small Palestinian population proved helpful in making comparisons with Sammu' village since, as shown elsewhere (Findlay and Samha, forthcoming), the emigration history and pattern of remittance usage of Palestinians and East Bank Jordanians is somewhat different.

Population density of most of Marka is over 20 persons per dunum, equivalent to the overcrowded and densely populated area of downtown Amman. The Amman-Balqa urban plan indicated that the quality of housing in Marka was in the lowest two residential categories of the conurbation, while service provision was amongst the poorest in Amman city. For example, the average distance to school was greater than for any other district in the conurbation (Amman Urban Region Planning Group, no date).

The surveys in Sammu' and north Marka were made possible only by the considerable assistance of Jordanian academics and students. In both surveys three types of migrant household were identified: return migrant, current migrant and "complex" migrant households (the latter containing both return and current migrants). The analysis below relates only to those households from which one or more persons were living and working abroad at the time of the survey. A systematic survey of Sammu' in early 1985 revealed the identification of 31 households which had one or more persons currently living abroad. Similarly, students carried out household surveys in early 1984 in several parts of the Amman conurbation including Marka. The data analysed below relate to 40 Marka households identified as having members currently absent and working abroad.

Some Characteristics of Temporary Labour Migration from Sammu' and Marka

Although Sammu' has had a long history of emigration for employment, recent labour outflow has been considerable. Over half of those currently abroad left the village after 1980, including nine emigrants who had been away for less than one year (Table 7.1). Emigration from Marka was greatest during the period 1975 to 1979, although a substantial number of persons left during the early 1980s. The Marka sample had a wider distribution of destinations than Sammu', which may reflect the timing of emigration from the two communities (Table 7.2). Marka migrants went to a more diverse range of destinations, including several countries in the Gulf, Libya, and also a significant number for "educational purposes" to Europe and the United States. Sixty-five

Table 7.1

YEAR OF MOST RECENT EMIGRATION OF CURRENT MIGRANTS

	Sammu'	Marka
Before 1975	0	6
1975-79	10	18
1980-81	5	7
1981-83	7	9
1984	9	n.a.
Total	31	40

Table 7.2

MIGRANT DESTINATIONS FROM SAMMU' AND MARKA

	Sammu'	Marka
Saudi Arabia	20	18
UAE	6	5
Kuwait	1	3
Other Arab	3	5
Europe and United States	0	9
Not stated	1	0
Total	31	40

per cent of current emigrants from Sammu' are in Saudi Arabia (particularly Riyadh). The United Arab Emirates (UAE) is the second most popular destination and, since the late 1970s, has eclipsed Kuwait as a major destination for Jordanian migrant workers. The number of new work permits issued to Jordanians in Kuwait fell by 64 per cent during the period 1977-81 (Seccombe, 1984). In the Amman survey, other sample areas which had participated at an earlier stage in the emigration process had higher proportions of their emigrants departing for Kuwait than occurred in Marka. In Sammu', Kuwait was the second most important destination in the early 1970s; only one migrant had left the village for Abu Dhabi prior to 1978. These changes in migration patterns in Sammu' and Amman are the result of declining relative wage rates in Kuwait (Al-Moosa and McLachlan, 1982) and the adoption of a more pro-Arab (rather than Asian) manpower policy in the UAE (Fergany, 1983).

International emigration from Jordan has been regionally selective for a number of reasons. The Amman region contained a large number of Palestinian refugee camps and hence the largest reserve of surplus labour on which Saudi Arabia and Kuwait could draw; but it was also the locus of government and the headquarters of many of the national institutions through which a proportion of the labour transfers were organised. Being the source of the best-educated and qualified persons on the Jordanian labour market, the capital city of Amman was the sector from which the oil-rich states chose to recruit. Indeed, the Jordanian Government encouraged the emigration of skilled and semi-skilled workers, viewing the economy's ability to export teachers, engineers, and professional personnel as a key element of its development plans. Inevitably this emphasis gave Amman, as the "training" centre for a large proportion of the nation's skilled population, a central role within the international migration process.

As opportunities for employment abroad became more restricted with changing labour market conditions in the Arabian peninsula and Gulf states, pre-migration employment in the public sector became an important avenue for prospective migrant workers. More than half the current migrants from Sammu' were employed in the public sector, primarily in the military and teaching professions, prior to emigration. The proportion is even higher (72 per cent) amongst emigrants after 1980. The public sector is similarly important as the major source of employment abroad for Sammu' emigrants. Nine of the current migrants were teachers, six of whom were on direct government secondment. Emigration is a favoured strategy among school teachers who, after a four-years training period and two years compulsory military service, receive relatively low wages (100-160 Jordanian Dinars/month). Those who had obtained a government scholarship to pay for their training were required to teach for two years in Jordan for each year of their funding before they were eligible for secondment abroad or to take up positions in the private sector.

In addition to the teachers, another eight current migrants from Sammu' were employed in the military or security forces abroad. For example, all the Sammu' villagers working in Abu Dhabi were employed in the emirates' armed forces. Although not on secondment to Abu Dhabi, they had obtained their employment abroad through army contacts; more than half were recruited directly via the Abu Dhabi embassy's military attaché in Amman. Emigrants serving in the military abroad are primarily skilled and experienced men with fifteen or more years service in the Jordanian army, and are recruited on retirement from the Jordanian forces. Only two of those serving in the military abroad were aged under 35, both of whom were on direct secondment (in Bahrain and Abu Dhabi). In addition to those in military service abroad, two migrants from Sammu' who had served as electricians in the Jordanian Army were employed abroad in the private sector as electricians.

In the Marka sample, emigrants who had left to study in Europe and the United States had not been previously employed. Amongst those emigrating to Saudi Arabia and the Gulf, the largest category had been involved in professional activities prior to emigration and also while abroad. The other two most important categories of current employment abroad were clerical and commercial activities. In both cases there had been a movement into these sectors from other forms of urban employment and underemployment held prior to emigration. In the urban sample there was some reluctance to admit to previous employment in the army, although military involvement was generally much less than in the rural sample.

Because many current emigrants from the village had acquired military and teaching experience, they were older than other emigrants. The modal age cohort for current emigrants from Sammu' (35-39 years) is five years older than the modal age cohort from Marka and ten years older than the age reported by the 1980 Royal Scientific Society migrant survey of Amman (Royal Scientific Society, 1983). The older age distribution of Sammu' emigrants may account for the low proportion of "never-married" (less than 10 per cent) and also the strong links that they maintain with the village. Table 7.3 shows a high frequency of home visits; one-third of current migrants visit the village more than once a year. The duration of such visits may also be quite long; school teachers spend up to three months vacation in the village each year. Interestingly, the three migrants who were abroad with their wives and children also visited the village at least once a year. The most frequent visitors were those whose initial departure had been in the 1970s; recent emigrants were less prone to frequent visits.

Table 7.3

FREQUENCY OF HOME VISITS TO SAMMU'

Year of departure	Frequency of visit		
	More than once per year	Once per year	No visit yet
1979 or before	6	4	0
1980-81	1	4	0
1982-83	3	4	0
1984	0	3	6
Total	10	15	6

Few village migrants were isolated at their destination, over two-thirds having reported contact with either a friend, neighbour or relative. Moreover, most migrants received some assistance during the migration process from contacts already at destination. While the role of family members in arranging employment for relatives declined after the mid-1970s, the presence of a relative or neighbour abroad remains of considerable importance in providing informal channels of labour market information to prospective emigrants. Although data in the tables relate to the eldest migrants from emigrant households in Sammu', the 31 households represented 46 migrants, while in Marka the 40 sampled households were in touch with 46 migrants working outside Jordan. Most emigrants from Sammu' received help from relatives and neighbours abroad in arranging residence permits and accommodation. As Table 7.4 indicates, only 14 emigrants received no assistance and all but one of these were in direct government employment.

The comparison of emigration from Sammu' with Marka, and the larger Amman survey (Findlay and Samha, 1985) has revealed a number of important differences, particularly with regard to employment. The concentration of occupations and destinations amongst the village sample makes the future of emigration from the village more unpredictable. As labour-receiving countries increasingly stress the need to reduce the foreign worker presence, it is likely that restrictions will be most readily applied to those public sector

Table 7.4

ASSISTANCE PROVIDED TO MIGRANTS BY FRIENDS, RELATIVES OR
NEIGHBOURS WORKING ABROAD (SAMMU')

	Number
Accommodation	12
Helping in the job search	10
Securing work permit, residence permit or entry visa	13
Loan of money	2
No assistance given	14
Not stated	1
Total	52 (a)

a)   Note that in all cases multiple assistance is reported.

occupations in which villagers are presently concentrated. In June 1983, for
example, the UAE cancelled its agreement to employ 200 Jordanian school
teachers. The greater diversity of occupations and destinations of emigrants
from Marka makes the future less uncertain than for Sammu'.

Although the rate of emigration for employment from Sammu' is high, it
must be set against the background of the region's long history of extra-
village employment and emigration. Prior to the early 1970s labour emigration
was primarily a response to agricultural (and later political) crises which
affected the Al-Kura region. In contrast, contemporary emigration for employment is largely a matter of choice, emigrants leaving because of opportunities
to earn higher incomes abroad and not because of unemployment. As Basson
suggests "... emigration is a preferred state, hoped for, planned for and well
integrated into family life" (Basson, 1984). The strong links between emigrants and their place of origin is emphasized by remittance flows and patterns of remittance usage.

Migrant Remittances

The volume of recorded worker remittances in the Jordanian economy
increased from Jordanian Dinars (JD) 7.4 million in 1972 to JD 440 million in
1984, a level substantially higher than the country's domestic exports and
accounting for between 25 and 33 per cent of both imports and GNP. This
growth reflects the financial and political stability that has prevailed
during the decade. In several years net remittances were higher than external
budgetary support and foreign aid. Furthermore, their importance has increased as signatories of the Baghdad Agreement renege on aid payments as a
result of the continuing Iraq-Iran war and the softening of world oil prices.

National dependence on emigrant remittances is magnified at the local
level. In addition to "current migrant" households, it is apparent that many
"never migrated" households also receive financial support from non-household

kin working abroad. As one would expect, not all respondents to the two surveys were willing to divulge the value of remittance receipts. In Marka the
cash sum remitted in the year previous to the survey was claimed to range from
JD 600 to over JD 4 000 (average JD 2 200). In Marka, only 18 per cent of
households depended on remittances as their sole source of income. Most
households with migrants currently working abroad claimed that remittances
accounted for less than 25 per cent of household income during the six months
prior to the survey, but this figure excluded the substantial value of consumer goods brought home by migrant workers during holiday periods. In
Sammu', by contrast, income from abroad was usually the major, and in some
cases the only, source of household income. Reported annual remittance levels
ranged from JD 600 to JD 4 800 (modal JD 1 500-2 000). Although average value
of remittances was less than in Marka, its overall significance was greater.
The majority (62 per cent) of households received remittances on a regular
monthly basis, usually in the form of a cheque or direct bank transfer. In
many cases these regular sums were supplemented by cash transfers occasionally
brought back to Sammu' by trusted "remittance agents" or by the migrant himself during a home visit.

Almost all households reported using remittances to settle debts
accumulated before or during the migration period, as well as debts incurred
by the migration process itself. Additionally, and somewhat surprisingly
given previous findings, half the sample reported retaining remittance
savings. A significant number (twelve) also indicated that Zakat (religious
donations) were made from remittance income. Use of remittances for these
purposes does not appear to vary with education level, household size or date
of first departure (Table 7.5).

More signficiant, in terms of both value and the large number of households involved, was the use of emigrant remittances for a variety of housing
projects. Nineteen of the 29 households reported using remittances for either
building a new house (eleven), adding new rooms (five) and buying land (usually small plots of 1 dunum or less) for residential building (three). As
Table 7.6 shows, consideration of planned remittance usage by recent emigrants
increases the likelihood of further investment in housing. Findlay and Samha
(1985) found a strong positive association between increasing length of residence abroad and the use of remittances for house construction and modification. Improved housing is still a priority remittance use amongst villagers
abroad on a secondment basis.

In Marka the use of remittances varied to some extent from other sample
areas in the rest of Amman. Although some respondents in the Marka sample had
built new houses with their remittances, a more popular usage was to purchase
a car, or invest in land or the family's education (Table 7.7). The native
East Bank population of the Marka area appears to have found less need for
housing improvement and house building than those in the city-wide sample
where 35 per cent of migrant households are involved in housing projects
(Findlay and Samha, 1985). This contrasts with the much greater use of remittances for housing noted in the Sammu' sample.

A major factor contributing to this rural/urban differential is the
extent of home ownership in rural areas. Almost 90 per cent of households in
Sammu' live in owned accommodation and only one household in the current
sample was living in rented accommodation. This compares with rates of home
ownership of 47 per cent for "below high income" urban areas and 42 per cent

Table 7.5

REPORTED USES OF REMITTANCE BY MIGRANT'S EDUCATIONAL LEVEL

Sammu' remittance use:	Higher	Secondary	Preparatory	Elementary	None	Not stated	Total
Debt settlement	5	6	7	5	--	1	24
Housing	1	4	5	9	--	--	19
Savings	3	4	5	2	--	2	16
Children's education	1	3	4	4	--	1	13
Zakat	3	3	1	4	--	1	12
Buying furniture	--	2	5	3	--	1	11
Buying electrical goods	1	1	2	1	--	1	6
Marriage payments	--	--	1	3	--	--	4
Investment in agriculture	--	1	1	1	--	--	3
Other uses	--	1	--	1	--	1	3
Uses not stated	1	--	--	--	1	--	2

Highest class of education completed

Table 7.6

REMITTANCE USE IN HOUSING ACTIVITIES BY EDUCATION LEVEL, SAMMU'

Highest class of education completed	Current use:			Planned use:			Total			
	Building new	Adding room(s)	Buying land	Building new	Adding room(s)	Buying land	Building new	Adding room(s)	Buying land	Total
Higher	1	--	--	3	--	1	4	--	1	5
Secondary	2	2	--	1	1	--	3	3	--	6
Preparatory	4	--	1	1	--	--	5	--	1	6
Elementary	--	3	2	1	1	--	5	4	2	11
Not stated	--	--	--	1	1	--	1	1	--	2
Total	11	5	3	7	3	1	18	8	4	30

120

Table 7.7

PERCENTAGE OF MARKA MIGRANT HOUSEHOLDS INVESTING REMITTANCES
IN DIFFERENT ITEMS

Building	17.5
Land	35.0
Car	45.0
Education	30.0
Industry	7.5
Agriculture	2.5
No "investment"	17.5

for "high income" urban areas of Amman (Saket, 1983). Basson (1984) also found a high rate (over 82 per cent) of home ownership in villages where housing is seen as a form of security and was given high priority amongst newly-married couples. In Sammu' new housing is designed either for the emigrant's own use on return to the village, or is intended as an independent unit for the migrant's son. The costs of new housing in rural areas (averaging JD 3-5 000 in Sammu') are substantially lower than in the Amman-Zarqa urban region where land prices rose 500 per cent and construction costs 170 per cent during the period 1970-76 (Kirwan, 1981). In Amman the construction of new housing is often preceded by land purchase, thus increasing costs and adding further to the time lag between emigration and investment in housing. In contrast, most of those building new houses in the village do so on land already owned by the family which has led to a rapid spread of housing units away from the village core and into surrounding fields, often some distance from roads and other housing units.

This use of family land holdings has enabled emigrants from rural areas to begin work on housing projects within the first three or four years of their initial departure. In contrast, in Amman non-ownership of land by migrants delayed commencement of house building by several years. Remittances were saved initially for land purchase and only later used for actual house building. Table 7.8, relating to the total Amman survey, shows the relationship between length of absence and propensity to construct or modify housing. Unlike Sammu', investment in housing in Amman is strongly associated with those who have been abroad for ten years or more.

Table 7.8

IMPORTANCE OF HOUSE-BUILDING AND MODIFICATION BY LENGTH OF
MIGRANT ABSENCE (ENTIRE AMMAN SAMPLE)

Period of absence (years)	Investment in house construction or modification (% of all emigrants)
1-4	37.5
5-9	30.4
10-14	65.4
15+	78.9

As Table 7.7 shows, lack of investment in housing in Marka was not accompanied by a significantly higher propensity to use remittances in productive projects in industry or agriculture. Remittances served instead to fuel demand for household consumables such as kitchen electrical appliances, radios, televisions and cassette recorders. This corroborates the results of the Royal Scientific Society's Survey (1983) which showed that one of the main consequences of the international migration experience was the transfer of urban "consumerism". Return migrants' expenditure patterns remained geared to the purchase of imported household consumables and was different in character from the expenditure patterns of households which had no contact with international migration.

Since Amman is the chief location from which imported consumer goods are distributed to the rest of the Jordanian economy, it also stands to prosper most from the "consumerism" promoted by international migration. As a capital city, it has been affected both directly by the expenditure patterns of emigrants from Amman itself, and indirectly by the "consumerist" behaviour of emigrants from other regions of the country.

Despite some differences in detail, the remittance-usage pattern in villages such as Sammu' is remarkably similar to that reported for Amman. The limited investment made by emigrants in the agricultural sector is not surprising given the long history of disassociation of the village economy from the agricultural sector. If emigration has reduced agricultural production, it is largely through changes in land use as a result of the expanding residential area than any apparent withdrawal of agricultural labour. Opportunities for the investment of remittance income in agriculture are limited, given the fragmentation and small size of holdings, together with the reluctance of villagers to sell inherited family lands and the low returns from dry-land agriculture.

There can be little doubt that the inflow of remittances to the Amman region has been partially responsible for the expansion of the built-up area. The rapid rate of Amman's growth has been accentuated by being host to a very large refugee population. The population growth of the city from 520 000 in 1971 to 823 000 in 1979 reflects continued in-migration from other regions of the country. This is entirely consistent with the demand for labour created in the construction and service sectors of Amman's economy as a result of remittance expenditures. Indeed, short-fall in labour within the Amman conurbation and the inadequate supply of labour through internal migration is reflected in the level of international immigration necessary to maintain the urban economy. In 1981 70 650 work permits were issued to foreigners in the Amman conurbation (Seccombe, forthcoming). Emigration of Jordanians from rural areas also led to replacement immigration. The 1983 Agricultural Census revealed that non-Jordanians accounted for 60 per cent of all paid employment in the agricultural sector, and in the Jordan Valley irrigated agriculture is maintained almost entirely by Egyptian immigrants (Seccombe, 1981). Immigrant workers are even found in small highland villages like Sammu' where the municipality employs twelve Egyptians as refuse collectors. Rising aspirations and wage demands, particularly among the younger, more educated Jordanian villagers, have encouraged employers to seek alternative and cheaper labour supplies (Seccombe, forthcoming).

Sammu' temporary emigrants generally do not, on their return from the Gulf, move to Amman or Irbid. This is not inconsistent with the findings of the Amman survey for it reflects the fact that Sammu' is relatively well-provided with services and has good road connections with Irbid (about 24 kilometres by road), Jordan's second largest city. A number of returnees from the village now work in commerce or services in the city while continuing to live in the village. Indeed, it could be argued that by increasing household incomes, improving housing conditions and increasing levels of consumerism within the village, temporary international labour migration is now seen by villagers as a preferable alternative to the more permanent rural to urban migration.

CONCLUSIONS

The results of the two surveys discussed in this paper reinforce the argument that international migration is associated with non-productive investment of remittances in consumer goods and in the construction sector. In an economy such as Jordan's, this pattern of remittance expenditure encourages very marked geographical changes in both villages and large urban settlements, but the morphological and functional changes that occur vary in significance according to urban hierarchy. The common link in all scales of settlement is that emerging patterns are determined by consumer rather than by producer behaviour, resulting in patterns of settlement change that are distinctly different from those found in settlement systems whose dynamics are governed by local patterns of production.

Acknowlegements

The authors would like to thank Professor M. Samha of the University of Jordan, and Dr. Ali Zaghal and Dr. R. Beni-Yassin of the University of Yarmouk for assistance with the larger surveys which made this comparative analysis possible. They are also grateful to the British Council, the Carnegie Trust and Ministère de l'Industrie et de la Recherche, which provided funding for the two surveys.

BIBLIOGRAPHY

AL-MOOSA, A. and K. McLACHLAN
"Wage Patterns Among the Foreign Labour Force in Kuwait", Arab Gulf Journal 2, 1982.

AMMAN URBAN REGION PLANNING GROUP
Planned Development in Amman Balqa Region 1981-1985, Amman, AURPG, no date.

ATKINSON K. and P. BEAUMONT
"Watershed Management in Northern Jordan", World Crops, 19, 1967.

BASSON, P.
"Male Emigration and Authority Structure of Families in North-west Jordan", unpublished paper, Irbid, Yarmouk University, 1984.

BIRKS, J.S. and S.E. LETTS
"Diqal and Muqaydah: Dying Oases in Arabia", Tijdschrift voor Economische en Social Geografia, Vol. 68, No. 3, 1977.

FERGANY, N.
Foreign Labour in the Arab Gulf States, Beirut, Centre for Arab Unity Studies, 1983.

FINDLAY, A.
"Migrant's Dreams and Planners' Nightmares", Cities 2, 1985.

"Regional Economic Disparities and Population Change in Morocco", Scottish Geographical Magazine, 102, forthcoming.

FINDLAY, A. and M. SAMHA
"The Impact of International Migration on the Urban Structure of Amman", Espace, Populations, Sociétés 3, 1985.

"Return Migration and Urban Change", in R. King, ed., Return Migrations and Regional Development, forthcoming.

KIRWAN, F.
"The Impact of Labour Migration on the Jordanian Economy", International Migration Review 15, 1981.

LEPELTIER, F.
"Les investissements immobilièrs des travailleurs migrants d'origine rurale dans la ville de Taza", in G. Simon, ed., Villes et Migrations Internationales de Travail dans le Tiers-Monde, Poitiers, Université de Poitiers, 1984.

PLASCOV, A.
The Palestinian Refugees in Jordan, 1948-1957, London, Cass, 1981.

ROYAL SCIENTIFIC SOCIETY
Workers Migration Abroad, Amman, RSS, 1983.

SAKET, B.K. et al.
Workers' Migration Abroad: Socio-economic Implications for Households in Jordan, Amman, RSS, 1983.

SECCOMBE, I.J.
Manpower and Migration: The Effects of International Labour Migration on Agricultural Development in the East Jordan Valley 1973-1980, occasional publications No. 11, Durham, CMEIS, 1981.

"Labour Migration to the Arabian Gulf: Evolution and Characteristics, 1920-50", Bull. Brit. Soc. Middle Eastern Studies, Vol. 10, No. 1, 1983.

International Labour Migration and Skill Scarcity in the Hashemite Kingdom of Jordan, Geneva, ILO working paper 14, International Migration for Employment Series, 1984.

"Emigration for Employment and Regional Disparity: Evidence from the Al-Kura District of North-west Jordan", paper presented to an Anglo-Dutch Symposium on regional disparity and migration in the Third World, Amsterdam, Free University of Amersterdam, 1985a.

"Labour Emigration Policies and Economic Development in Jordan: From Unemployment to Labour Shortage", in B. Khadar, ed., The Economic Development of Jordan, Louvain-la-Neuve, Université Catholique de Louvain, 1985b.

"Migrant Labour and the Early Oil Industry in the Arabian Gulf, 1930-50", Maghreb-Mashrek, 1986.

"Immigrant Workers in an Emigrant Economy: An Examination of Replacement Migration in the Middle East", International Migration, forthcoming.

SWANSON, J.C.
Emigration and Economic Development: The Case of the YAR, Boulder, Colorado, Westview, 1979.

TAYLOR, E.
"Egyptian Migration and Peasant Wives", MERIP Reports, No. 124, 1984.

WORLD BANK
Country Economic Memorandum on Jordan, Washington, D.C., World Bank, 1976.

B. CLANDESTINE

Chapter 8

IRREGULAR MIGRATION: AN EMERGING ISSUE IN DEVELOPING COUNTRIES

by

Reinhard Lohrmann (1)

INTRODUCTION

Since the early 1970s irregular migration, also labelled clandestine, illegal or undocumented migration, has become an issue of significant concern (United Nations, 1974;   Boehning 1983 and 1984).   The reason is not that irregular migration did not occur in earlier years;   what has changed is the overall impact of irregular migration in many countries and the perception of the phenomenon by state authorities.

Until the late 1960s foreigners frequently could enter countries where they obtained employment and established residence without any impediment. The labour markets in many industrial countries in Western Europe and North America, as well as in some upper middle-income developing countries and high-income oil exporting states in the Middle East, Africa and Latin America, readily absorbed a large number of unannounced migrants, in addition to those who were admitted legally as permanent or temporary immigrants.   Many irregular migrants regularised their status once they found employment.   Their arrival in the receiving country and/or their entering the labour market were not, in fact, viewed as illegal acts although they were contravening existing legislation.   Irregular migration was tolerated as a normal occurrence and regarded as inconsequential.   Though some countries took measures to reduce the number of irregular migrants, in particular by organising orderly recruitment under bilateral agreements, large-scale expulsion or deportation of irregular migrants, such as the expulsion from Ghana in 1969 of an estimated half a million people (mainly from Nigeria, Burkina Faso and Niger) was uncommon and due in part to specific political and social conditions in that continent.

The situation changed markedly in the 1970s when, due to changing economic conditions, overall demand for foreign labour declined in many migrant receiving countries where public opinion, sometimes reinforced by government statements, showed a growing awareness of and sensitivity to the presence of irregular migrants and their concentration in certain regions and sectors. Many governments curtailed immigration and reduced or abolished prevailing facilities for irregular migrants to regularise their status after arrival. Some countries introduced visa requirements for foreign nationals who previously could enter with only a passport.

The general decline in demand for foreign labour in some industrial receiving countries in the 1970s did not, however, apply to low-paid unskilled labour in sectors of persisting economic decline such as the service sector and agriculture. Thus, certain immigration flows of low-paid and unskilled workers, much of it irregular, continued. With curtailment of recruitment of legal foreign labour, irregular migration became the only remaining possibility, apart from family reunion, for persons to obtain employment in a receiving country.

The phenomenon also grew in developing countries. Increasing demand for labour in various oil-exporting developing countries was, to a large extent, met by irregular migrants. In other developing countries, political instability and natural disasters since the early 1970s have caused an unprecedented increase in the number of persons, including dependent family members, moving to other countries. Most border-crossing mass population movements of an irregular nature occurred in sub-Saharan Africa, Central America and parts of Asia. In a few developing countries in South America, long-established irregular migration flows continued in the 1970s. Widening income disparities and unequal economic development among developing countries, as well as persistent rapid population growth, were additional factors leading to irregular migration.

Developing countries reacted in different ways to the influx of irregular migrants. Some organised mass expulsions. Nigeria's policy in 1983 and 1985 is an example. Others, for instance Argentina and Venezuela, proceeded with legalisation campaigns and amnestied irregular migrants who reported to the authorities. Other countries imposed stricter border controls and tightened labour legislation by prohibiting and punishing employment of foreigners in an irregular situation. Even countries which had traditionally tolerated irregular migration because it satisfied persistent demand for unskilled labour in specific sectors of the economy, began to question its value.

The Perception in the International Community

The marked increase in irregular migration since the early 1970s has led to noticeable changes in attitude of the international community. The World Population Plan of Action approved by the United Nations World Population Conference at Bucharest in 1974 made a brief, one-paragraph reference to irregular migration in connection with the treatment of illegal aliens (United Nations, 1974). In the following year, the United Nations General Assembly adopted Resolution 3.449 (XXX) in which it called on the UN system to use the term "non-documented" or "irregular" in official documents to identify migrant workers who illegally enter another country to obtain work. The ILO World Employment Conference (1976), in its Declaration of Principles and Programme of Action, advocated sanctions against migrations in abusive conditions and measures to combat discrimination and illegal trafficking in manpower vis-à-vis those who take advantage of illegal movements of manpower.

In 1983, the Intergovernmental Committee for Migration (ICM) convened an international seminar in Geneva which analysed the characteristics of irregular migration in various world regions. Its conclusions emphasized the great variety of situations and recommended that the phenomenon be studied at the regional level. In 1984, the United Nations International Conference on Population in Mexico City, in referring to recent trends in international migration flows, included undocumented migrant workers among the three types of migrants to which greater attention should be given by the international community (International Conference on Population, 1984). Another United Nations initiative, which began during the late 1970s and addressed the treatment of undocumented migrants, became a major issue of controversy (United Nations, 1984). By the early 1980s, the mass exodus of unexpected flows of refugees, displaced persons and migrant workers had attracted much attention. In response to a Resolution of the UN Commission on Human Rights [Resolution 29 (XXXVII)], a Special Rapporteur on Massive Exodus and Human Rights was designated, and a Group of Experts on International Co-operation to Avert New Flows of Refugees was established (Sadruddin Aga Khan, 1981). The General Assembly has kept this subject on the agenda of all its sessions since 1981.

Irregular Migration Versus Refugee Migration

A problem faced by many developing countries is the relationship between economically motivated irregular migration and the migration of refugees who fall under the provisions of the 1951 United Nations Convention and the 1967 Protocol relating to the Status of Refugees. Some developing countries which have not signed the 1951 Convention consider as irregular migrants all foreign nationals not admitted as legal immigrants, irrespective of their personal situation. Consequently they deny those individuals the legal treatment usually granted to refugees.

States for which the 1951 Convention is binding apply the status of refugee to all those they deem qualified. In instances where refugee status is denied, the persons concerned are immediately considered irregular migrants to whom the general provisions of the foreigner's law apply. The situation is similar for individuals who enter the territory of a state other than their own and, although qualified in principle for refugee status, do not apply for it. Such cases are reported frequently. Indeed, for various reasons, some individuals prefer not to request refugee status. If they are not otherwise granted legal status, they are deemed irregular migrants by the receiving state.

Subsequent withdrawal of refugee status from individuals previously benefiting from it, because of changed conditions in the home country, may also create situations of irregular migration. Individuals concerned may prefer to remain in the host country instead of returning to their own country or may proceed to a third state.

It may therefore be concluded that many persons who apply unsuccessfully for refugee status, or who hold refugee status but later lose it, or who qualify for refugee status but do not apply for it, end up as irregular migrants. They represent an additional source of irregular migration to individuals who illegally cross international boundaries or who overstay authorised periods.

Patterns of Irregular Migration in Developing Countries

Patterns of irregular migration vary among developing countries in each continent.

Africa

In Africa, irregular migration is viewed by many scholars as an integral part of overall migration patterns on that continent. For centuries, pastoralists, invaders, pilgrims, refugees and traders have moved to lands far and near all over the continent (Ohadike, 1975). Adepoju (1983) notes that contemporary migration across land borders in Africa is largely undocumented and that such movements far exceed estimated legal flows. Migration occurs for a variety of political, religious, cultural, geographical, economic and related reasons. The political reasons stem from the colonial history of many African states which were established often with borders somewhat artificially drawn by colonial powers and did not take into consideration the ethnic and cultural links of populations. Geographical reasons include lack of physical barriers and the fact that many countries share borders with a number of other countries, thus rendering border control difficult and facilitating undocumented border crossing.

The most significant form of undocumentated migration in Africa during the last decade has been the spontaneous flows of refugees and displaced persons. This group of migrants has been and continues to be of primary concern to the international community not only because it requires material assistance for survival but also because it is expected to be self-supporting in the country of residence or first asylum. Since the 1970s, the number of such persons has consistently been between 2 and 3 million.

Irregular immigration based solely on economic motives generally follows the same pattern and directions as documented flows and usually as functional supplements to those flows (Adepoju, 1983). Many authors describe irregular migration in Africa as an extension of internal migration, with migrants crossing back and forth over international boundaries without documentation, particularly in areas where there are no distinct geographical barriers or where the same ethnic group inhabits both sides of the border (Brennan, 1984).

The most prominent streams of irregular migration are from poor countries to those offering better economic opportunities. In Southern Africa, the Republic of South Africa has attracted a large number of irregular migrants (Stahl, 1981). In West Africa, until 1969, Ghana attracted many migrants from Burkina Faso, Nigeria and Niger. Between 1975 and 1982, Nigeria received an estimated 1 to 3 million undocumented migrants, mainly from Ghana, Togo and Benin, although intake was drastically reduced after the Nigerian expulsion order of January 1983. Another important flow was from Burkina Faso and Mali to Côte d'Ivoire.

Mass expulsion of irregular migrants in Africa has been justified on the grounds that aliens are responsible for many of the social and economic ills being experienced by the receiving country. Adepoju (1983) shows that about ten major expulsions have occurred since the 1960s, the largest being Ghanaian nationals from Nigeria between January to Febraury 1983. Countries of origin of the expellees have also practised expulsion. For instance, Ghana expelled an estimated 500 000 aliens (mostly from Nigeria, Burkina Faso and Niger) who did not possess valid residence permits.

The most recent reported expulsion is of some 10 000 Niger and Mali nationals from Algeria during April and May 1986. Many had come to southern Algeria, were victims of successive droughts which have stricken the Sahara region, and were accused by the authorities of having been involved in illegal transfrontier trading (Le Monde, 24 May 1986). The principal reason may have been, however, that they had become a burden for the host communities and competitors in the service sector.

Asia

In Asia the main destination points of irregular migrants are the same as those of legal migrants. For example, during the 1970s, oil-producing states of the Middle East attracted both regular and irregular migrant labour from other Asian countries, incuding Arab as well as South Asian states. Irregular migration has declined considerably in recent years, partly because knowledge about authentic placement agents has spread more widely and governmental control of recruitment agencies has become more effective.

In Southeast Asia, Malaysia and Singapore have received many migrants from Indonesia; the Philippines and Thailand are major countries of out-migration. Irregular migrants are generally in agriculture and construction where documentary controls can more easily be evaded (Lin and Chan, 1983). A special situation prevails in Hong Kong. While a large number of Chinese nationals entered the crown colony illegally during the 1970s, stringent measures taken in October 1980, backed by co-operation from China, greatly reduced illegal flows (Lui, 1985). Another irregular flow is of Bengali Muslim settlers to India's Assam State. Though the migrants were accepted initially, they were later considered to be illegal, largely as a result of conflict over political power-sharing (Brennan, 1984). Aside from the Hong Kong and Assam situations, irregular migration in Asia is mostly of a temporary nature, especially migration to Singapore and Malaysia. Singapore intends phasing out the employment of all foreign workers by 1992 (Economist Intelligence Unit, 1984). A characteristic of irregular migration in Asia is the frequent involvement of illegal recruitment agents who sell required entry and identity cards to undocumented migrants at border crossings.

Latin America

In Latin America irregular migration is the predominant form of migration. By the late 1960s, it had reached considerable proportions and governments of many receiving countries, although in principle not opposed to accepting nationals from other Latin American countries, became concerned about the absence of effective controls over the movements.

The principal causes of intraregional migration in Latin America are income differentials and unequal availability of jobs. Since the 1960s, the main receiving countries have been Argentina and Venezuela, which have GNPs substantially higher than Bolivia, Uruguay, Chile and Colombia. Settlement areas chosen by migrants in Argentina are either in metropolitan areas or in provinces bordering the respective countries of origin (Direccion Nacional de Migraciones, 1983; Balan, 1985).

Irregular migrants in metropolitan areas are usually absorbed into industry, the construction sector or in household services. In bordering provinces they generally take employment as rural workers, but many later move to urban areas. A recent decline in the proportion of illegal migrants in Argentina from neighbouring countries has been attributed to the decline in purchasing power of workers' salaries (Villar, 1984). A similar decline in illegal migration to Venezuela has been attributed to economic problems caused by a reduction in oil production (Roy, 1984).

Large-scale intraregional irregular migration flows in Central America during the 1970s and early 1980s were caused by political tensions in several countries. An estimated 350 000 refugees and 1 000 000 displaced persons fled their homes between 1980 and 1984. Salvadorans comprise 68 per cent of refugees in the region and approximately 500 000 of the displaced. In 1984, Guatemalans comprised 18 per cent of the region's refugees and an estimated 100 000 to 500 000 displaced persons; a further 13 per cent of the region's refugees were from Nicaragua (Pessar, 1986). Various international humanitarian organisations, including UNHCR, ICM, ICRC and a great number of voluntary agencies, operate assistance programmes for displaced persons within the region.

Irregular migration is widespread among islands in the Caribbean. In 1981, 25 000 illegal Haitians were expelled from the Bahamas. Although seasonal labour migration of Haitians to the neighbouring Dominican Republic is deemed illegal, approximately 20 000-60 000 migrants enter the country each year to work on the sugar plantations (Fox, 1985). One result is labour insecurity; Haitians have no legal petitioning power to improve their conditions and their illegal status makes it easy for the government to deport them.

Characteristics of Irregular Migration

Irregular migration appears to occur more spontaneously in Africa and Latin America than in Asia, where border controls are more effective. Measures designed to regulate undocumented migration are undertaken more frequently in Latin America. Mass expulsion is more common in Africa.

It appears that the volume of irregular border-crossing migration to Malaysia, Singapore, Hong Kong, Argentina and Venezuela has been declining due to the economic downturn experienced over a number of years and/or to strengthened enforcement measures. However, mass displacement and exodus of people in Africa and Central America has led to an increase in irregular migration.

The involvement of agents/intermediaries in illegal trafficking varies between regions. In Southeast Asia the practice is reported to be widespread but less obvious than in African countries where border controls are neither as strict nor as effective. Controls on irregular border crossing between Latin American countries are easy to evade; nor is there much evidence to suggest that illegal trafficking is widespread.

Effects in Countries of Origin

Irregular migrants are in general more exposed to the risk of exploitation, lay-off and expulsion because of their characteristic unstable occupational situation and absence of legal status (Farooq-i-Azam, 1986). This situation exposes countries of origin to the risk of being suddenly faced with mass return movements of nationals and consequent difficulties of coping with their reinsertion. The massive return of over 1 million Ghanians from Nigeria in 1983 is an example of a situation in which a country of origin, itself stricken by great economic difficulties, was faced with the additional burden of resettling large numbers of returning nationals.

Until 1976/77, Colombia was one of the main supply countries of undocumented migrants in Latin America. The Colombian Government then established in border areas with Venezuela several reception centres for Colombian deportees. The measure was an immediate response to the burdensome problem of deportation of nationals. Between 1977 and September 1982, a total of 31 887 Colombians deported from Venezuela passed through reception centres established in three Colombian towns (Martinez, 1983).

Another effect of irregular migration for countries of origin is that they may become involved in problems relating to the treatment of their nationals abroad. Denial of basic human rights to irregular migrants may strain relations with countries of immigration. There may also be internal political debate about exploitation and illegal trafficking of nationals in and to foreign countries.

It has sometimes been argued that the very existence of the possibility of migration, even if on an illegal basis, diminishes the need for measures aimed at combatting poverty and unemployment in the country of origin (Koerner, 1986). Other scholars have asked whether the existence of such immigration opportunities have, in the final analysis, not worsened long-term structural problems in the countries of origin. For example, the development of labour migration between Colombia and Venezuela since the early 1980s has led to increased return migration at a time when Colombia was going through a severe economic crisis.

Effects in Developing Countries Hosting Irregular Migrants

Lin Lim Lean and Chan Tuck Hoong (1983) have noted the creation of a dependency upon undocumented migrants in Malaysia, especially in the implementation of land settlement schemes. Indeed, official forecasts of labour requirements and sources for the State of Sabah (East Malaysia) explicitly refer to dependence on such migrant labour and their descendants. The authors argue that the use of undocumented labour has had a retarding effect on the improvement of real incomes in these sectors.

In referring to the situation in Nigeria prior to the mass expulsion order of January 1983, Adepoju (1983) points out that where illegal immigration occurs on a large scale, and the participation of such immigrants in economic activity is thought to compete with that of natives, illegal migrants may become targets of hostility from the native population and sources of blame for whatever economic, social and political problem may arise in the country. The presence of a large number of aliens who are desperate for any means of livelihood provides a ready reserve of recruits for public disorder and other subversive activities.

The accusation that illegal aliens aggravate the host country's economic problems is often emphasized in Africa to justify expulsion orders. On the other hand, clandestine migrants tend to be employed in low paid occupations shunned by nationals. For example, it was reported that after the mass expulsion from Nigeria in 1983, many posts held by undocumented aliens remained vacant and were finally filled by other undocumented aliens (Adepoju, 1984). The acute labour situation in Ghana's cocoa farms following the enforcement of the alien's compliance order of 1969 is another case in point (Akomako-Sarfoh, 1974).

The very presence of undocumented migrants in developing countries may create or prolong situations of labour insecurity because irregular migrants have no legal petitioning power to rectify their conditions of employment. Their presence may also delay social progress and development, reinforce labour market dualism, exacerbate the underground economy and retard modernisation.

Irregular Migration in the Future Economic and Social Context

Income differentials between developing and developed countries (and between developing countries), displacement and mass exodus in developing countries, population growth and restrictions on legal immigration have contributed to the considerable increase in irregular migration during the last two decades. Forecasts for both developed and developing countries with continuously high unemployment rates and projected population growth suggest that irregular migration will continue in the near future. Countries with less structured labour markets and expanding parallel economies may be particularly affected by the phenomenon.

The extent to which these migration pressures materialise will depend on many factors, including the degree to which governments are prepared to effectively combat irregular migration flows and the employment of irregular migrants. Some receiving countries are prepared to accept irregular migrants in limited and controllable numbers. Lower wages, reduced social costs of irregular migrants and their higher mobility are attractive factors which in the past have outweighed the inconveniences. Much will depend also on the preparedness of migrant receiving countries to offer opportunities for legal immigration and on the effectiveness of bilateral and multilateral agreements. Although some factors tend to favour an expansion of irregular migration in developing countries in the future, low income differentials may reduce incentives for migration. In summary, wage differentials and unequal degrees of economic activity between developing countries will encourage irregular migration, while declining wage differentials and a uniform economic downturn are likely to produce the opposite effect.

CONCLUSIONS

Irregular migration was once tolerated as a normal occurrence, beneficial to both sending and receiving countries. It was regarded as a factor contributing to economic growth in both the sending and receiving countries.

Since the 1970s, however, increased volume of irregular migration has caused economic, social and political impacts which concern many recipient countries. Opportunities for regular admission and employment have declined in the face of high unemployment and slow economic growth. At the same time, in many developing countries of origin the potential for migration has continued to rise due to high population growth, low economic growth, political crises and natural and manmade disasters. Easy access to transport, increased tourist traffic, and the availability of cheap international communication facilitate mobility of people across national boundaries and, by extension, the occurrence of irregular migration.

In response to increased migration pressures, many developing countries have called for the adoption of coherent policies and measures at the national and multilateral (regional and global) levels to reduce the volume of irregular migration. Some developing receiving countries continue to benefit to a certain extent from irregular migration in view of the abundance of cheap labour. However, the lower wages and social benefits paid to irregular migrants are seen as disadvantages which contribute to delays in social progress. Developing countries of origin, although in principle interested in seeing some of their nationals obtain employment abroad, may suffer more than they benefit from irregular migration. The need to provide in periods of low economic growth for the reinsertion of more nationals returning than new emigrants departing reduces the benefits which these countries can obtain from irregular migration.

Irregular migration of both workers and dependent family members is becoming an issue of growing controversy in developing countries. The divergent interests of countries of origin and receiving countries affect bilateral relations. Solutions advocated and sought at national and international levels do not materialise easily. In many instances it is not possible to restrict effectively irregular migration by border controls. Marked differences in economic development and output between the economies of developing countries continue to determine push and pull factors for irregular migration. In the absence of strong economic growth in developing countries of origin, it is unlikely that irregular migration will decline in the future.

NOTES AND REFERENCES

1. The views expressed in this paper are those of the author and do not
    necessarily constitute an endorsement by the Intergovernmental Com-
    mittee for Migration (ICM).

BIBLIOGRAPHY

ADEPOJU, Aderanti
    "Undocumented Migration in Africa: Trends and Policies", Inter-
    national Migration, Vol. XXI, No. 2, 1983.

    "Illegals and Expulsion in Africa", International Migration Review,
    Vol. 18, Fall 1984.

AGA KHAN, Sadruddin
    Study on Human Rights and Massive Exodus, UN Doc. E/CN.4/1503,
    31st December 1981 and General Assembly Resolution 36/148 of
    16th December 1981.

AKOMAKO-SARFOH, J.
    "The Effects of the Expulsion of Migrant Workers on Ghana's Economy,
    with Particular Reference to the Cocoa Industry", in S. Amin, ed.,
    Modern Migrations in West Africa, London, Oxford University Press, 1974.

BALAN, Jorge
    "Las migraciones internacionales en el Cono Sur", Intergovernmental
    Committee for Migration, Hemispheric Migration Project, Geneva, 1985.

BOEHNING, W.R.
    For terminology and different forms of irregular migration see
    UN General Assembly Resolution 3449 (XXX), 1975.

    "Regularising the Irregular", International Migration, Vol. XXI, No. 2,
    1983.

    "A Typology of Contemporary Migration", Studies in International
    Labour, London, Macmillan, 1984.

BRENNAN, Ellen M.
    "Irregular Migration: Policy Responses in Africa and Asia", Inter-
    national Migration Review, Vol. 18, Fall 1984.

DIRECCION NACIONAL DE MIGRACIONES
"Specific Causes and Motivations of Illegal Migration", paper submitted to Sixth ICM Seminar on Adaptation and Integration of Immigrants, Information Doc. No. 20, MC/SAI/VI/INF/20, April 1983.

THE ECONOMIST INTELLIGENCE UNIT
Quarterly Economic Review of Singapore, Annual Supplement 1984, 1984.

FAROOQ-I-AZAM
"Working Conditions of Pakistani Migrant Workers in the Middle East", ILO Working Paper, International Migration for Employment, Geneva, ILO, doc. MIG WP.25, January 1986.

FOX, Robert
"From a Continent of Immigrants to a Continent of Emigrants", IDB News, Washington, D.C., May 1985.

INTERNATIONAL CONFERENCE ON POPULATION
Recommendations for the Further Implementation of the World Plan of Action, Mexico City, August 1984.

KOERNER, Heiko
"The Experience of European Sending Countries", paper submitted to the OECD Conference on The Future of Migration, Paris, 13th-15th May 1986.

LE MONDE
24th May 1986.

LIN, Lim Lean and P. CHAN Tuck Hoong
"Migrant Workers in ASEAN: A Review of Issues and Implications for Government Policies", International Migration, Vol. XXI, No. 2, 1983.

LUI, Ting Terry
"Undocumented Migration in Hong Kong", International Migration, Vol. XXI, No. 2, 1983.

"World Population Trends", 1983 Monitoring Report, Vol. 1, ed., United Nations Department of International Economic and Social Affairs, Population Studies, No. 93, New York, United Nations, 1985.

MARTINEZ, Julio Noé Cely
"Comments on the Causes of Undocumented Migration in Latin America", International Migration, Vol. XXI, No. 2, pp. 151-58 (155), 1983.

OHADIKE, P.O.
"African Immigration and Immigrants in Zambia: A Study of Patterns and Characteristics", in P. Cantrelle et al., eds., Population in African Development, Liège, IUSSP, 1975.

PESSAR, Patricia R.
"Report on the Inter-American Conference on Migration Trends and Policies", Hemispheric Migration Project, Occasional Paper Series, Centre for Immigration Policy and Refugee Assistance, Washington, D.C., Georgetown University, May 1986.

ROY, Ralph Van
"Undocumented Migration for Venezuela", International Migration Review, Vol. 18, Fall 1984.

STAHL, C.W.
"Migrant Labour Supplies, Past, Present and Future; With Special Reference to the Gold-mining Industry" in W.R. Boehning, Black Migration to South Africa, Geneva, ILO, 1981.

UNITED NATIONS
United Nations World Population Conference. Action Taken at Bucharest, World Population Plan of Action, New York, UN Centre for Economic and Social Information, November 1974.

Open-ended Working Group of the General Assembly on the Drafting of an International Convention on the Protection of the Rights of All Migrant Workers and their Families, Text of Preamble and articles agreed upon during the first reading, Doc. A/C. 3/39 WG.1/WP.1, 26th October 1984.

VILLAR, Juan Manuel
"Argentine Experience in the Field of Illegal Immigration", International Migration Review, Vol. XVIII, No. 3, Fall 1984.

WORLD BANK
World Development Report 1986 (and earlier years), New York, London, Oxford University Press, 1986 (and previous years).

World Development Indicators, New York, London, Oxford University Press, 1986 (and previous years).

C. TRANSIENT PROFESSIONALS

Chapter 9

LONG-TERM IMMIGRATION AND EMIGRATION: ITS CONTRIBUTION TO THE
DEVELOPING WORLD

With particular reference to movement between
Australia and Asia and the Pacific

by

Charles A. Price

For many years studies on international migration have focussed on the
movement of permanent settlers from Old World countries in Europe and Asia to
New World countries in the Americas and Australasia. Then came a switch of
interest to temporary migration, such as the officially organised guest-worker
schemes to western Europe and contract labour migration to oil-rich Arab
countries. Both types of migration have given rise to considerable short-term
flows, e.g., home visits to the old country and parental visits to sons and
daughters settled abroad. This type of migration has received much less
scholarly attention than other rapidly growing short-term movements such as
increased tourist movement arising from cheaper air transport and increasing
affluence in the industrialised world, and the increasing movement for conferences, business visits or professional exchanges which arise from the
spread of multi-nationals and the international exchange of information.

Short-term movements can have considerable impacts on developing
countries, particularly the tourist trade with its insatiable demand for
accommodation, food and leisure facilities. There is, however, another less-
conspicuous kind of temporary migration that affects the Third World, namely,
the long-term migration of professionally and technically qualified persons
who work in developing countries for periods ranging from a few months to
fifteen years. This movement is often counter-balanced by a reverse flow of
students and younger professionals or technicians from Third World countries
who spend several years in industrialised countries before returning home.

While this type of long-term migration is common between Western
Europe/North America and the developing countries related to them, there is
also considerable long-term movement between the developed countries themselves. Indeed, it is often difficult to distinguish the flows. A young
computer engineer from Scotland may go to the United States for further work
with IBM and, after two years, take a three-year job in Malaysia where he

143

advises on the establishment of computer systems in government departments; or an Indian statistician, having obtained a degree in Sydney, Australia, spends four years in a statistical institute in Canada before returning home to Bombay. Indeed, some persons move between developing and developed countries all their working lives and return to their native land only on retirement. Such persons were not formally recognised in migration literature until Anthony Richmond described them as "transilients", the term adopted in this chapter. Although this chapter concentrates on the impact of transilients, it is important to note the total long-term movement of such persons because it is from the total pool of transilients that moves from developed to developing countries occur.

One of the main reasons why so little research has been conducted on long-term migration is paucity of information and statistics. Few countries keep detailed information on such movements aside from officially-sponsored movements or those involving permanent settlement. Australia is one country which does keep reasonable statistics on long-term migration. It is therefore useful to examine these with a view to discovering important and interesting trends and patterns. Though the focus of this chapter is on long-term migration to and from developing countries, reference will also be made to the general pool of long-term migrants, and to comparable or contrasting movements between developed countries.

Australia, like many other countries, has seen a considerable increase in international migration since World War II. Permanent settler migration has averaged 80 000 a year (about 0.75 per cent of total population) and has been largely responsible for increasing the 1947 population of 7.6 million to 15.8 million in 1986. The short-term tourist, business and home visit migration -- here defined as less than six months in duration -- has increased dramatically; between 1939 to 1985 the number of residents travelling abroad increased from 56 000 to 1 420 000 and short-term visitors arriving increased from 66 000 to 1 063 000. Long-term movement -- here defined as any period from six months to fifteen years in duration (see Note) -- also grew substantially; the number of Australian residents moving abroad increased nearly ten-fold, from 15 000 to 147 000 a year, while visitors arriving increased nearly nine-fold from 13 000 to 114 000 a year.

The long-term movement of Australian residents falls into three distinct categories. First, foreign-born settlers or their Australian-born children who visit countries of origin, mostly in Western and Southern Europe, where they stay for up to two or three years during which they usually take temporary employment. Second, younger Australians who make long visits to advanced countries for higher education or advanced work experience, traditionally to North America and Western Europe, particularly the British Isles. Third, Australian residents who take their professional or technical skills or their capital and business experience to Third World countries. The fourth movement, to New Zealand, is a mixture: in many ways New Zealand counts as a developed country but it is considerably less industrialised than Australia and the temporary movement of Australians to that country has many of the characteristics of movements to developing countries.

Table 9.1 shows the volume and the changes of these movements between 1975 and 1985. The first two movements -- to Europe, North America and Japan -- increased in terms of numbers but decreased as a proportion of total movement, as did long-term migration to New Zealand. Conversely, long-term migration to developing countries increased both relatively and absolutely, from 30 700 to 53 000 a year and from 30.2 to 36.2 per cent of the total. In terms of Australia's relatively small population, and traditional links with Europe and North America, this long-term migration to the Third World is now substantial and significant.

Most of this migration is to developing countries near at hand, especially countries with which Australia has traditional links. Papua New Guinea, a former colonial dependency, still draws numerous long-term migrants but other island countries in the southwest Pacific, notably Fiji, also attract appreciable numbers. Countries of southeastern Asia, particularly Malaysia, also accept substantial numbers as do, for special reasons given later, Israel, Turkey and -- to a lesser extent -- Lebanon. Latin America and Africa (with the exception of South Africa, with its historic sea-faring and trading links with Australia dating back to the late 18th Century) draw few long-term Australian migrants, partly because of distance and partly because of the absence of major historical connections.

Data on duration of temporary movements to developing countries for the years 1975-77 show: six to twelve months 8.5 per cent; one to two years 39.5 per cent; two to three years 41.3 per cent; three to four years 7.9 per cent and four or more years 2.8 per cent. There are only minor differences between males and females and married and single persons. However there are somewhat greater differences between countries of destination. Long-term emigrants to Fiji include more persons going for three to four years (13.8 per cent), those to Malaysia had more for two to three years (56.3 per cent), and those to the Philippines more for one to two years (50.7 per cent). But the general picture is clear: the great majority of moves were for one to three years, thus giving the Australians concerned sufficient time to make a contribution to the Third World society before returning to Australia or moving elsewhere.

Sex and age distribution is also important as shown by Table 9.2 relating to males for the years 1976-78. There are striking differences between the migrations to developed and developing countries; whereas the flow to developing countries contained more adults aged 30-44, and children aged 0-14, the flow to developed countries contained more young adults aged 20-29, both male and female. With this went a clear distinction in marital status: amongst the 20-29 age group were more single men and women (82 per cent of males and 67 per cent of females) going to developed countries than to developing countries (57 per cent of males and 31 per cent of females); the same distinction held for those aged 30-59. Much of the long-term migration to developed countries clearly involves single men and women leaving for further education and work experience whereas migration to developing countries involves more married men accompanied by their wives and children.

Israel, India and South Africa are notable exceptions to this picture. In terms of age, for both males and females, long-term migration here resembled the flow to developed countries. Israel clearly draws young Australians of Jewish origin who want to make a contribution to the Zionist homeland before returning to Australia. South Africa has some of the characteristics of a developed country and has attracted some young Australians seeking further work experience, as has New Zealand. But India is more puzzling.

Table 9.1

AUSTRALIAN RESIDENTS DEPARTING: COUNTRY OF NEXT STAY
For intended absence of at least six months, not permanently

Country of next stay	1975-79 (a)	1985 (b)	Country of next stay	1975-79 (a)	1985 (b)
Developed countries:			**West Asia:**		
United Kingdom, Eire	34 349	40 284	Cyprus	227	338
Other Europe	20 391	26 925	Israel	673	999
Canada, United States	9 417	17 886	Lebanon	264	545
Japan	665	2 307	Turkey	518	1 734
			Other West Asia (f)	711	1 690
Total	64 822	87 402			
			Total	2 393	5 306
Percentage	63.8	59.5			
			Percentage	2.4	3.6
Pacific:			**South Asia:**		
Papua New Guinea (c)	10 194	14 975	India	696	1 044
Fiji	1 016	1 705	Sri Lanka, etc. (g)	434	1 043
Other Commonwealth	1 339	3 293			
Other Pacific	190	309	Total	1 130	2 087
Total	12 739	20 282	Percentage	1.1	1.4
Percentage	12.5	13.8	**Southeast Asia:**		
			Malaysia	3 523	6 628
			Indonesia	1 941	2 646
Americas, Central & South:			Philippines	652	1 148
Argentina	218	294	Thailand	434	1 144
Brazil	169	221	Other Southeast (h)	47	118
Chile	175	235			
Colombia	54	74	Total	6 597	11 684
Peru	64	88			
Uruguay	118	147	Percentage	6.5	7.9
Other	925	1 219			
			East Asia:		
Total	1 723	2 278	China	84	191
			Taiwan	119	294
Percentage	1.7	1.6	Hong Kong	1 671	3 454
			Singapore	1 772	3 086
Africa:			Korea, etc. (i)	351	823
Mauritius, etc. (d)	152	250	Total	3 997	7 848
Comm. East. Sth. (e)	353	734			
South Africa	946	1 293	Percentage	3.9	5.3
Comm. West (e)	121	191			
Egypt	184	397	New Zealand	6 138	6 571
Other Arab	157	250			
Other	239	397			
			Percentage	6.0	4.5
Total	2 152	3 512	Grand Total	101 691	146 970
Percentage	2.1	2.4	Percentage	100.0	100.0

a)   Annual average 1975-79 calendar.
b)   Adding estimates for 6-12 months to firm figures for 12 months and over.
c)   Includes Cocos-Keeling and Christmas Islands.
d)   Includes St. Helena and Seychelles.
e)   "Comm." and "Commonwealth" = "British Commonwealth".
f)   Jordan, Syria, Iraq, Iran and countries of Arabian Peninsula.
g)   Includes a few from Bangladesh, Pakistan, Afghanistan, Sikkim, etc.

Table 9.2

AUSTRALIAN RESIDENTS DEPARTING: COUNTRY OF NEXT STAY (a); BY AGE AND BY SEX: 1976-78
For intended absence of six months or more, not permanently; percentages

Country of next stay	Males aged							Females aged						
	0-14	15-19	20-29	30-44	45-59	60+	Total	0-14	15-19	20-29	30-44	45-59	60+	Total
United Kingdom, Eire	13.8	4.4	47.1	20.4	7.8	6.5	48 372	12.4	6.7	50.7	14.4	7.2	8.6	52 096
Other Europe	18.1	4.4	24.7	28.6	13.5	10.7	32 447	21.9	6.4	28.2	22.0	12.4	9.1	30 388
North America	19.5	5.8	33.2	30.5	8.2	2.8	15 438	20.7	9.2	34.3	23.5	7.1	5.2	13 931
Japan	14.5	7.7	28.2	34.3	13.4	1.9	929	17.2	28.9	23.0	20.2	9.6	1.1	1 010
Total	16.1	4.7	37.2	24.9	9.8	7.3	97 186	16.6	7.2	41.1	18.1	8.8	8.2	97 425
Israel	13.2	24.8	36.0	14.1	4.9	7.0	972	12.6	22.4	37.5	10.1	8.4	9.0	1 048
Turkey	27.7	7.7	16.1	41.4	4.9	2.2	1 052	38.4	6.2	18.5	31.3	2.9	2.7	912
Lebanon, Egypt	25.5	1.6	29.5	30.5	8.1	4.8	580	35.7	3.4	21.7	18.7	11.6	8.9	561
Other West Asia	13.9	3.2	23.2	38.3	18.8	2.6	1 247	32.6	4.1	24.2	31.5	5.5	2.1	1 014
West Asia	19.2	9.6	25.4	31.9	9.9	4.0	3 851	28.7	10.0	26.3	23.0	6.6	5.4	3 535
India	14.7	3.5	46.0	22.9	9.1	3.8	1 072	15.1	5.9	35.0	26.6	10.4	7.0	916
Malaysia	29.2	1.6	30.8	28.7	8.1	1.6	5 406	32.5	3.3	30.2	26.0	5.9	2.1	4 655
Indonesia	20.0	1.7	31.8	33.4	11.7	5.8	3 459	27.8	6.4	29.6	27.3	8.1	0.8	2 190
Philippines	25.2	2.7	14.8	33.0	18.5	5.8	958	25.8	9.6	21.8	21.3	14.3	7.2	958
Singapore	23.6	2.6	22.4	36.7	12.2	2.5	2 669	31.1	2.2	24.9	26.4	11.7	3.7	2 090
Hong Kong	26.2	1.8	16.5	38.1	11.6	5.8	2 597	28.6	1.7	21.1	30.0	12.9	5.7	2 551
South & East Asia (b)	23.9	2.0	28.1	32.2	10.9	2.9	18 529	27.8	4.0	28.9	26.7	9.1	3.5	15 226
South Africa	16.9	3.9	43.8	23.0	8.1	4.3	1 112	14.8	9.4	42.0	18.9	7.8	7.1	1 063
Other Africa	19.9	1.3	37.2	24.0	17.0	0.6	789	33.9	2.1	24.3	32.0	7.0	0.7	729
Africa	18.1	2.8	41.1	23.4	11.8	2.8	1 901	22.6	6.4	34.8	24.2	7.5	4.5	1 792
America (Cen., South)	18.9	3.5	31.6	32.0	10.1	3.9	1 808	23.9	7.2	28.8	26.9	7.9	5.3	1 501
Papua New Guinea (c)	23.8	1.0	27.5	35.8	10.0	1.9	16 877	32.3	1.4	29.1	28.7	7.1	1.4	12 287
Fiji	29.3	2.2	20.7	36.2	9.8	1.8	1 426	29.8	4.6	26.1	27.3	9.7	2.5	1 440
Comm. Pacific	36.9	1.4	20.6	30.5	9.3	1.3	1 759	31.2	0.7	27.8	28.0	8.3	4.0	1 509
Pacific (b)	25.2	1.2	26.4	35.3	10.0	1.9	20 357	31.7	1.7	28.7	28.4	7.6	1.9	15 497
New Zealand	11.8	9.7	49.8	20.0	6.1	2.6	8 552	12.7	19.3	47.6	10.7	5.8	3.9	7 389
Total (b)	18.6	4.2	35.0	27.3	9.8	5.1	157 425	19.7	6.9	38.1	20.1	8.5	6.7	146 272
Total Developed (d)	16.1	4.7	37.2	24.9	9.8	7.3	97 186	--	7.2	41.1	18.1	8.8	8.2	97 425
Total Developing (d)	24.4	2.4	28.4	33.0	10.4	1.4	51 687	28.2	4.0	29.3	26.5	8.3	3.7	41 458

a) Country of next stay = country in which resident will spend most time while abroad.
b) Smaller countries are included in total but not shown separately.
c) Includes a few from Cocos-Keeling and Christmas Islands.
d) Excludes New Zealand.

147

Table 9.3 shows that, in general, long-term emigrants to developing countries are more likely to be in the professional and business categories than those going to developed countries who are more likely to be skilled, semi-skilled and students. In terms of specific occupations, the group going to developing countries contains relatively more engineers, scientists, technicians, accountants and business executives, the economic areas where developing countries make their strongest appeal. These countries also attract significant numbers of doctors, dentists, teachers, office workers, ship and air officers, metal and electrical tradesmen.

Australians have also been attracted to industrial and building developments in oil-rich Arab countries. The appreciable flow of unskilled labourers to this region, however, is not to Arab lands but to Turkey (which takes 90 per cent of labourers heading for western Asia); these being unskilled Australian settlers originally from Turkey who make lengthy visits to their original homes. Some contemplate permanent resettlement, although on leaving Australia they are designated Australian residents making temporary visits abroad, so strengthening their right to re-enter Australia should they decide to return.

Of particular interest is the flow of persons with the occupational category police, fire brigade and armed services to mainly Asian countries. Singapore and Hong Kong attracted a number, but the majority of the 1 500 who went to Malaysia between 1976-78 were Australian air-personnel stationed at the Butterworth Air Base. Papua New Guinea also attracted appreciable numbers, a carry-over from the days when many police, fire and armed service officers served in the forces of Australia's colonial dependency. Though the political and strategic value of such arrangements is difficult to measure, there have been undoubted economic consequences in terms of capital and currency imports and of local spending by service personnel and their families. Another interesting category is "clergy"; including missionaries, teachers and nurses in religious orders. Though most went to nearby countries in Asia and the southwest Pacific, a few served with missionary organisations in Latin America and eastern Africa. With each of these occupational categories it must be remembered that Table 9.3 relates only to the years 1976-78; since then the long-term movement to developing countries has nearly doubled.

The occupations of Australian women moving long-term to developing countries are set out in Table 9.4. Apart from the 47 per cent employed in home duties, the main concentrations are in nursing, teaching and secretarial work. There are, however, some professional women (architects, engineers, scientists and doctors), an appreciable number of accountants and business executives and a few skilled tradeswomen. Again, the statistics refer to the years 1976-78, since when numbers have nearly doubled.

The general picture, then, is clear. Though long-term migration from Australia to the Third World is only a fraction of the flow to those countries from the United States, it is nevertheless significant, especially as it comprises mainly professionally and technically qualified persons, and businessmen who take their skills and experience for between one and three years mainly to developing countries in southeastern Asia and the southwestern Pacific.

Table 9.3

AUSTRALIAN RESIDENTS (MALE): OCCUPATION BY COUNTRY OF STAY
Departing 1976-78

Occupation: Males aged 15 and over	West Asia	Other Asia	Africa	Cen.Sth. America	Pacific	Total developing	%	Total developed	%
Architects, surveyors	47	258	33	18	294	650	1.8	1 491	1.6
Engineers	220	1 309	171	81	829	2 610	7.4	3 327	3.6
Scientists	55	299	104	47	308	813	2.3	1 776	1.9
Doctors, dentists	18	526	46	6	211	807	2.3	2 110	2.3
Nurses, paramedics	3	65	15	1	47	131	0.4	858	0.9
Technicians	55	315	39	37	404	850	2.4	1 235	1.3
Tertiary teachers	28	170	21	3	198	420	1.2	2 761	3.0
School teachers	59	296	51	36	686	1 128	3.2	4 358	4.7
Clergy	38	198	38	34	338	646	1.8	573	0.6
Lawyers	25	68	6	1	77	177	0.5	424	0.5
Other professionals	72	229	33	38	241	613	1.7	1 782	1.9
Total	620	3 733	557	302	3 633	8 845		20 695	
Percentage	19.9	26.6	36.0	20.6	23.9	25.0	25.0	22.3	22.3
Economists, accountants	37	574	56	14	793	1 474	4.2	1 760	1.9
Business executives	273	1 977	144	70	2 725	5 189	14.7	6 278	6.8
Office workers	108	449	67	70	1 482	2 176	6.1	5 264	5.7
Salesmen	57	221	54	53	281	666	1.9	3 475	3.7
Ship and air officers	35	205	19	4	474	737	2.1	617	0.7
Transport supervisors	69	134	11	50	215	479	1.3	2 387	2.6
Primary industry	23	146	42	35	235	481	1.4	1 693	1.8
Total	602	3 706	393	296	6 205	11 202		21 474	
Percentage	19.5	26.4	25.4	20.2	40.4	31.7	31.7	23.2	23.2
Metal tradesmen	127	812	122	188	1 330	2 579	7.3	6 792	7.3
Electrical, telecomm.	40	334	61	28	529	992	2.8	2 656	2.9
Building, woodwork	64	272	45	49	265	695	2.0	4 919	5.3
Process workers	108	162	36	75	185	566	1.6	2 587	2.8
Wells, cranes, earthmoving	39	208	22	12	96	377	1.0	1 111	1.2
Labourers	606	247	33	89	92	1 067	3.0	7 703	8.3
Total	984	2 035	319	441	2 497	6 276		25 768	
Percentage	31.6	14.5	20.6	30.0	16.4	17.7	17.7	27.8	27.8
Catering, personal	26	158	21	15	115	335	0.9	2 033	2.2
Police, fire, armed	68	1 985	9	1	872	2 935	8.3	1 472	1.6
Artists, entertainers	18	221	16	38	120	413	1.2	1 917	2.1
Recreation, sport	24	39	8	4	25	100	0.3	791	0.8
Other	20	77	2	52	64	215	0.6	879	0.9
Total	156	2 480	56	110	1 196	3 998		7 092	
Percentage	5.0	17.7	3.6	7.5	7.9	11.3	11.3	7.6	7.6
Government officials	76	523	51	61	872	1 583	4.5	1 542	1.7
Inadequately described	176	636	92	110	550	1 564	4.4	3 258	3.5
Students, 15 plus	412	659	52	92	182	1 397	3.9	6 695	7.2
Retired, independent	85	257	27	55	93	517	1.5	6 231	6.7
Total	749	2 075	222	318	1 697	5 061		17 726	
Percentage	24.1	14.8	14.4	21.7	11.4	14.3	14.3	19.1	19.1
Grand Total	3 111	14 029	1 547	1 467	15 228	35 382		92 755	
Percentage	100.0	100.0	100.0	100.0	100.0	100.0	100.0	100.0	100.0

Table 9.4

AUSTRALIAN RESIDENTS (FEMALE): OCCUPATION BY COUNTRY OF STAY
Departing 1976-78

Occupation: Females aged 15 and over	West Asia	Other Asia	Africa	Cen.Sth. America	Pacific	Total developing	%	Total developed	%
Architects, surveyors	5	23	3	--	54	85	0.3	314	0.3
Engineers	24	32	3	3	27	89	0.3	89	0.1
Scientists	19	54	7	8	56	144	0.5	439	0.5
Doctors, dentists	23	113	13	1	23	173	0.7	559	0.6
Nurses, paramedics	49	643	150	55	473	1 370	5.1	7 611	8.4
Technicians	8	58	12	1	26	105	0.4	894	1.0
Tertiary teachers	2	23	1	3	58	87	0.3	511	0.6
School teachers	131	720	114	98	769	1 832	6.9	7 334	8.1
Clergy, religious	2	101	24	15	308	450	1.7	102	0.1
Other professionals	22	246	37	2	145	452	1.7	2 175	2.4
Total	285	2 013	364	186	1 939	4 787		20 028	
Percentage	11.3	18.3	26.2	15.5	18.2	17.9	17.9	22.1	22.1
Economists, accountants	13	88	5	1	105	212	0.8	320	0.3
Business executives	47	244	16	5	285	597	2.2	1 463	1.6
Office workers	231	913	252	117	1 549	3 062	11.4	18 016	19.9
Saleswomen	29	113	21	9	100	272	1.0	2 446	2.7
Transport supervisors, etc.	13	19	5	--	41	78	0.3	216	0.2
Primary industry	2	28	--	3	5	38	0.2	329	0.4
Total	335	1 405	296	135	2 085	4 256		22 790	
Percentage	13.3	12.8	21.3	11.2	19.5	15.9	15.9	25.1	25.1
Metal tradeswomen	--	25	1	12	69	107	0.4	220	0.2
Electrical, telecomm.	12	33	3	2	23	73	0.3	648	0.7
Process, building workers	33	61	13	77	34	218	0.8	1 594	1.8
Labourers	10	12	3	3	2	30	0.1	542	0.6
Total	55	131	20	94	128	428		3 004	
Percentage	2.2	1.2	1.4	7.8	1.2	1.6	1.6	3.3	3.3
Catering, personal	40	255	54	20	243	612	2.3	3 321	3.7
Police, fire, armed	2	130	2	--	27	161	0.6	83	0.1
Artists, entertainers	14	120	15	4	36	189	0.7	1 317	1.4
Recreation, sport	12	8	1	1	2	24	0.1	318	0.3
Other occupations	4	29	5	32	47	117	0.4	956	1.1
Total	72	542	77	57	355	1 103		5 995	
Percentage	2.8	4.9	5.6	4.8	3.3	4.1	4.1	6.6	6.6
Government officials	20	122	12	19	167	340	1.3	676	0.8
Inadequately described	162	523	35	114	487	1 321	4.9	3 083	3.4
Students, 15 plus	420	634	116	121	231	1 522	5.7	6 342	7.0
Home duties	1 110	5 463	403	437	5 251	12 664	47.3	24 650	27.2
Retired, independent	63	152	65	38	27	345	1.3	4 107	4.5
Total	1 775	6 894	631	729	6 163	16 192		38 858	
Percentage	70.4	62.8	45.5	60.7	57.8	60.5	60.5	42.9	42.9
Grand Total	2 522	10 985	1 388	1 201	10 670	26 766		90 675	
Percentage	100.0	100.0	100.0	100.0	100.0	100.0	100.0	100.0	100.0

A very different picture appears when we turn to the other side of long-term migration from Third World countries to Australia (see Table 9.5). First, the number of visitor migrants, though still appreciably less than that of Australian residents going the other way, has increased more rapidly in recent years: from 9 660 a year in 1976-78, to 35 000 in 1985 whereas the reverse flow of residents increased from 30 700 to 53 000.

Second, though the regional distribution of visitors is broadly similar to that of residents -- relatively few persons arrive from Africa and Latin America compared with numbers coming from southeastern Asia and the south-western Pacific -- the countries most involved in long-term visitor migration are not exactly the same as those most involved in long-term resident migration. For example, Tables 9.1 and 9.5 show that in 1985 there were only 1 097 and 788 long-term visitors from Papua New Guinea and "other Commonwealth Pacific" countries respectively, compared with 14 975 and 3 293 Australian residents going the other way; and 1 726 visitors from Africa compared with 3 512 Australians going to Africa. In contrast, there were 13 851 visitors from Malaysia, and 3 086 from Indonesia, compared with 6 628 and 2 646 Australians going the other way.

Third, the occupational pattern is also very different, primarily because of the considerable inflow of student visitors from countries in southeastern Asia to the southwestern Pacific (see Table 9.7 for males and Table 9.8 for females). This type of inflow is reflected in age and marital status patterns; whereas the age-group 15-19 was relatively small for Australian emigrants to developing countries (2.4 per cent of males and 4 per cent of females, see Table 9.2) it was much more important for long-term visitors from developing countries (24.6 per cent of males and 25.1 per cent of females, see Table 9.6). So also with those aged 20-29, around 45 per cent of both male and female visitors compared with less than 30 per cent of Australians going the other way. As a consequence the proportion of those aged 30-44, and their children aged 0-14, was correspondingly lower. Here again there was some country variation, the contrast being very noticeable between certain Pacific islands (apart from Fiji) and countries such as Malaysia, Indonesia, Thailand and Hong Kong.

These data are indicative of the role Australia has been playing in providing secondary and tertiary education for neighbouring countries. Although over 20 000 students entered Australia from Third World countries during the last decade, the Australian Government recently decided that because tertiary education in Australia is provided free, at taxpayer's expense, the country was, in effect, subsidising many students from families well able to afford full fees, e.g., professional and merchant families in Hong Kong, Singapore, Penang and other prosperous towns in southeastern Asia. The government therefore introduced a procedure whereby private students from overseas (as distinct from students coming under government programmes such as the Colombo Plan) had to pay tuition fees ranging from $2 000 to $5 000 a year.

Many students enrol for post-graduate or trade certificate courses lasting one academic year only; or come for one academic year, return home for the summer holidays, and come back to Australia for the next academic year, so entering Australia as visitors intending to stay for nine or ten months only. This partly explains why one-third of visitors aged 15-19, and nearly half the visitors aged 20-29 from developing countries gave intended lengths of stay as between six and twelve months (see End Note).

Table 9.5

LONG-TERM VISITORS ARRIVING BY COUNTRY OF LAST STAY
For intended visits of at least six months but not permanently

Country of last stay	1976-78 (a)	1985 (b)	Country of last stay	1976-78 (a)	1985 (b)
Developed countries:			West Asia:		
United Kingdom, Eire	4 206	9 908	Cyprus	17	80
Other Europe	2 789	9 817	Israel	155	469
Canada, United States	6 231	15 611	Lebanon	23	160
Japan	1 966	9 177	Turkey	55	194
			Other West Asia (f)	82	366
Total	15 192	44 513			
			Total	332	1 269
Percentage	32.6	39.0			
			Percentage	0.7	1.1
Pacific:			South Asia:		
Papua New Guinea (c)	1 146	1 097	India	300	868
Fiji	416	1 726	Sri Lanka, etc. (g)	350	1 543
Other Commonwealth	365	788			
Other Pacific	95	137	Total	650	2 411
Total	2 022	3 748	Percentage	1.4	2.1
Percentage	4.3	3.3	Southeast Asia:		
			Malaysia	2 984	13 851
			Indonesia	730	3 086
Americas, Central & South:			Philippines	225	503
Argentina	30	57	Thailand	495	994
Brazil	55	137	Other (h)	90	411
Chile	30	69			
Colombia	10	23	Total	4 524	18 845
Peru	3	11			
Uruguay	15	34	Percentage	9.7	16.5
Other	122	274			
			East Asia:		
Total	265	605	China	33	149
			Taiwan	28	126
Percentage	0.6	0.5	Hong Kong	536	2 810
			Singapore	535	2 366
			Korea, etc. (i)	185	994
Africa:					
Mauritius, etc. (d)	25	69	Total	1 317	6 445
Comm. East. Sth. (e)	137	435			
South Africa	248	662	Percentage	2.8	5.6
Comm. West (e)	72	206			
Egypt	20	194	New Zealand	21 776	34 718
Other Arab	12	46			
Other	35	114			
			Percentage	46.7	30.4
Total	549	1 726	Grand Total	46 627	114 280
Percentage	1.2	1.5	Percentage	100.0	100.0

a) Annual average 1975-79 calendar.
b) Adding estimates for 6-12 months to firm figures for 12 months and over.
c) Includes Cocos-Keeling and Christmas Islands.
d) Includes St. Helena and Seychelles.
e) "Comm." and "Commonwealth" = "British Commonwealth".
f) Jordan, Syria, Iraq, Iran and countries of Arabian Peninsula.
g) Includes a few from Bangladesh, Pakistan, Afghanistan, Sikkim, etc.
h) Includes Burma, Laos, Kampuchea, Vietnam.

i) Includes a few from Mongolia.

Table 9.6

LONG-TERM VISITORS ARRIVING FOR INTENDED STAY OF SIX MONTHS OR MORE (NOT PERMANENTLY)
Country of last stay (a) by age and by sex for 1976-78 calendar years: percentages

Country of last stay (a)	Males aged							Females aged						
	0-14	15-19	20-29	30-44	45-59	60+	Total	0-14	15-19	20-29	30-44	45-59	60+	Total
United Kingdom, Eire	12.3	8.0	40.2	23.9	7.3	8.3	6 517	12.4	2.7	42.8	15.6	9.0	17.5	5 790
Other Europe	14.8	3.8	19.0	38.7	16.4	7.3	4 450	16.5	6.0	18.4	24.2	14.1	20.8	3 765
North America	18.3	13.7	24.3	28.2	13.5	2.0	10 582	23.3	10.2	30.8	23.7	9.9	2.1	7 563
Japan	16.8	3.4	16.4	50.3	12.2	0.9	3 649	27.9	15.0	21.1	28.5	6.9	0.6	2 115
Total	15.9	9.0	26.3	32.2	12.2	4.4	25 198	19.2	7.7	30.9	21.9	10.1	10.2	19 233
Israel	29.9	2.3	12.4	31.0	19.0	5.4	258	32.8	1.0	18.5	30.3	13.3	4.1	195
Turkey	26.8	7.3	30.5	25.6	8.6	1.2	82	19.0	6.3	46.9	17.7	7.6	2.5	79
Lebanon, Egypt	17.1	9.2	42.1	23.7	2.6	5.3	76	13.7	2.0	27.5	17.6	11.8	27.4	51
Other West Asia	32.3	1.5	26.3	25.6	13.5	0.8	133	28.0	6.5	33.7	29.0	0.9	1.9	107
West Asia	28.2	3.8	22.6	27.9	13.9	3.6	549	26.8	3.5	28.5	26.2	9.0	6.0	432
India	18.9	7.7	30.3	30.1	11.2	1.8	508	25.9	7.4	30.8	28.5	5.7	1.7	351
Malaysia	2.0	34.3	59.6	3.5	0.5	0.1	5 209	2.3	35.9	58.0	2.7	0.6	0.5	3 529
Indonesia	8.9	16.9	45.5	25.3	3.3	-	1 346	12.8	15.0	49.9	18.6	3.3	0.4	787
Philippines	9.3	16.4	36.0	27.6	10.7	0.8	214	4.3	9.4	60.0	18.2	5.4	2.7	445
Thailand	3.6	23.9	51.1	18.8	1.8	0.6	744	4.4	23.7	56.6	11.5	3.7	0.1	706
Singapore	4.2	12.6	67.5	11.5	3.6	1.1	816	5.6	18.1	66.9	7.7	1.0	0.7	756
Hong Kong	1.8	32.3	57.8	5.7	1.3	0.5	1 008	6.0	30.0	53.8	6.3	1.6	2.3	569
South & East Asia (b)	5.1	24.4	53.0	14.4	2.6	0.5	11 172	6.6	25.3	55.0	9.7	2.4	1.0	7 820
South Africa	16.9	9.2	19.4	29.4	16.4	8.7	391	30.4	19.4	20.3	17.0	7.8	5.1	335
Other Africa	12.9	5.1	44.2	32.7	4.7	0.4	532	23.9	6.3	37.5	13.7	16.1	2.5	285
Africa	14.6	6.8	33.7	31.3	9.7	3.9	923	27.4	13.4	28.2	15.5	11.6	3.9	620
America (Cen., South)	21.3	10.1	16.9	40.2	8.8	2.7	396	32.2	10.9	20.9	15.5	10.0	10.5	239
Papua New Guinea (c)	31.4	38.2	20.0	8.2	1.8	0.4	2 019	38.4	29.5	17.7	9.2	4.9	0.3	1 464
Fiji	6.8	31.5	55.3	5.2	1.1	0.1	859	12.6	36.9	34.9	14.2	1.1	0.3	358
Comm. Pacific	21.9	33.5	28.4	6.8	8.2	1.2	501	23.5	45.0	20.2	8.4	1.8	1.1	442
Pacific (b)	23.2	34.8	30.0	7.9	2.9	1.2	3 540	31.3	32.9	20.9	9.7	4.2	1.0	2 380
New Zealand	9.6	12.9	62.9	11.8	2.3	0.5	34 341	11.5	21.4	53.1	9.8	3.2	1.0	27 771
Total Developed (d)	15.9	9.0	26.3	32.2	12.2	4.4	25 198	19.2	7.7	30.9	21.9	10.1	10.2	19 233
Total Developing (d)	10.7	24.6	45.1	15.0	3.6	1.0	16 580	14.1	25.1	44.8	10.8	3.7	1.5	11 491

a) Country of last stay = country in which traveller regarded himself as living.
b) Smaller countries are included in regional total but not shown separately.
c) Includes a few from Cocos-Keeling and Christmas Islands.
d) Excludes New Zealand.

Older age groups also tend to come for shorter periods; for instance, about one-third of visitors aged 30-59 from Malaysia came for visits of between six and twelve months. The percentage duration of visits of persons aged 20 and over from developing countries for the years 1976-78 were: six to twelve months 48.7 per cent; one to two years 22.9 per cent; two to three years 9.6 per cent; three to four years 9 per cent; four years and over 9.8 per cent. This is a very different pattern to that presented for Australian residents moving to developing countries. Males coming for two or more years ranged from 50 per cent of all visitors from the Philippines, about 30 per cent for Malaysia, Thailand and Papua New Guinea, and about 20 per cent for Fiji and Indonesia. Women were in a shorter range: from 35 per cent for those from the Philippines and Fiji, 30 per cent for Malaysia and Hong Kong, 20 per cent for Indonesia.

Occupational data on non-student males appear in Table 9.7. An appreciable number were in the professional and general business categories (37 per cent and 25 per cent respectively), suggesting that non-student visitors include many seeking further work experience, as well as a number making exchange visits. The much greater movements of professional and businessmen from developed countries -- 25 000 in 1976-78 compared with 3 600 from developing countries -- includes persons sent by multi-nationals based in Europe, North America and Japan to establish branches in Australia, or to take over Australian businesses. Japan alone recently sent about 5 000 business executives, 2 000 office workers and 1 000 engineers and technicians each year in connection with the establishment and operation of Japanese motor-vehicle, electronic and kindred businesses in Australia. Additionally, many New Zealanders, being free to enter Australia without visas, have entered as long-term visitors to fill vacancies in professional and business occupations.

The occupations of women visiting Australia long-term appear in Table 9.4. Leaving aside more than half who were students, some 30 per cent of the remainder (that is, of non-students from developing countries) were housewives, another 37 per cent were professional women (mainly nurses and teachers) and 10 per cent had secretarial skills. The much larger number of women from developed countries (42 000 as against 9 600 from developing countries in 1976-78) had general business occupational classifications, including one quarter with secretarial skills. This pattern is also related closely to the practice of overseas-based companies sending staff to Australia for long-term employment.

Again, there were regional and country variations (see Tables 9.7 and 9.8). The small number of men from Africa and Latin America were mainly in the professions while about one-third of those from west Asian countries were in the general business category. The larger movements from southeastern Asia and the southwestern Pacific contained relatively more metal, electrical and other tradesmen from Papua New Guinea and the Pacific than from southeastern Asia. Malaysia, Indonesia and Thailand sent appreciable numbers of tertiary and secondary teachers. The clergy group were again interesting; nearly 10 per cent of non-student visitors from Latin America and nearly 4 per cent of these from the Pacific. Old missionary connections were involved, bringing missionaries and religious trainees in developing countries to Australia for further training and work experience.

Table 9.8 shows that 25 per cent of non-student female visitors from southeastern Asia were nurse and paramedics, compared with 10 per cent from

Table 9.7

OVERSEAS VISITORS (MALE): BY OCCUPATION AND BY COUNTRY OF ORIGIN
Arriving 1976-78

Occupation: Males aged 15 and over	West Asia	Other Asia	Africa	Cen.Sth. America	Pacific	Total developing	%	Total developed*	%
Architects, surveyors	--	27	6	1	6	40	0.3	517	0.9
Engineers	23	132	16	15	30	216	1.5	2 230	4.1
Scientists	17	74	34	19	10	154	1.1	749	1.4
Doctors, dentists	4	181	16	4	20	225	1.6	618	1.1
Nurses, paramedics	1	23	6	--	13	43	0.3	288	0.5
Technicians	4	65	8	1	34	112	0.8	867	1.6
Tertiary teachers	15	336	34	6	18	409	2.8	805	1.5
School teachers	23	219	45	--	94	381	2.6	1 266	2.3
Clergy	6	38	9	20	45	118	0.8	396	0.7
Lawyers	--	14	--	2	8	24	0.2	194	0.4
Other professionals	17	291	29	6	62	405	2.8	349	0.6
Total	110	1 400	203	74	340	2 127		8 279	
Percentage	28.0	13.2	43.8	31.9	12.5	14.8	14.8	15.1	15.1
Economists, accountants	3	112	11	7	10	143	1.0	692	1.3
Business executives	53	351	20	14	104	542	3.8	6 285	11.4
Office workers	17	227	11	5	135	395	2.7	2 470	4.5
Salesmen	21	15	1	5	7	49	0.3	2 355	4.3
Ship and air officers	--	79	--	--	30	109	0.7	231	0.4
Transport supervisors	8	97	--	5	14	124	0.9	2 315	4.2
Primary industry	13	11	4	2	50	80	0.6	2 057	3.7
Total	115	892	47	38	350	1 442		16 405	
Percentage	29.3	8.4	10.2	16.4	12.9	10.0	10.0	29.8	29.8
Metal tradesmen	5	31	7	4	131	178	1.2	4 963	9.0
Electrical, telecomm.	2	4	--	1	53	60	0.4	1 375	2.5
Building, woodwork	1	1	--	1	13	16	0.1	4 384	8.0
Process workers	7	9	9	--	1	26	0.2	2 028	3.7
Wells, cranes, earthmoving	--	1	1	--	5	7	--	677	1.2
Labourers	10	8	--	1	4	23	0.2	3 535	6.4
Total	25	54	17	7	207	310		16 962	
Percentage	6.4	0.5	3.7	3.0	7.6	2.1	2.1	30.8	30.8
Catering, personal	2	147	3	--	33	185	1.3	1 191	2.1
Police, fire, armed	--	339	--	--	74	413	2.9	1 665	3.0
Artists, entertainers	2	28	--	5	16	51	0.4	758	1.4
Recreation, sport	--	14	--	2	--	16	0.1	446	0.8
Other	--	5	--	--	2	7		477	0.9
Total	4	533	3	7	125	672		4 537	
Percentage	1.0	5.0	0.6	3.0	4.6	4.7	4.7	8.2	8.2
Government officials	44	392	52	35	103	626	4.3	1 198	2.2
Inadequately described	47	387	13	30	88	565	3.9	2 764	5.0
Students, 15 plus	42	6 914	126	37	1 479	8 598	59.7	3 932	7.2
Retired, independent	6	32	2	4	28	72	0.5	944	1.7
Total	139	7 725	193	106	1 698	9 861		8 838	
Percentage	35.3	72.9	41.7	45.7	62.4	68.4	68.4	16.1	16.1
Grand Total	393	10 604	463	232	2 720	14 412		55 021	
Percentage	100.0	100.0	100.0	100.0	100.0	100.0	100.0	100.0	100.0

* Including New Zealand.

Table 9.8

OVERSEAS VISITORS (FEMALE): BY OCCUPATION AND BY COUNTRY OF ORIGIN
Arriving 1976-78

Occupation: Females aged 15 and over	West Asia	Other Asia	Africa	Cen.Sth. America	Pacific	Total developing	%	Total developed*	%
Architects, surveyors	--	5	--	--	1	6	0.1	140	0.3
Engineers	1	9	1	4	--	15	0.1	133	0.3
Scientists	11	23	1	2	4	41	0.4	240	0.6
Doctors, dentists	--	47	1	1	6	55	0.6	143	0.3
Nurses, paramedics	1	709	6	4	77	797	8.3	3 632	8.6
Technicians	1	25	--	--	1	27	0.3	497	1.2
Tertiary teachers	--	60	--	4	3	67	0.7	200	0.5
School teachers	35	231	58	6	78	408	4.2	2 467	5.8
Clergy, religious	--	30	1	--	11	42	0.4	129	0.3
Other professionals	6	75	20	1	34	136	1.4	533	1.3
Total	55	1 214	88	22	215	1 594		8 114	
Percentage	17.4	16.6	40.7	13.6	13.2	16.5	16.5	19.2	19.2
Economists, accountants	2	48	--	--	2	52	0.5	311	0.7
Business executives	1	39	2	3	42	87	0.9	783	1.8
Office workers	1	173	14	2	160	350	3.6	9 516	22.5
Saleswomen	1	23	--	4	9	37	0.4	1 398	3.3
Transport supervisors, etc.	--	27	--	1	1	29	0.3	249	0.6
Primary industry	--	--	1	--	1	2		245	0.6
Total	5	310	17	10	215	557		12 502	
Percentage	1.6	4.2	7.9	6.2	13.2	5.8	5.8	29.5	29.5
Metal tradeswomen	--	--	--	--	1	1		155	0.4
Electrical, telecomm.	--	1	--	--	--	1		320	0.8
Process, building workers	2	5	--	2	3	12	0.1	1 615	3.8
Labourers	3	--	--	4	4	11	0.1	175	0.4
Total	5	6	--	6	8	25		2 265	
Percentage	1.6	0.1	0.0	3.7	0.5	0.3	0.3	5.4	5.4
Catering, personal	4	65	--	4	20	93	1.0	2 134	5.0
Police, fire, armed	--	8	--	--	5	13	0.1	227	0.5
Artists, entertainers	24	22	--	--	4	50	0.5	460	1.1
Recreation, sport	--	--	--	--	4	4	0.1	84	0.2
Other occupations	5	9	20	--	7	41	0.4	799	1.9
Total	33	104	20	4	40	201		3 704	
Percentage	10.4	1.4	9.3	2.4	2.4	2.1	2.1		8.7
Government officials	3	91	6	14	4	118	1.2	390	0.9
Inadequately described	44	313	4	16	48	425	4.4	2 201	5.2
Students, 15 plus	23	4 457	41	32	818	5 371	55.7	2 834	6.7
Home duties	142	776	35	38	266	1 257	13.1	9 081	21.5
Retired, independent	6	40	5	20	20	91	0.9	1 227	2.9
Total	218	5 677	91	120	1 156	7 262		15 733	
Percentage	69.0	77.7	42.1	74.1	70.7	75.3	75.3	37.2	37.2
Grand Total	316	7 311	216	162	1 634	9 639		42 318	
Percentage	100.0	100.0	100.0	100.0	100.0	100.0	100.0	100.0	100.0

* Including New Zealand.

Papua New Guinea and the Pacific and 3 per cent from Africa and Latin America. In contrast, over one-third of non-student women from Africa were school teachers while one-quarter of those from Papua New Guinea and the Pacific were business or office workers. Proportions in home duties also varied, ranging from two-thirds of non-student women from Lebanon and Egypt, one-half of those from India and Indonesia and one-third of those from Hong Kong, Papua New Guinea, Fiji and Latin America to one-sixth of those from Thailand, Malaysia, Singapore and the Philippines.

Thailand and the Philippines send a relatively large number of women to Australia as permanent settlers -- brides of Australian men who have worked in those countries or brides who have answered "lonely-heart" advertisements inserted by Australian men living in the outback or in other lonely circumstances. These brides may then receive long visits from single sisters or friends, or indeed picture-brides themselves may have arrived under the category "single women" making a long visit before changing status to "permanent resident" after marriage. Thailand and the Philippines also send appreciable numbers of women in religious orders to work in Australian branches of their organisations.

The migration statistics reveal a varied and fascinating picture of long-term migrants visiting Australia from different parts of the world. Again, it must be emphasized that data on age, marital status, occupation and duration of residence are available so far for 1976-78 only, and that since then the visitor movement from developing countries has more than tripled, now totalling well over 35 000 a year. By providing further work training and experience, Australia is making a small but significant contribution to the development of developing countries in Asia and the Pacific. The contribution of Australians migrating long term to work in developing countries has more impact because the volume is greater and the work visits are longer. Taken together, the two movements now total 90 000.

While other industrialised countries make a much greater contribution to developing countries than does Australia, their migration statistics are usually much less helpful than the Australian ones and, if available at all, rarely provide as much detail on age, marital status, occupation or duration of residence. The Australian data noted above show what can be done with reasonably full statistics and how important long-term migration is to the social and economic life of developing countries.

END NOTE

International statistical usage distinguishes between movements of less than one year, called "temporary" or "short-term" migration, and movements of more than one year, called "permanent" or "long-term" migration. For two reasons this is most confusing. First, using the word "permanent" to cover movements of one, two or three years and also movements for permanent settlement, combines two quite distinct migrations into one. Australia now splits the old "permanent" category into two, "long-term" and "permanent" or "settler" movements, so overcoming this first confusion.

Second, lumping all movements of less than one year into the single category "temporary" or "short-term" also combines several distinct kinds of migration. One of these is the true short-term movement of tourists, visitors coming for conferences or short business consultations, relatives visiting families for a few weeks or months, and so on. Quite different is the longer-term movement of students coming for the academic year of ten to eleven months, of professional, technical or business staff posted abroad for ten to twelve months, of scientists and academics working with an overseas institution for six to twelve months, and so on. These longer moves are quite unlike the true short-term movement and much more like the postings or visits of one, two or three years; which is why this chapter takes movements of six to twelve months out of the "short-term" or "temporary" category and includes them in the long-term but not permanent category. Such a change is essential if the contribution of long-term migration to developing countries is to be assessed. Ideally, governments should provide as much information on movements between six and twelve months as they do on movements of more than a year.

Chapter 10

INTERNATIONAL MIGRATION OF HIGHLY-SKILLED MANPOWER:
THEORETICAL AND DEVELOPMENTAL ISSUES

by

John Salt and Allan Findlay

INTRODUCTION

Major secular changes in patterns of international migration over the last few years have served to focus new attention on the geographical mobility of highly-skilled manpower. Only a handful of countries now encourage new settlement migration, and even that is increasingly selective (Kritz 1987). The era of mass migrations of relatively low-skilled labour also looks to be nearing its end, at least for the forseeable future, not because of a diminution in pressure to emigrate but because demand has faltered in the developed world and the Middle East. In contrast, migration by the highly skilled has, if anything, increased and should continue to do so for two main reasons. First, it is likely that in all countries economic development will require specialist skills and the experience of trained people. If they can be imported, thus obviating the need to incur training costs, so much the better. Second, the global economy functions through the movement of a highly-skilled elite, responsible for the transfer of knowledge from one part of the system to another. Already such transient labour is a major element in the migration pattern of many countries (Salt, 1983, Appleyard, 1985; Kritz, 1987). However, it has tended to slip through the net of most traditional migration analysis, largely because it has not been regarded as settlement migration, nor has its volume been particularly significant. This lack of attention belies its economic, social and political importance.

This chapter is concerned with two aspects of the migration of the highly skilled: developing an appropriate explanatory theoretical framework and assessing the impact on development of skill transfers through international migration. Following general observations on the migration of highly-skilled persons, a theoretical framework is proposed based on a system which addresses the new international spatial division of labour, the nature of careers, the role of internal labour markets and the lubrication provided by recruitment and relocation agencies. This is followed by new empirical evidence from US-based examples on the scale of relocation within transnational corporations (TNCs). The development impacts of the migration of the highly skilled are then considered by reviewing their role in development projects including the impact of skill transfer on indigenous populations. The final section, based on specific empirical examples, is a more general review of environmental and attitudinal impacts.

Significance of International Migration by the Highly Skilled

There is no accepted definition covering the various types of migration by the highly skilled. The phenomenon "brain drain" has long been known, and has frequently been regarded as a more or less permanent move (Committee on Manpower, Resources and Technology, 1967; Grubel and Scott 1965; Shearer, 1966; Glaser, 1978; Brydon and Gould, 1984). However "brain exchange" might now be a more accurate description because large numbers of highly-skilled workers move on a relatively short-term contract basis (Salt 1983). Appleyard (1985) has drawn attention to the ephemeral nature of much of this movement, combined with the high levels of skill of those involved, and referred to the movers as "professional transients".

Most of the literature continues to focus, however, on the concept of brain drain, especially on permanent moves from LDCs to MDCs. The debates have covered such aspects as degree of compensation to areas of origin of remittances, savings and training. Views differ as to both diagnosis and prescription; for example, through redistributive forms of taxation (Bhagwati and Dellafar, 1973) or some form of compensation system (Böhning, 1984). Issues of manpower and development planning are also important; for example, Bennell and Godfrey (1983) have raised the issue (in the African case) of the costs to countries of employing their own highly-skilled nationals at prevailing international rates of salary benefits.

Movement of the highly skilled between advanced industrial economies has also become a major element (Salt, 1983). Business trips of varying durations account for high proportions of border crossings, some of which resemble temporary migrations. Erlandsson (1979) drew attention to the relationships between communications possibilities, job functions and contract activity in countries whose major centres are becoming more accessible to each other. A highly-advanced and integrated modern economy such as Europe, with accessibility between major regions, requires transfer of productive, marketing, administrative and research skills. Indeed, the philosophy of corporate unity embraced by many large international corporations necessitates migrations within internal labour markets (ILMs) in order to improve communications and disseminate knowledge, experience and new technologies.

The existence of large transnational corporations with internal labour markets that are international has created new patterns of relocation of expertise. Periods of secondment abroad of a few months, even a few weeks, are common. Indeed it is becoming increasingly hard to distinguish between business travelling and international migration since the former may well substitute for the latter thanks to jet-age travel and modern communications. There is certainly greater fluidity among the highly skilled in international movement than we have come to expect even from fixed-term contract migration among the hewers of wood and drawers of water.

Difficulties of definition preclude accurate assessment of migration by the highly skilled without a rigid specificiation of time spent overseas. For example, excluding European Community and British nationals, the United Kingdom recorded a million business visitors in 1985; and of over 9 million non-immigrants admitted to the United States about 1.75 million were classed as temporary visitors for business, or foreign government officials or international representatives. It is also becoming clear that growing proportions of labour immigrants are highly skilled: 86 per cent of the United Kingdom's 7 067 long-term work permits issued in 1985 were to managerial and professional occupations; in the United States in 1984 19 per cent of the 225 000 temporary workers admitted were "workers of distinguished merit and ability" and a further 28 per cent were inter-company (i.e., corporation ILM) transfers. The ILM element was also important in the United Kingdom, accounting for 57 per cent of long-term work permit issues. Clearly, then, the scale of labour migration within TNCs justifies careful quantification, description and explanation.

There is some recognition in the Third World of the growing economic and political importance of brain migration [e.g., the bibliographies of Gould (1977) and Davis and Prothero (1981)]. This importance is likely to grow as Third World economies develop and demand more skills and the supply increases in response to training programmes and participation in modern economies. In these circumstances, the likelihood of migration between LDCs will increase in response to differences in levels of development. Brydon and Gould (1984) point out that growing economic disparities between countries in Africa may have been exacerbated by increased numbers of skilled workers moving to the economically more successful states from countries with internal economic and political difficulties. The principal destinations have been the oil-producing states within Africa, but also countries with more buoyant economies such as Côte d'Ivoire, Kenya and Malawi. Zachariah and Condé (1981) have also shown that countries with relatively depressed economies by African standards (Ghana, Guinea, Mozambique and Zambia) have experienced net losses of skilled manpower.

Highly-skilled manpower, unlike low-skilled, does not merely supplement the indigenous labour force, but can establish itself in positions of high sensitivity and dominance, with serious implications for the host country's political and economic systems. For example, instead of returning to the relative poverty of their own countries, expatriates may stay on and form their own political power groupings. In time this may affect political balance and stability, especially if highly-skilled migrant groups enjoy different rights and statuses from the host community. Such migrants can also be agents of change in other directions. By providing needed skills and expertise and purveying new technology and thinking, they may effect change by exposing indigenous populations to a wider spectrum of ideas, which may ultimately lead to change in social cohesion.

Theoretical Developments

Attempting to explain the migration of the highly skilled demonstrates the inadequacy of most existing migration models. The movement of relatively unskilled workers is more readily comprehensible in terms of marked differences in labour market conditions between countries of origin and destination, in modes and standards of living, and in the attitudes of potential migrants to the improvement of their situation, than it is to the smaller numbers of migrants with high levels of skill and expertise. Many of these persons move between advanced industrial economies in an interacting urban system, the interplay of which has developed brain exchanges. Others migrate between the more developed sectors of Third World economies and First World positions, in effect between constituent parts of a global economy. Migration theories based on concepts of distance, ideas of push and pull and gradients in wages and standards of living are inappropriate for explaining these exchanges. New approaches based on modern concepts of economic integration and on distinguishing specific occupational types and their relationship with labour market processes and institutions are required. It is suggested that four main elements require consideration.

International spatial division of labour

Discussion of world economic moves in recent years, especially the trend towards integration of Third World countries into the global economy, has seen increasing attention given to the "new international division of labour" (Frobel et al., 1980). While little consideration has been given to the impact of international migration on this trend, it must be considerable. It was certainly one of the main "emerging issues" identified at the IUSSP's Bellagio conference in April 1985.

The effects of a new international spatial division of labour are likely to be complex, involving movements of expatriates between and within Third World, First World (and even Second World) countries. For example, the growth of advanced manufacturing industries in LDCs requires immigration of highly-skilled expatriate staff; Third World nationals move to First and Second World countries for training; the development of indigenous multinational companies in Third World countries is increasingly leading to Third World -- Third World organisational-based migration. With economic integration come closer contact and flows of information. Highly-skilled personnel in one country can take advantage of their marketable skills by becoming better informed about improved conditions elsewhere.

Little is yet known concerning the extent to which this new phase of industrial organisation has contributed to uneven spatial development. Though there is a dearth of information on the consequences of this development, the work of Stahl (1984) on Singapore shows it can be important. Walton (1985) attempted to place contemporary trends in spatial divisions of labour into a temporal context by arguing that today's trends represent the third such transformation, although he did not assess the lessons from previous transformations concerning likely directions to be taken by international migration in the future.

At the heart of the new international spatial division of labour in recent decades is the internal spatial division of labour of the transnational corporation. The growth of the TNC has been instrumental in creating a global organisation of labour, much of it highly skilled, within which mobility takes place. The relationship between the two is unclear, though Hymer (1972) suggested that organisations create a division of labour between countries corresponding to the division between various levels in the corporate hierarchy with centralised high-level decision making in a few key cities in MDCs. Hymer's model is generally accepted, but study of corporate organisations has shown them to be highly complex and no single international division of labour with a neat hierarchical structure can be discerned. Indeed, the growth of Third World-based TNCs throws into doubt the general validity of the Hymer model, certainly as far as its assumption of paramountcy by TNCs from more developed countries is concerned.

As the large employing organisation grows, its functions become more specialised and its links more complex (Dicken 1986). Its ILM also reflects these developments. A hierarchical structure develops (see Figure 10.1) with a range of control functions, the principal ones at head office, others at lesser points in the organisational system. Links which develop between locations associated with these functions include geographical mobility of the skilled work-force. The international migration of the highly skilled may thus be seen as one expression of these links, with staff expertise moved to where it is required and in accordance with skills possessed by individuals.

The shape of the organisational system, and consequent staff relocation, is affected by the strategy being pursued, for example, toward horizontal expansion or vertical integration, both of which have implications for internal relations between the organisation's component parts, e.g., the extent to which units are created which are independent or interdependent [Dicken (1986)]. The latter would demand greater transfer of know-how which may be accomplished through a mobile professional transient work-force.

The degree of functional and spatial separation of the component parts of the organisation is related to the technology involved in its operations. Dicken argues that the particular spatial form of the organisation results from interaction between internal structure and technological forces. Different parts of the organisation have different locational needs and access to different technologies. For example, head and regional office, R&D, and production each requires its own locational type and has its own particular role within the organisation. Head office requires a strategic location, at the hub of communications and with easy face-to-face contacts. In a TNC a regional office may be a local country's head office. Regional offices have co-ordinating roles which depend on the corporate philosophy of who can rise to the top: for example, in some TNCs local nationals may control regional centres, in others their own nationals are in charge. The locational characteristics of R&D functions, depending largely upon the technology employed, determines whether the organisation is "organic" or mechanistic". In the former case firms operate on the frontiers of new technology, with continuing product and process innovation and the need to transfer technology specialists frequently and with speed; in the latter technology and production processes are more familiar, product lines longer and there is less need to relocate expertise.

The system and the career

An explanatory framework for international migration of the highly skilled should acknowledge the disaggregated nature of the modern labour market in which specialist skills and training mean that the work-force is segmented into self-contained non-competing groups (McKay and Whitelaw, 1977; Salt, 1983, 1986). Attempts at explanation must distinguish specific occupational types and examine their relationship with labour market processes and institutions. A close association exists between the career path of the

FIGURE 10.1: STRUCTURED INTERNATIONAL LABOUR MARKET

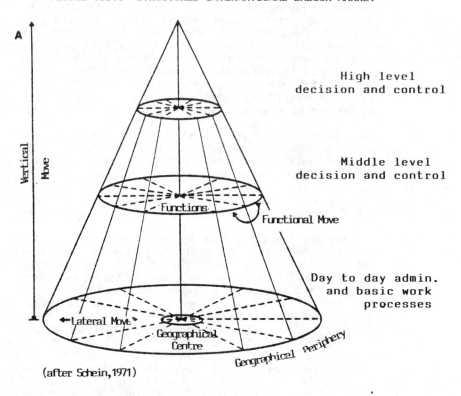

High level
decision and control

Middle level
decision and control

Functional Move

Day to day admin.
and basic work
processes

Lateral Move

Geographical
Centre

Geographical Periphery

(after Schein, 1971)

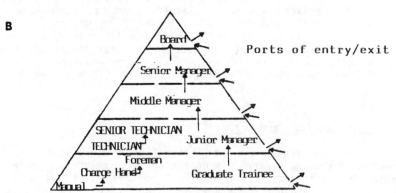

Ports of entry/exit

164

individual, the nature of the job and the migration demands imposed by the organisation of work and the internal structure of the employer.

Within the migration system that results the concept of career is most important. A career consists of a sequence of jobs held by an individual and related to each other by the acquisition of skill and experience. Mobility between jobs results from either task or locational change and may occur within an employing organisation or in movement between organisations. The career path can then be defined as the route taken by the employee through the sequence of jobs (tasks), occupations (collections of tasks), employers and locations. The choice of route broadly conforms to the idea that a career will progress upwards. We may hypothesize that on these career paths critical points will occur at which propensity to move increases and labour migration results. These are points which primarily reflect the nature of the occupation and the structure of tasks it contains, and the way in which an employer organises work and manages careers. The length and nature of career paths vary, and the interconnections reflect the organisation of work by the employer.

From the demand side the employer has a large system of fixed jobs into which must be fitted eligible people. Different policies exist for doing that. But such interaction cannot exist in isolation from supply side characteristics in the system, particularly attitudes to work and employee behaviour. There is some evidence that these attitudes vary between migration systems: American managers seem far more mobile than their European counterparts. Jennings (1971) has written of them as "mobilcentric". As an individual moves through his career his decisions about where to work, and what at, are affected by constraints and influences which operate at particular moments in time.

Geographical migration patterns are, therefore, determined on the one hand by the location decisions of employing organisations and the spatial division of labour they favour, and on the other by a group of eligible people with degrees of skill and experience already acquired. These are elements in a system the energy for which is provided by the need for employers to fill vacancies with the right sort of skills, and by the desire of employees for careers which present possibilities for promotion, job satisfaction and general improvement in life-style.

Migration in internal labour markets

The way in which migration occurs within the ILM can be explained with the help of Figure 10.1. The organisation is represented in A by a series of levels of operation, narrowing in size as higher-level decision and control is reached. At the heart is the head office, the geographical centre of operations. Peripheral operations may be widely scattered at far flung international locations. Within this system labour migration can take place in a number of ways. It may be a promotion, along the vertical axis in Figure 10.1(A); it may be lateral to a new post at the same grade; it may be between functions, perhaps from sales to production; it may be geographical, between organisational sites in the same or in different countries; it may also be some combination of these, e.g., with geographical relocation associated with promotion, lateral or functional movement.

Movement to and from the internal labour market occurs through a series of ports of entry/exit at different occupational levels. In Figure 10.1 (B) these are indicated in association with the promotional lines of movement of occupational groups. The permeability of any large organisation to the external labour market is determined by the degree of openness of these ports. In some cases employees may be freely recruited into the organisation at any level; in others entry is predominantly at the bottom, with a policy of filling vacancies higher up via promotional moves of existing staff. Within the organisation there are internal ports, diminishing in number up the hierarchy. Promotion through these may well involve geographical movement, but such relocation may also come from a lateral change of job within one of the "strata" depicted. For some employees such as manual workers, the promotional ladder is short; others, such as technicians, may come in at higher levels but progress is limited; graduates may enter at the bottom of the pyramid but expect that career development (and relocation) will move them upwards. The extent to which they are in competition with potential recruits from other organisations will depend upon the organisation's policy towards vacancy filling.

Movement within the organisational system may be for varying time periods. The likelihood of long-term migration overseas is now much diminished; the time when "our man" was permanently ensconced abroad is generally gone. Increasingly secondments are of short duration, perhaps two or three years at the most. What is also emerging is a tendency for corporations to use modern jet travel as a means of relocating expertise quickly and at short notice from an established base. The corporate labour market is increasingly able to substitute "business travel" for longer-term migration. In that way a special skill, like "trouble-shooting", can be on tap from the centre to a wide range of peripheral locations.

Lubricating the migration system

The mobility of the highly skilled is lubricated by efficient recruitment and placement systems and by generous relocation assistance. Recruitment may be within the internal labour market using local and central personnel functions, or through external agencies. Most large organisations have well-developed vacancy filling procedures where the work needs of the employer are related to the career development of the employee. Within the external labour market the recruitment services industry locates and places high-level expertise. Most recruitment agencies, at least those operating from the developed countries, are very specialised and meet particular types of labour requirements. Often, as a consequence, they tend to be highly selective in the geographical areas they deal with. They are essentially brokers, linking specific employers and types of employees and also particular origin and destination pairings. Some United Kingdom agencies, for example, work mostly at recruiting high-technology employees for the United States, others at sending a range of professional and managerial expertise to the Middle East. The role of recruitment agencies as organisers of the labour market for the highly skilled is reinforced by the selection procedures they use. They are an essential link in migration because managers, professionals and other specialists rarely engage directly in job search abroad, nor are prospective employers likely to take on at that level anybody who happens to turn up at the gate. About 50 per cent of the 110 000 British expatriates in the Middle East in 1981 were recruited through private agencies.

In addition to specialist recruitment advice the highly-skilled migrant is also assisted by (usually) generous relocation packages. These take several forms, normally including not only full financial recompense to cover expenses but advice and help in settling into the new environment. Increasingly TNCs are adopting world-wide job classification schemes to which salary levels are linked. A person who moves abroad, for whatever period, can thus keep his position in the corporate hierarchy; he also knows that a move overseas will adjust his status within it. Relocation agencies are increasingly offering their services to TNCs. For an agreed sum they will take over complete responsibility for the move, selling, finding or renting a house, providing information packs, dealing with administrative difficulties and covering all expenses. The relocation agencies may not provide the complete magic carpet but they are a lubricant of growing importance and TNCs think their sevices worth paying for if staff are relocated abroad with a minimum of aggravation.

Hence, within both internal and external labour markets services and schemes have been developed to ease overseas mobility. The hassle of going abroad may not have been completely eliminated, but the importance of frequent relocation has been recognised in the modern business world as has the need to eliminate as much of the friction as possible.

Migration of the Highly Skilled Within TNCs: The Case of the United States

There is little systematic evidence of the scale of migration of the highly skilled, and particularly of movement occurring within TNCs. Of special significance is the extent to which large corporations maintain expatriate staffs abroad and the scale of transfers associated with them. One of the few sources of data on these phenomena is the International Experience Index of the United States Employee Relocation Council.

In 1982 the ERC conducted a survey of its members, seeking details of their experiences in transferring staff to foreign countries. The resulting index provides, for each firm surveyed, data on numbers of employees in specified countries abroad, transfer volumes per annum and nature of the housing assistance provided. Those whose assignments are under six months are excluded. The data are subdivided into two employee categories: United States citizens assigned to a foreign locale (USE) and third country nationals (TCN) -- citizens of another country (not United States citizens) who are assigned to a country other than their own or the United States.

There are problems associated with using the Index as a source for studying the geography of the highly skilled. First, the data relate only to American firms and cannot be regarded as necessarily representative of all TNCs. However, since United States-based corporations are undoubtedly the most important on a world scale, the resulting pattern should be of interest. Second, the data represent only a sample of American firms, and may not be representative of total United States business. However, the large size of the sample and its sectoral catholicity should give a reasonable picture. Finally, the data are presented only in categorised form, making calculations of transfer rates difficult. A simple tabular presentation does allow a structure to be built by geographical region, of the main characteristics of expatriate professional and managerial level labour.

167

The sample lists data for 190 corporations in 114 countries in 1982, providing 2 719 records on annual scale of transfer and 3 065 records on numbers of expatriates employed. Tables 10.1 and 10.2 show that American firms use both USEs and TCNs, but that consistently USE staff are used and transferred more than TCNs.

Although it is not evident from the Tables presented, corporations do not necessarily use both USEs and TCNs in the same country; often, in fact, they use one or the other. Most firms are represented abroad by only one or two staff in any country, the vast majority employ under five (Table 10.1). About two-thirds of corporations with USE staff transfer less than one person per annum on average, while at that level the proportion for those employing TCNs is three-quarters (Table 10.2). Only two firms in the sample transferred over 100 USEs; three transferred over 100 TCNs.

These aggregate figures hide both similarities and differences between major world regions. The general pattern is for TCNs to be located and transferred in smaller numbers than USEs. In some regions numbers of expatriates employed are lower than average: Eastern Europe, Australasia, Central/South America and the Caribbean (Table 10.1). Larger numbers occur in the more developed regions, especially Western Europe where one-fifth of corporations employed between six and 25. The Middle East has the highest proportion of corporations with large expatriate staffs, reflecting the emphasis there on major structural projects and the oil industry. The Middle East and Western Europe too are characterised by greater use of TCNs than in the other regions. Western Europe stands out with a comparatively high level of transfers of USEs (Table 10.2) though only occasionally are there substantial numbers in a year, notably in the Middle East. Small numbers of USE transfers occur especially in Central/South America, Australasia and Eastern Europe. Among TCNs the Middle East tends to be involved in larger numbers of transfers than other regions, Central/South America and Eastern Europe in smaller ones.

Overall the analysis shows a very widespread global presence of highly-skilled expatriate labour employed by large corporations but with geographical differences. The pattern is for small pools of expatriates having a turnover of only one or two per year, but occasionally with larger numbers. The Middle East and Western Europe are the regions with the greatest tendency towards larger numbers, Eastern Europe being at the opposite extreme. In sum, it is clear that there are many global outposts incorporated into the ILMs of TNCs. Far more work needs to be done to explain the patterns, not least at the scale of individual countries and individual corporations. These results merely hint at the geographical complexities involved.

Development Impacts of Skill Transfers Through International Migration

The development impact on Third World countries of skilled international migration from the First World can be identified at two levels. First, projects to achieve the specific development of new services, infrastructure and large scale "modern" industries in Third World countries are often dependent on the import of appropriate skills from the more developed economies. At a second and more fundamental level skilled international migration has a development impact through its environmental and attitudinal influence on host societies.

Table 10.1

MAJOR WORLD REGIONS: PERCENTAGE OF EXPATRIATES EMPLOYED IN AMERICAN CORPORATIONS BY SIZE GROUP

(a) American Expatriates

Numbers of expatriates	Caribbean	Middle East	Western Europe	Central and South America	Africa	North America	Asia	Australasia	Eastern Europe	Total
1-2	59.0	55.3	53.4	65.4	55.2	54.4	56.3	67.2	87.5	57.6
3-5	15.7	21.1	19.0	19.5	26.9	23.4	24.1	14.6	6.3	20.6
6-10	6.0	7.3	11.9	7.2	6.7	14.0	10.8	8.0		9.9
11-25	10.8	7.3	10.8	5.1	6.0	6.4	5.4	4.4	6.3	7.4
26-50	8.4	0.8	2.3	2.1	2.2	1.2	2.0	3.6		2.3
>50		8.1	2.6	0.7	3.0	0.6	1.5	2.2		2.1
N	83	123	612	292	134	171	407	137	16	1 975

(b) Third Country Nationals

Numbers of expatriates	Caribbean	Middle East	Western Europe	Central and South America	Africa	North America	Asia	Australasia	Eastern Europe	Total
1-2	70.3	55.2	59.1	74.3	70.3	68.0	68.9	69.4	71.4	65.9
3-5	13.5	17.7	18.4	17.5	22.5	22.0	20.1	21.0	14.3	19.2
6-10	5.4	6.3	11.6	3.5	2.9	4.0	3.8	4.8	14.3	6.3
11-25	5.4	9.4	7.2	2.3	0.7		2.4			4.0
26-50		1.0	2.5	1.2	0.7		1.4	1.6		1.5
>50	5.4	10.4	1.3	1.2	2.9	6.0	3.3	3.2		3.1
N	37	96	320	171	138	50	209	62	7	1 090

Source: International Experience Index, US Employment Relocation Council.

169

Table 10.2

MAJOR WORLD REGIONS: PERCENTAGE OF EXPATRIATES TRANSFERRED IN AMERICAN CORPORATIONS BY GROUPED NUMBERS OF TRANSFERS PER ANNUM

(a) United States Expatriates

Numbers of transfers	Caribbean	Middle East	Western Europe	Central and South America	Africa	North America	Asia	Australasia	Eastern Europe	Total
Less than 1	61.8	63.6	58.8	76.9	64.0	66.9	65.2	70.4	100	65.4
1-2	26.3	17.8	26.7	15.4	22.0	21.7	24.2	19.2		22.5
3-5	6.6	7.5	9.1	5.8	6.0	8.9	2.0	5.6		7.4
6-10	2.6	3.7	4.3	0.8	3.0	1.9		3.2		2.9
11-25	2.6	2.8	0.9	1.2	4.0			0.8		1.0
26-50		1.9			1.0	0.6	0.3			0.3
51-100		0.9	0.2				0.8	0.8		0.3
More than 100		1.9								0.1
N	76	107	561	260	100	157	359	125	15	1 760

(b) Third Country Nationals

Numbers of transfers	Caribbean	Middle East	Western Europe	Central and South America	Africa	North America	Asia	Australasia	Eastern Europe	Total
Less than 1	72.4	64.4	69.9	83.3	75.6	79.1	70.7	69.8	85.7	72.7
1-2	17.2	18.4	22.7	13.5	19.5	18.6	20.1	24.5	14.3	19.5
3-5		6.9	4.6	1.9	1.6	2.3	4.0			3.9
6-10	6.9	1.1	2.1	0.6	0.8		2.9	1.9		1.8
11-25	3.4	5.7	0.7	0.6	0.8		1.1	3.8		1.5
26-50		1.1			0.8					0.2
51-100		1.1					0.6			0.2
More than 100		1.1			0.8		0.6			0.3
N	29	87	282	156	123	43	174	53	7	959

Source: International Experience Index, US Employment Relocation Council.

Development projects

Considering first the narrower and more direct development impact, it is evident that many developing countries have actively encouraged selective skilled immigration in order to accelerate progress with specific, and usually highly visible, development projects. Without external assistance unacceptable delays would emerge in the development process caused by the long period necessary to train the local population in appropriate skills. Consequently, foreign expertise is introduced often at considerable cost to the developing economies. For example, the rush to develop following the accumulation of oil revenues in many Arab states in the 1970s necessitated the immigration of many professional, technical and administrative skills in order to undertake projects such as water extraction and irrigation schemes at Kufra oasis, Libya and the multi-purpose water power and agricultural schemes on the River Lar, Iran (Marwick and Germond, 1975). Similarly basic urban infrastructural projects such as the renewal and extension of Cairo's public water supply and sewage system during the 1980s, perceived by most commentators as an extremely high-priority development project for the Arab world's largest city, rest upon the professional and technical expertise provided by a range of Western companies.

Many so-called "development projects" are designed neither to add value to the economy in which they occur through the transformation of the country's physical resources in the industrial process, nor improve the quality of life of the indigenous population through the improvement of national infrastructure. Instead they focus on the absorption of surplus labour arising from the rapid demographic growth of most developing countries. As has been indicated earlier, many multinational corporations have relocated a high proportion of their productive activity in Third World countries in order to take advantage of cheap labour resources (as well as of many other features of developing economies (Jenkins, 1984). It has been estimated that in 1980 multinationals employed 4 million workers in developing countries (Thrift, 1986, 46). In order to establish and efficiently supervise the production processes involving those workers, the multinationals have had to transfer skilled technicians and management staff from the more-developed to the less-developed countries. Once again developing countries have generally welcomed these skill transfers in the form of expatriate workers, viewing them as a necessary expedient to the establishment of labour-absorbing industries.

Skill transfers

The short-term impact of skilled immigration to facilitate industrial development has certainly been the creation of new job opportunities for certain groups in the indigenous populations (usually semi-skilled or unskilled female labour). The long-term impacts are less obvious. Following classical import-substitution theory one might have anticipated that developing economies would eventually succeed in replacing expatriates by local skilled labour, thus increasing the labour-generating functions of their involvement with transnational companies. There seems little evidence, however, of this switch having occurred.

Three reasons can be proposed for the relatively weak level of skill transfer to local populations from expatriate workers from developed economies. First, access to administrative and highly-skilled posts is controlled by the personnel strategies of large companies, and is not in the hands of host governments. The tightly-structured way in which multinational companies organise their internal labour markets favours the circulation of high-level staff between the company's head office and its branch plants. Skilled posts are filled from outside the local economy rather than by upward occupational mobility within one branch plant. This career system promotes a corporate image, encourages communication within the firm and provides opportunities for career advancement for staff from developing countries, but at the same time it militates against skill acquistion and managerial training for indigenous employees in branch plants.

A second reason for the limited level of skill transfer is the desire of large companies to protect their research and technological superiority. As Germidis (1978) pointed out, the multinational corporation has no incentive to transfer technological skills to the local labour force. Technical assistance is only provided to the minimum levels necessary to set up a production process at a particular location in the Third World. This is achieved by the secondment of technical experts to branch plants or to firms to whom work has been sub-contracted. On completion of the operation the experts are repatriated, thus protecting the firm's technological core from potential future competition from rival Third World companies who might "buy up" skills transferred to the local work force. It is therefore more correct to think of multinationals as "leasing" skills rather than transferring them to Third World countries.

The case of Tunisia serves as an interesting example of the problems faced by a branch plant economy. A government policy to encourage foreign investment in export-oriented industries resulted in an increase in the country's export of consumer goods from 3.0 per cent of all exports in 1968 to 18.9 per cent in 1980. This policy led to the creation of 23 000 jobs between 1973 and 1978, mostly concentrated in the textile and clothing sector (86.7 per cent of all new jobs) and mostly for low-skilled female labour (Findlay and Lawless, 1983). The new industries were administered mainly by staff from large European corporations, and the European principals carefully maintained control of product design and development and provided only minimal technical training to their Tunisian employees. The EEC decision in 1977 to impose high tariff barriers on foreign textiles had devastating effects. Nineteen of the new textile mills were closed in the following year involving the withdrawal of foreign capital and technical expertise. Germidis (1978) sums up the Tunisian experience:

> While the benefits of initial sub-contracting to the Tunisian economy are far from negligible in terms of jobs, earnings and foreign trade, their effects in terms of technology transfer is slow and fragmentary.

A third reason why the presence of skilled international migrants in developing countries has led to minimal technological transfer, and is therefore seen to have contributed to the "underdevelopment" of indigenous labour skills, has been that the relocation of production in the Third World has often been associated with the export of second-hand equipment which is technologically outdated. Even machine skills attained by employees are therefore of only limited value with the work-force remaining dependent on information from foreign management and technical experts about the most recent techniques being used in their industry in other parts of the world.

Environmental and attitudinal impacts of skilled migration

Many broad development implications arise from the ways in which Western expatriates affect the physical, economic and social environments into which they are inserted. It would appear that the stronger the cultural and political contrasts between the place of origin of the expatriates and their place of work, the greater the tendency for them to become a highly-segregated community. This is true not only for British and American staff working in the Third World but also for Japanese managerial and professional workers (Zielke, 1977). The tendency is strengthened by the policy of many multi-national companies and para-state organisations to provide housing for foreign staff, particularly in those parts of the world deemed less popular amongst expatriates (Table 10.3). By doing this they lubricate the international movement of skills, but also favour the isolation of expatriates in distinct residential units. The physical impact of this process on Third World cities has become of increasing importance, with the presence of expatriate residential districts in most capital cities paralleling to some extent the growth of colonial cities in the last century (King, 1976).

Table 10.3

LEAST FAVOURITE DESTINATIONS FOR BRITISH EXPATRIATES
(Percentages)

Africa	30
Middle East	18
South America	12
Asia	6
Australasia	5
Europe	5
North America	3
None	8
Other	11

Source: Overseas Recruitment Services, 1984.

Table 10.4 indicates the regional variations which exist in this form of intervention by American companies on behalf of their American staff working overseas. A majority of companies provide housing (either free or for rent) to American expatriates in the Middle East, while in Africa, South and East Asia and Eastern bloc countries over 40 per cent of companies intervened in this way in the housing market. The reasons for the higher level of provision in these parts of the world than in other regions seem to be two-fold. On the one hand Western expatriates experience much greater difficulties in finding and negotiating access to accommodation in alien cultural environments. On the other hand free or partially subsidised accommodation acts as a form of hidden financial bonus to entice expatriates to less popular destinations. It would appear from Table 10.4 that both factors are extremely important in the Middle East. The impact on urban areas in this region is heightened by the policy of some governments such as Saudi Arabia and Kuwait actively to encourage expatriates to live in separate districts or compounds

Table 10.4

HOUSING PROVISION FOR AMERICAN EXPATRIATES
(Percentage of American Companies by region)

	Free accommodation	Free housing or company housing available for renting
Middle East	33.0	55.1
Africa	20.4	42.8
Eastern bloc	19.4	41.9
South and East Asia (except Hong Kong and Singapore)	19.5	41.6
Japan	12.4	31.5
Hong Kong and Singapore	6.5	30.2
Caribbean	10.0	26.2
Central America and Mexico	9.8	25.9
Australia and New Zealand	8.9	22.9
British Isles	9.5	22.0
Latin America	8.2	20.9
South Europe	8.4	18.9
North and West Europe (except British Isles)	8.2	17.0
Canada	4.4	11.0

Source: International Experience Index, US Relocation Council.

in order to minimise cultural interactions between the host and immigrant populations (Al-Moosa and McLachlan, 1985). By contrast, some newly-industrialised countries such as Singapore and Hong Kong appear to be relatively popular amongst American expatriates with only 6.5 per cent of companies offering completely free accommodation to their staff, but nevertheless present difficulties to foreign workers in trying to find accommodation as illustrated by the moderately high involvement of companies in owning residential units for letting to their employees. It is interesting that purchase of housing stock by American corporations is relatively unusual in Latin America compared with other parts of the Third World.

The economic impacts resulting from the presence of skilled international migrants in developing countries are diverse and complex. The most apparent effects occur from the contact of highly-paid expatriate staff with local people. The conspicuous consumerist lifestyle of expatriates appears to act as a catalyst to domestic consumerism amongst the better-off elements of the local population, while to the poorer elements it may heighten a sense of injustice and inability to access the full benefits of urban living. It is perhaps significant that the Egyptian riots of 1986 saw the burning down of several international hotels in Cairo frequented by Western businessmen as well as tourists.

The presence of Western expatriates in very large numbers in several Middle Eastern countries during the 1970s and 1980s was responsible for the introduction of institutional innovations to the cities of the region. For example, in Saudi Arabia, supermarkets built to service Western expatriates were by the 1980s adapting their marketing techniques to lure the Saudi shopper away from traditional retail outlets. Evidence from a survey carried out in Tunis (Findlay et al., 1985) showed that supermarket shopping had been taken up selectively by the Tunisian population. Not surprisingly people from high-status occupations and people living in the suburbs of the capital city next to the expatriate population were more prone to adopt Western shopping habits than were low-status families living in traditional parts of the Arab city, such as the "medina". Similarly, the provision of English-speaking TV channels, showing Western films and documentaries, to service the expatriate population living in certain countries of the Arabian peninsula, has undoubtedly influenced the aspirations and outlook of much of the Arab population.

The social and cultural influence of skilled international migrants on host populations is difficult to quantify, but is quite distinct from the type of influence of colonial administrators and merchants. Unlike colonists, present-day expatriates do not represent one national ideology or one set of cultural values nurtured within a single nation state. Instead they represent the influence of transnational corporations whose economic and political interests seldom coincide with any one state and who promote cosmopolitan and supranational perspectives. Abstract but influential constructs such as Western capitalism, international mobility, and the image of the company man are transmitted through the presence of Western expatriates in a developing country.

Unlike merchants and businessmen of the colonial period, such as tea and cotton plantation managers, representatives of international companies today are seldom posted to the same location for more than four years. While the colonial populations had the opportunity to develop an in-depth knowledge of the places in which they lived and worked, contact between present-day expatriates and local populations is often relatively superficial and may be even covertly discouraged by the international companies for which they work.

These points can be illustrated from two surveys of British expatriates working in the Middle East (Findlay and Stewart, 1986a and b). In the first, a sample of British expatriates who had returned to the United Kingdom following the end of their overseas contracts were asked to report their international migration histories. No less than 58 per cent had worked not only in the Middle East but on some other previous contract overseas, reflecting the type of "professional transient" behaviour outlined earlier in this chapter, involving a career sequence with a chain of short-term overseas contracts at different locations. A significant proportion of the sample (46 per cent) intended to work abroad again and expressed a preference for this over working in the United Kingdom. Only 3 per cent of the sample said they would never contemplate working abroad again.

In the second survey some 77 British firms with offices in the Middle East were asked about their manpower policies. The modal contract length of British expatriates in the region was less than two years, and 91.9 per cent of firms felt no need to send their staff on a residential briefing course to prepare them for working overseas. The majority of British firms had no

British expatriates capable of speaking Arabic. The picture which emerges from the survey is one of companies expecting and encouraging the minimal possible level of social contact between expatriates and the indigenous population.

The lack of social contact between skilled international migrants and the local population strengthens the other forces outlined above which favour the ethnic segregation of Western populations living in developing countries. Far from minimising the development impact which international migration might have, this reinforces the alienating effects of the economic processes which have produced two circuits within Third World countries (Santos, 1979), and which have operated to "underdevelop" the human resources of Third World states.

CONCLUSION

This paper has touched on a wide range of issues, theoretical, empirical and policy-related. The theoretical framework presented needs elaboration and testing. In particular the nature of modern businesses and how they organise their supply of work in a globally interdependent economy demand attention. Definitions needs sharpening; e.g., when does business travel become temporary migration? Development impacts in Third World countries clearly covers a wide spectrum and much needs to be known about the way in which substitution of indigenous for expatriate skilled labour occurs. Perhaps the biggest problem is shortage of empirical information. Great forces are at work but we know little of their strength or direction.

BIBLIOGRAPHY

AL-MOOSA, A. and K. McLACHLAN
Immigrant Labour in Kuwait, London, Croom Helm, 1985.

APPLEYARD, R.T.
"Processes and Determinants of International Migration", IUSSP Seminar on Emerging Issues in International Migration, Bellagio, 1985.

BENNELL, P.A. and M. GODFREY
"The Professions in Africa: Some Interactions Between Local and International Markets", Development and Change, Vol. 14, 1983.

BHAGWATI, J.N. and J.W. DELLAFAR
"The Brain Drain and Income Taxation", World Development, Vol. 1, 1973.

BOHNING, W.R.
Studies in International Migration, London, Macmillan, 1984.

BRYDON, L. and W.T.S. GOULD
"International Migration of Skilled Labour within Africa: A Review and Agenda for Future Work", Liverpool Papers in Human Geography, No. 17, Department of Geography, University of Liverpool, 1984.

CASTLES, S. and G. KOSACK
Immigrant Workers and Class Structure in Western Europe, Oxford, Oxford University Press, 1973.

CASTLES, S., H. BOOTH and T. WALLACE
Here for Good, London, Pluto, 1984.

COMMITTEE ON MANPOWER, RESOURCES AND TECHNOLOGY
The Brain Drain, London, HMSO, 1967.

DAVIS, D. and R.M. PROTHERO
A Bibliography of Population Mobility in West Africa", Liverpool Papers in Human Geography, No. 6, Department of Geography, University of Liverpool, 1981.

DICKEN, P.
Global Shift. Industrial Change in a Turbulent World, London, Harper and Row, 1986.

ERLANDSSON, U.
"Contact Potentials in the European System of Cities" in H. Former and J. Oosterhaven, eds., Spatial Inequalities and Regional Development, The Hague, Nijhoff, 1979.

177

FINDLAY, A. and R. LAWLESS
"Offshore Industrialization in an Underdeveloped Economy" in B. Khader, ed., The Arab World and the International Division of Labour, Kuwait, Kuwait University Press, 1983.

FINDLAY, A. et al.
"An Appraisal of Retail Change within the Cultural Context of the Middle East", Working Paper 8506, Department of Business Studies, University of Sterling, 1985.

FINDLAY, A. and A. STEWART
"Migrations des travailleurs qualifiés britanniques sous contrat au Moyen Orient", Rev. Européenne des Migrations Internationales, Vol. 2, No. 1, 1986a.

"Manpower Policies of British Firms with Offices in the Middle East", Bulletin of the Committee for Middle East Trade, Vol. 20, 1986b.

FROBEL, F. et al.
The New International Division of Labour, Cambridge, Cambridge University Press, 1980.

GERMIDIS, D.
"International Sub-contracting and Transfer of Technology to LDCs" in A.B. Zahlan, ed., Technology Transfer and Change in the Arab World, Oxford, Pergamon,1978.

GLASER, W. et al.
The Brain Drain: Emigration and Return, UNITAR Research Report No. 22, Oxford, Pergamon, 1978.

GOULD, W.T.S.
"A Bibliography of Population Migration in Tropical Africa", African Population Mobility Project, Working Paper No. 31, Department of Geography, University of Liverpool, 1977.

GRUBEL, H. and A.D. SCOTT
"The International Flow of Human Capital", American Economic Review, Vol. 55, 1965.

HAGERSTRAND, T.
"On the Definition of Migration", Scandinavian Population Studies, Vol. 1, 1968.

HYMER, S.H.
"The Multinational Corporation and the Law of Uneven Development" in J.N. Bhagwati, ed., Economics and World Order, London, Macmillan, 1972.

JENKINS, R.
"Divisions Over the International Division of Labour", Capital and Class, Vol. 22, 1984.

JENNINGS, E.E.
The Mobile Manager, New York, 1971.

KINDLEBERGER, C.P.
Europe's Postwar Growth -- The Role of Labour Supply, Cambridge, Mass., Harvard University Press, 1967.

KING, A.
Colonial Urban Development, London, Routledge, Kegan and Paul, 1976.

KRITZ, M.M.
"The Global Picture of Contemporary Immigration Patterns" in R.T. Appleyard and Riad Tabbarah, IUSSP volume, forthcoming, 1987.

LUTZ, V.
"Foreign Workers and Domestic Wage Levels with an Illustration from the Swiss Case", Banca Nazionale del Lavoro, Quarterly Review, Vol. 16, 1963.

MABOGUNJE, A.
"Systems Approach to a Theory of Rural/Urban Migration", Geographical Analysis, Vol. 2, 1970.

McKAY, J. and J.S. WHITELAW
"The Role of Large Private and Government Organizations in Generating Flows of Inter-regional Migrants: The Case of Australia", Economic Geography, Vol. 53, 1977.

MARWICK, R. and J. GERMAND
"The River Lar Multi-purpose Project in Iran", Water Power and Dam Construction, Vol. 27, 1975.

OVERSEAS RECRUITMENT SERVICES
Pushed or Pulled?, London, ORS, 1984.

PETRAS, E.
"The Global Labour Market in the Modern World Economy" in M.M. Kritz, C.B. Keely and S.M. Tomasi, eds., Global Trends in Migration, Staten Island, New York, Centre for Migration Studies, 1981.

PIORE, M.J.
Birds of Passage: Migrant Labour and Industrial Societies, Cambridge, Cambridge University Press, 1979.

PORTES, A.
"Modes of Structural Incorporation and Present Theories of Labour Immigration" in M.M. Kritz, C.B. Keely and S.M. Tomasi, eds., op. cit., 1981.

SALT, J.
"High Level Manpower Movements in Northwest Europe", International Migration Review, Vol. 17, 1983/4.

"International Migration: A Spatial Theoretical Approach" in M. Pacione, ed., Population Geography: Progress and Prospect, Beckenham, Croom Helm, 1986.

179

SANTOS, M.
   The Shared Space, London, Methuen, 1979.

SHEARER, J.
   "In Defence of Traditional Views of the Brain Drain Problem, International Educational and Cultural Exchange, 1966.

STAHL, C.
   "Singapore's Foreign Workforce", International Migration Review, No. 18, 1984.

THOMAS, I.
   "Development and Population Redistribution" in J. Clark et al., eds., Population and Development Projects in Africa, Cambridge, Cambridge University Press, 1985.

THRIFT, N.
   "The Geography of International Economic Disorder" in E. Johnston and P. Taylor, eds., A World in Crisis, Oxford, Blackwell, 1986.

WALTON, J.
   "The Third 'New' International Division of Labour" in J. Walton, ed., Capital and Labour in the Urbanised World, London, Sage, 1985.

ZACHARIAH, K.C. and J. CONDE
   Migration in West Africa: Demographic Aspects, Oxford University Press for the World Bank, 1981.

ZIELKE, E.
   "Die Japaner in Düsseldorf", Düsseldorf Geographische Schriften, Vol. 19, 1977.

D. PERMANENT MIGRATION

Chapter 11

THE BRAIN DRAIN AND DEVELOPING COUNTRIES

by

D. Chongo Mundende

INTRODUCTION

During the 1960s and early 1970s the movement of highly-skilled workers received a great deal of attention from scholars of international migration. The term "brain drain", coined initially to describe the migration of British engineers and scientists to the United States, was later used to describe the migration of trained manpower in general (Watanabe, 1969: 40) and from developing to developed countries in particular. Some participants at the Expert Meeting of the World Population Conference in Tunisia in 1984 deplored the use of the term because it implied that only the migration of professionals was important. Participants felt that because other skilled workers were equally important, the term "transfer of talent" was more appropriate (POPCON, 1984). Another term that became popular after 1972 was reverse transfer of technology, deemed synonymous with transfer of talent.

Although the movement of trained personnel across national boundaries is not new, the scale of movement increased enormously after 1960, especially to the United States, United Kingdom, Canada, Australia, and Europe in general. Although these countries received large numbers of highly-trained workers from other developed countries after World War II, the salient feature of inflows after 1960 was that most of it came from developing countries. As brain drain migration created a great deal of controversy concerning its impact on developing countries, this chapter will examine and assess appropriate research during the last few decades. It should be pointed out, however, that the brain drain issue has received less attention during the present decade than it did during the 1960s and 1970s.

Causes of Brain Drain

Both the numbers of highly-trained and skilled workers from developing to developed countries, as well as the proportions of such persons from developing countries, increased significantly during the mid-1960s. This included persons who arrived from their home country, others who arrived from other developed or developing countries, and others who had entered developed countries as visitors or students and later had their status changed to immigrants. In 1977, these persons constituted 48.5 per cent of all professional immigrants and 10 per cent of all foreigners enrolled in the United States institutions of higher learning (Agarwal and Winkler, 1984: 814-815).

Although most migrants reach their decisions on the bases of economic, social, and political considerations at both origin and destination, several additional reasons have been ascribed to the movement of the highly-trained and skilled persons: they want to live and work in an environment where they are stimulated to apply their best efforts and where they are rewarded according to their expertise. Most often, developing countries are unable to provide the leadership, equipment, research facilities, and prestige required by professionals. Many therefore become frustrated and emigrate to countries where they feel they will be better rewarded and appreciated.

Some studies have concluded that many developing economies are unable to absorb their highly-trained manpower. As far as students studying abroad are concerned, the likelihood of their returning to the country of origin diminishes the longer they stay abroad, especially those on private, non-government scholarships. The chances of non-return are even greater if the student receives no communication from his country of origin. Under such circumstances, the student does not hear about job openings (Glaser, 1978, McKee, 1983a; UN, 1971); on the other hand, adverse or discouraging information from home may decide the student to stay abroad permanently (Mundende, 1982). Students can also be discouraged by news that there are no job openings (Grasmuck, 1984; McKee, 1983b). It seems that the higher the education he/she obtains, the lower the probability that the student will return (Glaser, 1978).

Income differentials are not only the major determinant of decisions to emigrate but they also greatly influence the choice of destination. The potential migrant weighs the costs and benefits of moving and if the latter outweigh the former, he/she will be likely to move (Grubel and Scott, 1977). Income differentials between home and any developed country outweigh all other factors for a potential emigrant from a developing country. Income differentials are certainly the major determinant of brain drain migration.

Political instability at country of origin has also encouraged many citizens to emigrate. For instance, studies on emigration from African, Caribbean and Andean regions (Bolivia, Chile, Colombia, Ecuador and Peru) indicate that many students studying in developed countries who cannot be assured of a peaceful political milieu upon return are unlikely to leave (McKee, 1983a, 1983b; Mundende, 1982).

Several factors operating in developed countries, and especially in the United States, tend to attract professionals from developing countries. For instance, although the American Medical Association was known to limit the number of entrants into medical fields before the mid-1970s, shortages did occur and many were filled as a result of active recruitment among students and other foreigners as well as from abroad (Watanabe, 1969: 420). In a bid to fill vacant professional positions, many developed countries have resorted to relaxing or waiving certain immigration rules and regulations. Developing countries simply cannot compete with developed countries in terms of the economic returns and other benefits that they can offer professionally-trained workers.

Impact

Several scholars have argued that emigration of skilled manpower adversely affects the national development process of developing countries in many negative and only a few, if any, positive ways. The country of emigration incurs costs of training and maintaining the emigrants even during their unproductive years (Watanabe, 1969). Indirect costs include the demonstration effect and tax revenue foregone.

According to the nationalistic viewpoint, migration of manpower from a developing to a developed country is bad because it inflicts irreparable losses on the former and robs it of irreplaceable, innovative individuals. Such migrations have been seen by some as "an act of treason and theft" (Zahlan, 1977: 320). Nationalists argue that human capital in international migration should not be compared to the movement of other factors of production. They argue that the movement is detrimental to the development process and is unidirectional -- from developing countries that have relatively few trained workers to developed countries with many. To nationalists, brain drain movements are helpful only if they move both ways. So long as they are unidirectional, from an area of shortage to an area saturated with trained manpower, brain drain movements are bad.

Nationalists further argue that brain drain leads to increased inequality; the rich countries continue to become richer while the poor countries become poorer. Ward (1975) considers brain drain as a manifestation of the exploitation of developing by developed capitalist societies and that the majority of emigrants become an exploited and marginal group. Immigrants often do not obtain jobs commensurate with their qualifications. At times job conditions are unpleasant and uncertain, even though the occupant obtains a higher income than at home.

Nationalists also argue that whereas a developed country may see brain drain as an ordinary commodity without special prestige and value, developing countries see it as a loss, a waste of resources, a skill bottleneck, that leads to a lesser rate of growth. Brain drain movements, they further argue, help developed countries to ease shortage of necessary skills and overcome bottlenecks.

Scholars of the international viewpoint contend that the world has become one market for highly-qualified manpower and that there is no such thing as a brain drain; only free movement of one factor of production. Labour simply locates in a country where it is most wanted and where it will give greater marginal productivity. Thus, the redistribution of highly-skilled workers leads to maximisation of world production on the basis of optimum productivity. Emigration is the most important means of transmitting information and technology (Grubel and Scott, 1977). Furthermore, the focussing on "drains" shifts emphasis away from more fundamental questions of the utilisation of talent, regardless of location, and discounts potential gains (Myers, 1967). In fact, developing countries are not stripped of badly-needed manpower, but are relieved of the surplus manpower they cannot use (Baldwin, 1970). Emigration ensures the optimum allocation of the world human resources.

The outflow of educated personnel reduces unemployment at the origin, raises the domestic capital-labour ratio, maximises the welfare of non-emigrants and increases productivity, income, and output. In addition, emigrants who go abroad return with better qualifications, training and experience. During their stay abroad, the emigrants may even return as consultants, researchers, or experts, thereby raising the prestige of their countries of origin (Grubel and Scott, 1977; Johnson, 1967; Kannappan, 1968; Sharma, 1976). Grubel and Scott (1977) argue that short-term losses due to brain drain are surpassed by remittances and by the spread effect of advanced research and technology derived by highly-trained and skilled manpower. Myint (1968) went even further by claiming that emigration reduced the gap between demand for and supply of manpower in developing countries and reduced the technological gap between developing and developed countries.

Focussing on international and nationalist arguments is not necessarily helpful. Ghosh (1985) distinguishes between brain overflow and brain drain. Conditions for brain overflow occur where the country trains more people than it can effectively employ. Brain overflow may be good for a developing country with high educated unemployment while brain drain may be bad for a country with manpower shortages, and especially for a developing country. Although this dichotomy is logical and has potential for clarifying aspects of the migration of talent, it is difficult to conceptualise. For instance, it is not easy to clearly distinguish brain drain and brain overflow. Even brain overflow movements have brain drain effects. As Stahl (1987) shows, long-term migration of talent may lead to ultimate stagnation and deterioration of an economy, although many observers tend to see any migration as an overflow simply because of the dearth of opportunities available at home.

Scholars representing the human viewpoint argue that an individual has the right to choose association, occupation, and residence of choice. Professionals may leave their country because they realise their international market value and conclude that their continued stay at home would lead to apathy and a loss of skill (Zahlan, 1977). According to the United Nations Human Rights Charter: "Everyone has the right to leave any country, including his own and to return to his country" (UN, 1973: 33). However, international migration is tightly controlled by both sending and receiving countries.

Overall Consideration of the Brain Drain Controversy

On the whole, brain drain migration has been found to be detrimental to developing countries. Most scholars agree that it removes strategic manpower from key positions in a country, causes loss of present and future production, present and future saving, taxes and potential innovations. Brain drain also involves the loss of money invested in the education, training and skill formation of the emigrants. Ghosh (1985: 355) estimates that for India the collective losses may have been as high as $5 billion, and DeVoretz and Maki (1980) showed that Canada saved a lot of money by recruiting professional and skilled workers in developing countries rather than training its own citizens.

The consequences of brain drain migration for developing countries are costly. For example, between 1964 and 1982 Zambia spent about K5 billion

186

(K = Zambian Kwacha) recruiting and maintaining expatriate accountants but only one-tenth of that amount training its own accountants. Nor are the consequences of brain drain migration confined to any one sector of the economy. In fact, they tend to affect the most important sectors, especially the technical, scientific and medical fields. Most of the emigrants from Africa to the United States have been in such scientific and science-based fields as physics, chemistry, electronics, chemical engineering, medicine, as well as in arts and social sciences. More than half of the African students in the United States in physics and chemistry in the 1960s never returned (UNESCO, 1984).

The frustration of brain drain migration is clearly reflected in the experiences of the University of Zambia. Since its establishment in 1966, the University, through its Staff Development Fellowship programmes, has been training nationals to replace expatriate professors. But most of the nationals who gain their doctoral degrees work for the university for only a short time before obtaining jobs outside the continent or elsewhere in Africa. This situation forced the university to indefinitely suspend the staff development fellowship programmes in 1986.

Shortages and scarcities of trained manpower in some developing countries are critical. While a country may continue to be served by a few educated persons, most of the highly-trained personnel emigrate elsewhere. In his study of emigration from the Commonwealth Caribbean to the United States, McKee (1983b: 58-59) concluded that the outmigrants were better educated than those who stayed behind. Previously, the movement included nurses, teachers, accountants and auditors, but engineers, lawyers, judges, physicians, surgeons and architects are now moving in increasing numbers to the United States (UNESCO, 1984: 434).

Some countries benefit from the remittances received from their nationals abroad. Indeed, Algeria, Morocco and Tunisia encourage their nationals to stay abroad as part of their solution to "population pressures" and to high rates of unemployment and underemployment (Bouvier et al., 1977; Ecevit, 1981; Sabot et al., 1981). Countries in the Caribbean and Andean region invoke similar policies even though they have shortages of workers in some professions (Grasmuck, 1984; McKee, 1983a, 1983b). Remittances can be substantial. Payments to India represented 8.5 per cent of the value of her total exports in 1973 and 14.8 per cent in 1977.

Mundende (1982) found that brain drain migrants from Africa used their savings to establish themselves in the receiving countries, unlike labour migrants who, faced with a finite stay abroad, were therefore conscious of the need to take some money with them upon return. Those authors who claim that emigration has reduced unemployment to almost zero per cent in Greece (Papademetriou, 1978) and Jordan (Kirwan, 1981) were referring to general labour migration rather than brain drain per se. POPINFO (1983), using data from World Bank studies, indicated that in Burkina Faso, Jordan and Yemen Arab Republic international remittances cover the cost of more than one-third of all imports and are equal to about 10 per cent of gross national product.

Few studies have been made of the use of remittances. Ghosh (1985: 360-361) reported that in certain villages in Kerala and Gujarat remittances were used to purchase consumption and durable goods and property, investment in securities, trade and business, including speculation. However, sustained growth had not been triggered by remittances. Moreover, very little money went into productive purposes. But according to Appleyard (personal communication), spending on consumption goods or investment is not necessarily the central issue. Instead, more attention should be given to assessing the impact of total payments on economic growth, to examining whether expenditure is made on foreign or locally-made goods, and evaluating the role and capacity of the national banking system to effectively "capture" and utilise funds remitted from abroad.

In her study of three agricultural communities in the Dominican Republic, Grasmuck (1984: 400) concluded that:

> [W]hile remittance payments made from abroad clearly aid selective families by raising th.ir standard of living, the net positive effects for the comm nities are questionable. Even in the case where potentially p sitive consequences were associated with emigration, the absence of any sort of local development has meant that migrants with investments were left to their own, often ill-informed, strategies.

Davis (1974) has argued that reliance on remittances is illusory in that they are subject to stoppage or control, especially in times of crisis.

Migration is a selective process confined mainly to persons of certain ages, occupations and education. Skilled manpower is needed to run the wheels of industry and to co-ordinate development efforts of the economy. Emigration creates vacancies where there should be none, and although the situation may not be critical in all sectors of the economy, it can lead to continuous dependence of developing countries on developed countries for manpower requirements.

It is generally accepted that brain drain creates shortages in skilled positions. For example, statistics from UNESCO (1980) indicate that Africa has shortages of medical, scientific and technical manpower and some countries rely on expatriate manpower. In some countries 60 per cent of persons in scientific and technical positions are not indigenous people. In addition, emigration has created shortages in less-skilled jobs, such as construction, public utilities and agriculture in Bangladesh (Ali et al., 1981) and Greece (Papademetriou, 1979).

Possible Solutions to the Brain Drain

Four measures to prevent trained workers in developing countries from migrating to developed countries have been articulated, namely: preventive measures, restrictive measures, restorative measures and compensatory measures. These are not necessarily mutually exclusive.

Preventive measures

By accelerating economic development and creating a conducive economic, political and social environment, developing countries could reduce the outflow of their nationals to developed countries. For instance, making facilities, equipment and incentives available to professionals could help solve the problem. Once in responsible positions, professionals should also be given decision-making power. Keeping in touch with nationals abroad and reducing the time lag between graduation and employment should be encouraged. Attractive salaries and good working conditions must also be provided if nationals are to be retained in the country of origin (Watanabe, 1969; Baldwin, 1970; Zahlan, 1977).

Restrictive measures

Immigration and emigration policies have been tightened since the early 1970s. Restrictive measures call for even tighter rules and regulations against the loss of highly-trained and skilled migrants from developing countries. Developed countries should be encouraged to eliminate or amend immigration laws and regulations that have the effect of encouraging the entry of professionals and other qualified manpower (Bohning, 1977: 315-316). However, it is recognised that restrictive measures are difficult to enforce and may also deny professionals and others the "cross-fertilization" of ideas that can only occur through constant contact with more developed centres of study. In the past, they have posed more difficulties than solutions (Bhagwati, 1976a: 720).

Restorative measures

Some authors argue that if developed countries are interested in the development of poor nations, they should encourage temporary rather than permanent settlement. Such a proposal would be costly because it would mean monitoring the movements of citizens from developing countries. It has also been suggested that developed countries should replace, through technical assistance, professionals whom they receive from developing countries. But how long could such an arrangement last? What countries would be interested in it? Would this not only perpetuate the same problem of dependence of developing countries on developed countries?

Compensatory measures

Some authors argue that if a developed country accepts immigrants from a developing country, it should repay the costs that the latter incurred in training and educating the migrants (Bhagwati, 1976b: 10). The developed country should be taxed and a fund created for use on developmental projects in the sending country. Stahl (1987) argues that since the expenditures would have been made in the past, they should be considered historical or sunk costs. Alternatively, an increase in aid and services should be made and/or the migrant required to pay a fee at the port of exit, although it is recognised that compensatory measures pose conceptual and statistical problems which would make their implementation difficult. However, taxing the brain drain may not be appropriate because by so doing it would be assumed that everyone emigrates for economic reasons. Immigration may arise from political and personal problems (Bohning, 1982).

CONCLUSION

The impact of brain drain migration on developing countries appears to be mainly negative in that they lose young, energetic, and well-trained workers. The net effect has been perpetual postponement of major development efforts because of manpower shortages and continuous dependence on expatriate manpower which has a high turnover. Nor is there sufficient evidence to suggest that brain drain and brain overflow coexist. In terms of preventing manpower drain, preventive measures appear to be more appropriate because they encourage improvement in economic and political conditions in developing countries.

The general conclusion that brain drain involves the flows of labour in one direction and flows of money in the opposite direction (POPINFO, 1983) is misleading. A neat two-way process does not exist in brain drain movements. For the brain drain to be beneficial, a two-way process must exist. Most developing countries have to import labour in order to fill the positions left vacant by emigrants. They also import even less skilled labour. For instance, Malaysia imports Indonesian labour to work in agriculture and construction employment in order to replace Malaysians who have migrated to Singapore and the Middle East (Lim quoted in POPINFO, 1983: M-264).

Note: Research Priorities

One of the most important deficiencies concerning studies on the brain drain are data on shortages of highly-trained personnel in given countries. Most of the data available relate to general immigration statistics or to samples of students residing in receiving countries. Much as these data are helpful in understanding certain aspects of the brain drain problem, they do not show scarcities.

Data on the situations of migrants before departure could be helpful in understanding the causes and impacts of brain drain on specific sending countries. It is often assumed that the migrants were unemployed whereas many leave important positions that remain unfilled or filled by inexperienced, less-educated replacements.

Data on the proportion of immigrants to graduates in countries of origin would assist in assessing manpower shortages.

Another important deficiency relates to data on remittances, especially on the contributions by professionals and other highly-trained persons.

BIBLIOGRAPHY

ADAMS, W., ed.
The Brain Drain, New York, Macmillan Company, 1968.

AGARWAL, V.B. and D.R. WINKLER
"Migration of Professional Manpower to the United States", Southern Economic Journal, Vol. 50, No. 3, 1984.

ALI, S.A. et al.
Labor Migration from Bangladesh to the Middle East, Washington, D.C., World Bank Staff Working Paper No. 454, 1981.

AMUZEGAR, J.
"Brain Drain and the Irony of Foreign Aid Policy", Economia Internazionale, Vol. 21, No. 4, 1968.

APPLEYARD, R.T.
"International Migration in a Changing World", International Migration, Vol. XXII, No. 3, 1984.

ARDITTIS, S.
The Assisted Return of Qualified Migrants to their Countries of Origin: The UNDP and ICM Multilateral Programmes, Geneva, ILO, International Migration for Employment, Working Paper, 1985.

BALDWIN, G.B.
"Brain Drain or Overflow?", Foreign Affairs, Vol. 48, No. 2, 1970.

BHAGWATI, J.N.
"The Brain Drain", International Social Science Journal, Vol. XXVIII, No. 4, 1976a.

"The International Brain Drain and Taxation: A Survey of Issues" in J.N. Bhagwati, ed., The Brain Drain and Taxation: Theory and Empirical Evidence, II, Amsterdam, North-Holland Publishing Company, 1976b.

"The Brain Drain, Compensation and Taxation", Economic and Demographic Change: Issues for the 1980s. Proceedings of the Conference, Helsinki, Finland, 1978, Vol. 3, Liege, International Union for Scientific Study of Population, 1979.

BHAGWATI, J.N. and K. HAMADA
"The Brain Drain: International Integration of Markets for Professionals and Unemployment: A Theoretical Analysis", Journal of Development Economics, Vol. 1, No. 1, 1974

BOHNING, W.R.
"The Migration of Workers from Poor to Rich Countries: Facts, Problems, Policies", International Population Conference, Mexico 1977, Vol. 2, Liege, International Union for the Scientific Study of Population, 1977.

"The Idea of Compensation in International Migration", Population and Development in the Middle East, Baghdad, United Nations Economic Commission for Western Asia, 1982.

BOUVIER, L.F., H.S. SHRYOCK and H.W. HENDERSON
"International Migration: Yesterday, Today, and Tomorrow", Population Bulletin, Vol. 32, No. 4, 1977.

DAS, M.S.
"Brain Drain Controversy and African Scholars", Studies in Comparative International Development, Vol. 9, No. 1, 1974.

DAVIS, K.
"The Migrations of Human Populations", Scientific American, 132, 1974.

DeVORETZ, D. and D. MAKI
"The Size and Distribution of Human Capital Transfers from LDCs to Canada: 1966-1973", Economic Development and Cultural Change, Vol. 28, No. 4, 1980.

ECEVIT, Z.H.
"International Labor Migration in the Middle East and North Africa: Trends, Effects and Policies" in M.M. Kritz, C.B. Keely and S.M. Tomasi, eds., Global Trends in Migration: Theory and Research on International Population Movements, Staten Island, Centre for Migration Studies of New York, 1981.

ECEVIT, Z.H. and K.C. ZACHARIAH
"International Labour Migration", Finance and Development, Vol. 15, No. 4, 1978.

ECONOMIC COMMISSION FOR AFRICA
International Migration in Africa: Past, Present and Future Prospects, Addis Ababa, Population Division, 1981.

GHOSH, B.N.
"Brain Migration from Third World: An Implicative Analysis", Rivista Internazionale di Scienze Economiche e Commerciali, Vol. 34, No. 1, 1985.

GLASER, W.A.
The Brain Drain: Emigration and Return, Oxford, Pergamon Press, a United Nations Institute for Training and Research Study Report, No. 22, 1978.

GRASMUCK, S.
"Impact of Emigration on National Development: Three Sending Communities in the Dominican Republic", Development and Change, Vol. 15, No. 3, 1984.

GRUBEL, H.G. and A. SCOTT
   The Brain Drain: Determinants, Measurement and Welfare Effects,
   Waterloo, Wilfrid Laurier University Press, 1977.

ICM (Intergovernmental Committee for Migration)
   Evaluation Report on the Implementation of the Project "Reintegration
   of Qualified African Nationals", Seminar on Reintegration of Qualified
   African Nationals, Nairobi, 1st-4th December 1986, ICM Information
   Paper No. 2, 1986a.

   ICM Activities in Latin America, Geneva, Intergovernmental Committee
   for Migration, 1986b.

JOHNSON, H.G.
   "Some Economic Aspects of Brain Drain", Pakistan Development Review 7,
   1967.

KANNAPPAN, S.
   "The Brain Drain and Developing Countries", International Labour
   Review, Vol. 98, No. 1, 1968.

KIRWAN, F.X.
   "The Impact of Labor Migration on the Jordanian Economy", International Migration Review, Vol. 15, No. 4, 1981.

McKEE, D.L.
   "Some Specifics on the Brain Drain from the Andean Region", International Migration, Vol. 21, No. 4, 1983a.

   "Some Specifics on the Loss of Professional Personnel from the Commonwealth Caribbean", Inter-American Economic Affairs, Vol. 37, No. 3,
   1983b.

MUNDENDE, D.C.
   African Immigration to Canada Since World War II, unpublished
   M.A. Thesis, Department of Geography, Edmonton, University of Alberta,
   1982.

MYERS, R.G.
   "'Brain Drains' and 'Brain Gains'", International Development Review,
   Vol. IX, No. 4, 1967.

MYINT, H.
   "The Underdeveloped Countries: A Less Alarmist View" in W. Adams, ed.,
   The Brain Drain, New York, Macmillan, 1968.

OECD (Organisation for Economic Co-operation and Development)
   Migration, Growth and Development, Paris, OECD, 1979a.

   "Economic Consequences of Migration from North Africa to France",
   Development Digest, Vol. 17, No. 4, 1979b.

PAPADEMETRIOU, D.
   "Greece" in R.E. Krane, ed., International Labor Migration in Europe,
   New York, Praeger, 1979.

POPCON (International Conference on Population)
Population Distribution, Migration and Development, New York, Department of International Economic and Social Affairs, 1984.

POPINFO (Population Information Program)
"Migration, Population Growth, and Development", Population Reports, Series M, No. 7 XI (4), Special Topics, 1983.

ROMANS, J.T.
"Benefits and Burdens of Migration (with Special Reference to the Brain Drain)", Southern Economic Journal, Vol. 40, No. 3, 1974.

SABOT, R.H., L. TAYLOR and Y. BOUTROS-GHALI
Labor Force Growth, Employment and Earnings in Egypt: 1966-1986, Washington, D.C., World Bank, 1981.

SALT, J. and A. FINDLAY
"International Migration of Highly Skilled Manpower: Theoretical and Developmental Issues", paper presented at the Migration and Development Seminar organised jointly by the OECD Development Centre, ICM and CICRED, Paris, 17th-19th February 1987.

SHARMA, G.D.
"Brain Drain Controversy: A Survey", Mainstream, Vol. XV, No. 11, 1976.

STAHL, C.W.
"Labor Emigration and Economic Development", International Migration Review, Vol. 16, No. 4, 1982.

"Economic Perspectives on the Consequence of International Migration for Third World Development", paper presented at the Migration and Development Seminar organised jointly by the OECD Development Centre, ICM and CICRED, Paris, 17th-19th February 1987.

UN (United Nations)
The Brain Drain from Five Developing Countries, New York, United Nations Institute for Training and Research Study Report No. 5, 1971.

The Determinants and Consequences of Population Trends, Vol. 1, New York, Population Division Studies No. 50, 1973.

UNESCO (United Nations Educational, Scientific, and Cultural Organisation)
Statistical Yearbook, 1980, London, UNESCO, 1980.

"Brain Drain or the Migration of Talent and Skills" in International Conference on Population, Population Distribution, Migration and Development, New York, Department of International Economic and Social Affairs, 1984.

WARD, A.
"European Migratory Labour: A Myth of Development", Monthly Review, Vol. 27, No. 7, 1975.

WATANABE, S.
"The Brain Drain from Developing to Developed Countries", _International Labour Review,_ Vol. 99, No. 4, 1969.

ZAHLAN, A.B.
"The Brain Drain Controversy" in _International Population Conference, Mexico 1977, Vol. 2,_ Liege, International Union for the Scientific Study of Population, 1977.

Chapter 12

THE BRAIN DRAIN ISSUE IN INTERNATIONAL NEGOTIATIONS

by

J. d'Oliveira e Sousa (1)

INTRODUCTION

The movement of human beings endowed with specific skills and knowledge across national boundaries has been an abiding phenomenon in history. Skilled migrants have not only contributed to increased output and welfare in recipient countries, but in some cases have reshaped the latter's cultural and economic environments. Such migrants have also occasionally been important agents of technological change and transformation (2).

Such a contribution to the welfare of the recipient country has often been met with a sense of loss by the country of origin. Indeed, as early as A.D. 150, Atheneus complained about "the drain of Greek brains to Alexandria" (Dedijer, 1968), although it was not until 1962 that the term "brain drain" was coined in a report by the British Royal Society in reference to the outflow of engineers, scientists and technicians from Britain to North America. Since then, the term has been widely used, particularly in connection with the migration of skilled manpower from developing to developed countries.

The UNCTAD III Conference in Santiago de Chile in 1972, in requesting the Secretary-General of UNCTAD to initiate work on "brain drain", referred to it as a "reverse transfer of technology". The new terminology added a conceptual dimension by shifting emphasis from loss of "brains" to the resource content of skill flows. The term implies that skilled migrants, who embody capital and knowledge, constitute a transfer of resources and technology in the reverse direction, i.e., from those countries that are usually technology recipients to those that are predominant technology suppliers (Papademetriou, 1984).

Reverse transfer of technology, or brain drain, is a complex and multifaceted phenomenon which can be approached from many angles. Because it involves mobility of human beings and freedom of choice to pursue their welfare, it cannot fail to raise philosophical, ideological and human rights issues. A vast literature on the subject deals mainly with economic, statistical, demographic, humanitarian and social aspects.

The numbers and specific skills of persons moving across national borders are determined largely by the policies of recipient countries. The brain drain not only requires decisions and choices by individuals who migrate, including their assessment of costs and benefits incurred or expected from their movement, but it also has an impact on both recipient and sending countries.

This chapter attempts to show how the brain drain issue and its impact on developing countries have been dealt with in international negotiations. The first part deals with the rise of international concern since the early 1960s and provides data on gross flows of skilled migrants from developing to selected receiving developed countries during the last quarter of a century. The second part examines several policy proposals made in the course of international debates in different fora. The third part reviews recent attempts by the international community to reach agreement on an integrated approach to the reverse transfer of technology.

The Rise of International Concern

Significant numbers of skilled persons have emigrated from developing to several industrialised countries since the early 1960s. Table 12.1 shows that about 700 000 scientists, engineers, doctors, professors and other highly-skilled persons emigrated from developing countries to three countries for which data are available for the period 1961-83. Had appropriate statistics been available for other countries, gross flows of skilled migrants from developing to receiving developed countries would have exceeded 1 million during the last quarter of a century.

Although there has been a declining trend since the mid-1970s, the share of skilled migrants from developing countries in total skilled immigration to the United States and Canada has increased steadily during this period. For the United States, the percentage rose from 37 per cent for the period 1961-65 to 77 per cent for 1971-83. A similar trend occurred in Canada: 20 per cent for the period 1961-65 to around 30 per cent for 1971-79.

The determinants and destinations of brain drain migration are attributed to both "push" and "pull" factors:

Those flows reflected the relatively high rates of economic growth in the industrialized countries concerned; the inadequacy of output of their own professionals; the consequently selective nature of their immigration regulations, biased in favour of admitting those with skills; and the very high rate at which the output of Third World graduates and professionals were expanding. (Godfrey, 1976.)

While the causes of the phenomenon seem to be well understood and relatively widely accepted, divergent views have been expressed in academic circles concerning the impact of such migration on both receiving and sending countries. Neo-classical welfare economists of the "internationalist" school see the international circulation of human capital based on free choice as

Table 12.1

SKILLED MIGRATION FROM DEVELOPING COUNTRIES TO THE UNITED STATES,
CANADA AND THE UNITED KINGDOM
Gross flows

Year	Number of skilled migrants from developing countries to:				Share of developing countries in total skilled immigration (percentage)		
	United States	Canada	United Kingdom	Total	United States	Canada	United Kingdom
	(1)	(2)	(3)	(4)	(5)	(6)	(7)
1961-65	9 655 (a)	2 049 (b)	10 205 (c)	21 909	37	20	26
1966	13 941	5 930	10 812	30 683	46	23	26
1967	23 061	8 614	8 156	39 831	55	25	21
1968	28 263	7 489	9 418	45 170	58	24	23
1969	27 437	8 286	9 932	45 655	68	28	22
1970	33 684	6 867	8 635	49 186	73	27	19
1971	38 448	6 195	7 843	52 486	79	31	18
1972	38 963	7 070	8 833	54 866	80	36	19
1973	31 882	6 180	--	38 062 (d)	77	25	17
1974	27 719	7 631	--	35 350 (d)	78	27	15
1975	29 830	6 362	--	36 192 (d)	77	25	14
1976	31 588	4 842	--	36 430 (d)	77	24	--
1977	34 537	--	--	34 537 (e)	77	--	--
1978	37 737	--	--	37 737 (e)	77	--	--
1979	29 561	3 273	--	32 834 (d)	75	38	--
1980	--	--	--	--	--	--	--
1981	--	--	--	--	--	--	--
1982	34 636	--	--	34 636	77	--	--
1983	30 212	--	--	30 212	77	--	--

a) Average for 1961-65.
b) Average for 1963-65 only.
c) Average for 1964-65 only.
d) Canada and the United States only.
e) United States only.

Source: UNCTAD Statistical Pocket Book, New York, 1984 (United Nations Sales No. E.84.II.D.20). Estimates for the United States in 1982 and 1983 were made by the author on the basis of data provided by the Statistical Yearbook of the Immigration and Naturalization Service of the United States of America, 1982 and 1983.

resulting in optimisation of individuals' productivity and therefore of overall welfare. Johnson (1968) argued that "in the absence of any pervasive evidence to the contrary ... there is no significant probability of world loss from the international migration of educated people". The "nationalist" school represented by Grubel and Scott (1977) begins from different premises, but reaches similar conclusions: that if nations aim at maximising income per head, emigration should cause no loss if the income of the individual migrant increases and if the income of those left behind does not decrease by the fact of migration.

The neo-classical approach in its "internationalist" and "nationalist" versions has been challenged by Bhagwati and Hamada on grounds that it dealt with the response of individuals to a number of variables without taking adequate account of the structures within which individual decisions were made and of the relevant interdependence and dynamic effects.

In fact, choices and decisions made by individuals to optimise their welfare may be at variance with the objectives and interests of society as a whole. This applies with particular relevance to long-term or permanent migration and to skilled rather than to unskilled emigrants. In the case of the former:

> The long-term losses generated by their emigration would be even more pronounced. First, insofar as they serve as vehicles for the dissemination of skills and technical knowledge, their emigration would reduce the rate of human capital. Thus, not only are the skills lost in the short run, but long-term skill formation may be stifled. Second, insofar as their savings are higher than the per capita average, investment per capita will decline with detrimental consequences for income growth. Third, although their departure initially reduces the size of the population, if their rate of family formation was less than average, the rate of population growth will rise. In the longer term, this implies, for a given rate of investment, a decline in capital per worker and hence productivity and income per capita. Fourth, as higher than average income earners, the permanent emigrants may have paid a level of taxes higher than their consumption of public goods. Fifth, insofar as permanent emigration causes skill bottlenecks, the economy's capacity to respond to growth-promoting stimuli is reduced while the risk of inflation and balance of payments problems associated with any stimulus are enlarged concomitantly. (Stahl, 1982).

By the mid 1960s, the impact of the brain drain on development was being discussed in international fora. Its initial consideration in the General Assembly and the Economic and Social Council was related to the need for training national technical personnel for the accelerated industrialisation of developing countries. Delegates thought it contradictory that while developing countries badly needed qualified human resources for their development, significant numbers of their most dynamic and trained personnel were migrating to industrialised countries. General Assembly resolution 2259 (XXII) of 1967 took account of "the importance of considering the problem of the drain of such personnel at all levels from the developing countries" and in its resolution 2350 (XXII) decided "to keep the subject under constant review".

It soon became clear that the brain drain was a symptom of imbalances in the international economic system and of the technological gap between developing and developed countries. In its resolution 2417 (XXIII) of 1968, the General Assembly requested the Secretary-General to "formulate suggestions for ways of tackling the problems arising from the outflow of trained personnel at all levels from developing to developed countries within the framework of the proposed strategy for development of the Second United Nations Development Decade". In spite of this specific request, no reference to it was made in General Assembly resolution 2626 (XXV) of 1970 containing the Strategy for the Second United Nations Development Decade. It was not until a decade later that the brain drain issue was incorporated in the text of the Strategy for the Third United Nations Development Decade (paragraph 123 of General Assembly resolution 35/56 of 1980). This outcome reflected efforts by the international community to better understand the phenomenon and its impact on developing countries as well as to reach agreement on appropriate policies to deal with its effects.

The Negotiating Setting: Diagnosis and Proposals

If the late 1960s set the stage for intergovernmental consideration of the brain drain, the 1970s witnessed an intensification of the debate in a great variety of fora. While specific aspects of the phenomenon have been discussed at specialised fora, impact at the systems level has been discussed in general assemblies. For example, the World Population Conference held in Bucharest in 1974 debated the implications of international migration, particularly of skilled migration from developing to developed countries, for economic development. In paragraph 51 of its Plan of Action, the Conference recommended that while governments and international organisations should facilitate voluntary international movement, paragraph 57 warned that:

> Since the outflow of qualified personnel from developing to developed countries seriously hampers the development of the former, there is an urgent need to formulate national and international policies to avoid the "brain drain" and to obviate its adverse effects, including the possibility of devising programmes for large-scale communication of appropriate technological knowledge mainly from developed countries to the extent that it can be properly adjusted and appropriately absorbed.

Consideration of reverse transfer of technology was also initiated at UNCTAD during the 1970s. Consideration moved from diagnosis to proposals from three sessions of the Conference itself and a first meeting of governmental experts on reverse transfer of technology (February/March 1978). The International Labour Office also addressed the problem in the context of migration for employment; UNESCO and UNITAR have supported diagnostic studies. One UNESCO study (1971) concentrated on the movement of scientists and UNITAR supported research on both country studies and the motives of individuals who comprise the brain drain (Henderson, 1970; Glaser, 1978). The World Health Organisation has conducted studies on the impact on developing countries of the migration of doctors and nurses to developed countries (Magia, Pizurki and Royston, 1979), and the Plan of Action prepared at the United Nations Conference on Science and Technology for Development at Vienna in 1979 referred to reverse transfer of technology in connection with the mobilisation of human and financial resources for the technological development of developing countries.

Finally, the Third United Nations International Development Strategy declared that:

> Concerted efforts will be made by the international community early in the Decade to take comprehensive and effective action, as recommended by the United Nations Conference on Trade and Development at its fifth session, at the national, regional and international levels, aimed at minimizing the negative impact of the migration of skilled personnel so that such migration from developing countries will constitute an exchange in which the interests of all parties concerned are adequately pro- tected. The international community should consider examining, early in the Decade, in the light of relevant United Nations decisions, arrangements whereby developing countries experienc- ing large-scale outflows of their skilled nationals which cause economic disruption could secure assistance in dealing with the adjustment problems arising therefrom. (General Assembly resolution 35/36, Annex.)

The concepts embodied in this strategy, namely "comprehensive" action on reverse transfer of technology, and "assistance" to developing countries suffering from the brain drain, had been fashioned during a decade of dis- cussions on both losses and gains from the brain drain and on proposals that receiving countries should compensate sending countries for the losses that they had incurred.

Losses and gains

A study prepared by the Secretary-General of the United Nations, in response to General Assembly resolution 3017 (XXVII) of 1972, reviewed the main causes and identified the most significant effects of the brain drain in both sending and receiving countries (United Nations, 1972). It argued that "one obvious category of loss for developing countries pertains to the financial cost which has already been incurred in educating the migrants", and emphasized that "the financial loss is only the visible tip of the iceberg since the effects upon the process of development are as important, if not more so". The study also indicated that several skill-receiving countries had obtained "large benefits from the immigration of trained persons from the developing countries. These gains consist of: (a) what the developed countries would have to spend to train people if the immigrants were not available; (b) the goods produced or services rendered by them minus goods and services consumed by them; and (c) the vitality and breadth of the research contribution made by them".

The gains accruing to developed countries were of three types: "oppor- tunity costs" or savings in investment for training domestic skills required in the absence of migration; net increase in national output; and the effect of "reverse transfer of technology". Although the study was very restrained in its calculation of losses and gains, regarding health personnel it con- cluded that "the total gain for major receiving countries should be considered as being in hundreds of millions of dollars".

However, a study by the Congressional Research Service of the United States House of Representatives (1974) was less cautious in its conclusions. In addition to providing a very well-documented historical review, the study attempted to estimate both the losses incurred by developing countries and the gains obtained by the United States from the migration of skilled manpower during fiscal years 1971 and 1972. Using data provided by the National Science Foundation, it calculated that on the basis of average educational costs per skilled migrant being US$20 000, developing countries had lost some US$646 million for the biennium. Concerning opportunity costs saved by the United States, it estimated US$1 718 million for the biennium 1971-72. In Canada, DeVoretz and Maki (1980) concluded that the replacement value of the transferred human capital from developing countries between 1967-73 ranged from C$ 1 billion to C$ 2.4 billion at 1968 prices.

Since the passing of resolution 32/192 of 1977 by the General Assembly, "that the development process of developing countries, particularly their capacity to strengthen their domestic technological potential, is crucially dependent on the supply of highly trained personnel, and that the outflow of such personnel represents a significant loss to these countries", several proposals have been made concerning redistribution of benefits accruing to countries of immigration. At the sixty-ninth session of the International Labour Conference in 1983, Mr. Hozin Mubarak, President of the Arab Republic of Egypt, proposed the establishment of an International Fund for Vocational Training "to enable those countries which suffer manpower outflows to implement programmes for training substitute elements, thus filling the gap left behind by migration" (International Labour Conference, 1983). In his address to the Governing Council of UNDP in June 1984, the Rt. Hon. Edward Seaga, Prime Minister of Jamaica, indicated that his country had lost US$194 million in trained skilled migrants over the period 1977-80 and proposed the creation of an International Fund for Manpower Resources "to finance the recruitment of skilled manpower on a medium-term basis with whatever concessions may be affordable from the use of grants, operational projects or any other concessional resources available to the Fund".

Proposals

Proposals may be divided into three categories: compensatory schemes; taxation proposals; voluntary contributions. Compensation is based on the assumption that net benefits accrue to developed receiving countries from the immigration of skilled personnel from developing countries and these should revert to the countries of origin to offset the financial costs incurred by such migration. At the sixty-third International Labour Conference in June 1977, His Royal Highness Crown Prince Hassan bin Talal of Jordan proposed the establishment of an International Labour Compensatory Facility (ILCF) along the lines of the Trust Fund for Compensatory Facilities of the International Monetary Fund. "The proposed facility would draw its resources principally from labour-importing countries, but in a spirit of solidarity and goodwill, other ILO members may contribute to it. The accumulated resources would be diverted to developing labour-exporting countries in proportions relative to the estimated cost incurred due to a loss of labour." (International Labour Conference, 1977). While the proposed facility was designed to cover migration in general, it was especially applicable to the brain drain.

As a follow-up to the above proposal, a report was prepared by the Secretary-General of the United Nations at the request of the General Assembly and one study was prepared by the International Labour Office (Böhning, 1982). In his report to the thirty-fifth session of the General Assembly, the Secretary-General examined alternative compensatory schemes, outlined measures for international co-operation and concluded that "principally, the facility is expected to undertake efforts to continuously assess the dynamics of migration of trained and skilled personnel, collect and evaluate data on a uniform and consistent basis, evolve policy measures for consideration at national and international levels, assist in the implementation of steps to reduce the adverse effects of migration." (United Nations, n.d.).

In his final report on the subject to the thirty-sixth session of the General Assembly (document A/36/483), the Secretary-General examined alternative models for compensatory schemes in the light of views which had been expressed on the principles of compensation, the extent of resources and the scope of ultimate benefits that could be derived from such a facility, and suggested that in view of the complexity of the issue, it should be considered by a group of governmental experts. While no consensus has emerged, the proposal has remained at the centre of intergovernmental attention in the area of reverse transfer of technology (UNCTAD TD/B/AC.35/6). In 1979, the United Nations Conference on Science and Technology for Development specifically established a link between financing the technological development of developing countries and resources that may accrue from the proposed establishment of an international labour compensatory facility. Paragraph 113 of the Vienna Programme of Action on Science and Technology for Development agreed that the "financing system may enter into arrangements with international, regional and other public and private financial institutions with a view to the generation and channeling of additional resources to the developing countries for scientific and technological activities, including research and development, and the commercialization and acquisition of technology". Paragraph 115 specified that "additionally, the system may use other resources, such as ... (b) resources that may accrue from the proposed 'international labour compensatory facility' related to the reverse transfer of technology".

Taxation proposals

Taxation proposals are of two main types: revenue-sharing arrangements and the levying of taxes on the incomes of migrants. Under the former a portion of the income taxes paid by skilled migrants in the host country would be shared with the home country. Several modalities of revenue-sharing arrangements have been identified such as tax treaties, tax deductions and credits and direct assessment on host countries. A tax could either be levied by the developed country of residence (as originally proposed by Bhagwati) or the developing country of origin/citizenship. The rationale for the latter type according to Guhan (1978) is:

> That in a world of unequal educational opportunities and imperfect mobility, individuals who have had the opportunity to migrate could be reasonably required to share some part of the increased personal benefits accruing to them in order to improve welfare to those left behind in the poorer developing country of origin; accordingly, such a tax would be an

extension of the principle of progressive taxation to all nationals of the developing country, whether resident in or outside that country.

Such proposals have met with serious objections and reservations on the part of industrialised countries on grounds of discrimination and double taxation (UNCTAD, 1978).

Voluntary contributions

It has also been suggested that contributions could be made through international human resource funds (IHRFs). The legal basis of these organisations would vary according to their source of authority, but all would be non-profit and exempt from taxes on their receipts. IHRFs may contribute to general development, education purposes or be linked to specific development programmes designed to ameliorate factors causing the international migration of skilled personnel.

Towards an Integrated Approach to International Skill Exchange

The idea that brain drain problems should be resolved by a combination of measures at national, bilateral and multilateral levels was suggested in the report of the Secretary-General to the General Assembly (E/C.8/21). In addition to recommending specific action at national levels, the report argued that "bilateral and multilateral agreements between nations are one of the most efficient means of taking corrective action relevant to the outflow of trained personnel from developing to developed countries". It was also suggested that "the United Nations system could also play a role in evolving an internationally accepted code of conduct in the matter of migration of trained personnel from developing countries" (3).

It was not until 1978, however, that the spectrum of recommendations for national action and bilateral and multilateral proposals described above were considered by a group of governmental experts in Geneva under the auspices of UNCTAD. For the first time, the whole range of issues relating to the brain drain were considered. Sharp differences in approach were taken by experts from the industrialised countries of immigration and experts of developing countries. These related mainly to diagnosis of the causes of brain drain and the scope for national action, conceptual and empirical issues relating to the measurement of flows, and legal and humanitarian considerations related to policy proposals (4). In spite of the divergences, the Group of Governmental Experts reached important conclusions and made recommendations to governments of both developing and developed countries. The group also identified directions for future activity by governmental experts. One obstacle to implementing multilateral policy proposals had been lack of methodological and empirical tools for measuring the skill flows. The group therefore concluded, inter alia, that "in view of the inadequacy of statistical data and differences in views, further work by the United Nations system, in a co-ordinated manner, on international resource flow accounting at an expert level should be directed towards clarifying the methodological aspects of the concepts and procedures to be developed for its practical application".

How can brain drain be measured?

An Intergovernmental Group of Experts on the Feasibility of Measuring Human Resource Flows met in Geneva between 30th August and 6th September 1982 under the auspices of UNCTAD and on the basis of documentation submitted by the Secretary-General of UNCTAD (1982). It considered the conceptual, methodological and empirical aspects of measuring international flows of human resources in general and of skilled personnel from developing countries in particular.

Two types of measurement were reviewed: problems relating to statistical measurement (numbers of migrants, professional categories, directions of flows) and the economic valuation of flows. Despite the important work done by the United Nations Statistical Commission and Statistical Office, data on such flows is scanty. It is collected systematically only by a few countries of immigration and in these cases lack of common processes and definitions make international comparability hazardous. Furthermore, data are lacking on return flows. UNCTAD suggested a number of ways for improving data collection and analysis.

Although economic valuation of skill flows is to some extent interdependent on availability of statistical data, it raises some complex problems of its own. From the outset, a distinction has to be made between "the value of the human capital embodied in the migrants and the value of the effect in welfare terms which this capital movement caused. The former measures only the value of what is transferred, while the latter is concerned with the economic, or even non-economic effects that the transfer produces in both countries involved" (UNCTAD, 1982). The study dealt only with the former aspect of measurement.

Alternative approaches and methodologies for imputing values to skill flows were reviewed, namely the "historic cost" approach and the "present discounted value" (PDV) approach (d'Oliveira e Sousa, 1985). According to the former, the migrant is seen as an asset whose value is estimated by accumulating the direct costs of education and the indirect costs (foregone earnings) incurred prior to migration. The procedure of estimating the historical costs becomes, in fact, an opportunity cost approach from the immigration country's point of view. In the PDV approach, the human capital embodied in the migrant is measured by projecting the present value of his productive capacity over his expected life span and discounting expected future earnings, year by year.

In spite of considerable efforts made by all parties concerned, it proved difficult to reach common agreed conclusions and recommendations among the regional groups. The Group of 77 and Group B presented separate conclusions and recommendations (UNCTAD, 1982a), and while the attempt by the Chairman to reconcile viewpoints was successful, agreement could not be reached concerning appropriate terms of reference for the following meeting of governmental experts. The position of the Group of 77 was that:

> The study submitted by the UNCTAD secretariat in document TD/B/C.6/AC.8/2 shows that the measurement of international human resource flows is conceptually and technically feasible; while there is always room for further diagnostic work, this should not delay consideration of policy-oriented action by the

international community at the national, regional and international levels ... The basis has now been laid to reach agreement on the relevant principles, measures, concepts, procedures and conventions required for the practical application of international resource flow accounting, and the consideration of policy-oriented measures at the national, regional and international levels. (Annex 1.)

Group B concluded that "the study submitted by the UNCTAD secretariat in document TD/B/C.6/AC.8/2 shows several alternative ways and methods for the measurement of international human resource flows". However, "further detailed study of the problem and of the requirements for realistic measurement of human resource flows is therefore required before any definitive decision on the issue could be taken." (Annex II.)

The need for an integrated programme of action on reverse transfer of technology

The above disagreement was reflected in General Assembly resolution 37/207 of December 1982, the first on this subject to be adopted by a roll call vote. Developing countries, socialist countries and China voted in favour. Group B, with the exception of Turkey, which voted in favour, and Greece, which abstained, voted against. The main point of contention was operative paragraph 5 which requested "the Secretary-General of the United Nations Conference on Trade and Development to convene the requisite meetings of governmental experts ... to formulate recommendations on policies and concrete measures, with a view to mitigating the adverse consequences for the developing countries of the reverse transfer of technology, including the proposal for the establishment of an international labour compensatory facility".

Pursuant to the above General Assembly resolution and to General Assembly resolutions 38/154 and 39/211, three meetings of governmental experts on reverse transfer of technology were held in 1983, 1984 and 1985 under the auspices of UNCTAD. Countries of Group B, with the exception of Turkey (which participated actively) and Finland, Norway and Sweden, did not participate in the meetings.

From the first meeting it was clear to governmental experts that the problem of reverse transfer of technology is so complex and multifaceted that it had to be tackled in an integrated fashion, i.e., by relating policy formulation to data treatment and the refinement of measurement techniques (UNCTAD, TD/B/AC.35/2). The experts also realised that some of the difficulties encountered in discussions on the feasibility of measuring brain drain were not solely of a technical nature but related to lack of common standards, definitions and principles. The experts finally concluded that in view of the problem's complexity, policy action would have to be formulated at different levels. Regarding multilateral proposals, long-term solutions to the brain drain had to be sought in a blending of different proposals and implemented in a flexible way (UNCTAD, TD/B/1973-TD/B/AC.35/14).

Several important results were achieved at the Third Meeting of Governmental Experts in 1985. First, a preliminary set of guidelines on all aspects of the reverse transfer of technology were identified and formulated; these could be the basis for future discussion (UNCTAD, TD/B/AC.35/12 and Corr. 1).

Second, a questionnaire on quantitative and qualitative aspects of the reverse transfer of technology was formulated (UNCTAD, TD/B/AC.35/13). The experts recommended that the results should be key components of an integrated programme of action.

Constructive results achieved at the three meetings were instrumental in setting the stage for consensus on the future agenda for international negotiations on brain drain. At the fortieth session of the General Assembly, resolution 40/191, premised on the belief that outflow of skilled personnel from developing countries seriously hampers their development, declared an urgent need to formulate national and international policies to avoid the brain drain and to obviate its adverse effects. The Secretary-General of the United Nations Conference on Trade and Development was requested to convene a meeting of governmental experts:

> To review the current situation with respect to all aspects of the international migration of skilled personnel from developing countries; the governmental experts should focus, in their study, on the nature, scale and effect of such flows taking into account the concern of all parties, with a view to proposing to the Conference and, as appropriate, other international organizations, further work that they may carry out to mitigate adverse consequences of this phenomenon, especially as it affects the developing countries, also taking into account, as appropriate, the work done thus far by governmental expert groups, and any other relevant material.

The above resolution, adopted by 124 votes to one, was seen as a significant step towards consensus on appropriate ways of dealing with the problem. Terms of reference of the next meeting (tentatively scheduled for 1987) reflect growing recognition that the brain drain needs to be tackled in "all its aspects" in order to permit adequate policy formulation at different levels.

CONCLUSION

During the last twenty years the brain drain issue has figured prominently in international negotiations on development questions. Because of its complexity and the implications of control on the freedom of individuals, international agreement regarding appropriate action to mitigate negative consequences for developing countries has been difficult to achieve. In particular, serious reservations have been expressed by some developed countries concerning redistribution schemes such as the International Labour Compensatory Facility.

However, systematic consideration of the subject in different fora has permitted identification of linkages between the brain drain and such related issues as population, economic development, employment, human rights, science and technology and health. Complex technical, conceptual and methodological aspects of the phenomenon, including the tools for its measurement, have also been explored. Intensive multilateral negotiations have led to better understanding and hence a more balanced and integrated approach to development aspects of brain drain. The great challenge is to find appropriate solutions for mitigating the negative effects of brain drain for developing countries which take into account the interests of all parties involved as well as the basic right of human beings to move freely.

NOTES AND REFERENCES

1. The author is a member of the UNCTAD secretariat. The views expressed in this article are his own and not necessarily those of the UNCTAD secretariat.

2. "For example, the geographical transfer of textile technology, like that of printing and publishing, is alleged to have been accomplished by the flight of specialists. That these two industries are believed to have expanded and shifted in this way is important for general economic history, for they are usually said to be among the leaders, or even harbingers of general economic growth." (Grubel and Scott, 1977.)

3. More recently, J. Bhagwati argued for the adoption of a "Code of Conduct on International Migration" to regulate the flow of migrants, which he sees as a "major issue in the management of the world economy". (New Haven Register, Tuesday, 1st March 1983.)

4. The spokesman for Group B stated, inter alia, that the "accounting of brain drain flows was very complex and raised several very difficult conceptual and practical problems. It was, therefore, premature to use estimates of the type presented by the UNCTAD secretariat in order to explain the magnitude and economic impact of the brain drain" (TD/B/C.6/28-TD/B/C.6/AC.4/10, p. 7). The Group of 77 was "of the view that measures for a better sharing of gains and losses associated with the brain drain, on the basis of reciprocity, should help to improve the chances of developing countries to augment their skilled personnel" (idem., p. 10).

BIBLIOGRAPHY

BHAGWATI, J.N.
The Reverse Transfer of Technology (Brain Drain): International
Resource Flow Accounting, Compensation, Taxation and Related Policy
Proposals, UNCTAD, (TD/B/C.6/AC.4/2).

BOHNING, R.
Towards a System of Recompense for International Labour Migration,
International Migration for Employment Working Paper, Geneva, ILO,
mimeo., restricted, February 1982.

DEDIJER, Steven
"Early Migration", in W. Adams, ed., The Brain Drain, New York,
Macmillan, 1968.

d'OLIVEIRA e SOUSA, J.
"The Measurement of Human Resource Flows: Methodology and Approach",
Trade and Development -- An UNCTAD Review, No. 6, 1985.

DeVORETZ, D. and D. MAKI
"The Size and Distribution of Human Capital Transfers from LDCs to
Canada: 1966-1973", Economic Development and Cultural Change, 1980.

GLASER, W.
"The Brain Drain: Emigration and Return", (UNITAR/RR/22), 1978.

GODFREY, Martin
The Outflow of Trained Personnel from Developing Countries. "Brain
Drain": The Disengagement Alternative, E.CN.5/L.421, 12th November
1976.

GRUBEL, Herbert G. and Anthony SCOTT
The Brain Drain. Determinants, Measurement and Welfare Effects,
Ontario, Canada, Wilfried Laurier University Press, 1977.

GUHAN, S.
Migrant Labour and Brain Drain, Secretariat Paper No. 8, prepared for
the Fourth Meeting (25th-28th August 1978) of the Independent Commission on International Development Issues.

HENDERSON, G.
"Emigration of Highly Skilled Manpower from Developing Countries",
(UNITAR/RR/3), 1970.

INTERNATIONAL LABOUR CONFERENCE
Provisional Record, Sixty-ninth session, Geneva, 1983.

Record of Proceedings, Sixty-third session, Fourteenth special sitting,
ILO, Geneva, 1977.

JOHNSON, Harry G.
"An 'Internationalist' Model", in W. Adams, ed., The Brain Drain, New
York, Macmillan, 1968.

MAGIA, H., H. PIZURKI and R. ROYSTON
Physician and Nurse Migration -- Analysis of Policy Implications,
Geneva, WHO, 1979.

PAPADEMETRIOU, Demetrios G.
"International Migration in a Changing World", in International Social
Science Journal on Migration: World Trends, Localised Flows and Their
Absorption, Vol. XXXVI, No. 3, UNESCO, 1984.

POMP, Richard and Oliver OLDHAM
The Reverse Transfer of Technology (Brain Drain): Legal and Adminis-
trative Aspects of Compensation, Taxation and Related Policy Measures:
Suggestions for an Optimal Policy Mix, UNCTAD, (TD/B/C.6/AC.4/7).

SEAGA, Rt. Hon. Edward
"Towards an International Fund for Manpower Resources", an address to
the Governing Council of UNDP, Geneva, 12th June 1984.

STAHL, Charles W.
"Labour Emigration and Economic Development", International Migration
Review, Special Issue, International Migration and Development, Centre
for Migration Studies, Staten Island, N.Y., Vol. 16, Winter 1982.

UNCTAD
Possible Elements for a Questionnaire on Quantitative and Qualitative
Information on the Reverse Transfer of Technology, (TD/B/AC.35/13).

Preliminary Outline of a Set of Guidelines on the Reverse Transfer of
Technology, (TD/B/AC.35/12 and Corr. 1).

Proposals and Concrete Measures to Mitigate the Adverse Impact of
Reverse Transfer of Technology on Developing Countries, (TD/B/AC.35/6).

Report of the Group of Government Experts on Reverse Transfer of Technology, Geneva, (TD/B/C.6/28), February/March 1978.

Report of the Intergovernmental Group of Experts on the Feasibility of
Measuring Human Resource Flows, Geneva, 30th August-6th September 1982,
(TD/B/C.6/28-TD/B/C.6/AC.8/3, Annexes I and II), 1982a.

Report of the Third Meeting of Government Experts on the Reverse Transfer of Technology, held at Geneva, 20th August-4th September 1985
(TD/B/1973-TD/B/AC.35/14).

The Feasibility of Measuring International Flows of Human Resources, (TD/B/C.6/AC.8/2), 1982.

Towards an Integrated Approach to International Skill Exchange: Proposals for Policy and Action on Reverse Transfer of Technology, (TD/B/AC.35/2).

UNESCO
Scientists Abroad, Paris, 1971.

UNITED NATIONS
Economic and Social Council, Outflow of Trained Personnel from Developing to Developed Countries, Report by the Secretary-General, (E/C.8/21), 1972.

Establishment of an International Labour Compensatory Facility, Report of the Secretary-General, (A/35/198), no date.

UNITED STATES HOUSE OF REPRESENTATIVES, Sub-Committee on National Security Policy and Scientific Developments, Foreign Affairs Division, Congressional Research Service, Brain Drain: A Study of the Persistent Issue of International Scientific Mobility, Library of Congress, Washington, D.C., 1974.

Chapter 13

THE IMMIGRATION POLICIES OF DEVELOPED COUNTRIES AND THE "BRAIN DRAIN" FROM DEVELOPING COUNTRIES

by

Chen Chin Long

Since World War II, traditional structures of production in industrialised countries have undergone major changes. The decline of such industries as iron and steel, chemicals and automobiles has led to a decline in employment.. Although large numbers of displaced workers have been relocated in new industries, even in the United States the development of industries based on new technologies such as computers, micro-electronics, fibre optics, telecommunications and biotechnology have not been able to compensate for the overall reduction of jobs caused by the decline of old enterprises. Besides, the new industries require workers with highly-specialised skills.

Post-War Immigration Polices of Developed Countries and Economic Restructuring

In response to these changes, the immigration policies of developed countries have undergone significant changes. In 1862, the United States provided immigrants with free farmland and Australia, New Zealand, Brazil and Argentina either paid their travel costs and/or provided them with subsidies. But after the 1930s, the policies of "traditional receiving" countries became very restrictive, thereby protecting their own labourers from competition by immigrants. Changes in their immigration policies after World War II may be summarised as follows:

a) Revision of immigration legislation directed against racial discrimination. The United States, Canada and Australia have traditionally preferred immigrants from Europe. However, sustained criticism of policies which gave little encouragement to non-Europeans led receiving governments to initiate changes. As a result of significant changes in Canada's policy after 1962, the proportion of Asian immigrants in total intake rose from 4 per cent in 1963 to 8 per cent in 1965. The United Kingdom had been the main source country of immigrants into Australia and New Zealand but after World War II, mainly as a result of a limited supply of migrants from that country, Australia and New Zealand negotiated migration agreements with the Governments of the Netherlands, the Federal Republic of Germany, Greece, Italy and Malta. Then, after 1966, non-European immigrants were admitted for permanent settlement;

b) Priority given to the immigration of highly-skilled and professional persons. Research institutions and private and public enterprises have attracted foreign senior scientists, technical experts and managerial personnel with good working conditions, research equipment, and much higher salaries than were generally available in their own countries. Since World War II, Europe, which had traditionally lost technical personnel to the United States, has become an importer of technical personnel.

Changes in United States immigration law in 1965 stipulated seven "categories" of immigrant, including four with priority status:

a) Relatives of American citizens or relatives of foreign nationals residing in America;

b) Senior scientific and technical personnel, including scientists and artists with distinguished talent and those specially trained in professions;

c) Persons who could fill jobs for which Americans were unavailable;

d) Refugees.

Categories (b) and (c) have provided entry for thousands of highly-skilled and professional workers from developing countries.

In Canada, changes in immigration law in 1967 provided for persons with no relatives in Canada being appraised on the basis of their education, skill, professional title, age, mastery of English and French, and destination. Of these conditions, the first two were specially emphasized and led to a rapid increase in numbers of immigrants from the Caribbean area, India and Pakistan.

Talent and the Economic Development of Developing Countries

During the early post-war period, it was widely believed that the development of education, culture, health and technical education was necessary to promote economic growth. At an address at Harvard University in 1963, Clark Carl declared that knowledge-concentrated industries may become the central factor in promoting the development of national economies. Railways had been the medium for economic growth during the late 19th Century and automobiles an additional impetus during the 20th Century. It is most likely that knowledge-concentrated industries will play a similar role during the latter part of the 20th Century.

Knowledge concentration is closely linked with the development of education and the strengthening of "human capital" investment. Professor Seodo Schultz, a pioneer in the theory of intellect development, divided capital into human and non-human, and attempted to assess the contributions made by education to economic growth. In the case of the United States, he concluded that 40 to 45 per cent of long-term economic growth could be attributed to human capital. Thus, in addition to paying careful attention to non-human capital and simple unskilled labour, it is necessary to give careful attention to the development of human capital through education and scientific research.

What then is the present situation of intellectual resources and development in developing countries? Is it adequate for their economic growth? Although developing countries have a large supply of manpower, the quality is typically unsuitable for economic growth. Until the 1970s, many adults in developing countries were illiterate: i.e., Bangladesh 70 per cent; Egypt 56 per cent; and Brazil 25 per cent. Education budgets of many developing countries were frequently cut. While developed countries spend approximately 6 per cent of their gross national products on education, the target for developing countries is only 4.3 per cent. In 1977, the average educational expenses per capita in developed countries was US$314 (for North America it was US$528); whereas the figure for developing countries was only US$24. Books published in developing countries amount to only 16 per cent of the world's total. Developing countries are already short of people working in education, culture and science but, what is worse, losses through emigration are large and persistent.

On the basis of experience by developing countries since World War II, it is clear that development should incorporate social as well as economic objectives. Kuwait, an oil-abundant country, topped the table of countries on the basis of average gross national product per capita in 1978 (US$15 970) but four adults out of ten in that country are illiterate. Developing countries should give more attention to social development (employment, education and culture) in their plans for long-term growth. They should also consider the relationship between intellectual development and the restructuring of their economies, start from their present situation and take feasible measures necessary for steady reform. Developing countries require enormous investments in education, culture, health, science and technology. Returns from these investments, in turn, provide the knowledge and techniques necessary to promote production. Many developing countries have already made large investments in intellectual capital. Thirty-six per cent of Singapore's national budget in 1980-81 was earmarked for house-construction and education; and the number of professional and technical personnel in that country was reported to have increased by 8.6 per cent.

"Brain Drain" and its Consequences for Developing Countries

In 1982, about 25 per cent of Egypt's labourers worked abroad. Among them, about 350 000 worked in Canada and the United States, 800 000 in Saudi Arabia, one million or more in Iraq and 250 000 in Kuwait. In Saudi Arabia, an Egyptian doctor, lawyer, teacher or engineer can earn US$1 500 to US$2 000 per month and enjoy free housing and other welfare facilities, whereas in Egypt the government pays the same professional only US$50 per month. Even though private enterprise may offer a higher salary, it would also be much less than what the professional could earn in a foreign country. In 1981, some doctors, college teachers, civil engineers and agronomists who had emigrated from Sudan to oil-producing countries in the Middle East and to Western countries were earning up to ten times the incomes that they had earned at home.

Employment and working conditions at home are also poor. While many developing countries follow the educational systems of developed countries, they tend to overlook ordinary and technical middle education. As a result many domestically-trained people of talent are unable to effectively apply their skills to the economy.' Indeed, many experience great difficulty in finding a job let alone finding a job commensurate with their professional qualifications. In the 1970s, the unemployment rate of certain types of engineers and technicians in Pakistan was estimated to be 45 per cent. Furthermore, working conditions in the cities are far worse than those abroad, and although the countryside badly needs technical people, few are willing to work in places where working conditions are worse than those in the city. In India, 80 per cent of doctors live in cities but 80 per cent of India's population live in the countryside. Finding a job is difficult in Argentina because it suffers from economic stagnation, and although farming and animal husbandry are major industries, the unemployment rate of agronomists is about 50 per cent. It is therefore understandable that, in the absence of appropriate policies, emigration of technical people and professionals increased substantially after the 1960s. To the beginning of 1982, about 250 000 scientists, technicians and professionals had emigrated: 64 per cent to America, 16 per cent to Spain and 12 per cent to Canada.

Immigration policies of developed countries is the major reason for emigration of people of talent from developing countries. Between 1961 and 1976, 400 000 experts emigrated from developing to developed countries. Those going to America, Canada and Britain from the Southern Hemisphere included 61 000 doctors and surgeons, 123 000 technical personnel (or workers equal to technical personnel) and 100 000 engineers and scientific workers. At the beginning of the 1970s there were 2.2 doctors for every 10 000 persons in India, but 15 000 Indian doctors (about 13 per cent of the country's total) were practicing medicine mainly in developed countries. Over 9 500 doctors from the Philippines settled in Northern Hemisphere countries. According to estimates of the United Nations Trade and Development Council, developing countries suffered a loss of US$46 billion as a result of manpower losses to the United States, Canada and Britain between 1961 and 1972. This figure was equal to the amount of development aid officially provided by developed countries during the same period.

Developing countries should devise strategies of socio-economic development suitable for their national conditions in order to resolve the brain drain problem. These could include reform of the education system so that graduates can utilise their skills, improved working conditions and increased salaries for persons with special professional skills, and attempt to maintain a balance between population, resources and employment.

E. REFUGEES

Chapter 14

THE CONSEQUENCES OF INFLUX OF REFUGEES FOR COUNTRIES
OF ASYLUM IN AFRICA

by

A. Adepoju

INTRODUCTION

Africa is the home of millions of refugees. Both the magnitude and
rapid increase in numbers of refugees pose serious problems for countries of
asylum and for organisations concerned with the welfare of refugees. The
refugee problem in Africa has generated considerable economic and social
misery and dislocation and resulted in untold human suffering. It is also one
of the most complex and agonising of Africa's problems (Adepoju, 1982; Gould,
1974). This chapter examines the consequences of refugee influx for major
countries of asylum in Africa.

Africa's Refugees: A Human Tragedy

Africa has experienced the "most acute refugee problems in terms both
of magnitude and complexity" (UNHCR, 1982). With an estimated 6 million or
more refugees and internally displaced persons Africa, the poorest of all
regions, is home to one of every two of the world's refugees (Adepoju,
1984c). They originate from and settle in countries designated as the least
developed in the world, countries that are plagued with problems of famine,
war, drought, and political instability (Kennedy, 1982; RPG, 1983).

Varying estimates of the refugee population in Africa reflect different
definitions of the category. The Organization of African Unity (OAU) definition (1) includes internally displaced persons (who find themselves in a
"refugee-like" situation). On this basis, Africa, within a short time span,
has become the continent with half the world's refugees; from less than a
million in the early 1960s to probably over 6 million today (Gould, 1974,
Rogge, 1985). Situations that have contributed to this massive increase
include the struggle for independence in Algeria, Guinea Bissau, Mozambique
and Angola; sessionist movements in independent nations (Shaba province,
Zaire (1977); Biafra in Nigeria (1966-70) and the struggle for autonomy

within Eritrea and southern Sudan. Apart from refugees resulting from political situations in newly independent countries undergoing severe internal political and military strife, and others still under colonial or white minority regimes, ecological factors (drought, famine) and breach of fundamental human rights have become major causes. Drought in Ethiopia, Somalia and the Sahel; internal strife in Chad, Mozambique, Uganda and Ethiopia especially in the Eritrean region; war in Ogaden between Somalia and Ethiopia have created additional waves of refugees (UN, 1981, 1984; Adepoju, 1982a).

Nearly 43 per cent of all refugees in Africa have in fact been displaced by natural disaster, drought, ecological problems, internal conflict or wars of liberation. Hence these refugees include children, women, old persons, mostly of rural background. In general, refugees are poor (or have been rendered so); in the process of flight, they have lost the little possessions they have -- land, cattle, etc.

Women refugees are particularly vulnerable. They face and have to solve "problems of abandonment of their homes, insecurity, privations, the burden of looking after a family when the head of the family is not there" and many more (UNHCR Refugees, No. 18, June 1985). Large numbers of such "refugees" are in Uganda, Tanzania, Zimbabwe, Ethiopia and Sudan. The Horn of Africa has the largest refugee population in Africa: about 1.3 million in Somalia, 0.75 million in Sudan, and several thousands uprooted by war and natural disaster in Ethiopia (Adepoju, 1982b).

The dilemma of Africa's refugees is that they are drawn from one of the poorest regions of the world and seek asylum in equally poor countries in the same region. Countries of asylum face unpredictable problems of drought and food deficits. Famine and war have become common. Thus, Somalia, itself a poor country, accepts a large and increasing number of refugees from Ethiopia, an equally poor country. Sudan's refugees originate in Chad, Ethiopia and Uganda. The countries of asylum, especially Sudan and Somalia, have had to bear heavy refugee burdens, in spite of their frail economies. In the case of Somalia, for instance, the situation is amply described as "a crushing burden for the vacillating economy of a country classed among the ten poorest on the planet "(UNHCR, 1981).

Indeed, it is now obvious that Somalia has "perhaps one of the most serious refugee problems anywhere" (UNHCR, 1981a). Shortage of water and deterioration of existing water supplies resulting from prolonged drought have threatened the lives and health of an estimated 850 000 refugees in 24 camps in southern Somalia (Melander, 1980; ICIHI, 1985, 1986a, b). The situation is worsened by the fact that 60 per cent are children under age 15 and 30 per cent are adult females. The influx of a large number of refugees of Somalie ethnic origin, mostly uprooted nomads and their animals, placed severe strains on water supply and grazing areas. While most refugees initially live among local populations, government long-term policy is to promote voluntary repatriation where possible, but in the short term to improve the refugees' living standards and assist them to become self-supporting (Melander, 1980; UNHCR, 1980, 1983; Khasiani, 1984).

Africa's position with respect to other world regions is the weakest. Economically, it is the most backward in food production in spite of abundant land resources. Per capita income is the lowest in the world; Africa can hardly feed, educate and provide adequate shelter and remunerative jobs for its rapidly increasing population, a situation that is exacerbated by internal strife, natural disaster, drought and famine (Adepoju, 1984b). In these circumstances, the incidence of the refugee problem is overwhelming: in Somalia, Ethiopia and Djibouti, for instance, the proportion of needy refugees (in the organised camps) to the local population in mid-1982 ranged from 1:5 to 1:6. Other estimates put the ratio of refugees to the total population as 1:3 in Somalia, 1:17 in Ethiopia and 1:18 in Djibouti (USCR, 1982).

Among the world's twelve countries with the highest proportion of refugees to local population in 1981, eight were in Africa -- Somalia, Djibouti, Burundi, Cameroon, Sudan, Swaziland, Zaire and Angola. Somalia stands out in the group, not only because it has the highest ratio of refugees, but also because it is the poorest of the twelve countries.

One striking feature of the refugee situation in Africa is that countries that generate refugees also provide shelter for refugees. Thus, Sudan received refugees from neighbouring Ethiopia, Uganda, Chad and Zaire but, prior to 1972, also generated refugees (who sought asylum in Ethiopia) and displaced persons. Zaire opened her doors to refugees from Uganda, Angola and Zambia while refugees from Zaire have sought asylum in Angola, Sudan, Uganda and Zambia (Gould, 1974; Adepoju, 1984a).

Such open-handed hospitality is not surprising, as reported by a recent Report on Refugees (January, 1985):

... there is a very special set of historical circumstances attached. First, the people are related tribally on both sides of the border, and then the Sudanese (during their own long civil war) had themselves taken asylum in Uganda. Thus they felt a special duty to offer asylum to their fellows from Uganda when they in turn came across.

The refugee situation in Africa is fluid and highly unpredictable; while old problems are being solved, new ones surface. The increasing desertification in the Sahelian region, drought in eastern, central and southern Africa, Chad, Uganda and Mozambique, and the war of liberation in South Africa and Namibia, have generated and will continue to generate new or increased waves of refugees (Adepoju, 1984c; Rogge, 1985).

Impact of Refugee Influx on Countries of Asylum

It is generally agreed that the solution to the refugee problem in Africa is voluntary repatriation. It is much preferred to such other long-term solutions as settlement in countries of first asylum on the basis of self-reliance, or resettlement in new "homelands" (Adepoju, 1982a). Refugees whose situation makes repatriation difficult, but who have effectively integrated into the local community, may find naturalisation, as pioneered by Tanzania, a viable strategy.

Rural refugees

The influx of refugees of rural background in the early 1960s, from Rwanda, Congo (now Zaire), Portuguese Guinea (now Guinea-Bissau) and

Mozambique marked the beginning of assisted rural settlements in Africa. A variety of settlements have been established: relief camps (Djibouti), assisted spontaneous settlements (Zaire), unassisted spontaneous settlements (Tanzania), organised rural settlements (Tanzania and Sudan) and quasi-urbanised settlements (Sudan) (UNHCR, 1981a). Rural settlements designed to consolidate refugees in viable communities have been established in Tanzania, Mozambique, Zambia, Sudan, Swaziland, Angola and Zaire.

In Tanzania, about 146 000 refugees from Burundi live in three rural settlements (Ulyankulu, Mishamo and Katumba) on land donated by the government. These refugees constitute 70 per cent of the total refugee population. While refugees in Tanzania constitute only 1 per cent of the country's population, in Mpanda district (where Mishamo and Katumba settlements are located) the proportion is as high as 50 per cent (UNHCR Fact Sheet No. 4, March 1986). By mid-1983, about 160 rural settlements in 14 African countries held over one million refugees.

In Africa, perhaps more than elsewhere, the strains on refugees have been minimised -- and the process of adjustment to refugee life considerably eased -- by ethnic and kinship ties between refugees and people in the country of asylum (United States Department of State, 1983). In fact, spontaneous, "self-settling" refugees constitute about 60 per cent of rural refugees in Africa. These relocate among villagers of similar ethnic stock near their national frontier. Where refugees belong to the same ethnic or social group, speak the same language and practise the same religion, adaptation and assimilation into the host society become easier as was the case of the Fang refugees from Equatorial Guinea who were readily absorbed spontaneously by the Fangs in Cameroon and Gabon. This contrasts sharply with the attempt to settle skilled refugees of diverse ethnic origin in the Mbandjock Sugar agro-complex with Cameroonians and others from the Central African Republic -- an experiment that precipitated a major inter-group confrontation in 1975 (Gwan, 1983). In fact, it has been argued that Burundi "fundamentally, will only accept refugees of similar ethnic and linguistic background" like the Tutsis from neighbouring Rwanda (UNHCR, 1981a).

Self-settlement appears to relieve both the host government and voluntary and international agencies concerned with refugee issues of aid and assistance. Conventional thinking assumes that refugees who settle spontaneously amongst their kith and kin rarely experience problems in the relocation process. However, as Stein (1982) reminds us, the host population "bears the main load of emergency aid, it welcomes, feeds and cares for the refugees as part of traditional hospitality". However, the host population may also live at subsistence level and the large influx of refugees -- and the sharing of the limited resources -- invariably results in severe hardship for both refugees and their hosts (Kibreab, 1983; D'Souza, 1980).

This argument is countered by situations where the construction of roads, or upgrading of existing infrastructure, especially clinics and schools, also benefit the local population as happened in Zaire. Nevertheless, one is inclined to ask the following questions: are refugees in Africa special because they are Africans? What distinguishes African refugees from other refugees? How easily are they absorbed into the local community and with what consequences at the micro and macro levels? Are refugees solely dependent on external assistance for survival? What makes the African refugee problem unique? To what extent has the worsening economic situation adversely hampered the warm reception refugees traditionally expect -- and do in fact receive -- from their hosts? These questions become even more pertinent in relation to Coles' observation:

> At the moment, there seems very little prospect of a significant diminuition of the basic needs of the African refugees. Without solutions to these refugee situations, and with the refugee situation worsening, it will be difficult to avoid this assistance becoming not only an indefinite and recurring expense but a growing one as well. (Coles, no date)

War, natural disaster and drought readily render the continent a beggar for food aid. Recent examples include the war in Chad, the Ogaden crisis and drought in the Sahel. The threat of famine in 1983 in the Sahel region, Zambia, Uganda, Ghana, etc. following late or zero rainfall further increased dependence on food aid (ICIHI, 1985). Rapid population increase is one cause of this predicament. By 1980, African countries imported five times as much food compared with 1975. Failure to attain self-sufficiency in food production means that refugees become a severe burden.

While good land has been made available to refugees in Tanzania, Zambia and southern Sudan, President Nyerere summarised the dilemma facing most countries hosting refugees:

> I want to make it clear that Tanzania is perfectly willing to take over refugee settlements from UNHCR and absorb them into the normal life of the country. ... However, when about 50 per cent of all Tanzanian villages still lack an adequate supply of pure water, when so many of our roads and bridges are still unusable in the rainy season, it is just not possible for us to give top priority to the development of refugee settlements. (Refugees Magazine, No. 5, 5th December 1983.)

Refugees' immediate needs are for shelter, food and sometimes clothing. Later they require land, basic tools, seeds (for farmers) and viable employment. Donor agencies often provide for immediate needs in the hope that transition to so-called self-sufficiency will be attained as soon as local situations permit. However, major refugee influxes have severely disrupted the normal development activities of Sudan, Tanzania and Somalia. Inadequate resources also mean that increasing refugee populations exert tremendous pressure on housing, health and educational facilities. This generally increases resentment and hostility against refugees as in Sudan's urban areas (UNHCR, 1986a; Rogge, 1985).

Sudan's refugee population burgeoned as drought and war forced thousands of Eritrean and Tigrayans to seek refuge across the border. Wad Sherife, a camp designed to accommodate 5 000 refugees, actually held over 100 000 and Wad Kowli increased from 40 000 to more than 60 000, situations that led to growing animosity toward refugees and strained local resources (Refugees, May 1986).

Feelings of resentment by local populations can also be aroused by facilities provided for refugees -- schools, hospitals/clinics, bore holes, etc. -- which do not benefit them. In refugee settlements in Sudan each (Ugandan) refugee family is given a plot of land of about eight acres (depending on its quality) to help them attain self-sufficiency. Each settlement also has a primary health care unit, dispensary, primary school and sometimes a community hall. Community development activities are designed to assist refugees to learn such trades as carpentry, masonry and shoe repairs. Farmers are also provided with tools and seeds, and encouraged to enrol in such programmes as training to use oxen teams, or learn poultry, pig and fish farming. About 320 kilometres of roads have been built (both inside and outside the settlements) and shallow wells and improved springs and other natural sources have complemented bore holes to increase water supply to about 20 litres per person per day.

In large refugee receiving countries -- Somalia and Sudan, in particular -- increasing deforestation caused by open-air refugee concentrations has been one of the neglected but most devastating acts of environmental damage. Most camps are surrounded by semi-arid scrubland where refugees rely on wood as a source of fuel. As few are supplied with charcoal, trees and bushes have been rapidly depleted, thereby hastening desertification (Refugees, No. 18, June 1985).

Urban refugees

Urban refugees (educated and skilled adults) who compete for limited opportunities, pose a greater challenge to countries of asylum in Africa. Sudan and Djibouti are examples: in 1980, 49 per cent of urban refugees in Djibouti lived in the capital; overall they constituted 10 per cent of the urban population (UN, 1982). Sudan is reported as having the largest urban refugee population in Africa which poses a serious problem as they compete with Sudanese citizens for very scarce resources: employment, health services, schools. In 1981, not more than 10 per cent of refugees in the capital city of Khartoum were gainfully employed (UNHCR Fact Sheet, 1981).

By the end of 1983, an estimated 200 000 refugees had settled spontaneously in Port Sudan, Gedaref and Khartoum. Of these, about 50 000 lived in the capital (Refugees, 1985). Most were Ethiopians; a few were Zaireans and Ugandans. According to current regulations in Sudan, only refugees who are self-sufficient may live in the capital: material assistance is guaranteed only in the camps. In theory, refugees in Sudan enjoy the same employment rights as Sudanese except in key sectors. In practice, most are unable to find openings that match their qualifications, partly because few are able to speak Arabic. Moreover, global economic recession has created high unemployment (Refugees, No. 24, December 1985).

An estimated 85 per cent of refugees in Kenya live in and around Nairobi, the capital. Kenya has the largest urban refugee population in Africa. Most of the refugees are of urban background. Unlike neighbouring Tanzania, Kenya does not permit large-scale settlement; besides, refugees cannot own land. In 1984, it was estimated that only 1 per cent of the refugees had found employment in Nairobi (Refugees, No. 23, November 1985).

In general, urban refugees are expensive to maintain and difficult to integrate. In Port Sudan, where they constituted 12 per cent of the town's population in 1980, the majority were unemployed. In Kenya where over 80 per cent of the refugee population live in Nairobi, only 19 per cent of the urban refugees (14 per cent in Nairobi and 56 per cent in the provinces) were employed. In addition to being unemployed, they also experienced loneliness and problems of integration. The establishment of semi-urban settlements in Sudan has not solved these problems (Adepoju, 1983; UNHCR, 1983).

There are nevertheless positive aspects of the urban refugee situation. Although some Sudanese resent urban refugees in general, many skilled refugees (especially technicians) have replaced skilled Sudanese who migrated to the Gulf and have thereby contributed to the alleviation of critical manpower shortages (Refugees, No. 34, December 1985).

In Search of Durable Solutions

The refugee problem in Africa has both long-term and short-term perspectives. Short-term solutions include provision of emergency aid calculated to ensure the refugees' survival: food, shelter, clothing and medical assistance. Long-term solutions are of three kinds: voluntary repatriation to their countries or origin; settlement in countries of first asylum and resettlement in new homelands. Of these solutions, voluntary repatriation is perhaps the most durable (Adepoju, 1982a).

The number of refugees with professional skills who need placement in the country of asylum is relatively small. Rural refugees usually settle spontaneously among local populations (as in Somalia) or are assisted in settling (as in Sudan, Senegal and Tanzania). Spontaneous settlements have been facilitated by ethnic affinity between refugees and resident populations, the receptive attitudes of governments, and the availability of land enabling refugees to continue their normal occupations.

The refugee burden is far from evenly shared between sub-regions and countries in Africa: only 18 of the 51 member states of the Organisation of African Unity accommodate 90 per cent of refugees. Yet these countries are among the least developed and "most seriously affected" by recent adverse economic conditions (Kibreab, 1983).

In Sudan, for example, refugees from Ethiopia, Uganda, Chad and Zaire have stretched to the limit the country's meagre resources. One of the poorest countries on the continent, Sudan has also suffered from both floods and drought. The enormous magnitude of the refugee problem in Africa, especially in Somalia, Sudan and Zaire and of internally displaced persons in Ethiopia and Uganda, has severely drained the limited resources in these countries. Ethiopia, Chad, Rwanda and Zaire have generated most refugees in recent years while, paradoxically, Somalia and Sudan in that order (two very poor countries) are major countries of asylum. By virtue of their geographical location, countries surrounding refugee-producing countries are obvious destinations for refugees. Zaire is bordered by nine countries and Sudan by eight, including Uganda, Angola, Chad, Ethiopia, Rwanda and Burundi which have generated thousands of refugees. At the moment, countries in central and east Africa bear the brunt of the refugee problem. The exceptions are Senegal, Nigeria and Cameroon which have received a large number of refugees from Chad, Equatorial Guinea and Guinea (Adepoju, 1982, 1983).

The general principle of burden-sharing was a major recommendation of the Arusha refugee conference in 1979 (Erikson and others, 1981). This was later ratified by the Organization of African Unity's Council of Ministers.

By adopting this strategy, African countries that do not harbour refugees will make financial contributions to those that provide asylum to large numbers. So far, however, the recommendation has not been implemented by many African governments.

While the search for a durable solution to the refugee problem continues, the problem is unlikely to disappear during the next few decades. Newland (1981) has warned that "there is really no such thing as preventive action specific to refugee problems". Besides, refugee movements are unplanned and highly unpredictable.

It is not only the sheer magnitude of numbers of refugees and internally displaced persons in Africa but also the concentration of refugees in a few countries with frail economies that pose major problems of resettlement. While a number of developed countries have resettled refugees from Asia and Latin America, resettlement of African refugees has been done mainly by African countries. As the Emergency Committee for African Refugees (1982) concluded, "the opportunity for an African refugee to settle outside the first country of asylum is almost non-existent. For instance, out of 500 000 refugees that the United States agreed to resettle in 1980 and 1981, only 4 500 were Africans. This is less than 1 per cent of the total refugee population admitted to the United States". Furthermore, most of these refugees were highly skilled, the conventional brain drain phenomenon. Much greater international commitment and aid programmes need to be devoted to African refugees if only because it would be a cheaper solution for donors and psychologically more satisfying for the refugees themselves to be resettled within Africa. Aid of this kind could be closely linked to overall development programmes and therefore extend beyond immediate survival of refugees who, once self-reliant, would contribute positively to the economies of host countries.

Although African refugees are characteristically illiterate and unskilled, there are skilled, educated, young and aspiring refugees who could contribute, and indeed have contributed, significantly to the development of host economies. For example, refugees from Equatorial Guinea in Gabon and Ugandan refugees in southern Sudan whose proficiency in agriculture has been emulated by the host population (Smythe, 1982).

Refugees in Africa normally hope to return home when conditions permit. General amnesty in Zaire in 1980, change of regime in Uganda, Equatorial Guinea and Central African Republic, the attainment of independence in Mozambique (1975), Guinea Bissau (1974) and Angola (1975) promoted large-scale repatriation of refugees to their home countries (Adepoju, 1982a). Recent instances include mass repatriation to Chad (1981 and Zimbabwe (1980) and from Djibouti to Ethiopia (1983). For some refugees, the possibilities for repatriation are remote. These situations call for a reorientation of objectives by those agencies that offer assistance to refugees (Rogge, 1985). So far, the main emphasis has been on immediate relief -- food, medical facilities, shelter. It should progressively be focused on long-term developmental activities which may include education and vocational training and agricultural projects to facilitate job placement in host countries. Other activities such as child welfare and health nutrition have also been suggested (Smythe, 1982; ECAR, 1982). Refugees should be assisted to become fully self-supporting. Once integrated, they become assets to the host community and their self-image is enhanced.

Mishamo settlement in Tanzania is a unique example of successful resettlement. Established two decades ago, the settlements vary from single villages of 3 000 to 4 000 (as in the case of Mwese for Rwandese settlers recently granted Tanzanian citizenship) to vast communities like Katumba, which is 100 kilometres south of Mishamo, housing 80 000 Burundis, probably the largest of its kind in Africa (UNHCR, 1985, 1986). Of Mishamo, the UNHCR Refugees magazine (January 1985) reports:

> Like earlier refugee settlements, Mishamo is beginning to yield distinct benefits for both refugees and host community now that the arduous task of establishment is nearly complete. Mishamo's residents now enjoy standards of health care, education and water provision at least as good as the surrounding district. With each family cultivating their own (five-hectare) plot, Mishamo was virtually self-sufficient in food after only two farming seasons. And with the cultivated area increasing by 2 000 hectares each year, the settlement raked in an impressive 4 500 000 shillings from surplus crop sales and 3 000 000 shillings in tobacco sales, the main crop, last year. Each village centre is the focus of community life based around the rural development centres, churches and co-operative groups, many of whose buildings were constructed on a self-help basis by the villagers themselves. The several busy markets which burst into life twice a week throughout Mishamo also testify to the rising standards of living the settlers are beginning to enjoy.

It is also claimed that Tanzania benefitted from the hospitality she provided refugees. Located in thinly populated and most inaccessible western regions, the government ingeniously promoted regional development and expanded food production. In doing so, it succeeded in mobilising international aid to provide most of the investment required. In 1984, Mishamo's surplus food crops alleviated shortages in drought-stricken neighbouring regions of Mwanza and Shinyanga (UNHCR, January 1985).

Economic development in the Mpanda district, the largest in Tanzania, with more refugees than citizens, has been greatly facilitated by dynamic settlement schemes. Local business has boomed and refugees, widely referred to as "businessmen", (a grudging compliment to their ability to work hard and make money) have stirred local farmers to greater efforts. Hence an erstwhile remote, neglected and underpopulated part of the country has been transformed into "one of the greatest remaining agricultural potentials in Africa (UNHCR, January 1985).

Helping Africa's Refugees

In designing relevant assistance programmes for Africa's refugees, the first step should be to ascertain approximately how many there are, where they are located and their specific, immediate and long-term needs. Accurate estimates of refugee populations (and internally displaced persons) in Africa are hard to come by. Indeed, few African countries have accurate information on their own populations. Moreover, most refugees -- about 60 per cent -- live outside organised camps and are widely scattered amongst local populations. Numbers fluctuate rapidly as new refugee flows emerge and others repatriate.

Estimates of refugees and internally displaced persons are therefore bound to be imprecise; from between 3 million and 6 million at the end of 1983 (UNHCR, 1983; USRC, 1983). Because it is believed by some that the number of refugees is often inflated by the host governments in order to attract attention and obtain substantial aid (Christensen, 1982), it is necessary to indicate official estimates in the main countries of asylum in Africa.

As of Janauary 1986, UNHCR estimated that there were 1 164 000 refugees in Sudan. Of this number, 637 500 were assisted by the Commission -- 448 000 Ethiopians, 124 000 Ugandans and 65 000 Chadians. About 380 000 spontaneously settled in rural areas, with a few in towns (Kassale, Gedaref, Port Sudan and Khartoum). Also at that time there were 283 000 refugees in Zaire, mostly Angolans (235 000) who lived in the provinces of Bas, Shaba, and Bandundu (Zaire), and in Kinshasha. Tanzania hosted 209 000 refugees, mostly from Burundi. In Somalia, about 700 000 Ethiopian refugees were located in 36 camps in the regions of Gedo, Hiran and Lower Shabelle. About 80 per cent of the refugees were women and children. In Swaziland, a country of about 650 000 population, about 11 000 refugees were registered; Zambia hosted 100 000 refugees (UNHCR Fact Sheet No. 13, March 1986).

Solutions to Africa's refugee problem must take account of the fact that the majority are located in the Horn of Africa and the Sudan -- countries not only ranked among the least developed in Africa but also plagued by drought, war and political instability. Second, because most refugees relocate spontaneously among local populations "thousands of refugees go unnoticed because of Africa's traditional hospitality" (United States Committee for Refugees, 1981). Indeed about half or more of Africa's refugees live with local populations in the country of asylum (sometimes near the border) outside organised settlements (UN, 1982). In Sudan and Somalia, over 60 per cent of refugees settle spontaneously in rural areas, making assistance difficult. In fact, the 35 established settlements in Somalia and the estimated 25 in Sudan accommodate probably no more than one-quarter of the refugees in these countries. As a result, they do not avail themselves of the services and relief materials provided specifically for refugees by host governments and concerned agencies, both voluntary and international. Third, African refugees are confined to the continent for, as Stein (1982) remarked, "a key feature of African refugee problems is that virtually all the refugees stay within the continent and are assisted by their fellow Africans".

The majority of refugees are of rural background -- farmers, pastoralists, nomads and traders who need access to (fertile) land which in Africa is becoming increasingly depleted by drought through deforestation. This process may well limit the feasibility of settling refugees in countries of asylum in Africa.

Arguments in favour of organised settlements include the need to control and concentrate assistance efforts, that governments may settle refugees away from sensitive border posts, and provide land and related infrastructure to settlements. Two undesirable effects of organised settlements are the feeling of sustained dependence of refugees on donor agencies and the disparity in conditions inadvertently generated between refugees and local populations especially with respect to access to education, health facilities, water and food. Hence to avoid resentment, refugee settlements should not be enclaves, enjoying additional benefits and privileges that are generally unaccessible to local populations (Adepoju, 1984a).

In some cases, the assisted refugees appear to be better off than local host communities. For example, refugees at the Mishamo settlement in Tanzania have greater access to health and adult education facilities than the average Tanzanian. Infant mortality is much lower there than in the rest of Tanzania (Refugees Magazine, February 1984). In the Mayukwayukwa camp where about 500 Angolan refugees and Zambian children attend the same village school, Zambians feel that refugee children who receive free school uniforms enjoy preferential treatment. It is also contended in Djibouti that "the numerous feeding, health and education programmes afforded the refugees are not available to Djiboutians, and it is widely held that the refugees live better than most nationals" (United States Department of State, 1983:9).

Refugees in Zambia's towns who have access to international assistance but nevertheless compete for the few jobs, are envied by locals. Where support of international agencies has enhanced the productive capacities of refugee settlements, as in western Tanzanian agricultural settlements, benefits which refugees receive create disparities between them and the locals who also require improved services, health, education and sometimes housing services. Situations such as these have cautioned governments to request that refugee assistance be integrated with development aid so as to benefit both the refugees and local inhabitants. An editorial in Refugees Magazine (No. 3, March 1984) aptly summarises this sentiment: "for social, psychological and political reasons, it is impossible to create such opportunities for refugees while ignoring the needs of their hosts. What is needed, therefore, are projects which aim at providing new income-earning opportunities for the whole area where the refugees live ...".

One of the key issues raised during ICARA II (the Second International Conference on Assistance to Refugees in Africa) was the need to strengthen the infrastructure of countries receiving refugees and returnees. For instance, poor access roads and inadequate storage facilities often caused bottlenecks in the delivery of international relief in countries like Ethiopia and Sudan. As Africa's refugees originate from -- and settle in -- poor countries, sustained development of these countries is potentially a powerful tool in solving the refugee problem -- both in arresting the factors that generate refugees and in increasing the capacity of receiving countries to adequately accommodate refugees.

The consensus at the International Conference on the Emergency Situation in Africa held in Geneva (March 1985) was that we should look beyond the current emergency and program long-term measures designed to reduce the causes of refugee influx. Attention should henceforth be focused on agricultural and infrastructural development and desertification and deforestation (Refugees, No. 17, May 1985).

SUMMARY

The African refugee situation is a human tragedy. Refugees are victims of war, drought, famine and related problems. They consist predominantly of young persons, women and the elderly. More than one-half settle spontaneously in rural areas in countries of asylum. They originate from and settle in countries ranked among the poorest in Africa. Though they are regarded primarily as an African problem, their reception has taxed available resources of asylum countries which not only provide land for settlement but in some cases avail refugees of the option of naturalisation in situations where repatriation appears unlikely. Because refugees originate and relocate within the continent, long-term solutions have to be pursued as part of the continent's economic/demographic condition. The causes of refugee movements are fluid and highly unpredictable; likewise, long-term efforts to accommodate or reduce its consequences require concerted effort, planning and substantial financial resources.

NOTES AND REFERENCES

1. The Organisation of African Unity (OAU) defines refugees as "every person, who owing to well founded fear of being persecuted for reasons of race, religion, nationality, membership of a particular social group or political opinion, is outside the country of his nationality and being outside the country of his former habitual residence as the result of such events is unable or, owing to such fear, is unwilling to return to it". In its wider perspective, it "also applies to any person who, owing to external aggression, occupation, foreign domination or events seriously disturbing public order in either part or the whole of his country of origin or nationality, is compelled to leave his place of habitual residence in order to seek refuge in another place outside his country of origin or nationality". This definition has been accepted by OAU member states (Melander and Nobel, 1978).

BIBLIOGRAPHY

ADEPOJU, A.
"The Dimensions of the Refugee Problem in Africa, African Affairs, Vol. 81, No. 322, 1982a.

"The Refugee Situation in the Horn of Africa and Sudan", ISSUE, (A Journal of Africanist Opinion), Vol. 12, Nos. 1/2, Spring/Summer, 1982b.

"Refugees in Africa: Problems and Prospects", paper presented at the Symposium on Causes and Consequences of Refugee Migrations in the Development World, Manitoba, 1983.

"Assisting Africa's Refugees: Issues and Challenges in the 80's", paper prepared for the Seminar on Assistance to Refugees in Africa, Cambridge, 1984a.

Redistributing Population: Challenges and Prospects: Inaugural Lecture No. 66, University of Ife Press, 1984b.

International Migration in Africa South of the Sahara, Project Report to UNESCO, Population Division, Paris, 1984c.

CHRISTENSEN, H.
Survival Strategies for and by Camp Refugees, report on Six-week Exploratory Sociolgical Field Study into the Food Situation of Refugees in Camps in Somalia, Geneva, UNRISD, 1982.

COLES, G.J.U.
Problems Arising from Large Numbers of Asylum-Seekers: A Study of Protection Aspects, International Institute of Humanitarian Law, no date.

D'SOUZA, F.
The Refugee Dilemma: International Recognition and Acceptance Report No. 43, London, Minority Rights Group, 1980.

EMERGENCY COMMITTEE FOR AFRICAN REFUGEES (ECAR)
"US Policy and the Current Refugee Crisis in Africa", ISSUE, (A Journal of Africanist Opinion), Vol. 12, Nos. 1 and 2, 1982.

ERIKSON, L.G., G. MELANDER and P. NOBEL, eds.
An Analysing Account of the Conference on the African Refugee Problem, Arusha, May 1979, Uppsala, Scandinavian Institute for African Studies, 1981.

GOULD, W.T.S.
  "Refugees in Tropical Africa", International Migration Review (Special
  Edition on International Migration in Tropical Africa), Vol. 18, No. 3,
  1974.

GWAN, E.
  "International Migration in Central Africa", unpublished manuscript,
  Yaounde, 1983.

HANRELL, S. ed.
  Refugee Problems in Africa, Uppsala, Scandinavian Institute for African
  Studies, 1967.

INDEPENDENT COMMISSION ON INTERNATIONAL HUMANITARIAN ISSUES (ICIHI)
  Famine: A Man-made Disaster?, New York, Vintage Books, 1985.

  The Vanishing Forest: The Human Consequences of Deforestation, London
  and New Jersey, Zed Books Ltd., 1986a.

  The Encroaching Desert: The Consequences of Human Failure, London and
  New Jersey, Zed Books Ltd., 1986b.

KENNEDY, J.C.
  "Refugees in Africa: The Continuing Challenge" in USCR, World Refugee
  Survey 1982, New York, 1982.

KHASIANI, S.A.
  Refugee Policies, Programmes and Research in Somalia, Ethiopia and
  Tanzania: A Review, Project Report for International Development
  Research Centre, Nairobi, unpublished, 1984.

KIBREAB, G.
  Reflections on the African Refugee Problem: A Critical Analysis of
  Some Basic Assumptions, Research Report No. 67, Uppsala, Scandinavian
  Institute of African Affairs, 1983.

KNIGHT, D.
  Refugees: Africa's Challenge, a special report by Christian Aid,
  London, Christian Aid, 1978.

MELANDER, G.
  Refugees in Somalia, Research Report No. 56, Uppsala, Scandinavian
  Institute of African Studies, 1980.

MELANDER G. and P. NOBEL, eds.
  African Refugee and the Law, Uppsala, Scandinavian Institute of African
  Studies, 1978.

NEWLAND, K.
  Refugees: The New International Politics of Displacement, World-watch
  Paper No. 43, Washington, D.C., 1981.

ORGANISATION OF AFRICAN UNITY
Report of the Administrative Secretary-General on the Conference on the Situation of Refugees in Africa held in Arusha (Tanzania) from 7-17 May 1979, Council of Ministers Thirty-third Ordinary Session, Monrovia, 1969.

REFUGEE POLICY GROUP (RPG)
Refugees in Africa, Background Brief for Refugee Policy Group Meeting on Refugees in Africa, Washington, D.C., 1983.

ROGGE, J.R.
"Refugee Migration and Resettlement", in J.I. Clarke and L.A. Kosinski, eds., Redistribution of Population in Africa, London, Heinemann, 1982.

"Africa's Displaced Populations: Dependency or Self-sufficiency," in J.I. Clarke, M. Khogali and L.A. Kosinski, eds., Population and Development Prospects in Africa, London, Cambridge University Press, 1985.

SMYTHE, M.M.
"African Refugees: Their Impact on Economic Development in Countries of Asylum", ISSUE, (A Journal of Africanist Opinion), Vol. 12, Nos. 1 and 2, 1982.

STEIN, B.N.
Refugees and Economic Activities in Africa, paper presented at Seminar on Refugees, Khartoum, 1982.

UNITED NATIONS
The Refugee Situation in Africa: Assistance Measures Proposed, International Conference on Assistance to Refugees in Africa, Geneva, 1981.

Second International Conference on Assistance to Refugees in Africa, ICARA II, Geneva 9th-11th July, Geneva, 1984.

UNITED NATIONS ECONOMIC COMMISSION FOR AFRICA (UNECA)
Report of the Conference on the Legal, Economic and Social Aspects of Africa's Refugee Problem, Addis Ababa, 1969.

The Refugee Child, Geneva, 1979.

UNITED NATIONS HIGH COMMISSION FOR REFUGEES (UNHCR)
UNHCR: The Last Ten Years, Geneva, 1980.

Managing Rural Settlements for Refugees in Africa, Geneva, 1981a.

Refugees, (several issues), Geneva, 1981b.

Report of the Seminar on the Problems of Refugees in Zaire, Geneva, 1982.

Refugees, (several issues), Geneva, 1983.

Refugees, (several issues), Geneva, 1984.

Refugees, (several issues), Geneva, 1985.

Refugees, (several issues), Geneva, 1986a.

UNHCR Fact Sheet, (several editions), Geneva, 1986b.

UNITED STATES COMMITTEE FOR REFUGEES
World Refugee Survey 1981, New York, 1981.

World Refugee Survey 1983, New York, 1983.

UNITED STATES DEPARTMENT OF STATE
Country Reports on the World Refugee Situation, Washington, D.C., 1983.

WINTER, R.P., 1983
"Refugees in Uganda and Rwanda: The Banyarwanda Tragedy" in World Refugee Survey 1983, New York, USCR, 1983.

Chapter 15

THE IMPACT OF REFUGEES IN RECEIVING COUNTRIES IN AFRICA: THE CASES OF REFUGEE WOMEN AND REFUGEE PROFESSIONALS

by

Shanyisa Anota Khasiani

INTRODUCTION

A refugee is any person who seeks the protection of another country out of fear of persecution due to race, religion, nationality, social affiliation or because of events disturbing public peace in his country (Organization of African Unity, 1969). Africa hosts more refugees than any other region in the world: the number of officially recognised and assisted refugees on the continent is estimated at about 3 million. Africa has witnessed an unprecedented increase in the refugee population, attaining the record figure of 5 million towards the end of the last decade. The situation has improved as a result of positive events on the continent: many Zimbabweans were repatriated following Independence of their country and thousands of Ugandans and Angolans voluntarily repatriated after their countries declared general amnesty. In addition, more than 36 000 former Rwandese refugees were granted citizenship by the United Republic of Tanzania; likewise, the Botswana Government granted citizenship to 2 000 former Angolan refugees.

Despite these achievements, the refugee problem in Africa continues to worsen, and the factors which generate refugees continue to intensify. One of the main causes of the refugee problem in southern Africa is the apartheid policy of the Republic of South Africa which promotes racial segregation, oppression and exploitation of the majority non-white by the white minority. This has resulted in numerous uprisings, violence and the flight of non-whites into neighbouring independent states as refugees. Linked with the South African apartheid regime is her continued occupation of Namibia. South Africa controls the economy and exploits and discriminates against black Namibians who consequently flee to front line states. While the intensified liberation struggles in South Africa and Namibia further increase the number of refugees, influxes in independent African countries have also increased in the last decade. The causes are varied and include inter-state conflicts, coups, repressive regimes, ethnic and religious differences, foreign intervention and violation of human rights.

Refugee statistics are scanty and unreliable; nonetheless reasonable estimates can be made. Available data shows that eastern, southern and central sub-regions shoulder the heaviest burden of refugees (United Nations, 1984). Countries like Somalia (700 000), Sudan (700 000), Zaire (304 000), Burundi (256 000), Tanzania (180 000), Uganda (173 000), Algeria (167 000) and Namibia (103 000) have refugees who constitute large proportions of their local populations. The largest refugee proportion is in Somalia where they account for 30 per cent of the total population (Kibreab, 1981). In some regions of Somalia refugee proportions reach 50 per cent. In Burundi, there is probably one refugee for every 17 citizens.

Host societies have continued to share with refugees their limited resources: land has been made available for refugees to settle with their families; education and employment opportunities, medical services and housing facilities have been extended to refugees. In the major host countries where refugee populations have been for long periods, an immediate impact is the heavy demand made on the host country's resources, often at the expense of national progress (Smith, 1982). The marginalisation of sub-sections of refugee populations arises from limited and often inappropriate integration programmes and facilities, as a result of which able-bodied and sometimes well-trained refugees lack the means to attain self-reliance. They eke their living from inadequate hand-outs and increase the pool of poor, dependent persons in host countries. This is well demonstrated by cases of refugee women and refugee professionals in Africa.

The Case of Refugee Women

Refugees result from various factors. In the period before and during flight, many men are killed or captured; others take advantage of their greater mobility to seek their fortune further afield. This situation leaves women, children and the aged as the dominant groups among refugee populations. Existing refugee statistics and research rarely give data on gender and age. The dominance of women and children in refugee settlements, in camps and in transit centres is, however, evident. Estimates made for ICARA II, for instance, show that as much as 90 per cent of the refugee population in Somalia are women and children under 15 years (United Nations, 1984). In Mishamo settlement in Tanzania, women and girls over 14 years of age constitute 51 per cent of the refugee population (Adepoju, 1982). Women probably constitute between 50 and 60 per cent of all refugees in Africa.

The turbulent conditions that generate refugees cause women to flee with their children. In refuge, many women are forced to assume new roles as heads of households and sole income earners. In Somalia more than 75 per cent of refugee families are headed by women (Adepoju, 1982). In Mishamo settlement, 25 per cent of families have female heads (Palmer, 1982). In Uganda, during recent disturbances, many men were killed, kidnapped or forced to join guerilla fighters; as a result many refugee families are headed by women (Khasiani, 1985).

Most of the women are of rural background and settle in rural areas. They suffer attendant problems of large families, poverty, limited literacy and productive skills and poor health and are often assisted by the United Nations and international agencies, as well as local agencies and host governments. Subsequently, some engage in activities that can promote their integration and contribute to the development of host communities.

Integration assistance takes the form of counselling, health, education and income-generating facilities and services. Integration programmes constitute a burden on host governments. Furthermore, inaccessibility of most refugee women to these programmes, due to their inadequacy and sometimes their inappropriateness, relegates the women to poor dependent status in the host population.

Counselling services

To facilitate the integration of refugees, counselling services have been established to provide guidance in health, social welfare, employment and education programmes. Where necessary, they make material assistance available to those in need, the aim being to help refugees to understand their situation in the light of available resources.

Counselling services are provided by UNHCR, national and international voluntary agencies. Efforts are made to reach all refugees. For refugee women, orientation counselling determines the appropriate assistance for each new arrival who is provided with limited relief assistance while efforts are made to achieve integrative solutions. During the integration stage, counselling services are provided to promote self-reliance by developing the economic potential of refugees, and identifying suitable self-help activities, strengthening their abilities to cope with domestic roles and promoting good health. When refugee women have problems, they are expected to communicate with counsellors who determine the nature of the case and recommend appropriate action. Counselling then becomes a continuing process until refugee women are fully integrated into the host community.

Most countries have established religious-based institutions through which they channel appropriate counselling. Since most counselling services are provided only for urban refugees, most women in rural areas are not reached. Even when counselling services have penetrated the female refugee caseload, they remain disadvantaged for a number of reasons: ignorance concerning services available to them; lack of experience in seeking help; suspicion of strangers; and lack of time to receive the services due to childcare responsibilities. In Sudan in 1982, 70 per cent of counselling service clients were males (Palmer, 1982). This situation further marginalises women because integration programmes are established without recognising and taking account of their special needs.

Due to shortage of staff, most of the countries with established counselling services have no formally-established posts of interpreter. Communication with most refugee women is made difficult by high rates of illiteracy and lack of knowledge of the local language. Furthermore, the content of counselling and guidance programmes for women is often inappropriate. It has been found that the concept of "vulnerability" is applied indiscriminately so that able-bodied women and widows are lumped together with the aged and disabled with the result that efforts are diverted into unproductive traditional marginal welfare activities (United Nations, 1982). Motivation for self-reliance is stifled and a marginal group of women is created. Recently, more emphasis has been placed on combining individual with group counselling.

Health services

Conditions of refugees exacerbate poverty and ill health among female heads of households. Promotion of the health of these women would also enhance the welfare of their families. Most host governments and the international community provide health services to refugees, sometimes as part of national health programmes. In Kenya, maternal and child health clinics exist and serve all women in the country while additional medical services for refugees are provided when recommended by counsellors. In Somalia, the government has established a Refugee Health Unit within the Ministry of Health to administer, co-ordinate and set priorities and guidelines for refugee health; additional mother and child health centres have been established in refugee camps. Special health measures include preventive health education through rural clinics; and feeding centres provide supplementary and therapeutic feeding to pregnant and nursing mothers.

These services, however, cover only a small proportion of needy women. Despite existing primary health care programmes, problems of maternal health and infant mortality resulting from lack of sufficient health services still exist. In Somalia, increased health facilities reduce the high mortality resulting from unattended and complicated deliveries. Mortality levels in refugee regions are high; crude death rates of around 20 per thousand population and infant mortality between 150 and 170 per thousand births (United Nations, 1984). The major health problems include diarrhoeal and upper respiratory diseases; measles and malnutrition are widespread among children.

Large concentrations of refugees who have settled spontaneously pose tremendous problems for host countries. In Eastern Sudan for instance, the 170 000 refugees who settled in and around the towns of Kassala and Gadaref constitute over 45 per cent of the total population. The limited health services of these towns have been stretched to the limit, resulting in chronic water shortage and inadequate health and sanitary facilities (United Nations, 1984).

Sudan has requested external funding through ICARA II for a project to improve hospitals which service national and refugee populations in Kassala and Gadaref. The project in Gadaref includes construction of an additional well-equipped gynaecological and paediatric department to cater for women and children. Kenya has requested assistance to construct and equip an additional maternity unit at Kangemi estate which has the largest concentration of refugees in Nairobi. A request by Somalia for assistance through ICARA II to establish community-oriented hospitals, including training facilities and outpatient clinics, is aimed at providing primary and secondary health care. In Burundi, where the influx of refugees also exerts pressure on existing health programmes, shortage of medical personnel and supplies persists in spite of progress in national health programmes. Partly because of this, mortality among refugee women is very high.

Education and training

Education plays an important role in the successful integration of refugees, especially women and children. Efforts to improve the literacy of refugees has focused on national educational schemes. At the primary school level, projects are often run by refugees themselves assisted by national and international agency personnel. In Tanzania, refugees are eligible for the same free primary education enjoyed by nationals. Primary schools have been built in refugee settlements and teachers include Tanzanians and refugees. In Somalia, attempts are being made to meet the educational needs of refugee children by establishing schools in and around camps.

In principle, educational assistance is available equally to male and female refugees; in practice however socio-cultural factors in asylum countries favour males. Female participation rates in primary education tend to be highest in settlements where they predominate. A study (United Nations, 1984) of primary school enrolment in the two camps (Adi Addeys and Lugh Jellow in Somalia) showed that enrolment in the national system favours males. The situation is worse in spontaneously settled urban and peri-urban communities where refugees compete with nationals for limited educational facilities.

Educational projects at the primary school level for refugees are inadequate to meet their needs both with respect to quality and quantity of services available. Although a large budget is allocated to education, only a small percentage of children of primary school age attend school. In Ethiopia the percentage of children of primary school age currently enrolled is very low in the refugee areas of Eritrea (17.5 per cent) and Harraghe (14.5 per cent), largely because of a shortage of educational facilities even for the local children (United Nations, 1984). Attempts to expand existing school facilities have been constrained by inadequate classroom equipment. In Somalia, severe overcrowding in refugee schools has forced the government to abandon its policy of compulsory attendance at primary school level.

Inadequate primary school facilities for refugees is compounded by shortage of staff. Refugee teachers often are inadequately trained while trained national personnel are usually in short supply which, together with inadequate teaching materials, has had adverse effects on the quality of refugee primary education.

A substantial number of refugee women are involved in post-primary education and organised vocational training programmes. United Nations and other agencies provide assistance through scholarship programmes for a limited number of eligible students; the largest educational assistance programmes in 1984 financed 6 000 refugee students in post-primary academic vocational and technical disciplines in Sudan. In Tanzania, admission of refugees to secondary schools is by a non-citizen quota of 2 per cent of the places available in Form 1. Post-primary education in which refugees in Somalia engage includes secondary education and an in-service Teachers Training Programme. Secondary schools do not exist in refugee camps in Somalia, and so refugees have to compete with nationals for limited secondary school places available outside refugee camps. In addition, refugees have to compete with nationals for limited scholarships.

In the main, secondary and tertiary education scholarships discriminate against women (Khasiani, 1984). Even though more men than women obtain scholarships, participation of refugee women in educational projects has improved. In the 1974/75 academic year, 15 per cent of refugee students were women and girls; by 1979/80 it was 20 per cent (UNHCR, 1980). Field observations from several countries show that adult and functional literary programmes are biased in favour of women. This is justified in view of the large numbers of female illiterates in refugee populations. Requests presented to

ICARA II include plans to expand post-primary educational facilities to accommodate more refugees, especially women. Although some educational refugee programmes are established with women as the primary beneficiaries, they lack support from the international community. In all cases, the majority of elderly refugee women who stay at home receive little or no training. They lack knowledge of the local language and are not reached by refugee counsellors.

Income-generating activities

All major countries of asylum have policies that promote self-sufficiency for refugees settled in both urban and rural areas. In urban areas, the main forms of assistance are provided through supporting projects for self-employment and employment in both the formal and informal sectors. Most refugees obtain the lowest-paying menial jobs. Urban refugee women, who constitute most of the unskilled urban labour force, face serious unemployment problems. Domestic responsibilities further restrict refugee women from access to viable job opportunities. In Port Sudan, Nairobi and several towns in Zambia, Zaire and West Africa, many refugee women resort to petty trade and prostitution. A survey in urban and suburban areas of eastern and central Sudan, found that 27 per cent of single mothers who were heads of households had resorted to prostitution as a source of income (UNHCR/ILO, 1983).

Most refugee women live in rural areas. This, combined with lack of education, makes agriculture the only viable source of employment and income. Integration requires policies that encourage settlement on land. Refugee families are usually given land by the host government to produce for their subsistence and sell the surplus for extra income. In major asylum countries (Tanzania, Zambia, Somalia, Sudan and Ethiopia) they are also provided with farm implements and seeds to encourage self-reliance. Agricultural projects have been established to enhance the standard of living of refugees. In Senegal, the United Nations in co-operation with local agencies has funded an agricultural and fisheries project for 5 000 Guinea-Bissau refugees; part of the project's funds is earmarked for the integration of refugee women into the economic life of the country (UNHCR, 1984). In Somalia, the Refugee Agricultural Unit co-ordinates and implements refugee agricultural activities which include irrigation schemes and vegetable gardens for women. In Burundi, plots have been made available for a Land Development Agricultural Extension project. In Ethiopia, attempts are being made to find suitable agricultural land for recently-arrived refugees.

The location of settlements far from borders to avoid raids and reprisals, tend to alienate women and isolate them from the support of the extended family and familiar cultures. Agricultural projects also fail to take into consideration the composition of refugee families. Little attention is paid to the fact that most households are headed by females and that the refugee family consists predominantly of children and women. Scarcity of good agricultural land has been given as the reason why refugees are usually assigned to unproductive marginal land, a situation that leads to poor harvests, the destruction of the ecology through deforestation and over-use of marginal lands.

Experience in Africa indicates that many female-headed households in rural settlements may never attain self-sufficiency in food while they continue to depend on insufficient food rations. Handicrafts and small-scale industries have been considered as another means of promoting refugee integration, generating income and improving the nutrition of refugee families. In refugee settlements in eastern and central Sudan, several projects have been specifically designed to integrate female heads of refugee households into co-operative ventures designed to break womens' isolation and develop their self-reliance (UNHCR/ILO, 1983). The projects provide cottage-based industries for women with childcare responsibilities and outdoor activities for those without. In Somalia, several agencies have funded a number of income-generating projects. In Zimbabwe and Zambia, the United Nations provides grants to individual refugees to start small businesses. ILO is also implementing various income-generating activities for refugees in Kenya, Zaire and Lesotho.

Problems experienced in implementing these projects include finding raw materials for production and markets for finished products. This partly reflects the tendency to conceptualise and establish projects within the confines of traditional sex-specific roles and in the absence of adequate information. Even when women are channeled into traditional enterprises like knitting and basketry, their potential is not fully exploited to generate adequate income, thus leaving many women bored, isolated and marginalised. Conceptual confusion also exists over cultural preservation of activities and promotion of economically progressive income-generating activities. Activities like fancy needlework serve neither purpose but frustrate, disillusion and marginalise refugee women.

The Case of Refugee Professionals

Professionals are another marginalised section of refugee populations (Khasiani, 1985). Refugee professionals are defined as highly-qualified people who are currently pursuing undergraduate and post-graduate studies, high-level technical training or have completed tertiary training. They are capable of promoting development through research and other activities and constitute a manpower resource that is in short supply in Africa. Their training and skills can be channeled to benefit both the refugee professionals and the host societies. This has not been done because host governments generally view their stay as temporary and consider repatriation the only durable solution. Few countries have policies designed to incorporate refugee professionals as a resource in development planning.

Refugee professionals include former lecturers, researchers, highly-skilled government officials and students with urban backgrounds who seek employment in urban areas. Although host governments recognise the need for highly-skilled personnel, they are handicapped by limited capital and institutional capacities and give priority to their nationals. Many refugee professionals are therefore unemployed or settle for jobs unrelated to their training. They also suffer discrimination with respect to training and research programmes. Out of extreme frustration, some resettle outside Africa, often in the West thereby adding to the brain drain.

241

Education and training

Agencies that have responded to the needs of refugee professionals include United Nations Education and Training Program for South Africans, All Africa Conference of Churches, United Nations Council for Namibians, Lutheran World Federation, World University Service, African American Institute, Phelps-Stokes Fund, Otto-Benecke Stiftung, Commonwealth for Technical Co-operation, and the Organization for African Unity. Most of these agencies restrict their award of scholarships to legally recognised refugees and South African and Namibian members of liberation movements. For instance, UNHCR sponsors only professionals who are legally recognised refugees from independent African states and South African refugees who are non-party affiliates. The United Nations Commission for Namibians restricts its scholarships to refugees for Namibia. The Organization of African Unity Bureau of Refugees provides scholarships for refugee professionals from all over Africa, with most scholarships going to South Africans and Namibians. Restrictions of sponsorship are occasionally relaxed to fit prevailing conditions in a host country.

For some donor agencies, a condition for sponsorship is that the candidate qualify for college entrance. Failure to be accepted by a college disqualifies the candidate from UNHCR sponsorship. Some sponsoring agencies negotiate with colleges to relax admission criteria for refugee professionals. Agencies such as Lutheran World Federation, World University Service and Phelps-Stokes Fund, which sponsor refugees from South Africa, usually negotiate on behalf of students who fail to meet college entrance criteria. Under these circumstances, the colleges administer internal tests to determine whether or not the candidates qualify for entrance.

Most sponsoring agencies discourage post-graduate training. Restrictions to sponsoring a first degree is based on the desire to train more refugees at lower levels of tertiary training. An exception relates to refugees under liberation movements. For these refugee professionals, sponsorship is dictated by the manpower needs of the future republics of Namibia and South Africa as defined by liberation movements. Recently, however, in the wake of intensified localisation of posts in most countries, there has been increasing recognition of the need to sponsor refugees for higher degrees to enable them to compete favourably with citizens of host countries.

Most agencies award scholarships that cover education and personal costs. Partial scholarships are few, though some agencies supplement insufficient scholarships to ensure completion of training. The number of scholarships available for refugee professional training is determined by several factors. First, the budgets of the sponsoring agencies restrict the number of scholarships awarded. Most agencies involved in education and training of refugee professionals have small budgets for higher training, a situation worsened when unexpected costs are created. The number of places allocated to refugee professionals also limits the number of scholarships awarded. Foreign quotas range from 1 to 20 per cent of all places available in colleges. This partly reflects the limited institutional capacities of tertiary training in host countries. A final limitation results from the failure of candidates to qualify for entrance. The number of scholarships for Southern African and Namibian refugee professionals are only restricted by the needs of the liberation movements.

Scholarships for professional training are equally open to refugee women and men. There are, however, more men than women in scholarship programmes, reflecting the disadvantages women experience in education and training programmes from an early age. Many women also have childcare responsibilities and scholarships generally do not cater for dependents.

Most refugee professionals are young adults in their thirties and forties. While most donors do not specify age limits for candidates to qualify for their scholarships, a few, such as the United Nations Education and Training Program for Southern African refugees, sponsors candidates under the age of 32.

Many donor agencies, including the Orangization for African Unity and United Nations High Commissioner for Refugees, sponsor only students in African institutions. Other agencies like Lutheran World Federation and African American Institute award scholarships that are tenable in training institutions both inside and outside Africa. Outside Africa, most of the scholarships are tenable in the United States, Canada, United Kingdom and West Germany. To reduce costs, most sponsors give preference in scholarship awards to students choosing to study in Africa. Refugee professionals sponsored for training outside Africa are required to return after their training, except for refugee professionals who are members of liberation movements. On completing their training, these professionals may be posted to liberation movement offices anywhere in the world. The United Nations High Commissioner for Refugees helps refugee professionals procure appropriate documents for travel.

Educational counselling involves guiding students to take courses with which they can cope. Selected courses are designed to make graduates employable. In countries where unemployment is very high, counsellors discourage enrolment in social science courses. Sponsors may also restrict their award of scholarships to fields where a need exists to promote manpower development, including education, engineering and agriculture.

Employment conditions

Employment conditions of refugee professionals depend on the situation in host countries which, in turn, influences the employment policies and practices of host societies and the attitudes of nationals towards the employment of refugee professionals (Khasiani, 1985).

Most African countries face a bleak and deteriorating employment situation. Refugee professionals are therefore employed in areas that lack high level manpower, e.g., medicine, engineering, agriculture and teaching. The public sector, parastatal institutions, universities and other research organisations are the main employers but opportunities are limited by shortage of funds for expansion. Few refugee professionals trained in the social sciences are employed because these fields are saturated with local professionals. Refugees from South Africa and Namibia usually enrol in law, administration and nuclear physics in preparation for future nationhood, skills that are not related to employment opportunities in host nations. This leads to high unemployment among these professionals who then appeal to their liberation movements for any kind of employment.

In conformity with the principle of burden-sharing propounded by the Organization of African Unity, and reiterated in most African refugee meetings, most countries in Africa have adopted legislation that guarantees refugee employment. There is, however, lack of specific policies concerning the employment responsibilities of countries of first asylum to refugees (Khasiani, 1984). Thus refugee professionals cannot legally challenge discrimination. In signing the Organization for African Unity and the United Nations Conventions, some countries reserved the right to make jobs available to refugees. Most countries with policies specifying refugees' rights to employment also have other policies that contradict them. Such policies include the localisation of posts which was adopted by most African countries at independence whereby foreigners are not allowed to hold senior positions in most organisations. Where they do, they are ultimately replaced by qualified nationals. This affects the employment conditions and opportunities of refugee professionals, who, along with other foreigners, are also excluded from jobs that are considered to be sensitive.

The employment practice towards refugee professionals in both the public and private sectors reflects the host country's employment conditions. In the face of unemployment, governments understandably make no attempt to expand employment opportunities for refugee professionals; non-government agencies and the international community are expected to tackle this issue. The employment policies of parastatals and other research organisations which employ refugee professionals are influenced by the desire to maintain international standards. In practice, these organisations not only favour nationals but are also under pressure to localise high-level positions.

Employment conditions of refugee professionals may also be worsened by the attitudes of local populations. In the face of limited job opportunities, local populations portray negative attitudes towards refugee professionals. These are generally strongest amongst those professionals who compete for the same jobs, who feel threatened and therefore press for preferential treatment. The intensity of these sentiments vary and are strongest in countries with large urban refugee populations.

Although private firms emphasize merit criteria in recruiting employees, few have information on refugee professionals. Some have employed refugee professionals without discriminating while others argue that refugee professionals, along with other foreigners, often lack commitment to their work, being preoccupied with plans to repatriate.

Despite their high qualifications, many refugee professionals remain unemployed for long periods. Others are underemployed partly because of a mismatch of their jobs and skills. Most refugee professionals who are members of liberation movements have trained in fields which are considered sensitive; such professionals often have to settle for jobs unrelated to their training. Those trained in fields for which no jobs are available are forced to take jobs unrelated to their skills. The process of getting work permits may be time-consuming and result in loss of job offers. Other refugees, in sheer desperation to earn some income, take any available job (Khasiani, 1985).

Some agencies have assisted refugee professionals in securing employment. Southern African refugee professionals who are members of liberation movements are assisted by these organisations. The liberation movements also enter into bilateral and multilateral relations with governments and other organisations. Most United Nations High Commissioner for Refugee branch offices assist refugee professionals to secure employment (Khasiani, 1985). The Organization for African Unity collaborates with African governments to provide employment for refugee professionals. Some donor agencies such as the African American Institute assist graduates whom they sponsored to secure employment. In Tanzania, the Ministry of Manpower Development recruits at high-level manpower for government ministries and parastatals; refugee professionals along with other foreigners are recruited in the same way.

However, when refugee professionals obtain appropriate employment their terms are often inferior. Many countries employ them on short contracts and on terms which make their tenure insecure. In the unstable economies of host countries, merit criteria may be secondary to preference for nationals. Furthermore, some donor communities discriminate against refugee professionals through policies which award research grants and training to nationals affiliated with local institutions (Khasiani, 1985).

These factors have meant that local professionals have a better quality of life than their refugee professional counterparts. In addition to being disadvantaged in their employment, refugee professionals are newcomers to the host economy. They have had to build everything from scratch and, unlike nationals at comparable levels, lack a network of kinship and friendship ties. Refugee professionals also have the added responsibilities of assisting fellow refugees from their countries, most of whom have low standards of living. Although many of them feel that they would get better jobs and terms of service in their home countries, they are not prepared to repatriate for employment and would prefer to resettle in Western countries where there are better employment opportunities and terms of service. The United Nations High Commissioner for Refugees policy discourages this. Instead, migration to other African countries for purposes of employment is encouraged. Because African host governments discourage this, many refugee professionals finally migrate to the West for employment. Refugee professionals who are members of liberation movements cannot return to South Africa or Namibia and therefore remain in other African countries or live outside Africa where many have resettled for security reasons.

CONCLUSION

Africa's resources are scarce and unevenly distributed. Rampant poverty is compounded by rapidly increasing populations. The problems of refugees are therefore superimposed on other development problems. The large number of refugees, including women and professionals, constitutes a burden on the economies of receiving countries. Limited resources lead to the establishment of inadequate and often inappropriate integration programmes which marginalise able-bodied refugee women and highly-skilled refugee professionals. The latter are discouraged from migrating to other African countries or resettling in the West for employment. Those who do migrate to the West constitute a loss of manpower resources for Africa.

The most important contribution made by refugee-producing African countries relates to amnesty laws for their nationals in exile to return home, including refugee women and refugee professionals. Another activity has been the adoption of regional legal instruments intended to reduce the refugee problem. The 1969 Organization of African Unity Convention Governing the Specific Aspects of the Refugee Problems in Africa is the regional complement of the 1950 United Nations Convention on Refugees.

The problem of refugee women and professionals is primarily a problem for countries of asylum which provide emergency relief and integrative assistance. Because needs can be assessed only on the basis of accurate information on the size and characteristics of target populations, there is a need for country-sponsored studies on refugee women and refugee professionals.

In keeping with the principle of burden sharing, the problems of refugee women and refugee professionals will have to be solved on a regional basis. There is need for regional co-operation in addressing these issues. The Organization of African Unity has the political machinery necessary for this purpose, especially for the integration of refugee women and refugee professionals. Existing collaboration between the Organisation of African Unity and United Nations agencies involved in refugee matters should enlarge integration assistance to these groups. At the same time, United Nations Development Program could use its co-ordinating role in the United Nations system to introduce programmes for refugee women and refugee professionals on a complementary regional basis. Establishing appropriate regional programmes for refugee women and refugee professionals requires a solid data base.

Within both countries and regions, women's groups and professional organisations can create awareness of problems by clearly defining them and initiating integration assistance by mobilising the political and economic resources at their disposal.

African countries which host refugees are among the poorest and least developed countries in the world. They have fragile agricultural economies and insufficiently developed resources and infrastructure. People who lack most of the basic needs in life are being called upon to share the little they have with refugees. Furthermore, Africa is now bearing this huge burden of refugees at a time of unprecedented socio-economic crisis. Unfavourable external circumstances in the last decade have exerted strong pressure on weak African economies. The cumulative impact of severe and extended droughts, desertification and other natural disasters, civil strife and slow economic growth is threatening a downward spiral of economic decline, poverty and hunger. It is in response to this, and recognition that the refugee problem is an international problem, that the international community should co-operate in the search for a permanent solution.

The assistance already provided by the international community should continue and also expand to include women and professionals as special problem groups. There should also be co-operation and collaboration among donor agencies in funding and implementing projects. Such activities would establish the vital link between relief and integration assistance. Promotion of participation by refugee populations in planning and implementation of programmes would increase their relevance and success and eliminate the loss of resources associated with marginalisation of refugees in host countries and migration to the West.

BIBLIOGRAPHY

ADEPOJU, A.
"The Dimension of the Refugee Problem in Africa", Africa Affairs, Vol. 81, No. 822, 1982.

KIBREAB, G.
"Reflections on the African Refugee Problem: A Critical Analysis of Some Basic Assumptions", Research Report No. 67, p. 30, Table V, cited from International Conference on Assistance to Refugees in Africa, Geneva, 1981.

KHASIANI, S.A.
"Refugee Policies, Programs and Research in Somalia, Ethiopia, and Tanzania: A Review", report submitted to the International Development Research Centre, Nairobi, 1984.

"The Nature and Scope of Education Training and Employment Problems of Refugees and Displaced Professionals in Eastern and Southern Africa", report submitted to the International Development Research Centre, Nairobi, December 1985.

"The Situation of Refugee and Displaced Women in Independent African States", report to the Economic Commission for Africa, African Training and Research Centre for Women, and The Organization of African Unity, Addis Ababa, 1985.

OAU
Convention Governing the Specific Aspects of Refugee Problems in Africa (Article 1), 1969.

Report of Mission of the Commission of Fifteen on Refugees in Africa to the Thirty-sixth Ordinary Session of the Council of Ministers, 1983.

PALMER, I.
"Women Refugees in Urban and Rural Settlements", unpublished paper, 1982.

REPORT of the Secretary General on Detailed Description of Needs, Project Outlines and Background Information on Refugee Situation (A/CONF.125/2) to the Second International Conference of Assistance to Refugees in Africa, Geneva, 9th-11th July 1984.

SMYTHE, M.M.
"African Refugees: Their Impact on the Economic Development in Countries of Asylum", ISSUE, (A Journal of Africanist Opinion) Nos. 1 and 2, African Studies Association, 1982.

UNHRC

"World Conference of the United Nations Decade for Women. Equality, Development and Peace", Copenhagen, The Situation of Refugee Women the World Over, Copenhagen, A/CONF.94/24, 1980.

Fact Sheet Nos. 1-3, 6, 8 and 10, 1984.

Fact Sheet, West Africa No. 1, June 1984.

"Refugee and Refugee Assistance in Tanzania", General Information Paper, March 1984.

Map of Refugees in Africa, Spring 1984.

UNHCR/ILO

"Self Reliance for Refugees in Sudan: A Program for Action", draft report of the UNHCR/ILO.

Report of Income-Generation Activities for Refugees in Eastern and Central Sudan submitted to the Khartoum Workshop 17th-20th April, No. 82/AP/SUD/LS/26/ILO, Vol. 1.

Overview, Geneva, March 1983.

UNITED NATIONS

Report of the Secretary General on the Situation of Refugees in Sudan (A/37/178) of 15th April 1982.

Report of the Secretary General on Detailed Description of Needs, Project Outlines and Background Information on the Refugee Situation (A.CONF.125/20) to the Second International Conference on Assistance to Refugees in Africa, Geneva, 9th-11th July 1984.

Research Institute for Social Development, "Survival Strategies for and by Camp Refugees", a report on a Six-Week Exploratory Sociological Field Study Into the Food Situation of Refugees in Camps in Somalia, Geneva, 1984.

"Second International Conference on Assistance to Refugees in Africa" (ICARA II), Geneva, 9th-11th July. United Nations General Assembly Distr. A/CONF.125/2, 23rd March, Report of the Secretary General, 1984.

Chapter 16

AUSTRALIAN REFUGEE POLICY AND DEVELOPING COUNTRIES:
EVOLVEMENT OF AUSTRALIAN REFUGEE POLICY, 1945-85

by

D. Cox

Although Australia's involvement with refugees goes back to the 1830s, the period of significant involvement dates from the end of World War II when the government responded very positively to the needs of refugees from Eastern and Central Europe. Australia's support was due in part to its policy of admitting numbers of immigrants each year equal to 1 per cent of total population but also due to a genuine sympathy for the persons involved. By 1952 over 170 000 Eastern European refugees had arrived in Australia. The Displaced Persons programme, as it was known, conformed with Australian Government conditions that all immigrants meet health, security and employment requirements and be of European race (Price, 1980, 3-4). Having "no local family ties, no property and few effective civil rights ... they (were) allocated to those economic sectors which had great difficulty attracting locally-born labour" (Jupp, 1984, 11).

Between 1947 and 1976 Australia, responding to various European crises that resulted in refugee movements, as well as to the more or less continuous stream of refugees from Europe, admitted over 350 000 refugees, including White Russians from China (Price, 1979, 153). Yet throughout this period it was criticised frequently for exploiting the refugee situation for population-building and work-force purposes, for taking far too few of the "hard-core" cases and very few non-European refugees (Price, 1979, 153-4). The latter criticism became increasingly pertinent as the number of European refugees dwindled and numbers in other parts of the world increased. This period of refugee immigration to Australia was perceived by the 1977 Green Paper on immigration policy as not having imposed intolerable strains on community resources nor hindered the achievement of national economic or other objectives (APIC, 1977, 41-2). The Council supported a call for a refugee policy separate from the normal immigration policy.

The refugee policy announced in Parliament in May 1977 was based on four principles:

i) Australia fully recognises its humanitarian commitment and responsibility to admit refugees for resettlement;

ii) The decision to admit refugees must always remain with the Government of Australia;

iii) Special assistance will often need to be provided for the movement of refugees in designated situations or for their resettlement in Australia;

iv) It may not be in the best interests of some refugees to settle in Australia. Their interests may be better served by resettlement in countries elsewhere. (Mackeller, 1977, 2.)

The statement accompanying the policy described several new mechanisms for responding to refugee situations and monitoring the response. It specifically rejected a completely separate refugee intake or a clear distinction being made between criteria to be applied for refugees and all other immigrants (Cox, 1979, 8-9).

While pressure for a refugee policy had been mounting, the 1970s saw the dismantling of the White Australia policy, leaving Australia theoretically free to respond to the many refugee situations outside Europe. After 1975, the major situation to which Australia did respond was in Southeast Asia from where she accepted some 95 000 Indo-Chinese refugees between 1975 and June 1985 (DIEA, 1985, 68). Increasingly, however, concern was expressed about the genuineness of the latter waves of refugees from this region. In 1982 the then Secretary of the Department of Immigration stated that "the arrangements for individual determination of refugee status, and a general tightening of our refugee policies are now ensuring that only genuine refugees are settled here under Australia's programs" (ACPEA, 1982). Such comments tempered the strong moral overtones of earlier statements. For example, in 1980 the then Minister for Immigration stated:

We have only to compare the affluence, the material security and the political freedom which we enjoy with the plight of refugees in many parts of the world. It would make a mockery of any claims by Australia to Christian or humanitarian principles if we were not to respond with generosity to world refugee situations. Ours is a nation and a lifestyle of great abundance. We have no moral alternative but to share some of that abundance with those who have faced persecution and deprivation as a result of racial, religious and political discrimination. (ARAC, 1980.)

What was constantly being sought at the policy level was a balance between the exercise of humanitarian responsibilities and, to use a much-favoured phrase, Australia's "capacity to absorb" refugees. Successive governments in the 1970s and 1980s were very conscious of the country's continuing high unemployment and inflation and of the possibility that many Australians might attribute these difficulties in part to the refugee intake.

The final development that should be noted is the increase during the 1980s in the number of source countries from which refugees were accepted. Although most refugees continued to come from Indo-China and Eastern Europe,, by 1985 persons of over 30 different nationalities had been accepted. Significant programmes were underway in Europe, Asia, Latin America, the Middle East and Africa (DIEA, 1985, 67). The distribution of refugees who arrived between 1983 and 1985 can be seen in Table 16.1. Despite the wide range, however, many regions provided only a few refugees.

Table 16.1

REFUGEE ARRIVALS (a) BY REGION OF LAST RESIDENCE

	1983-84	1984-85
Britain and Ireland	16	17
Northern Europe	1 257	940
Southern Europe	1 141	1 261
Middle East	563	1 326
North Amererica	4	11
Central and South America	837	1 866
Africa	41	35
Asia	10 909	9 339
Total	14 769	14 803

a)   Includes the Special Humanitarian Programme.

Source: DIEA, 1985, 64.

Australia's refugee policy can be understood by examining the way criteria for resettlement of refugees have evolved. Prior to 1977 the absence of any formal refugee policy was seen as inhibiting a speedy and appropriate Australian response (Senate Committee, 1976, 82-83). The purported overriding criterion was humanitarian: "Australia accepts refugees largely because of humanitarian considerations and international obligations" (DIEA, 1979). However, for many years an overall immigration policy that excluded non-Europeans suggested that racial balance of the population was more important than humanitarian principles. Second, humanitarian considerations were linked with international obligations. In part this reflects the fact that Australia is a party to various international conventions that impose obligations regarding refugees. It also reflects Australia's relations with specific foreign countries. The intake of more Vietnamese than Kampucheans and Laotians, and more Vietnamese from Malaysia than from Hong Kong and even Thailand, reflected the significance of external political relations in determining response to the Southeast Asian refugee situation.

A commonly-stated third factor is Australia's capacity to resettle refugees effectively. This is a complex factor and embraces both economic realities and the domestic political scene. "Australia's capacity to resettle was more importantly constrained by political factors: the absolute numbers of refugees and the pace at which they arrived would draw approval, indifference or concern from Australians with consequent political effects for the government" (Viviani and Lawe-Davies, 1980, 13). Moreover, "the political colour of any refugee group influences their acceptability to a reigning political party ... We are naive if we ignore the realities of foreign relations, a government's political survival at home and the responsible handling of economic and demographic developments which must be a part of any government's concern" (Cox, 1979, 13). Humanitarian motivations have clearly been tempered by other considerations.

How does the operation of these criteria relate to Australia's response to refugee situations in Third World countries where a combination of social, economic and political factors frequently give rise to refugee populations? An Australian journalist has suggested that Australia faces three broad types of refugee situations (Hastings, ARAC, 1980). First, a situation in which Australia is required only to contribute money, for example, the general African refugee situation. Second, where it is in Australia's interest to accept refugees for settlement, for example, from Eastern Europe, the Middle East and Indo-China. Third, in situations where hidden social costs may ultimately prove quite high such as white refugees from Zimbabwe, Indians from Fiji, white refugees from New Caledonia and boat people from an impoverished Pacific country such as Kiribati (Hastings, 1980, unnumbered).

The implications of Hastings' typology would seem to be that Australia will differentiate between, first, those refugees where resettlement outside the region or in a third country is seen to be appropriate and those where it is not; second, between those situations where it is under political pressure to accept a specific type of refugee, and can do so without adverse consequences, and those where it is not; and, finally, those situations where Australia is virtually obliged to accept a group of refugees, despite the likely costs, and those where it can avoid doing so. The arrival of boat people in Darwin alerted Australia to its vulnerability as a country of first asylum for boat refugees.

An examination of refugee policy statements and of refugee arrivals since World War II indicates that neither the severity of particular refugee situations nor economic conditions in the refugees' host country have been major determining factors in Australia's refugee resettlement policy. Yet this policy emphasis could well have been anticipated. The common tendency is for a country to respond to outsiders with whom there already exists some affinity. Moreover, the political realities are that governments are unlikely to spend the money necessary to resettle refugees if the public considers the expenditure unjustified. This is likely to occur where racial differences exist and when the extent of human tragedy involved is not appreciated.

The Settlement of Refugees in Australia, 1947-85

Australia has resettled in excess of 400 000 refugees during the last forty years. The following extracts from a government booklet reflect the composition of that programme:

-- 170 000 from Europe, including 63 400 from Poland, 34 700 from Estonia, Latvia and Lithuania, and 23 500 from Yugoslavia between 1947 and 1954, displaced as a result of the war;

-- 14 100 Hungarians following the 1956 uprising in Hungary;

-- 5 700 Czechoslovakians, after similar events in their country in 1968;

-- 13 300 White Russians from China;

-- 700 Iraqi Christians;

-- 88 112 Indo-Chinese between April 1975 and June 1984;

-- 21 300 East Europeans since 1978.

Other groups assisted under relaxed criteria and special humanitarian programmes include:

-- 17 000 Lebanese since 1975;

-- 5 500 Timorese since 1975;

-- 4 800 Soviet Jews since 1973;

-- 1 100 Central and South Americans since 1983; and

-- More than 100 Africans in 1984." (DIEA, 1985b).

These figures indicate the strong European bias in Australian immigration until the 1970s when the government initiated nine fundamental principles underlying immigration policy. One of these was that "immigration policy and selection are non-discriminatory" (Mackeller, 1978). The implementation of this policy increased the range of source countries.

In the 1970s Australia offered resettlement to refugees and quasi-refugees from Lebanon, Iraq, Timor and elsewhere, but predominantly from Indo-China. Then, in 1984, a public debate occurred in Australia over Asian immigration when Professor Geoffrey Blainey stated that "the pace of Asian immigration is now far ahead of public opinion" (Blainey, 1984, 25). As might be expected the speech drew a range of comments for and against the broadening of Australia's intake from Asian source countries. The Prime Minister stated clearly the government's position in a speech to Parliament in May 1984:

> Over the past decade we have buried the White Australia policy forever. We have shown our capacity to accept people from Asian cultures ... This Government does not consider that a balance or mix in our migration programme determined on racial grounds can have any place in our society ... It categorically rejects any proposals to introduce covert discrimination through differential standards in selection criteria (Hawke, 1984).

The Department of Immigration's 1985 Review presented the refugee programme as a global one "which seeks to respond to the needs of refugees and others in human rights difficulties in most major refugee situations" (DIEA, 1985a, 67). That Review reported having accepted refugees from Sri Lanka "following the communal violence"; from Central America including

El Salvador, Cuba, Guatemala and Nicaragua; from "South America 752 people were accepted for resettlement, most from Chile ... reflecting the Government's continued concern about the human rights situation there"; "in 1984-85, Australia accepted 1 882 people, notably Iranian Baha'is, from the Middle East for resettlement"; "a total of 943 Lebanese were visaed under these special entry arrangements"; and "Australia accepted 144 Africans, most of them Ethiopians", but there were also refugees from Uganda, Somalia, Angola and South Africa (DIEA, 1985a, 68-9). While the numbers from outside Europe and Indo-China were small, Australia's refugee resettlement programme included persons from many countries.

An early study of European refugees in Australia stressed the diversity and complexity of the settlement process (Martin, 1965). Generalisations must therefore be regarded with care. Martin herself concluded that refugees intermarried with Australians and other Europeans more than did other immigrants, tended to live outside ethnic concentrations and were not therefore a part of ethnic institutions, and made few demands of Australian social service and other systems. Other studies have stressed the downward social mobility experienced by many refugees related to the then poorly-developed facilities for learning English, a very low rate of acceptance of their professional and trade qualifications and a measure of discrimination against newcomers. Related to this social and occuaptional demotion was a high incidence of certain psychiatric disorders among East European refugees in Australia (Jupp, 1966, e.g., 55 and 116; Cox, 1975, 82-6). Sexual imbalance of intakes from some Eastern European countries exacerbated social difficulties. For example, in the 1950s many refugee single men worked on hydro-electric schemes in Tasmania where limited contact with females led to low marriage rates and high rates of alcoholism. Despite these conditions many survived to retirement age. Now, obliged to retire and move out of their protected camp environments, they face considerable difficulties.

While ethnic groups have generally been supportive of new arrivals, early European refugees did not have the support of established groups. Widespread settlement patterns isolated them from ethnic group developments and also restricted developments of a formal nature. Moreover, it was noticeable that some political refugees deliberately avoided ethnic activities for fear of retribution by the regimes from which they had fled. High rates of out-marriage lessened cultural ties and undoubtedly created many marginal persons. Moreover, ethnic group developments that did occur tended to be beset by internal conflict, as one of Martin's studies revealed, and were generally short-lived (Martin, 1972; see also Jupp, 1966, 178).

Eastern European refugee settlement in Australia in the 1950s and 1960s reflected to some degree the social conditions prevailing in Australia at that time. Was it a successful movement for the individuals involved? There are certainly many individual success stories. On the other hand, there are undoubtedly many who may well have been happier had they remained in Europe. Those who formed part of cohesive and active community groups, especially among the Jewish refugees, appear to have experienced a more rewarding life in Australia than those who did not. However, overall the movement was, as Martin stressed, very diverse.

Of the 95 000 Southeast Asian refugees who arrived between 1975 and 1985, the majority were refugees from Vietnam, mainly ethnic Chinese (Viviani, 1984, 130 ff). High masculinity ratios and predominance in semi-skilled or unskilled occupations characterises this group, although there were also some educated persons who faced considerable difficulties in having their qualifications recognised (Cox, 1983; see also Fry Committee, 1983).

There is little doubt that a large proportion of Indo-Chinese refugees in Australia have experienced many difficulties, although again generalisations are dangerous. Difficulty of acquiring a reasonable knowledge of English has certainly contributed to high unemployment rates. Tensions have also existed both within and between Southeast Asian ethnic associations and one study found that at least 20 per cent of Australians hold racist attitudes towards Indo-Chinese (Keys-Young, 1980, 74). On the whole, however, it is difficult to know how Indo-Chinese themselves perceive their settlement in Australia and their prospects for successful integration. Studies of the kind conducted by Viviani leave many questions largely unanswered (Viviani, 184, 273-5).

It therefore appears that many Australian-born, and many immigrants, remain ambivalent towards Asians, with working-class persons and European immigrants being more ambivalent than others. This ambivalence turns readily to rejection when economic well-being is threatened. It may also be concluded that non-Europeans are obliged to conform to social systems that are Anglo-Celtic or European in origin. Despite its rejection as policy, assimilation remains a strong force in Australia. Retention of cultural values in the private sphere and in ethnic group life is accepted, so long as it is not too intrusive or known to reflect values that are unacceptable to European-Christian values.

In the short term, it appears that a considerable proportion of Indo-Chinese refugees will not be able to integrate in any full sense at linguistic, social and economic levels within mainstream Australian life. Some will find an alternative niche within comparatively self-sufficient Asian enclaves, as the Chinese have frequently done around the world, and other Australians may well accept this. Other Asians will remain in marginal situations and perhaps project their hopes onto their children. None of these phenomena is peculiar to Asian immigrants; the same developments have been experienced by other groups.

As already noted, the 1980s have seen a considerable broadening of the range of source countries from which refugees have come. It is also likely that Australian immigration officials have been highly selective in determining those eligible. Although statistics are not available, many refugees have been well-educated and have possessed a high level of ability in the English language. Their settlement potential is therefore high; individual difficulties seem to relate mainly to recognition of overseas qualifications, the rental housing market and the employment situation. However, these difficulties seem to slow the refugee's integration rather than obviate his ultimate success.

It should not be assumed that only the more poorly-educated individuals require the support of appropriate socio-cultural structures. A majority of immigrants will desire to affiliate with some form of religious, cultural, sporting or social organisation, and frequently they will insist or prefer that the organisation possess an ethnic orientation. This may be in terms of the language used, the manner in which activities are organised or the backgrounds of other members. Yet small ethnic populations, unless highly-concentrated geographically, have great difficulty developing an organised group life. Hence many of the more recent refugee arrivals have been left largely dependent on the openness of the wider Australian society and their own cultural attributes. That openness remains fairly limited. It would be surprising if the small numbers of Ethiopians, Afghans, Ba'hai Iranians, Salvadoreans and others who arrived during the past few years have been met with open arms for either themselves or their organised cultures.

In very general terms, the economic settlement of these people has depended mainly on their skills and their determination to succeed. On the whole the refugee population has been highly motivated, has accepted initially poorly paid and relatively unattractive employment and, by dint of hard work and sheer determination, the majority has fared reasonably well.

Where economic hardship has occurred among refugees, it has usually been due to personal misfortunes of various kinds, or related to membership of clearly defined categories of refugees. One category has been adolescent arrivals, especially if migrating alone but often as members of families. Refugee adolescent arrivals frequently had their development impaired in the years prior to departure. Australian systems have never catered well to adolescent arrivals, let alone deprived or disadvantaged refugee adolescents. Hence the opportunities for successful integration for this category are limited.

A second category has been single adult refugee arrivals. A significant proportion of these people has experienced psychiatric illness, alcoholism and a lack of family life; crime rates among some sections of this single-on-arrival population may have been higher than average in the community (see Krupinski, 1966, 271-3; DIEA, 1970; Krupinski and Stoller, 1966; Francis, 1981, 156-7). Reasons for the difficulties experienced by this category of refugee are complex. Some relate to previous psychiatric and social problems or to a pattern of drifting already established; many suffer greatly from lack of family life in Australia and many experience difficulty in establishing meaningful social contacts in either their ethnic group of origin or in the wider Australian society (Cox, 1973). Migration and settlement in third countries may not be the best solution for such refugees, despite the possible initial reaction of some that single refugees will find settlement in third countries easier than will families.

Finally, it should be noted that refugee families which experience breakdown in family functioning will, like most immigrants, tend to experience more difficulties than the Australian-born. These are exacerbated by such events as the death of a breadwinner, an industrial or road accident leading to a physical disability, prolonged periods of illness or difficulties with intra-familial relations. The support systems operative in such situations tend to disadvantage immigrant clients, while lack of personal support networks that characterise the situations of many refugees aggravate the initial problem. While in one sense immigrants in Australia in such situations will be better off then in their homeland or in a country of first asylum, in other ways their often intense isolation leaves them worse off than they might have been. Freedom from starvation is very important, but bare economic survival by itself does not constitute living.

While the economic settlement of refugees in Australia has been successful (and that of their children even more successful) their vulnerability and hardships along the way should not be overlooked. The social aspects of refugee resettlement are less well understood and probably underrated. It seems likely that ethnic group development is more difficult within typical refugee populations. Possible reasons for this would include a comparative lack of initial economic resources; a need to work very hard since return is usually out of the question; frequently high levels of anxiety about relatives left behind or who have disappeared, and sometimes about their own safety; high levels of factionalism with reactions to past events being projected on to leaders and others in the settlement situation; the frequently dispersed nature of the settlement, especially given the absence of chain migration together with the common preponderance of isolated nuclear families and single persons; and a prevailing sense of uncertainty regarding attitudes towards them in the host society. Comparative absence of ethnic group support is an extremely important factor in the Australian context, given the highly significant roles played by ethnic group structures (Cox, 1975).

However, there is a further important dimension to refugee settlement, and that is the individual's acceptance of the move and of life in the new country. It appears that many refugees possess overt or repressed negative attitudes towards their move. It may be a sense of having made the wrong decision; it may be a bitterness that circumstances beyond their control forced the move; or it may be a deep-seated nostalgia or homesickness that is never overcome. Of course other immigrants can experience such feelings, but they have a way out. Voluntary migrants can return and, judging from Australian statistics, many do. Most refugees either cannot return or know that they would be returning to impossible conditions. The propensity of refugees to take any job and to work hard is not always a positive feature. It can represent a desperate effort either to convince themselves of the appropriateness of the move or to escape pervasive negative feelings. When this is the case there comes a time when work will no longer serve either purpose. Many refugees find support from fellow refugees; however, for many such refugees support is not readily available, and they are obliged to battle on alone.

The basic question underlying refugee settlement in Australia is whether refugees from developing countries are likely to experience greater difficulties than other refugees. At the economic level, past experience suggests that a combination of relevant skills, a positive approach by refugees stemming from reasonable levels of satisfaction, and reasonably positive attitudes towards the refugee group in question on the part of employers and others are essential. If members of a refugee population possess few skills (including English), are preoccupied with the personal and social aspects of settlement and are not positively viewed by the majority of employers, their economic settlement will be precarious.

At the social level the issue is not so much the development status of the countries whence they come, although this is a factor, but rather the individual refugee's background. Depending on such factors as acceptance of mobility and separation, the importance of organised culture and the degree of affinity that a culture has with others, there is likely to be considerable variation among refugee groups in social integration, although much depends on the individual. Fortunately, recent developments in Australia and internationally may improve the social integration of refugees in the future. As Australia becomes increasingly multicultural and multiracial, few groups will feel completely isolated in the future. Mobility between countries is now much greater and more refugees may regard their settlement in a third country as a temporary sojourn. Involvement in any country's politics from outside that country is probably now easier, and such activity may be increasingly used by refugee settlers as a defence against preoccupations with guilt, anger and resentment.

On the other hand, both excessive mobility in the form of returning and involvement from within Australia in another country's politics are unlikely to be viewed favourably by Australian residents. Overall, it appears that refugees from Third World countries are more at risk in the settlement process in Australia than are other refugees or voluntary immigrants.

Australia's Refugee Policy and Developing Countries

An analysis of refugee resettlement in Australia suggests strongly that refugees from impoverished backgrounds in developing countries experience considerable difficulty in resettling satisfactorily in Australia. The more divergent their backgrounds the greater will be the extent of difficulty and the more problematic appear to be both ethnic group and local support. What, then, should be Australia's response to refugee situations in developing countries? Such situations occur from a combination of political and economic factors (Goodwin-Gill, 1980, 21). Consideration of economic factors may lead a government to question the genuineness of claims to refugee status. Many people believe that the move to a developed country by people in a developing country is "very attractive economically, even if they are in no danger" (Rivett, 1979, 138). Many Australians were highly suspicious of the later waves of refugees from Vietnam for this reason. Yet this may not be a valid assumption. Writing of potential refugees from Latin America, Schneider (1980, 143) argued:

> If we find relatively few refugees from the more disadvantaged sectors of these communities it is not because they had no reason to flee but because (i) they have a strong cultural resistance against leaving their country, (ii) they often have insufficient education and training to reach the standards of acceptance imposed by countries such as Australia, and (iii), maybe more importantly, they often consider repression simply as one more of the many difficulties through which they have to survive, together with unemployment, crime, under-nourishment and lack of decent housing.

Political factors behind refugee movements seem to evoke a more positive response than do the economic factors. It has been argued that by accepting refugees from a repressive regime a country is in practice aiding and abetting repression. Some persons argued that too positive a response in resettlement terms would encourage Vietnam to continue to expel an ethnic minority.

Although refugee situations in developing countries result from well-understood economic and political factors, one cannot assume that potential countries of resettlement such as Australia will automatically respond positively. Both sets of factors may present difficulties at the point of acknowledging either the genuineness of the refugee movement or the appropriateness of responding to it in resettlement terms. This is partly why Australian policy statements in recent years have increasingly stressed the importance of non-resettlement solutions to refugee situations. In 1982 the then Secretary of the Department of Immigration and Ethnic Affairs explored some of the other options open to Australia:

A variety of solutions are available, and Australia is taking an active and vigorous role in pursuing these, particularly voluntary repatriation of these people to their former homes ... Aside from resettlement we are heavily involved in the process of providing care, assistance and protection for refugees and displaced persons around the world. Last year Australia contributed some A\$ 49 million to these activities ... Australia is working with the international community through the UNHCR to seek long term solutions for those who have not been resettled in third countries ... Another aspect of our approach is the normalising of migration outflows from refugee source countries. (Menadue, 1982, 2/4-2/5.)

If the desire is to see resettlement in third countries as a last resort rather than a first option, refugees might languish for years in refugee camps either while these alternative solutions are explored by the international community or until complex political situations in countries of origin are resolved.

One group of people commonly affected by political repression and upheaval are well-educated individuals who become leaders and activists within political movements that are unacceptable to the ruling body. Such persons are usually middle class or elite, "whose experience and skills represent a human capital of considerable importance" (Schneider, 1980, 142). If they flee and resettle elsewhere they represent a considerable loss to their country. Nor are they likely to return to their country until a change of regime occurs. They represent a considerable asset to the country of resettlement acquired at virtually no cost. Initially their past involvement in political activities may result in a preoccupation with events in their country of origin but, unless change is seen to be imminent and return possible, the majority soon divert their energies to achievement in the country of resettlement. Australia has never been adverse to accepting such refugees unless the political affiliations of the group in question were considered likely to constitute a destabilizing force within Australian society.

A second group of people likely to be a part of a major refugee exodus are those living in areas affected by major upheaval. These are likely to be rural or village people whose lives of subsistence are easily jeopardised and whose capacity to be influenced by mass hysteria is high. In developing countries most of these people will possess minimal education and strong traditional cultural bonds. In the country of first asylum, their desire is to return home. Both their capacity to assess resettlement prospects in a third country and their capacity to adjust to a very different environment are limited. For such people it would seem that safe return should be negotiated if possible, or alternatively that resettlement in situations not too dissimilar or too distant geographically from the ones whence they came should be sought. It is unlikely that resettlement in Australia would represent a good solution. While they would be safe and would not starve, it is highly unlikely that they will integrate in any full sense of that word.

The third type of refugee in past and potential refugee movements from developing countries is expelled minorities who require a new homeland. Australia has already admitted White Russians from China, Armenians and Assyrians from various Middle East countries, Christians and others from Iran and Iraq, Asians from Uganda and Chinese from Vietnam. The potential for such movements in Australia's geographical region is high. Feith (1979, 22) observes that ASEAN governments' main concern seems to be to facilitate the emigration of people who could be politically troublesome at home. And Grant (1979, 82) argues that of "the main exodus of 163 000 people who left Vietnam between March 1978 and mid-1979 for nearby non-communist countries, 65 per cent were from Vietnam's Chinese minority. In the same period about 250 000 Chinese left Vietnam for China. Clearly, an explanation for the exodus must be sought, at least partly, in the position of the Chinese in Vietnam". Hastings (1980) wrote that the one great lesson that Vietnam taught the world was the "extraordinary success, if that is the word, of a policy of deliberate expulsion of a particular ethnic group".

Confronted with refugee situations involving the expulsion of ethnic minorities, especially those occurring within its region, Australia is likely to be under considerable pressure to respond, especially when alternative solutions to resettlement may be very difficult. The controversy in Australia in recent years over Asian migration suggests, however, that the ready absorption into Australian society of ethnic minorities of non-European origins may not be a straightforward matter. Yet Australia may have little choice but to offer resettlement opportunities. Moreover, several factors could contribute to the ultimate success of such programmes. First, minority groups are often adept at surviving under adverse conditions. Second, the groups likely to be expelled may have considerable economic resources which assist greatly the resettlement process. Third, such movements are likely to lead to close settlement patterns and institutional developments, both of which are usually very supportive.

In each of these three situations the impact on countries from which the refugees have come will be mixed. Departure of both community leaders and ethnic minorities represents loss of a considerable economic asset even though rulers benefit from the exodus. Only if the communal tensions that caused the exodus were having a devastating effect on the country would the refugee exodus be likely to have long-term benefits. If the exodus comprised "typical" citizens, it could be followed by return movement. However, the absence of refugees for a period, especially from rural areas, and their return, would be costly. Not only would refugees who resettle in third countries be unlikely to send back large remittance payments but the amounts would probably decline after the first few years.

Australia is far more likely to accept political, economic and social leaders who are forced to flee as refugees and members of ethnic minorities expelled by governments within its region than large numbers of unskilled refugees from developing countries. If it is pressed to accept the third category of mass refugees, as it was in Eastern Europe and Southeast Asia, it will be as selective as possible. One could therefore conclude that the resettlement of refugees from the Third World has not been, and is unlikely to be, of significant benefit to countries of origin. On the other hand, it largely has been, and is likely to continue to be, of benefit to Australia.

While the process of selecting refugees is, in the case of Australia, more disadvantageous than advantageous to Third World countries, it is possible that the longer-term benefits for Third World countries of their refugees settling in Australia may be more advantageous than has been supposed. For example, remittance payments have not been insignificant and refugees, like all other Australian residents, are entitled to nominate for settlement relatives of specified degrees of affinity. For example, the resettlement in Australia of refugees from Vietnam has made possible the Orderly Departure Program from Vietnam of relatives of these refugees. While such family reunion movements often present short-term social and economic problems within Australia they may represent more assistance to the country of origin than did the original refugee movement.

Even more significant for the Third World countries than the emigration of comparatively small numbers of people to Australia could be the stronger bonds forged between the two countries as a result of the movement. As more people from a specific Third World country settle in Australia, their country becomes better known to Australians. This occurs in a variety of ways. Individual Australian residents meet the newcomers and learn of their country of origin; the mass media frequently cover specific migration situations and eventually school curricula may incorporate something from that country.

Other linkages may also develop. Refugee enterpreneurs will forge trade and other linkages in their region of origin. Such linkages are likely to be economically beneficial for both regions. For example, a 1985 report on Asian refugees from Uganda in the United Kingdom indicated that some had prospered by building business contacts with Africa (UNHCR, 1985). Whether Asian refugees in Australia will achieve the same degree of success is difficult to say, but given their achievements so far it is highly likely that they will do so.

Refugees in Australia also operate as pressure groups on the Australian Government seeking its involvement in specific international situations. For example, Palestinian refugees have sought to influence Australia's role in Middle Eastern affairs, Tamil refugees in Sri Lankan affairs, various Vietnamese and Cambodian groups in Southeast Asian political developments, and refugees from Africa in the affairs of various African countries. Political interest may lead to development aid or better trade arrangements or a change in a Third World political situation and thus create a greater degree of economic stability or a higher level of economic growth.

CONCLUSION

Several conclusions may be drawn from this brief analysis of the impact of Australia's refugee resettlement policy on Third World countries. First, it is unlikely that Australia will accept large numbers of refugees from Third World countries. The numbers accepted from any situation will depend mainly on the degree to which Australia is under pressure to offer resettlement opportunities and such pressure is likely to be greatest when the refugee situations are within Australia's geographical region.

Second, for reasons that relate mainly to its own economic and political realities, Australia is likely to carefully select refugees who are best able to adapt to Australian conditions. Such policies will therefore benefit Australia more than Third World countries of origin.

Third, the short-term consequences of refugee settlement in Australia will probably be negative for the country of origin. Refugees represent a loss that low level remittances will not offset.

Fourth, the fact that refugee groups have tended to integrate economically, socially and politically into Australian society will have long-term benefits for the countries of origin: more trade and business links, better levels of understanding and perhaps some positive contributions from Australia through more enlightened foreign policies. For these reasons, even small movements of refugees from Third World countries to Australia for resettlement should not be regarded as insignificant for the countries of origin; they are certainly not insignificant for the individual refugees.

BIBLIOGRAPHY

AUSTRALIAN COUNCIL ON POPULATION AND ETHNIC AFFAIRS
    Regional Refugee Consultations, Canberra, DIEA, 1982.

AUSTRALIAN POPULATION AND IMMIGRATION COUNCIL
    Immigration Policies and Australia's Population, Canberra, AGPS, 1977.

AUSTRALIAN REFUGEE ADVISORY COUNCIL
    National Consultation On Refugees, Canberra, DIEA, 1980.

BLAINEY, G.
    All For Australia, Sydney, Methuen Haynes, 1984.

COX, D.R.
    "Problems of the Single Male Immigrant", in N. Parker, ed., Focus On
    Migrants, Sydney, ACOSS, 1973.

    "The Role of Ethnic Groups in Migrant Welfare", Welfare of Migrants,
    Canberra, AGPS, 1975.

    "Australia's Immigration Policy and Refugees", in R. Birrell
    et al., eds., Refugees Resources Reunion, VCTA Pub., 1979.

    "Refugee Settlement: An Australian Case Study", in C.A. Price, ed.,
    Refugees: Challenge of the Future, Canberra, Academy of the Social
    Sciences in Australia, 1981.

    "Professionally Qualified Refugees from Vietnam", Australian Journal of
    Social Issues, Vol. 18, No. 4, 1983.

DEPARTMENT OF IMMIGRATION
    Survey of Immigrants in Psychiatric Institutions, Canberra, 1970.

DEPARTMENT OF IMMIGRATION AND ETHNIC AFFAIRS
    Australia's Policy on Refugees, Canberra, 1979.

    Review '85, Canberra, AGPS, 1985(a).

    A Land of Immigrants, Canberra, 1985(b).

FEITH, H.
    "Australian Immigration Policy and Asia", in R. Birrell et al., eds.,
    Refugees Resources Reunion, Melbourne, VCTA Pub., 1979.

FRANCIS, R.D.
    Migrant Crime in Australia, St. Lucia, University of Queensland Press,
    1981.

FRY COMMITTEE OF INQUIRY
The Recognition of Overseas Qualifications in Australia, Canberra,
AGPS, 1983.

GOODWIN-GILL, G.
"The Refugee Situation Today", in C.A. Price, ed., Refugees: The
Challenge of the Future, Canberra, Academy of the Social Sciences in
Australia, 1980.

GORDON, M.M.
Assimilation In American Life, New York, Oxford University Press, 1984.

GRANT, B.
The Boat People, Penguin, 1979.

HASTINGS, P.
"Australia and the World Refugee Problem", Australian Refugee Advisory
Council, National Consultation on Refugees, Canberra, DIEA, 1980.

HAWKE, R.J.
Parliamentary Hansard, 10th May 1984.

JUPP, J.
Arrivals and Departures, Melbourne, Lansdowne Press, 1966.

"Australian Immigration 1788-1973", in F. Milne and P. Shergold, eds.,
The Great Immigration Debate, Sydney, Federation of Ethnic Communities'
Councils of Australia, 1984.

KEYS-YOUNG, M.S.J.
The Settlement Process of the Vietnamese, Lao, Kampuchean and Timorese
in Sydney, Canberra, DIEA, 1980.

KRUPINSKI, J.
Sociological Aspects of Mental Ill-health in Migrants, paper presented
to the Sixth World Congress of Sociology, Evian, France, 1966.

KRUPINSKI, J. and A. STOLLER
"Family Life and Mental Ill-health in Migrants", in A. Stoller, ed.,
New Faces, Melbourne, Cheshire, 1966.

MACKELLAR, M.J.R.
Refugee Policy And Mechanisms, Parliamentary Debates, 24th May 1977.

Statement to Parliament on A New Immigration Policy, Parliamentary
Debates, 6th June 1978.

MARTIN, J.I.
Refugee Settlers, Canberra, ANU Press, 1965.

Community And Identity, Canberra, ANU Press, 1972.

MENADUE, J.
"Refugee Programs and Priorities", Australian Council on Population and
Ethnic Affairs, Regional Refugee Consultations, Canberra, DIEA, 1982.

NORMAN, N.R. and K.F. MEIKLE
    The Economic Effects Of Immigration In Australia, Canberra, Committee
    for Economic Development of Australia, 1985.

PRICE, C.A.
    "Family Reunion and Refugees", in R. Birrell et al., eds., Refugees
    Resources Reunion, Melbourne, VCTA Pub., 1979.

    Introduction, in C.A. Price, ed., Refugees: The Challenge of the
    Future, Canberra, Academy of the Social Sciences in Australia, 1980.

RIVETT, K.
    "Towards a Policy on Refugees", The Australian Outlook, August 1979.

SCHNEIDER, H.J.
    "Latin America: Lands of Refuge, Lands of Exile", in C.A. Price, ed.,
    Refugees: The Challenge of the Future, Canberra, Academy of the Social
    Sciences in Australia, 1980.

SENATE STANDING COMMITTEE ON FOREIGN AFFAIRS AND DEFENCE
    Australia and the Refugee Problem, Canberra, AGPS, 1976.

UNITED NATIONS HIGH COMMISSIONER FOR REFUGEES
    Refugees, September 1985.

VIVIANI, N.
    The Long Journey: Vietnamese Migration And Settlement in Australia,
    Melbourne, MUP, 1984.

VIVIANI, N. and J. LAWE-DAVIES
    Australian Government Policy on the Entry of Vietnamese Refugees, 1976
    to 1978, Griffith University, Centre for the Study of Australian-Asian
    Relations, 1980.

F. RETURN

Chapter 17

ROLE MODELS AND PARALLEL LIVES:
MEXICAN MIGRANT WOMEN RETURN HOME

by

A. Perez-Itriago and S. Guendelman

INTRODUCTION

It is commonly believed that America is the land of milk and honey, of freedom and opportunity in which many dispossessed people want to settle permanently. However, many immigrants enter the United States on a temporary basis and then return home to their local communities. Few systematic data have been collected on return migration which has been consistently over-shadowed by studies on permanent immigration (Gmelch, 1980). Furthermore, as the impacts of migration appear in the receiving country long before they affect the sending country (Murillo Castano, 1984), it is perhaps not surpris-ing that these have only recently received scholarly attention.

Return migration streams are difficult to determine largely because returnees have not been precisely identified. Some estimates of return have been based on actual counts while others have relied on the migrants' expec-tations. Furthermore, most of the research has been based on the experiences of males; the contribution of females has been neglected (Gmelch, 1980; Guendelman and Perez-Itriago, forthcoming (1)). This chapter therefore focuses on the role of women in the return process, specifically the experi-ences of seasonal workers who travel back and forth between Mexico and the United States, their processes of adjustment once they return and their influence on the home community.

Return in the Context of Seasonal Migration

Return migration has been defined as a movement of migrants back to their homelands to resettle (Bovenkerk, 1974; Feindt and Browning, 1972; Gmelch, 1980). When movement between two places includes multiple returns, it is referred to as circulation. Seasonal migration is a specific type of circulation in which multiple returns for varying lengths of time occur at different stages of a person's life. Recurrent trips create seasonal

269

lifestyles in which each successive return constitutes a temporal event in the migratory experience. Some individuals break this cycle by resolving not to return or by returning home permanently. However, "permanent" resettlement is often tentative and many returnees express a strong desire to return to the host country (Gmelch, 1979a, Lianos, 1975; Paine, 1974). Others voice strong intentions to resettle in their country of origin while continuing to return only on a temporary basis. Because actual and potential returnees have been included in studies of return migration, definitions and denominators have been obscured (Weist, 1979).

Whether defined according to permanence, residence, motivation or return ideology, returnees cannot be studied in isolation from historical and socio-political factors. Migrants' decisions to return are couched in a complex macro structure. For instance, the seasonal migration of Mexicans to the United States is predominantly a response to job opportunties and better wages available in the north. The Bracero Program, formalised in 1942, was designed to alleviate manpower shortages in the agricultural sector. Seasonal male workers were hired for an average eight months per year in large-scale agricultural complexes in the southwestern United States. During its twenty-two years existence, the programme attracted approximately 550 000 Mexican migrants (Garcia y Griego, 1983).

Although the Bracero Program was officially terminated in 1964, economic disparities between Mexico and the United States sustained significant flows of seasonal workers. Legal migration triggered illegal migration which increased with the help of social networks that had been established in the United States. Women joined these streams in increasing numbers, suggesting a high dependence on male migration patterns and opportunities in labour-intensive United States' markets (Dinnerman, 1982; Fernandez-Kelly, 1983).

The persistence of seasonal migrant flows suggests that once initiated, migration streams take on a life of their own. They are hard to stop despite policy changes in the host society (Tapinos, 1983). Seasonal migration triggers multiple returns and successive cohorts in search of better and new opportunities join the flow of temporary workers abroad. Moreover, for many cohorts that return home, changed lifestyles and expectations of higher standards of living require further migrations (Weist, 1978). Seasonal migration thus induces recurrent returns on a temporary basis while strengthening intentions of permanent return when basic and surfeit needs can be steadily satisfied.

The interdependency between the individual's decision to return and the broader macro structure is further reflected in the ideology of return. This refers to a cognitive model that guides migrant behaviour, shapes ideals and reconciles differences between dreams and realities of the migration experience (Philpott, 1971, 1973). It is a strategy that migrants use to hold on to their fantasies and expectations of maintaining close ties with their homelands while undergoing changes in a host society. It also serves to order various elements of the migration process within society. For example, the sending communities of Jalisco have institutionalised "el dia del ausente", a festivity that honours those migrants living abroad who maintain close social ties with the community and upon which an economic dependency has been established.

The strong interdependency between Mexico and the United States influences the return ideology. Decisions to return to Mexico are often deferred by low wages, lack of job opportunities and reluctance to return to work in agriculture (Weist, 1979; Gmelch, 1979b, 1980; Bustamante, 1978; Bennett, 1979; Brettel, 1979). Dissatisfaction with traditional life at home and difficulties in readjusting to home values and norms are cultural barriers operating against a permanent return. Immigration policies in the host society also intervene. Although immigration without documentation is considered illegal by the United States Immigration and Naturalization Service, holding a job is not sanctioned under the law. This contradiction encourages immigration and delays the decision regarding permanent return to Mexico. Finally, as more women and children participate in international migration and join the United States labour force, the incentive to return is weakened. Women become reluctant to return to Mexico where they would be confined to the home. Children react to being uprooted from their peers and their schools. However, since women are very dependent on family bonds and on household decisions, they generally follow their spouse's decision on whether and when to return. Hence for women, it seems that affective considerations weigh heavily in the decision to return.

The Impact of the Return

The impact of return migration has been studied from two general standpoints: individual and societal effects including economic impact and changes in social values, expectations and social relations. Although consistency of evidence bolsters confidence in these studies, many suffer from methodological shortcomings. The prime difficulties relate to quantifying the concept and that most studies confuse wishes or intentions to migrate with actual behaviour. Because most studies rely exclusively on self reports to access information on return, the validity of measurement should be questioned. Furthermore, almost sole reliance on the experiences of men may limit the relevance of the findings to women. These shortcomings not withstanding, the following evidence distills what is known about the impact of return which may be relevant for understanding the experiences of women.

Individual adjustment

It has been widely assumed that migration is a stressful experience which taxes individual coping mechanisms. Several studies suggest that individuals go through such stages of adjustment as incorporation of new values and behaviour and accommodation and assimilation into society (Colson, 1975; Graves and Graves, 1974). However, these studies characteristically fail to determine whether the stresses related to seeking work, establishing friendships, adjusting to old values; and whether these stemmed from the migration process itself, the characteristics of the home society or the returnee's personal attributes; and the extent to which interaction contributed to the return experience. In the specific case of seasonal migration, a strong ideology of return and the community's receptivity to returnees are important factors influencing adjustment. Evidence suggests that the stronger the ideology of return, i.e., the stronger the expectation of return, culminating in an actual return, the higher the likelihood of adaptation. Likewise, a stronger community responsiveness to returnees makes adjustment easier.

Evidence culled from European and Caribbean studies suggests that the individual adjustment of returnees depends mainly on four characteristics: (i) the locus of control in the decision to return; (ii) reasons motivating the return; (iii) the extent to which return expectations fit reality; and (iv) the distance between the values and norms acquired in the host society contrasted with those in the home society.

i) Locus of control: The decision to return may be planned or unplanned according to whether it was inner-directed or imposed by external factors. Return to get married or to reinforce social ties is an example of a planned return; deportation, unemployment or lay-off are examples of unplanned returns. When a relocation, whether of a temporary or permanent nature, culminates in a planned return, the coping strategy is considered successful (Gmelch, 1980). When the return has been involuntary, subject to conditions beyond individual control, the return is likely to trigger maladaptive behaviour or prompt re-emigration;

ii) Reasons motivating the return: Cerase (1974) has identified four types of returnees. First, returnees of failure, i.e., those who had been unable to satisfy the needs that motivated them to leave the society of origin. The second are returnees of conservatism who return home with savings which they seek to invest or spend. The third are innovative types who return home because they see the possibility of implementing their new skills and of additional earnings. Finally, there are returnees who seek to retire;

This typology is not exhaustive and in the case of seasonal migrants the ideology that motivates return may not be solely to invest and consume. Many returnees to Mexico expect to enjoy leisure. The opportunity to be indulged by family and friends in communities where dollars "stretch further" makes home an appealing "vacation land". If communities are eager to receive these returnees, not only because they bring back earnings but also because they liven up depressed towns drained by massive emigration, then the emotional refueling derived from social supports is even stronger;

iii) Realistic expectations: The extent to which returnees have realistic expectations of what the home society can provide is another factor influencing adjustment. Vacations to the homeland, letters from loved ones, nostalgia and childhood memories often shape unrealistic fantasies about the homeland. The wider the gap between fantasy and reality, the greater the likelihood of maladjustment problems. For instance, Puerto Rican adolescents returning from New York experienced school adjustment problems, lack of identity and low self-esteem undervaluing the Puerto Rican school system and perceiving school, teachers and self to be more positive in the United States (Seilhamer and Prewett-Diaz, 1983). These experiences are sometimes referred to as reversed culture shock (Gmelch, 1979a; King, 1978; Rhoades, 1978);

iv) Values and normative distance between host and home societies: Evidence suggests that the wider the dissimilarities in values and norms acquired in the host culture compared with those in the home culture, the greater the cultural conflict experienced by returnees (Kasl and Berkman, 1983; Gmelch, 1980). Dissenting evidence suggests that stress and role conflict are not necessarily by-products of migration, especially when migration occurs between societies in which individuals share common values and attitudes that facilitate adjustment (Maingot, 1985). With respect to seasonal migrant women, we have found that they rely strongly on networks to bridge the cultural gap as they move back and forth between Mexico and the United States (Arizpe, 1983; Mortimer and Bryce-Laporte, 1981). Furthermore, desire to maintain family cohesiveness can be an important reason for migrating (Guendelman and Perez-Itriago, forthcoming). To what extent then, does migration enhance psychological well-being rather than add stress? This study seeks to address this important issue.

Impact on the social structure

Economic impacts have received the most attention. Several authors argue that emigration serves to improve the standard of living of individual migrants and their families (Bennett, 1974; Palmer, 1983; Weist, 1978, 1979; Swanson, 1979; Gmelch, 1980); although there is less consensus concerning the extent to which it enhances the long-term economic development of sending societies (Swanson, 1978; Rhoades, 1979; Rubenstein, 1982). For instance the claim that emigration from Mexico is a safety valve that alleviates economic and population pressures and helps quell political unrest (Bustamante, 1984) should be set against loss of human capital investment for Mexico. Nor does emigration always trigger increased productivty; it often creates depressed towns and villages inhabited by women, children and the frail who become largely dependent on remittances.

Estimates by Martin (1985) indicate that migrants remit an average $2 000 annually to their families and estimates by Cornelius (1982) indicate that Mexican workers send an average of $170 per month back home and then take approximately $300 in savings when they return. Remittances are directed to basic consumption needs to guarantee survival rather than to the development of local economies (Wood, 1982). They are seldom used on productive investments or innovative machines and tools that increase productivity (Gmelch, 1980; Swanson, 1979). With few exceptions, most of the money is spent on food and clothing or on conspicious consumption such as the building of large and elaborate housing (Weist, 1979, 172). When productive investments are made, allocations go into small land plots or businesses. Land acquired is seldom exploited to capacity and businesses either encourage further surplus consumption or merely add to the supply of services already available in the community (Griffiths, 1979). Some scholars argue that such investments serve to enhance the social prestige of returnees rather than foster local industrialisation (Cerase, 1974; Brana-Shute, 1982). An exception is investment in housing which generates employment in housebuilding. However this activity is often sporadic and unstable, since it depends on continued remittances.

Remittances symbolise a sense of obligation towards family and community, as well as a symbol of success. During absences abroad remittances serve to extend the migrant's presence in the family. Furthermore, savings are usually channeled into concrete expressions of success such as elaborate housing and furnishings which set returnees apart from the rest of the community. Since the community is the principal judge of a returnee's success, returnees ensure that the economic rewards they have reaped abroad are ostensibly displayed (Rhoades, 1978, 1979; Bennett, 1979; Philpott, 1968). Remittances may also represent the most important expression of an intention to return.

The extent to which migrants learn skills that can be transferred to less developed societies is problematical. Weist (1975, 1978) found that many of the skills acquired by Mexican bracero workers in large-scale agriculture could not be transferred to small-scale agriculture in Mexico. The few skills that seem transferable are house-design, self-appearance, nutrition and sanitation (Cerase, 1974).

In sum, remittances are primarily used to improve personal or family lifestyles rather than for capital investment and community development. Murillo Castano (1984) suggests that the real benefits of migration accrue over time. As migration patterns become more established, future generations may reap the advantages of a well-established lifestyle.

Social values, expectations and social relations

In migration-oriented societies returnees are assigned a special value because of their economic contributions and new ideas. However, homogeneous traditional societies tend to resist quick innovation and insist on maintaining the status quo. While returnees may be valued as successful, upwardly mobile entrepreneurs, they are also a source of envy and threat to those who do not have access to their purchasing power. This leads to social disparities and tensions in the community. Evidence suggests that non-migrants become suspicious and resist innovations brought home by European returnees (Gmelch, 1980; Cerase, 1970; Dahya, 1973; Davison, 1968; Rhoades, 1978).

The conservative orientation of most returnees also counteracts change (Cerase, 1974). The dream of migrants is to work with their hands in the host societies so that they can either stop working or work in non-manual activities when they return (Brettel, 1979). For instance, many see Mexico as a place of leisure and the United States as a place of work. Consequently, migrants want to protect the status quo by investing in a plot of land or small business rather than changing society. They also want to preserve their familiar culture which reassures identity and provides emotional refueling. Those returning with innovative ideas on how to run a business, or organise and improve community resources can be resented. Local power groups and limited economic resources tend to block innovations (Rhoades, 1979).

Studies from Europe, Mexico and the Caribbean also suggest that despite migrant dreams of climbing the social ladder, returnees seldom achieve social mobility. Their gains are usually circumscribed to enhanced prestige and temporal economic power which, as it dries out, pushes returnees back to their original status within society (Cerase, 1974; Stinner, Albuquerque and Bryce-Laporte, 1982; Weist, 1979; King, 1978). A decrease in standard of living triggers re-emigration. The rising expectations and impact of migrant behaviour in the community makes them powerful role models for others. As non-migrants become aware of the limited opportunities to improve their standards of living they try to emulate migrants by joining the migratory flow (Rubenstein, 1979).

In sum, existing evidence based primarily on the experiences of males indicates that returnees are seldom carriers of lasting social change. The extent to which women contribute to change either in the family realm or in the broader social system has not been documented. The present study explores this neglected issue.

Methodology and Fieldsite

Information for this study was collected using two techniques: a survey questionnaire and in-depth interviews. Quantitative data were obtained from 80 women living in the United States in 1983 who returned to their home towns as single, unaccompanied adults or spouses. It is a sub-sample of a larger household survey of 386 seasonal workers and their families.

Two rural towns located in the outskirts of Guadalajara, Mexico were used as fieldsites. They are known to be important sending communities of migrants to California. Each of these towns relies mainly on agriculture, livestock and milk production. Many farmers live off small plots of eroded, rain-fed land; a few are employed by large surrounding private farms or own small businesses. Women in these communities generally do not work outside the home. Those who do, perform mainly vocational or clerical services.

The sample was drawn from the censuses of both towns of approximately 4 100 and 1 850 persons. Each household that reported a member in the United States during 1983, the baseline year, and who returned to Mexico by early 1984 was interviewed (Guendelman, 1985; Guendelman and Perez-Itriago, forthcoming). A total of 250 household interviews were conducted; response rate was 98 per cent. Whereas quantitative data were collected when Mexicans returned home for family reunions and annual town festivities, qualitative data were obtained during periods of low emigration in order to fully explore the experiences of long-term returnees. In-depth interviews of returnees were first conducted in Mexico in May and June 1985. Women were interviewed in the absence of their family members. This technique yielded rich information on conjugal relations and decision-making within the family. Physicians, nurses from two health centres, a local priest and the town's delegate were also interviewed. Two key informant women who had not travelled to the United States provided rich information on women's issues and the town's mores.

Follow-up interviews with the same returnees were conducted in Mexico a year later. Several focus group sessions (Folch-Lyon and Trost, 1981) of six to seven informants were audiotaped. Changes in opinions, expectations and new insights on the impact of immigration were discussed. This technique allowed for a deeper understanding of women's perceptions, preferences and role expectations after their return. The qualitative data provided the basis for an assessment of women's individual adjustment after returning to their home communities and an initial discussion of the influences they exert on the broader society.

Findings

Sample characteristics

Most of the women returning to Mexico in 1983 were between 21 and 30 years of age (Table 17.1). Whereas 75 per cent had acquired only primary education, 25 per cent had attained higher levels, indicating that a higher proportion of educated females emigrated and returned compared with the educational achievements of the populations of the two Mexican towns. Only 10 per cent of the rural population had attained secondary or higher education (IMSS-Coplamar, 1984). Over 70 per cent of the returnees were in their child-bearing years, 75 per cent were married and of these 50 per cent had left their children behind, thus increasing the likelihood of return.

On average, women had returned to their towns 4.3 times, beginning the shuttle process as early as 1974, suggesting that seasonal return was a pattern established during the last decade. Although only 4 per cent of the sample had participated in the Mexican labour force, 39 per cent did so in the American, earning an average median wage of $2.70/hour (Guendelman and Perez-Itriago, forthcoming). This ten-fold increase suggests a shift from minimal work-force particiaption in Mexico to incorporation into the American labour force. Over one-third of the women had entered the paid labour system for the first time.

One-third of returnees reported having no documentation in the United States; nor did the others necessarily enter the country with legal documents. Many reported having relied on their husband's documented status acquired through a temporary working permit. Illegal status in the United States hampered return; crossing the border with the help of a "coyote" or professional smuggler is risky and scary, particularly when there are children involved. Returns were therefore often delayed.

Whereas reasons for migrating to the United States were predominantly economic, the reasons reported for returning were affective. Women longed for family and friends, for community ties, and particularly for settling in their own houses. The expectation of return while abroad was always present. Our qualitative data show that although reasons for return did not change after the first year, expectations for re-emigrating increased with the family's shrinking economic resources. Lack of jobs and income followed by the husbands' feelings of anguish and despair as he increasingly became an inadequate provider were reported as major considerations in potential relocation. A woman who had already experienced this process put it succinctly: "The first time we came back we stayed over a year but my husband became desperate. After the second month he wanted to leave again. Finally, we left and after the hardships of re-emigration all we wanted was to save money to come back home!".

The return home: women and men live parallel lives

Resettlement induces marked changes in male and female social and work environments which have significant repercussions on the way they perceive and relate to each other. Spouses are sometimes pushed into parallel spheres of control when, as a consequence of split family migration, one spouse temporarily leaves the other behind. Studies have shown that women who are

Table 17.1

SAMPLE CHARACTERISTICS OF WOMEN RETURNEES

Age	Number	(%)
16-20	12	(15.0)
21-30	25	(31.3)
31-40	20	(25.0)
45-50	9	(11.2)
51 over	14	(17.5)
Total	80	(100.0)
Education		
≦ Primary	60	(75.0)
Secondary	17	(21.2)
College (technical and professional)	3	(3.8)
Total	80	(100.0)
Marital Status		
Single	14	(17.5)
Married	60	(75.0)
Widowed	4	(5.0)
Consensual union	2	(2.5)
Total	80	(100.0)
Number of returns		
$\bar{x}$ = 4.3		
S.D = 3.50		
Legal status in the United States		
With some documents	54	(67.5)
Without documents	19	(23.8)
Missing	7	(8.4)
Total	80	(100.0)

left behind often take over control of both private and public responsibilities in the home country (Abern et al., 1985; Mueller, 1977). In this case, their parallel spheres of control are delineated by geographical and temporal boundaries. But what about those situations in which both spouses migrate and return home? Do they also experience parallel roles?

The impact of changing lifestyles upon return is reflected in marital relationships. Our qualitative data suggest that women experience significant role shifts as they move from one society to the other and that work is a strong determinant of this process. Both the stay in the United States and the return to Mexico are experienced differently by those who joined the United States work-force compared with those who remained unemployed. Although substantial individual differences exist, the dynamics of these two groups suggest different patterns worthy of examination.

Working couples tended to establish co-operative roles which facilitates increased sharing in decision making and activities within the family and more interaction with other people. Similar work habits facilitate this co-operation. For instance, working in the same place, usually in the fields, sharing similar work hours, pooling incomes, and jointly deciding how the money should be spent drew couples closer together. Decisions involving childcare arrangements and shopping for food and household goods were other areas of co-operation achieved through increased male participation in household maintenance. These joint decisions and activities bridged the traditional gender distance between spouses and served to balance power relationships within the family. Such co-operation also seemed to enhance women's feelings of autonomy, as they became aware that they were independently contributing to all aspects of the family's welfare, and were not limited to childrearing, childbearing and household management. As Maria, a working woman expressed it: "When you first come back with all that money you feel in heaven, superior to other women. Once this money is spent you begin to feel like the rest ...".

Return to Mexico produced a sudden role shift which markedly changed the conjugal relationship. Specifically, a shift occurred from co-operative to parallel roles in which decision making and activities once again became highly segregated and demarcated. Husbands regained a dominant position in the family's transactions with the outside world, but were peripheral to childrearing and household responsibilities. Wives, in turn, recaptured the dominant position in the domestic realm. As a result, the distance between spouses increased. Rather than turning to each other, they sought same sex peers for support and validation. This shift in the relationship was clearly expressed by a woman who claimed that while in the United States "we ran errands together, ate together, went to church together; even Sundays we spent together. Here (in Mexico) we don't even see each other on Sundays. Since it is customary to gather at the main square our kids know that they can see their father there if they want to".

The change from co-operative to parallel conjugal roles was frequently cited by women in this study as a stressful period. Our impressions are that both the psychological distance and the redistribution of power between couples are important sources of stress. Further research is needed to support this contention.

The process of resettlement on the conjugal relationship of non-working women showed a markedly different pattern. Non-working women in the United States tended to become very isolated and reclusive, often feeling helpless due to language, transportation and economic barriers. Hence, they became increasingly dependent on their husbands for such daily activities as shopping, going to the laundromat, interacting with the medical care system and deciding how minor earnings would be spent. These families were characterised by female dependent roles and a tendency by the husband to intrude and even usurp the wife's domestic roles due to her difficulties in negotiating the new society. The wife who had characteristically assumed childrearing and household responsibiities became increasingly dependent on her spouse's participation to carry out her role. The husband, who characteristically had assumed a dominant position with respect to the broader social role, now additionally had to take over some traditional family responsibilities, such as overseeing the child's school work or taking the children shopping. This increased asymmetry in power distribution and increased role dependency seemed to be very stressful for non-working women. Many reported increased psychosomatic symptoms, and then experienced improved psychological health after returning to Mexico. They felt freer in Mexico; feelings that were distinctly opposite to the oppressive feelings reported by working women upon their return.

This tension reduction among non-working women could perhaps be explained by a role shift in the conjugal relationship from dependent back to parallel roles, a shift which re-established an expected balance in the relationship. Dependent women recaptured their dominant position with respect to childrearing and household responsibilities: men no longer intervened in the domestic realm but allowed them to make autonomous decisions. Lupe put it this way: "Here we do not need our husbands. They give us the money and we administer it. Here we are far more independent. Here, we go our way and they go theirs ...". In this transition, women became reincorporated into a rigid rural society where couples live parallel, asymmetrical lives, separated by strong sexual stereotypes and marked gender norms. For non-working women this social arrangement seemed to be less stressful and more satisfying than the highly-constrained and dependent lifestyle experienced in the United States. These women, not surprisingly, expressed less readiness to cross the border and join their husbands on the next trip.

The double life

These strong subjective experiences suggest that seasonal migration, and hence continuous resettlement, alter women's lifestyles as they move from one culture to the other. Marked transitions in coping with the demands of each society resulted in "double lives"; double because each successive relocation requires a metamorphosis in order to adapt to the counter demands imposed by different social and economic contexts. The return home, regardless of whether it is temporary or permanent in nature, triggers individual readjustment.

The experience of "double lives" is most accentuated among working women. Their access to work brings forth sharp contradictions in marital roles. Moving from a dual to a single paycheque family, from permeable to rigid family roles and from a complementary to a segregated maritial relationship requires readjustment. As one women said: "In California my husband was like a mariposa", meaning a sensitive, soft, responsive butterfly. "Back here in Mexico he acts like a distant macho". Having to cope with these transitions and the contradictions that they create suggests that one adaptive response to seasonal migration (and henceforth, seasonal returns) may be found in the adoption of "seasonal roles". Such versatility may represent a safety valve that responds to the temporary, but cyclical nature of their lifestyles. Another adaptive response may emerge from the dissatisfaction of working women upon returning to a traditional sex-segregated life. This dissatisfaction may induce them to search for alternative marital relations. One indication of this trend lies in women's yearnings for their husbands to remain as soft and sensitive as butterflies. Another indicator is found in some working women's expressed desire to return to the United States in order to resume more co-operative relationships.

Women as role models: their contribution to the community

Women's economic contribution through remittances or investments appears to be marginal. Their earnings are small (due to low wages and part-time employment in the United States) and merely enhance family purchasing power abroad rather than contribute to savings or investment back home. Despite this marginal role, women participate actively in administering family savings: "When we lived in the United States I used to earn some dollars cooking food for men working in the fields. This money went towards the purchase of a car. With the money my husband made we managed to save some and sent it to my father-in-law who helped us build a house. I saw to it that we had enough money to buy a few animals and household equipment".

The responsibilities for administering these earnings are even larger for those women who stay in Mexico while their husbands' venture out again. They often have to take over farming or business responsibilities in addition to household management. It seems therefore that female returnees tend to enhance men's economic roles by reinforcing their conservative orientation to invest and to spend their earnings at home. Men and women jointly place at the core of their return the task of house building and furnishing, emphasizing display of acquisitions brought from the north such as electrical appliances, records, furniture and clothing.

Since opportunities for female work in rural Mexico are so limited, women are seldom able to apply new techniques to the workplace. However, several women found that they gained in confidence as a result of migrating, and had established small business ventures such as "lemonade stands" or had prepared "birthday cakes" as alternatives to making money. The idea of remaining confined to home, particularly when economic resources became scarce, was just no longer satisfying.

Women's main contributions, however, lie mainly in the social sphere. They act as powerful role models for other women who see temporary migration as a way out of poverty. Furthermore, for women who yearn to work and explore new roles, returnees open horizons that are closed to them at home. The stigma of an employed woman is still strong in rural Mexico. Men tend to perceive females working outside the home as "fast" and "looking for affairs". This attitude often changes in the United States as men become more accepting of the image of an employed wife. Thus, returnees not only reinforce aspirations of improved standards of living, but also of modernising traditional female roles.

Returnees also make powerful role models because they display modern behaviour and acquisitions which reinforce behaviour and consumer orientations transmitted on television. Hence they help to bridge the gap between screen and rural life, demonstrating that many expectations are indeed realisable. Among the salient behaviour patterns that seem to distinguish returnees from non-migrants are new hairstyles, modern apparel and make-up, increased personal hygiene and more concern about health. For instance, returnees often demand that health providers make annual cervical pap smears to screen for cancer. Returnees also appear more inquisitive about their health and that of their children, asking more questions and demanding better answers from providers. Such health behaviour represents a diffusion of new ideas among providers who are beginning to modify their traditional authoritarian approach, providing more opportunities for self-care and control among migrant patients.

Although we have stressed the modernising effect of returnee role models, it is important to mention that not all returnees are bent on social innovations. Many women return disappointed at the isolating, dependent lifestyles they engaged in the United States and long to consolidate their traditional roles at home. These returnees adjust quickly to the confines of their home, alerting their networks about the pitfalls of emigration. They diffuse ideas that help to keep the "ideology" of migration within more realistic bounds.

There is a danger in reducing women's social impact to either modernising or conservative extremes. A wide spectrum of responses to the home community exist and these are not always consistent. Women may act as innovative role models in health care but be very traditional with respect to the definition of the female role as wife and mother. Others may have modern orientations regarding work outside the home but remain traditional with respect to household management decisions in Mexico.

The scope of responses suggests that the experience of return is largely dependent both on individual adjustment skills and on the effect that family and community exert on women by way of social pressures, cultural expectations to conform and economic reality.

The contradictions that arise through continuously absorbing and adjusting to values of two cultures increase the likelihood of role conflict among migrant women. Returnees are particularly vulnerable to experiencing contradictions in roles and lifestyles involved in moving back and forth between a slowly developing rural community and a highly-industrialised environment. Each return home seems to exacerbate these contradictions, which when confronted, open up opportunities for social change.

NOTES AND REFERENCES

1. This is a slightly modified version of the section "The Impact of Work on Women's Lives", Guendelman and Perez-Itriago, Journal of Women's Studies, forthcoming.

BIBLIOGRAPHY

ABERN, S., B. DEXTER and R. BACA
"Migracion y La Mujer Fuerte", Migration Today, Vol. 13, No. 1, 1985.

ARIZIPE, L.
"The Rural Exodus in Mexico and Mexican Migration to the United States", in P. Brown and H. Shue, eds., The Border that Joins. Mexican Migrants and US Responsibility, Totowa, N.J., Rowman and Littlefield, 1983.

BENNETT, B.
"On Intra-European Migration", Current Anthropology, Vol. 19, 1974.

"Migration and Rural Community Viability in Central Dalmatia (Croatia), Yugoslavia", Papers in Anthropology, Vol. 20, No. 1, 1979.

BOHNING, W.
"Some Thoughts on Emigration from the Mediterranean Basin", International Labour Review, Vol. 111, No. 3, 1975.

BOVENKERK, F.
The Sociology of Return Migration, The Hague, Nijhoff, 1974.

BRANA-SHUTE, R. and G. BRANA-SHUTE
"The Magnitude and Impact of Remittances in the Eastern Caribbean: A Research Note", RIIES Occasional Papers No. 3, 1982.

BRETTELL, C.
"Emigrar para voltar: A Portuguese Ideology of Return Migration", Papers in Anthropology, Vol. 20, No. 1, 1979.

BUSTAMANTE, J.
"Commodity-migrants: Structural Analysis of Mexican Immigration to the United States", in S. Ross, ed., Views Across the Border. The United States and Mexico, Albuquerque, University of New Mexico Press, 1978.

"Migracion interna e internacional y distribucion del ingreso. La frontera norte de Mexico", Comercio Exterior, Vol. 34, No. 9, 1984.

CERASE, F.
"Nostalgia or Disenchantment: Consideration of Return Migration", in S. Tomasi and M. Engels, eds., The Italian Experience in the United States, New York, Centre for Migration Studies, 1970.

"Expectations and Reality: A Case Study of Return Migration from the United States to Southern Italy", IMR, Vol. 8, 1974.

COLSON, E.
The Social Consequences Of Resettlement, Manchester, Manchester University Press, 1975.

CORNELIUS, W.
"Mexican and Caribbean Migration to the United States: The State of Current Knowledge and Priorities for Future Research", Monographs in US-Mexican Studies No. 1, La Jolla, California, Centre for US-Mexican Studies, University of California, San Diego, 1982.

DINERMAN, I.
"Migrants and Stay-at-Homes: A Comparative Study of Rural Migration from Michoacan, Mexico", Centre for US-Mexican Studies Monograph Series, No. 5, La Jolla, California, University of California, San Diego, 1982.

DAHYA, B.
"Pakistanis in Britain: Transients or Settlers", Race, 14, 1973.

DAVISON, B.
"No Place Back Home: A Study of Jamaicans Returning to Kingston, Jamaica", Race, 9, 1968.

FEINDT, W. and H. BROWNING
"Return Migration: Its Significance in an Industrial Metropolis and an Agricultural Town in Mexico", International Migration Review, 6, 1972.

FERNANDEZ-KELLY, M.P.
"Mexican Border Industrialization, Female Labor Force Participation and Migration", in J. Nash and M. Fernandez-Kelly, eds., Women, Men and the International Division of Labor, Albany, State University of New York Press, 1983.

FOLCH-LYON, E. and J. TROST
"Conducting Focus Group Sessions", Studies in Family Planning, Vol. 12, No. 12, 1981.

GARCIA Y GRIEGO, M.
"The Importation of Mexican Contract Laborers to the United States, 1942-1964: Antecedents, Operation and Legacy", in P. Brown and H. Shue, eds., The Border That Joins. Mexican migrants and US Responsibility, Totowa, N.J., Rowman and Littlefield, 1983.

GMELCH, G.
Return Migration and Migrant Adjustment in Western Ireland, Irish Foundation for Human Development, 1979a.

"Irish Return Migration: The Socio-demographic Characteristics of Return Migrants", Papers in Anthropology, Vol. 20, No. 1, 1979b.

"Return Migration", Ann. Rev. Anthropol., 9, 1980.

GRAVES, N. and T. GRAVES
"Adaptive Strategies in Urban Migration", Ann. Rev. Anthropol., 3, 1974.

GRIFFITHS, S.
"Emigration and Entrepreneurship in a Philippine Peasant Village", Papers in Anthropology, Vol. 20, No. 1, 1979.

GUENDELMAN, S.
"Children's Health Needs in Seasonal Immigration", Journal of Public Health Policy, Vol. 6, No. 4, 1985.

GUENDELMAN, S. and A. PEREZ-ITRIAGO
"Double Lives: The Changing Role in Seasonal Migration", Journal of Women's Studies, forthcoming.

IMSS-Coplamar
Tepehuaje Health Centre Report, 1984.

KASL, S. and L. BERKMAN
"Health Consequences of the Experience of Migration", Annual Review of Public Health, 4, 1983.

KING, R.
"Return Migration: Review of Some Cases from Southern Europe", Mediterranean Studies, Vol. 1, No. 2, 1978.

LIANOS, T.
"Flows of Greek Outmigration and Return Migration", International Migration, Vol. 13, No. 3, 1975.

MAINGOT, A.
"The Stress Factors in Migration: A Dissenting View", Migration Today, Vol. 13, No. 5, 1985.

MARTIN, P.
"The Economic Effects of Temporary Worker Migration", Migration Today, Vol. 13, No. 1, 1985.

MORTIMER, D. and R. BRYCE-LAPORTE, eds.
"Female Immigrants to the United States: Caribbean, Latin American and African Experiences", RIIES Occasional Papers No. 2, 1981.

MUELLER, M.
"Women and Men, Power and Powerlessness in Lesotho", Signs, Vol. 3, No. 1, 1977.

MURILLO CASTANO, G.
"Migrant Workers in the Americas. A Comparative Study of Migration between Colombia and Venezuela and between Mexico and the United States", Monograph Series, 13, San Diego, Centre for US-Mexican Studies, University of California, 1984.

PAINE, S.
Exporting Workers: The Turkish Case, London, Cambridge University Press, 1974.

PALMER, R.
"Migration from the Caribbean to the States: The Economic Status of the Immigrants", RIIES Occasional Papers No. 1, 2nd printing, 1983.

PHILPOTT, Stuart
"Remittance Obligations, Social Networks and Choice Among Monter-servation Migrants in Britain", Man, 3, 1968.

"The Implications of Migration for Sending Societies: Some Theoretical Considerations", proceedings of the Annual Meeting of the American Ethnological Society, 1970, Seattle, University of Washington Press, 1971.

West Indian Migration: The Montserrat Case, London, LSE Monographs on Anthropology, 1973.

RHOADES, R.
"Intra-European Return Migration and Rural Development: Lessons from the Spanish Case", Hum. Organ., Vol. 37, No. 2, 1978.

"Toward an Anthropology of Return Migration", Papers in Anthropology, Vol. 20, No. 1, 1979.

RUBENSTEIN, H.
"The Return Ideology in West Indian Migration", Papers in Anthropology, Vol. 20, No. 1, 1979.

"Return Migration to the English-speaking Caribbean: Review and Commentary", RIIES Occasional Papers, No. 3, 1982.

SEILHAMER, S. and J. PREWETT-DIAZ
"The Return and Circulatory Migrant Student: A Perception of Teachers, School and Self", Migration Today, Vol. 11, No. 1, 1983.

STINNER, W., K. ALBUQUERQUE and R. BRYCE-LAPORTE, eds.
"Return Migration and Remittances: Developing a Caribbean Perspective", RIIES Occasional Papers, No. 3, 1982.

SWANSON, J.
"Some Consequences of Emigration for Economic Development in the Yemen Arab Republic", Middle East Journal, Winter, 1978.

"The Consequences of Emigration for Economic Development: A Review of the Literature", Papers in Anthropology, Vol. 20, No. 1, 1979.

TAPINOS, Georges
"European Migration Patterns: Economic Linkages and Policy Experiences", in Mary Kritz, ed., US Immigration and Refugee Policy, Man., Lexington Books, 1983.

WEIST, R.

"Wage-labour Migration and the Household in a Mexican Town", J. Anthropol. Res., 29, 1975.

"Rural Community Development in Mexico: The Impact of Mexican Recurrent Migration to the United States", University of Manitoba Anthropol., Paper No. 21, 1978.

"Anthropological Perspectives on Return Migration: A Critical Commentary", Papers in Anthropology, Vol. 20, No. 1, 1979.

WOOD, Ch.

"Migration Remittances and Development: Preliminary Results of a Study of Caribbean Cane Cutters in Florida", RIIES Occasional Papers No. 3, 1982.

Chapter 18

OCCUPATION AND STATUS IN THE IDEOLOGY OF CARIBBEAN RETURN MIGRATION

by

E.M. Thomas-Hope and R.D. Nutter

INTRODUCTION

Return has long been an integral component of Caribbean international migration. Movements to Central America in the 19th and early 20th Centuries, and migrations to Europe and North America since the mid-20th Century have been associated with a distinct pattern of reciprocal flow. Even in cases of "permanent" settlement, except where there has been a political reason for not returning home, significant return migration has persisted.

For the majority of Caribbean people, migration has come to be regarded less as a means of severing relationships with the homeland and family than a strategy for temporarily extending island opportunities to overcome constraints on upward mobility imposed by the system at home, a system stamped with the legacies of slavery and the plantation (Thomas-Hope, 1978). The periodicity of movement and the duration of stay overseas varies as much with the circumstances of the individual as with the wider opportunities and constraints of the source and destination areas. Thus whatever the specific characteristics of the movement, return remains an important component. Social institutions have evolved to accommodate emigration and return and, over the years, they have become firmly established in the ideology of achievement and success.

In Caribbean societies, as in all others, the meaning and manifestations of achievement and success vary between groups, especially on the basis of class. Though material well-being is acknowledged by all classes to be an essential ingredient of success, class-related cultural and social norms that signal achievement range from certain standards of public behaviour in the lower social strata to specific expectations in terms of occupational status in higher echelons.

Almost all migrants aspire to improving their occupational status if they return home prior to retirement. But while capital and occupational change may guarantee improved personal circumstances, it is rarely sufficient to bring about transformation in class status. This has traditionally been achieved through education. As a consequence, the acquisition of formal qualifications is regarded as critical for upward mobility and particularly valued by socially aspiring persons on the margins of two classes. For persons in these situations, education is a fundamental component of the migration ideology.

Not all migrants return to the Caribbean; some because they never intended to do so and others because the opportunities available in the receiving country overwhelmed their original intentions. The initial migration goals become replaced by new goals and commitments; contacts at home are maintained through visits and remittances (Rubenstein, 1983; Thomas-Hope, 1980 and 1985).

Goal Orientation and Return Migration

The identification of a number of different migration types in the Caribbean demonstrates variation in characteristics as well as in the principal goal objectives of each group (Table 18.1). Although the concept of return is not discussed here, an essential consideration is that duration of stay overseas and periodicity of movement are not in themselves critical issues in determining the impact of migration. It is the goal orientations of migrant groups, their pursuit, and even more important their achievement, which determine the impact of return.

Migration for short periods abroad precludes most opportunities for obtaining educational qualifications; migrants in this category are almost entirely oriented towards capital accumulation. Vendors travel overseas for the purpose of purchasing goods for sale in the informal retail sector back home. Although informal, this is a highly-organised pattern of international circulation in several Caribbean islands. Each island group has established its own profitable circuit. For example, most Leeward Islanders go to the Virgin Islands, while Haitians go to the Bahamas and Puerto Rico and Jamaicans to Haiti as well as to Cayman, Panama and Miami. This migratory activity provides opportunity for capital accumulation and thus the potential for increased status in an otherwise essentially rigid system controlled by traditional groups of entrepreneurs. However, it permits upward mobility between the various strata only at the lower class; it is not an accepted means of achieving middle class status.

Contract workers, unlike vendors, are agricultural labourers, construction workers, or waiters who obtain contracts for a specified period and for a specific purpose. A number of Caribbean destinations are involved in this movement as well as the United States and Canada. For example, thousands of Haitians are contracted each year to work as labourers on sugar estates in the Dominican Republic. Barbadians and others from the eastern Caribbean obtain agricultural jobs in various parts of the United States and Canada. Contract workers do not characteristically upgrade their skills overseas, but back home, like the small traders, they are frequently able to upgrade their status through the capital they have accumulated.

In contrast to these formally contracted workers there is a small number of other itinerant labour migrants, principally men, who travel

Table 18.1

CARIBBEAN INTERNATIONAL CIRCULATION

Type of migrant	Occupational change	Residential change	Process of goal achievement
1. Transients or shuttle migrants			
a) International vendors	Upgrading of entrepreneurial activities	Rural-urban Urban-urban	Capital accumulation
b) Contract workers	Trades or small small farming to entrepreneurial activity	Rural-rural	Capital accumulation
c) Other itinerant labour migrants	No significant change	No significant change	Capital accumulation
d) Business commuters	White collar employment to self-employment	Rural-rural Rural-urban Urban-suburban	Capital accumulation
2. Long-stay migrants			
a) Settler workers	Agricultural and trades to blue collar Blue collar to white collar	Rural-rural Urban-urban	Capital accumulation and education
b) Dependants	Blue collar to white collar (managerial)	Rural-urban Urban-suburban	Education
c) Students	White collar to white collar (professional or para professional)	Rural-suburban Urban-suburban Suburban-suburban	Education
d) Long-term circulators	Blue collar or domestic to service	Rural-rural Urban-suburban	Capital accumulation

Source: Thomas-Hope, 1986.

seasonally across national boundaries to nearby locations in search of work. The low level of skill required for the casual work in which they engage means that little difference is made to their occupational chances back home. The chief benefit of these migrations to the individual is derived from the money earned, which is small in cash terms but when converted into local currency can provide the main economic base of the migrant's household.

International business commuters are a middle class variation of the circulating worker. In most of the islands, people engaged in business travel within the region or to North America on a regular basis effectively maintain two households (Thomas-Hope, 1983). In some instances the family remains resident in the Caribbean and business is conducted by one or more members overseas, while in other cases, the reverse situation occurs. The pattern of occupational change associated with this group is complex and difficult to research. However, like the contract workers, business commuters either enter a dual occupation situation or enhance their occupational status back home through the capital they accumulate from commercial involvement overseas. Only in exceptional cases is the amount of capital accumulated so great that an inter-class shift in status is perceived to have taken place.

The goal of capital accumulation dominates in the cases of workers who settle at the destination for several years and those who circulate on a regular basis. Settlers are known as persons who, for varying periods of time and at least more than a year, establish their principal household at the migration destination. A Barbadian study showed that the average period spent overseas was thirteen years (Gmelch, 1984). Whatever the duration, remittances continue to be sent home for as long as the intention to return remains (Rubenstein, 1983; Thomas-Hope, 1985).

A small number of long-stay migrants return home after retirement, but the great majority return to continue working. Gmelch found that 85 per cent of returnees in his Barbadian study intended working. Although occupational change typically results in the enhanced status of the returning long-stay migrant, unless it is based on a significant increase in material wealth, then it is only brought about through formal education. Neither of these situations is common among returning long-stay migrant workers who typically return to rural areas to engage in agriculture or start their own business, invariably a retail shop. Urban returnees are also found in various forms of self-employment, especially in the retail and transport sectors.

Some long-stay migrants return on a regular basis but effectively maintain households in the Caribbean. Meanwhile, they spend more time in a temporary setting in the United States or Canada than "at home". These migrants usually acquire no specialised skills and, at least in the first instance, work in private domestic or nursing jobs. They transfer large amounts of consumer goods, especially household equipment and clothing, and also remit substantial sums of money which are invested in housing, used for the education of their children, or for supplementing family income and financing continued travel expenses. The impact of remittances on improved residential location, housing quality and standard of living is very considerable. Moreover, the financing of education enhances the prospects for their children.

Dependents of workers who go abroad at an early age, as well as those who go specifically to study, are two groups whose circumstances on return are related directly to their educational qualifications. The objective of inter-generational advancement through education pervades the goal orientation of family units. While migrants may be oriented towards capital accumulation in the short term, the single most important underlying factor in their move-ment is the educational advancement of their children. In some cases children are taken abroad at the time of migration or "sent for" once initial problems of adjustment have been overcome.

Groups at the top of the social hierarchy, whose parents are able to finance their foreign education, or those whose qualifications earn them scholarships, constitute the student category. This group migrates indepen-dently of their families; their rate of non-return is high but for those who intend to (or do) return, their goal is specifically educational achievement. However, notwithstanding variation relating to class, upward social mobility on return is a universal goal of the Caribbean migration process. Inter-generational occupational mobility through education may also be an important feature of some short-term circulators. In particular, the achievement of migrants who spend only brief periods abroad is also considerable, not only in terms of savings but also because of the longer-term implications for inter-generational upward social mobility.

Education and Return Migrant Status

The literature on return migration to the Caribbean focuses upon remit-tances of capital and goods (Frucht, 1968; Brana-Shute, 1982; Rubenstein, 1983; Gmelch, 1984; McCoy, 1983; Griffith, 1983). The return of migrants whose enhanced occupational status reflects the role of education in migration ideology has been largely ignored. An explanation for this bias is the rural emphasis of previous studies, especially impact on the home society of remit-tances and the uses to which they are put. The difficulties of attempting to evaluate the impact of education and skill acquisition among return migrants are also considerable. There is no doubt that both the short-term and long-term implications of return must be addressed if total impact is to be known.

While this paper makes no claim to providing a formula for precise measurement, it draws attention to the role of education in the long-term strategy of migration. Further, it seeks to demonstrate that there are groups whose migration and reasons for return are frequently characterised by edu-cational objectives. A sample of return migrants from the United Kingdom employed in the industrial sector of the Kingston Metropolitcan Area (KMA), Jamaica, serves to illustrate the point. A total of 93 returnees were ident-ified from a 20 per cent sample of all manufacturing and retail establishments in the KMA. Men comprised 59 per cent and women 41 per cent of the sample; ages ranged from 18 to over 60, with 48 per cent in the 36-50 age group.

The type, size and location of premises at which the returnees worked showed that they were not distributed equally between types of establishment or uniformly in various districts of the city. For instance, of 77 premises employing returnees, 59.1 per cent were employed in three industrial cate-gories, yet these categories contained only 33.3 per cent of total sample premises (Table 18.2). Furthermore, returnees were usually employed in larger establishments which tended to be associated with the modern industrial sector

(Table 18.3). An analysis of returnees' employment by area of the KMA revealed a similar tendency towards clustering. Nearly 80 per cent of returnees
were employed in four areas of the KMA (Spanish Town Road; Southwest, Central
and North Central St. Andrew) although these areas contain only 46.5 per cent
of sample premises (Figure 18.1). By contrast, Downtown Kingston with
30.5 per cent of sample premises provided employment for only 9.7 per cent of
returnees.

These data show that returnees were chiefly employed in one of the
three modern industrial sectors -- principally financial, and in one of four
areas of the KMA -- all in the newer development zone of Central Kingston.
Older areas, such as Downtown Kingston and the traditional industrial sectors,
had been largely avoided by returnees (Nutter, 1985). Furthermore, a striking
feature of returnee occupation was the extremely high proportion in professional and managerial positions (Table 18.4). Nearly 55 per cent of the
returnees were in this category and 83.9 per cent were employed in white
collar occupations compared with 8.34 per cent of the 1982 Jamaican work-force
(National Planning Agency, 1983). It appears that returnees represent a
significantly skilled minority.

By tracing the emigration patterns of the group of returnees and their
educational achievements in the United Kingdom, it was possible to evaluate
the way in which emigration and return reinforce a set of values held concerning migration and the education of both migrants and non-migrants in Jamaican
society.

Fifty per cent of returnees in the sample had originally migrated as
young dependents with, or soon after, other family members. An additional
12 per cent were housewives who had not worked prior to their departure for
the United Kingdom so that only 38 per cent of the sample had been economically active at the time of their departure. Subsequent occupational structure
of the group after their return was almost entirely the result of educational
qualifications obtained abroad. Thirty-seven per cent of the sample had been
trained to degree, Higher National Certificate or Diploma level and a further
24 per cent had obtained at least one A level subject (Advanced level school-
leaving certificate). Of those in white collar occupations, 60.3 per cent had
gained their educational qualifications wholly or largely in the United Kingdom as second generation or dependant migrants.

The majority of returnees had also worked in the United Kingdom usually
in positions similar to those they occupied after their return. Some had held
professional and managerial posts (19 per cent) or clerical posts (29 per
cent) prior to their return. Occupational mobility was therefore related to
their experience abroad; it was not associated solely with Jamaican labour
force demands. The single underlying factor for the occupational success of
both groups seems to have been their high level of educational achievement
while abroad.

Alternative explanations for the success of returnees may be advanced
in terms of selectivity of the migration process. The argument could be
advanced that many emigrants were more ambitious and faced better prospects
than non-emigrants so that their later success would have occurred in any
event. While there is no way of knowing what a person would have achieved had
he or she not migrated, there was a definite positive relationship between
duration abroad and degree of occupational success on return. Seventy-two per

Table 18.2

EMPLOYMENT OF RETURNEES BY INDUSTRIAL CATEGORY

Industrial category (a)	Sample premises % total	Premises employing returnees	Returnees No.	%	Returnees per establishment
Food and beverage manufacturing	9.7	20.7	13	14.0	0.22
Textiles and clothing manufacturing	12.0	11.1	9	9.7	0.12
Wood and paper manufacturing	11.9	8.4	7	7.5	0.10
Chemicals and miscellaneous manufacturing	11.2	6.0	5	5.4	0.07
Metal and metal products manufacturing	17.4	21.2	29	31.2	0.28
Retail and wholesale	31.6	11.1	17	18.3	0.13
Financial and financial services	6.2	27.0	13	14.0	0.35
Total	100.0		93	100.0	

a)   Industrial categories based on Ministry of Industry Industrial Classification, Ministry of Industry, Kingston, (no date).

Table 18.3

EMPLOYMENT OF RETURNEES BY SIZE OF PREMISES

Work-force size	Sample premises % total	Premises employing returnees	Returnees No.	%	Returnees per establishment
10-14	54.0	6.0	17	18.3	0.06
25-49	25.5	18.1	28	30.1	0.20
50-74	11.1	23.9	22	23.7	0.36
75-99	4.7	28.6	9	9.7	0.35
Over 100	4.7	43.6	17	18.3	0.65
Total	100.0		93	100.0	

FIGURE 18.1

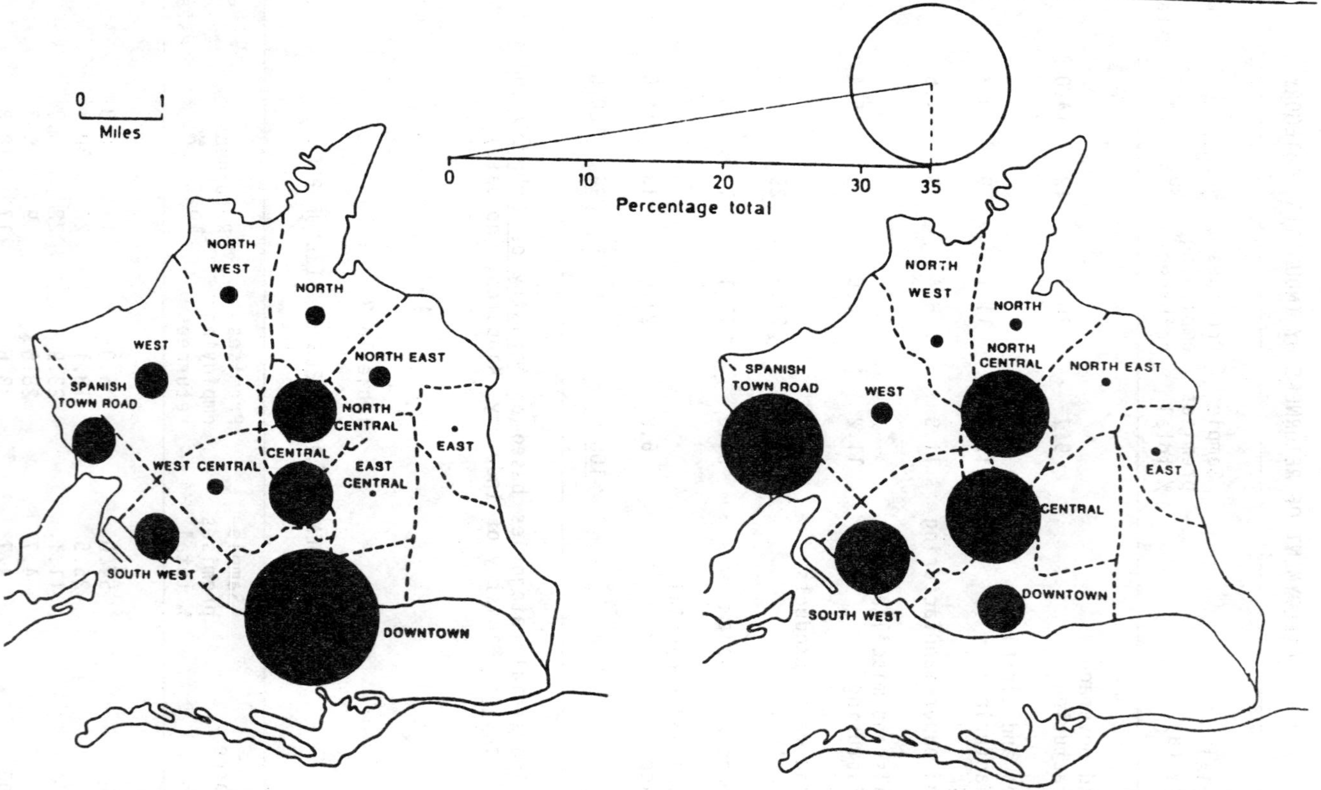

Percentage total

0 10 20 30 35

LOCATION OF PREMISES BY SAMPLE AREA OF KMA

LOCATION OF RETURNEES BY SAMPLE AREA OF KMA

Table 18.4

RETURNEE OCCUPATION BY INDUSTRIAL CATEGORY

| Occupation (a) | Industrial Category | | | | | | | Total | |
	Food mfct.	Text. mfct.	Wood mfct.	Chem. mfct.	Metal mfct.	Retail	Finance	No.	%
Professional & managerial	6	1	4	4	18	11	7	51	54.8
Clerical	2	5	1	1	7	5	6	27	29.0
Processing	5	--	--	--	1	--	--	6	6.4
Machine trade	--	1	1	--	--	--	--	2	2.1
Benchwork	--	1	--	--	--	--	--	1	1.1
Structural	--	--	--	--	3	--	--	3	3.2
Miscellaneous	--	1	1	--	--	1	--	3	3.2
Total	13	9	7	5	29	17	13	93	100.0

a)   Based on United States Department of Labor, Dictionary of Occupational Titles, 1977.

cent of those in professional and managerial positions and 70 per cent of those in clerical posts prior to return had remained abroad for ten or more years. By comparison, only 52 per cent of the total sample had remained abroad for this length of time. Amongst those who remained abroad sixteen years or more, 81 per cent were employed in the top two occupational categories. Empirical data strongly suggest that occupational status was affected in a positive way by the migration experience and would have been lower for these individuals had they not migrated.

One issue which cannot be resolved by empirical evidence is whether the more successful migrants stay abroad longer or whether the longer they stay the more successful they become. However, as far as the home countries are concerned, the answer is irrelevant for, in either case, the implications are the same. Returnees are perceived by themselves and by others as having been successful if they have achieved an occupational status higher than their status prior to their migration.

The extent to which return migration focused upon occupational status achieved through education has influenced Caribbean migration ideology, and its impact on the perpetuation of the migration process, is more difficult to assess. The emigrant who achieved social and economic advancement through emigration, education and hard work and returned to an enviable and prestigious position within the home society regarded himself as successful

and greatly valued his foreign experience. Such achievement clearly strengthens the strands of an ideology which sees emigration and return not only as a
necessary part of individual development but also as a prerequisite to social
and economic advance. It contributes strongly to the idea inherent in Caribbean migration ideology that a person is somehow better for having been
abroad, and therefore increases the likelihood that emigration will continue
to be a much sought after goal in Jamaican thought and consciousness.

The meaning and relevance of education to social status has its roots
in the colonial history of the region (Norris, 1962; Brown, 1979; Morrissey,
1982). The continuing dominance of overseas educational values and the continuing status of foreign education can be at least partially explained by the
pattern of elite education in Jamaica. Of the 1 433 individuals listed in two
directories of Caribbean personalities for the years 1978 and 1982, 54 per
cent had been educated abroad (Dickson, 1982; Levy and Jacobs, 1978), especially in the United Kingdom (Figure 18.2). Almost 80 per cent of those in
technical positions and higher education and 70 per cent of those in government, legal and medical professions -- the three professions that provide the
core of colonial heritage in Jamaica -- had been educated abroad.

The characteristics of returnees and the ideology of return raise two
important issues -- one relating to analytical models applied to the Caribbean
migration process, the other concerning the implications of international
migration for the region's development. Characteristics of returnees question
the adequacy of either the equilibrium-type model or the classic historical-
structural model to explain the migration process. Subjective evaluation in
migration decision-making can create a gradient of desirability running
counter to the objectively measured gradient of opportunity or of population
potential. At the same time, decisions to return are not based solely on
personal motives; they are made within a wider set of values held by the
family unit of which the migrant is a member.

The historical-structural approach also proves inadequate as the sole
explanatory model for Caribbean migration when the return component is considered. Although outward migration streams move in the direction of periphery to centre, specific patterns are influenced by historically determined
structural factors. However, return again demonstrates the relevance of
social and subjective values as important elements in the migration process.
These values and their related ideology -- so central to the return process --
must therefore be incorporated into explanatory models.

Contradictory assumptions have been made concerning the role of the
return migrants and the implications for Caribbean societies on the basis of
observations of different types of return migrants. Where analysis has been
confined to migrant groups principally oriented to capital accumulation, then
the element of conspicuous consumption and negligible improvements in relevant
skills dominate conclusions. The study presented here demonstrates that there
is a significant repatriation of skills which must have some short-term beneficial effects in the industrial context and longer-term benefits through
increased educational advantages for the next generation. However, it has
also been shown that the traditional value placed on overseas education is
reinforced by the experience of returnees, thereby strengthening the pervasive
part that international migration continues to play in Caribbean external
orientations and metropolitan dependence.

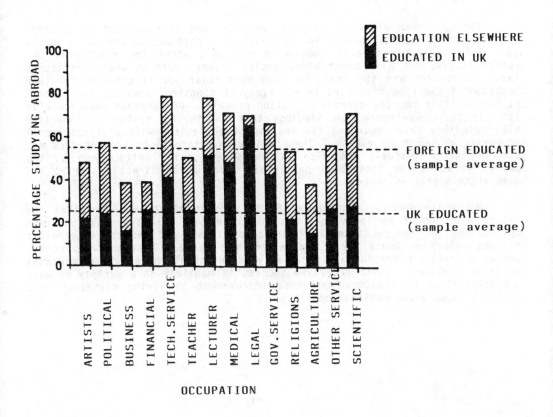

FIGURE 18.2:   FOREIGN EDUCATION AND ELITE OCCUPATIONS

CONCLUSION

The Caribbean migration process supports, and is supported by, a wider system of social values which form the basis of a distinctive migration ideology. This ideology contains judgements not only about the meaning of migration itself, but also about wider social issues, such as what constitutes status or success and the goals of each particular social grouping. Return migration of the type discussed in our study of Kingston, Jamaica, has important implications for the overall migration process. Of foremost importance is its role in strengthening an ideology that combines a system of inherited values (in this case regarding the meaning of education) with distinct social judgements of worth or esteem. These values and judgements are embedded not just in the individual, but also in the wider social units, such as the family, in which the individual participates and which directly support and nurture the migration process.

While the success experienced by this group might be regarded as the goal or ambition of an individual migrant, return of this type has long-term implications for the persistence of migration itself and for the externally-oriented values on which local evaluations are based. The short-run consequences of return migration are undeniably advantageous to individual migrants and their families. Their perceived success is manifest in a variety of ways -- modernisation of consumer patterns, improvement in living standards and, not least, upward occupational mobility.

BIBLIOGRAPHY

BRANA-SHUTE, Gary and Rosemary
    "The Magnitude and Impact of Remittances in the Eastern Caribbean: A
    Research Note", in William S. Stinner, Klaus de Albuquerque and Roy
    S. Bryce-Laporte, eds., Return Migration and Remittances: Developing a
    Caribbean Perspective, Washington, D.C., Research Institute on Im-
    migration and Ethnic Studies, 1982.

BROWN, Aggrey
    Color, Class and Politics in Jamaica, New Jersey, Transaction Inc.,
    1979.

DICKSON, R., ed.
    The Jamaican Directory of Personalities 1981-82, Kingston, Gleaner Co.,
    1982.

FRUCHT, Richard
    "Emigration, Remittances and Social Change: Aspects of the Social
    Field of Nevis, West Indies", Athropologica, Vol. 10, No. 2, 1968.

GMELCH, George
    "From London to Bridgetown: The Motives and Readjustment of Return
    Migrants in Barbados", unpublished paper, 1984.

    "Work, Innovation and Investment: The Impact of Return Migration in an
    Eastern Caribbean Society", unpublished paper, 1984.

GRIFFITH, David C.
    "The Promise of a Country: The Impact of Seasonal US Migration on the
    Jamaican Peasantry", unpublished Ph.D. thesis, University of Florida,
    1983.

LEVY, A. and H. JACOBS, eds.
    Personalities Caribbean 1977-78, Kingston, Personalities Ltd., 1978.

McCOY, Terry L.
    "The Impact of Seasonal Labor Migration on Caribbean Development: A
    Case Study", conference paper, The American Political Science Associ-
    ation, 1983.

MORRISSEY, Mike
    "A Preference for America: The Country Preferences of School Children
    in Seven Caribbean Territories", unpublished paper, 1982.

NATIONAL PLANNING AGENCY
    Economic and Social Survey Jamaica, Kingston, Government Printer, 1983.

NORRIS, Katrin
Jamaica: The Search for an Identity, London, Oxford University Press, 1962.

NUTTER, Richard D.
"Implications of Return Migration for Economic Development in Kingston, Jamaica", in Russell King, ed., Return Migration and Economic Development, London, Croom Helm, 1985.

RUBENSTEIN, Hymie
"Migration and Underdevelopment: The Caribbean", Cultural Survival Quarterly, Vol. 7, No. 4, 1983.

THOMAS-HOPE, Elizabeth M.
"The Establishment of a Migration Tradition. British West Indian Movements to the Hispanic Caribbean in the Century after Emancipation", in Colin G. Clarke, ed., Caribbean Social Relations, Liverpool, Centre for Latin American Studies, Monograph Series, No. 8, 1978.

"Hopes and Reality in the West Indian Migration to Britian", Oral History: The Journal of the Oral History Society, Vol. 8, 1980.

"Off the Island: Population Mobility among the Caribbean Middle Class", in Arnaud F. Marks and M.C. Hebe, eds., White Collar Migrants in the Americas and the Caribbean, Leiden, Department of Caribbean Studies, 1983.

"Return Migration and Its Implications for Caribbean Development", in Robert Pastor, ed., Migration and Development in the Caribbean, Boulder, Colorado, Westview Press, 1985.

"Transients to Settlers: Varieties of Caribbean Migrants and the Socio-economic Implications of Their Return", International Migration, Vol. 24, No. 3, 1986.

Chapter 19

COLOMBIAN IMMIGRANTS IN VENEZUELA

by

A. Pellegrino

The Background of Colombian Immigration to Venezuela

Since World War II, Venezuela and Argentina have been the main countries of immigration in South America. Unlike Argentina, Venezuela did not receive large flows of migrants during the 19th Century and the first half of the 20th Century. But exchanges of population between Venezuela and Colombia had been common in their border regions for over a century and a half.

Towards the end of the 19th Century the expansion of coffee-growing in the Andean border regions led Colombians to move into Venezuela. The shared culture of the Andean population in both countries, coupled with the fact that for much of the 19th Century the border areas international trade was shipped through Maracaibo, gave the region an economic unity and made it comparatively autonomous of other economic channels in Colombia and Venezuela.

Until the end of World War II, when a considerable number of European immigrants arrived, Colombians were the largest body of foreigners in Venezuela. In the 1960s European immigration came to a halt (except from Portugal), while the number of Colombians entering Venezuela began to increase substantially. The proportion of illegal immigrants became significant during this period. In the 1970s, and particularly after 1974 when financial expansion was triggered by higher oil prices, immigration was fuelled largely by flows from South America and the Caribbean, with Colombians again strongly represented (43.3 per cent of all immigrants in Venezuela, according to the 1981 census).

Legal Aspects and Definition of Immigrants in Venezuela

There is no explicit definition of an illegal immigrant (in Venezuela the term used is "indocumentados" -- people without proper papers). In practice, an illegal immigrant is a person residing in the country who did not enter on a transit or resident's visa or who entered as a tourist and failed to comply with formalities.

301

During the 1960s and 1970s the government pursued selective immigration policies, using agreements involving agencies. After 1973 special arrangements were made with ICM. A Selective Immigration Office was opened in the Labour Ministry and in 1976 the National Council for Human Resources was established, one purpose being to formulate selective immigration policies in line with the country's needs and priorities.

Immigration law contains no specific definition of an "illegal worker", and lays down no job reservation criteria vis-à-vis the foreign population (1). The 1937 Aliens Act bars from entry any person working as a "hawker, pedlar dealer in cloth and trinkets and, in general, any foreigner who earns his livelihood by petty exploitation of the working classes".

The expansion of agriculture and stockbreeding in the 1960s, with agro-food enterprises developing in the sector, led to a decline in subsistence farming and an increase in larger-scale production units. Together with the growth of manufacturing industry and services, this hastened movement to towns in Venezuela (the urban population rose from 31.3 per cent in 1941 to 79.2 per cent in 1981) (2), leading to labour shortages in the rural sector, especially at harvest time. This provided opportunities for Colombian workers who mostly found rural employment in border areas during the initial period.

In terms of migration policy, a number of instruments were devised to regulate inflows through bilateral agreements between Colombia and Venezuela. The 1959 Tonchala Treaty (3) states that both governments would regulate the status of their nationals residing in the other country, subject to identification by consular officials and providing they were engaged in "lawful employment". The Treaty also provided for "agricultural cards", being issued to farm workers for six months, renewable. The 1963 agreement on trade and economic development between Venezuela and Colombia carried forward this undertaking on the same conditions, and proposed special programmes for the registration of workers without proper papers. Within the framework of the Cartagena Agreement, which led to the Andean Pact to which Venezuela acceded in 1973, the Simon Rodriguez Convention signed in that year included among its objectives "harmonization of social and economic policies and national legislation in relevant areas". Finally, under the Cartagena Agreement, the Andean Migrant Labour Instrument was signed in 1977. Three categories of migrant worker were defined: skilled, border and temporary workers. The agreement laid down specific standards for labour contracts, specified rights and obligations, and defined administrative arrangements for the exchanges. The two countries further agreed to regulate the status of all immigrants without proper papers, provided they were engaged in lawful employment, held identity papers issued by one of the member countries, and had entered the country before the instrument came into force.

In 1980, by Presidential Decree and in accordance with the Andean Migrant Labour Instrument and the Aliens Act, Venezuela decided to establish a General Aliens Register. While the Decree was designed primarily to grant temporary identity papers to nationals of the Cartagena Agreement signatories it also applied to nationals of other countries who registered and produced papers which entitled them to apply for residence. This arrangement regulated the status of those who registered; they were issued transit identity cards valid for one year, renewable. As a rule, the transit pass was converted into a resident's pass after two years in the country although the period has varied on several occasions. Recently it has become more difficult to obtain a transit pass and to convert it into a resident's permit. In addition, the transit card is now issued for six months only, and the cost of renewing it has been raised to 1 000 bolivars (US $70). This will certainly mean that many lesser-skilled immigrants will be unable to renew their papers and will have to return to their home countries or join the ranks of the illegals.

It should be noted that between 1961 and 1981, according to Interior Ministry data, there were 559 352 "legalisations" (4) and 170 582 deportations. Of the first figure, 266 795 were people on the General Aliens Register. Deportations were higher than legalisations in 1977 and 1978 (Torrealba, 1985).

Estimating the Number of Colombians in Venezuela

The larger numbers of immigrants who entered after 1974 tended to concentrate in urban areas, especially the Caracas Metropolitan Area. This aroused government concern over the number of foreigners in Venezuela, in particular illegals. The press published a number of speculative estimates, some of which were taken up by official agencies. The estimates for illegals ranged between 1 and 4 million.

Estimating the number of illegals in Venezuela is no easy matter. Most of them are Colombians, and the border between the two countries runs for over 2 000 km. Jean Papail (1984) estimated that the net inter-census balance was in the region of 500 000 persons, and that the net balance for Colombians was 270 000. Another estimate, based on projections from the 1971 population and the 1981 census (corrected for omissions), leads to a residual balance of between 550 000 and 600 000 (Bidegain and Pellegrino, 1985).

The net migration balance obtained from the 1971 and 1981 censuses is 478 174 overall and 328 022 for Colombian nationals (Table 19.1) (not corrected for the overall rate of omission in the 1981 census, put at between 7.0 and 7.6 per cent for the national total). There is a difference of some 70 000 to 120 000 between the estimated maximum assumptions for the residual balance and the inter-census migration balance. Moreover, it cannot be assumed that illegals were not included in the census.

The present analysis is based on a study of the Colombian population, which at the time of the 1980 Aliens Register made up over 92 per cent of all immigrants who applied for migrant status. It should be borne in mind that this population as a whole is highly mobile, coming as it does from a neighbouring country with easy overland access. It is made up of a number of types of flows:

1. Fairly permanent migration settling in urban regions, where work is predominantly in industry, trade and services;

2. Permanent migration settling in border regions, with work in farming and stockbreeding or "urban-type" jobs;

3. Flows of seasonal immigrants, crossing the frontier at harvest time.

Table 19.1

POPULATION BORN ABROAD BY COUNTRY OF BIRTH

Country	1971			1981		
	Male	Female	Total	Male	Female	Total
Colombia	84 524	95 620	180 144	243 144	264 889	508 166
Chile	1 453	1 640	3 093	13 212	11 988	25 200
Argentina	1 882	2 089	3 971	6 009	5 532	11 541
Uruguay	469	553	1 022	3 692	3 315	7 007
Bolivia	674	778	1 452	1 222	1 079	2 301
Ecuador	2 923	2 316	5 239	10 895	10 627	21 522
Peru	1 137	1 046	2 183	12 462	8 654	21 116
Dominican Rep.	809	992	1 801	6 949	10 770	17 719
Cuba	5 345	5 070	10 415	6 606	6 508	13 114
Caribbean Islands	3 379	3 556	6 935	4 529	4 996	9 525
Others America	12 029	11 755	23 784	15 131	15 177	30 308
Spain	80 688	69 059	149 747	79 469	65 036	144 505
Italy	55 171	33 078	88 249	51 009	28 993	80 002
Portugal	35 091	24 529	60 430	56 312	36 717	93 029
Others Europe	16 626	14 798	31 424	17 149	14 441	31 590
Not stated	94	159	253	9 013	9 030	18 043
Others	15 774	10 539	26 313	24 113	15 828	39 941
Total	318 878	277 577	596 455	561 049	513 580	1 074 628

Source: Tenth and Eleventh Population and Housing Censuses.

The first two groups represent the bulk of Colombian immigrants; their totals are probably around the estimates mentioned above.

It is more difficult to gauge the volume of seasonal immigrants who cross legally (with a border pass) or illegally to work in agriculture. Table 19.2 shows that Colombians represent 98 per cent of all foreigners employed in farming and stockbreeding, and 9.6 per cent of the labour force in that sector. For seasonal Colombian workers (assuming none were recorded in the census), if a contingent as large as the stable population were to be hired, 100 000 extra workers would come in every year for the harvest (seasonal workers rarely bring their families). That figure seems very high, given that there are 257 671 agricultural labourers in the country as a whole, because it would mean an additional 40 per cent would be taken on, not counting local manpower. The figures mentioned are even less likely when we consider that Colombian workers take seasonal jobs largely in the border areas (even though they have moved into other parts of the country in the last ten years). While it is difficult to estimate the floating population of Colombians in Venezuela, figures of 1-4 million are unfounded.

Table 19.2

EMPLOYMENT IN AGRICULTURE AND STOCKBREEDING

Countrywide			534 585
Foreigners			53 644
Colombians			50 755
Countrywide employment in agriculture, stockbreeding, hunting, forestry and related activities			523 891
Foreigners			51 158
Colombians			50 212

	Total	Born abroad	Colombians
Economically active population in Tachira (a)	209 664	60 407	(c)
Economically active population in Zulia (b)	522 754	80 655	67 079

	Total	Foreigners	
Agricultural employment in Tachira	44 253	(c)	
Agricultural employment in Zulia	58 542	22 011	

Labourers in agriculture, etc., countrywide		257 671
Colombian labourers in agriculture, etc., countrywide		39 341

a)   Tachira, bordering on Colombia, predominantly agricultural; 21 per cent of the Colombians in the country reside there.

b)   Zulia, bordering on Colombia, predominantly agricultural; 22.4 per cent of the Colombians in the country reside there.

c)   Information not yet available.

Source: Eleventh National Population and Housing Census, 1981. The data for Colombians are taken from a special section in the census.

Features of Illegal Colombian Immigration

The sole source of information on illegal immigrants is the Aliens Register. Registration took place between August and December 1980, and 266 795 people over the age of nine were accepted. Of these, 246 192 (92.3 per cent) were Colombians, and the balance included 16 721 (6.3 per cent) from South and Central America and the Caribbean.

Comparison of data on Colombians in Venezuela from the census conducted in October 1981 with the Aliens Register shows that Colombians on the Aliens Register are among the least-skilled group of Colombians in Venezuela. The geograhical distribution shown by the Register and the 1981 census (see Table 19.3) indicates that illegals were concentrated mainly in border or nearby states. This confirms the hypothesis that illegals are much more of an issue in border states than in urban areas and the Caracas Metropolitan Area.

Table 19.3

GEOGRAPHICAL DISTRIBUTION OF COLOMBIANS IN VENEZUELA

	1971 Census	1980 Register	1981 Census
Federal District and State of Miranda (a)	20.3	11.4	29.65
Aragua and Carabobo (b)	4.0	6.9	9.86
Tachira and Zulia (c)	60.1	56.2	43.33
Barinas and Mérida (d)	7.1	17.0	7.13
Others	8.5	8.5	10.03
	100.0	100.0	100.0

a) This region includes the Caracas Metropolitan Area; government, services and some industry.
b) States with recent industrial development.
c) States bordering on Colombia.
d) States close to the frontier, predominantly agricultural.

Source: OCEI. National Population and Housing Censuses, 1971 and 1981.
DIEX. Aliens Register, 1980.

Table 19.4 shows that the level of education of Colombians on the Aliens Register was substantially lower than for all Colombians in Venezuela, and that the overall educational level of Colombian immigrants was similar to the Venezuelan population as a whole.

The age structure of persons on the Aliens Register, compared with all Colombians in the 1981 census, shows a far higher proportion of young people among illegals than for Colombians as a whole (Table 19.5).

The proportion of males is higher in the Aliens Register than in the 1981 census. There are a number of reasons for this. The 1981 census and the 1981 Migration Survey showed that Colombian women tend more to go to the Caracas Metropolitan Area, whereas men tended to remain in the border states (Bidegain, Papail and Pellegrino, 1984).

Furthermore, high female participation in the domestic service sector doubltess gave them better opportunities for regulating their status without going through the Aliens Register procedure as they can usually count on assistance from their employers. At any rate, according to the Aliens Register, 78.6 per cent of working women were in the service sector. Unfortunately the Register does not allow comparisons between occupations or sex and geographical spread.

Data on family composition in the Register are very confused. They show the number of children reported by each individual, but not how many live under the same roof. The total number of children may be duplicated if both parents register. What can be seen from the data is that 39.2 per cent of women on the Register stated that they "had children". Of the children

Table 19.4

EDUCATIONAL LEVEL OF THE COLOMBIAN POPULATION AND
THE TOTAL POPULATION OF VENEZUELA

| | Colombians | | Total Venezuela |
	Register (a)	1981 Census (b)	1981 Census (c)
Illiterate/no education	17.1	10.5	11.0
Primary	66.2	56.3	59.1
Secondary	16.4	29.4	24.9
Higher	0.2	3.8	5.0
	100.0	100.0	100.0

a) Population aged nine and over.
b) Population aged five and over.
c) Population aged seven and over.

Source: OCEI. Eleventh National Population and Housing Census, 1981.
DIEX. Aliens Register, 1980.

Table 19.5

AGE STRUCTURE OF COLOMBIANS

| | Register 1980 | | | 1981 Census | |
	Absolute	Relative		Absolute	Relative
			0-9	32 611	6.42
9-14	18 565	7.6	10-14	27 280	5.37
15-20	40 219	16.3	15-19	41 839	8.23
21-30	102 345	41.6	20-24	73 570	14.48
31-40	46 536	18.9	25-34	160 185	31.52
41-60	32 784	13.3	35-54	138 085	27.17
61 and over	5 743	2.3	55 and over	34 596	6.81
Total	246 194	100.0		508 166	100.00

Source: OCEI, Eleventh National Population and Housing Census.
DIEX, Aliens Register, 1980.

declared 31.4 per cent were born abroad and lived there; 19.9 per cent were born in Venezuela and lived abroad, and 43.7 per cent were born in Venezuela and lived there. Of the men, 35.2 per cent declared that they "had children". Of these children, 46.3 per cent were born and lived outside Venezuela, 18 per cent were born in Venezuela and lived abroad, and 35.7 per cent were born and lived in Venezuela (5). In other words, over half the children of the illegals who registered were living apart from their parents. The 1981 Migration Survey indicated that 39 per cent of the Colombians were married and 22 per cent were together; there were more unmarried women than men.

In the 1981 census, indices of demographic and economic dependence for Colombians and those born in Venezuela were as follows:

	Colombians			Born in Venezuela		
	Total	Male	Female	Total	Male	Female
Demographic (a)	16.51	16.61	16.63	84.22	85.49	82.98
Economic (b)	40.29	19.34	59.34	69.79	56.19	83.29

a)   Demographic dependence: $\dfrac{\text{Aged 0-15 + 65 and over}}{\text{Aged 15 - 64}}$ X 100

b)   Economic dependence: $\dfrac{\text{Non-active population}}{\text{Total population}}$ X 100

These data confirm that Colombian migration in Venezuela is made up essentially of workers who usually do not bring dependents. Participation rates (*) are as follows:

	Total	Male	Female
Colombians	59.6	80.5	40.5
Born in Venezuela	46.2	67.7	25.3

*) $\dfrac{\text{Active population aged 12 and over}}{\text{Total population aged 12 and over}}$ X 100

Turning to employment, Tables 19.6, 19.7 and 19.8 show that people on the Register were heavily concentrated in agriculture, and in crafts and factory work.

The concentration of women in services, and the low participation rate in other types of employment, is clear in the Aliens Register although census data show not insignificant numbers in other sectors (offices 10.6 per cent, crafts and factory workers 9.4 per cent) (6).

Table 19.6

TYPES OF EMPLOYMENT, ACCORDING TO THE 1981 CENSUS (COLOMBIANS ONLY) AND THE ALIENS REGISTER

	Register (a)						1981 Census					
	Male	%	Female	%	Total	%	Male	%	Female	%	Total	%
Professional and technical	2 040	1.54	192	0.38	2 232	1.22	7 758	3.96	4 588	4.28	12 346	4.07
Management and public services	194	0.15	20	0.04	214	0.12	3 978	2.03	792	0.74	4 770	1.57
Office employees, etc.	479	0.36	1 935	3.81	2 414	1.32	5 846	2.98	11 364	10.60	17 210	5.68
Sales, etc.	3 794	2.86	1 154	2.27	4 948	2.70	17 790	9.08	9 174	8.56	26 964	8.90
Agriculture, livestock, fishery	28 765	21.67	203	0.40	28 968	15.79	49 415	25.23	797	0.74	50 212	16.57
Transport and communications	671	0.51	4	0.01	675	0.37	6 286	3.21	282	0.26	6 568	2.17
Miners, quarriers and related	377	0.28	2	0.00	379	0.21	415	0.21	7	0.01	422	0.14
Craftsmen, factory workers and related	60 977	45.95	1 861	3.67	62 838	34.25	72 622	37.08	10 054	9.38	82 676	27.28
Other crafts and trades	26 816	20.21	3 184	6.27	30 000	16.35	11 879	6.06	59 725	55.72	71 604	23.63
Workers in services, etc.	3 483	2.62	39 889	78.59	43 372	23.64	18 670	9.53	7 932	7.40	26 602	8.78
Not stated or identified	5 117	3.86	2 312	4.56	7 429	4.05	1 205	0.62	2 475	2.31	3 680	1.21
Seeking work for the first time												
Total	132 713	100.00	50 756	100.00	183 469	100.00	195 864	100.00	107 190	100.00	303 054	100.00

a) The data on employment in the Register are for all aliens registered.

Sources: DIEX, Aliens Register, 1980.
OCEI, Eleventh National Population and Housing Census, 1981.

309

Table 19.7

PARTICIPATION OF COLOMBIANS BY SECTOR, ACCORDING TO THE 1980 ALIENS REGISTER AND THE 1981 CENSUS

Sector	Male	%	Female	%	Total	%	Male	%	Female	%	Total	%
Agriculture, hunting, forestry and fishing	30 189	22.75	208	0.41	30 397	16.57	50 755	26.07	2 001	1.1	52 756	17.62
Oil and gas, mines and quarries	373	0.28	2	0.00	375	0.20	800	0.41	92	0.09	892	0.30
Manufacturing industry	69 038	52.02	4 755	9.37	73 793	40.22	35 295	18.13	13 075	12.49	48 370	16.16
Electricity, water, gas and services		0.00		0.00	0	0.00	1 002	0.51	149	0.14	1 151	0.38
Construction	18 694	14.09	272	0.54	18 966	10.34	31 598	16.23	1 437	1.37	33 035	11.03
Trade and financial institutions	4 339	3.27	3 011	5.93	7 350	4.01	31 037	15.94	21 902	20.92	52 939	17.68
Transport, storage and communications	283	0.21	3	0.01	286	0.16	5 787	2.97	789	0.75	6 576	2.20
Public and private services	4 781	3.60	40 168	79.14	44 949	24.50	25 329	13.01	58 607	55.97	83 936	28.04
Not stated or identified	5 016	3.78	2 336	4.60	7 352	4.01	13 056	6.71	6 663	6.36	19 719	6.59
Total	132 713	100.00	50 755	100.00	183 468	100.00	194 659	100.00	104 715	100.00	299 374	100.00

Source: Aliens Register, realigned on the classification in the 1981 Census. To approximate the labour force we have excluded "home" (60 531) and "student" (22 795). Eleventh National Population and Housing Census, 1981.

Table 19.8

ECONOMICALLY ACTIVE POPULATION AGED 12 AND OVER, BY TYPE OF EMPLOYMENT

	Register		1981 Census			
	Total 1981	%	Born abroad 1981	%	Colombians 1981	%
Professional and technical	425 869	9.07	46 332	7.32	12 346	4.34
Management, public services	107 540	2.29	41 832	6.61	4 770	1.68
Office employees, etc.	493 162	10.51	45 934	7.26	17 210	6.05
Sales, etc., agriculture, livestock, fishery	466 497	9.94	92 045	14.54	26 964	9.48
Transport and communications	523 891	11.16	60 342	9.53	50 212	17.66
Miners, quarries and related	10 635	0.23	1 098	0.17	422	0.15
Craftsmen, factory workers and related	1 041 738	22.19	150 602	23.80	82 676	29.07
Other crafts and trades	284 480	6.06	32 644	5.16	7 910	2.78
Workers in services; etc.	563 596	12.01	112 862	17.83	71 604	25.18
Not stated or identified	630 037	13.42	43 786	6.92	6 595	2.32
Seeking work for the first time	146 323	3.12	5 413	0.86	3 680	1.29
Total	4 693 768	100.00	632 890	100.00	284 389	100.00

Source: Eleventh National Population and Housing Census, 1981. Data realigned on the 1971 classification.

Of the economically active population in the Aliens Register, 76.6 per cent were in employment, 7.2 per cent were self-employed and 16.2 per cent were unemployed. According to the 1981 census, the breakdown was rather different: 3.9 per cent of the total were unemployed, 15.3 were self-employed and 73.1 per cent were in employment including domestic service (the remaining 7 per cent were largely "not stated").

In employment terms it is, therefore, clear that Colombians, and especially illegals, have tended to replace local manpower in the farming and stockbreeding sector, where local participation has been declining in absolute terms since the 1961 census. They have also followed the growth in "modern" sectors, crafts and factory work, and services. In these two areas they represented 7.9 and 12.7 per cent respectively.

Features of Employment in Venezuela and Colombian Integration

Oil brought about a substantial transformation of Venezuela's economy. Although it outstripped coffee as the leading export by the end of the 1920s, significant growth in employment tied to the "urban" sector did not occur until the 1950s. At the same time, especially from 1960 onwards, the farming and livestock sector gradually shifted towards entrepreneurial production units. Linked with these developments was an increasing trend towards manpower "dependence". Wage-earning and salaried employment rose from 54.8 per cent in 1976 to 68.2 per cent in 1980 (Chen, 1984).

Employment in the farm sector fell by some 100 000 people between 1950 and 1981. In relation to the economically active population, the fall was extremely significant (41.9 per cent in 1950, 11.2 per cent in 1981). Urban employment expanded steadily in both secondary and tertiary sectors. The sharpest rise was in the tertiary sector, from 35.0 per cent of the labour force in 1950 to 56.7 per cent in 1981. In the secondary sector, employment increased from 15.7 per cent of the labour force in 1950 to 25.9 per cent in 1980 (Chen, 1984).

During the 1970s construction achieved an annual growth of 9.4 per cent, far in excess of any other part of the secondary sector. The highest growth rate in the tertiary sector was in trade and financial institutions, real estate and business services (6.4 per cent a year between 1950 and 1980).

The State has also played a role in generating employment both in services and in industry, especially in the 1970s. Wage-earning and salaried government employment increased from 20 per cent of all employment in 1971 to 24.4 per cent in 1981 and rose by 550 000 jobs in absolute terms; one-third of overall growth in the economically active population was in the public sector. Foreign participation in this sector was only 2.8 per cent.

This shift certainly affected foreign participation in areas where local manpower switched from the private to the public sector. The case of women seems more typical in this respect. Since they were more widely represented in the services sector, whether born in the country or abroad, the movement of Venezuelan women into public-sector jobs allowed more foreign women to participate in the private sector, especially in domestic service. Wages in the least-skilled jobs in the public sector were no higher than in domestic service, but meant greater freedom, less dependence on employers, and additional income in the form of social security and bonuses.

Despite the modernisation of Venezuela, domestic service, which has traditionally drawn on female internal migration, is still significant. It employs 3.4 per cent of the economically active population and 11.8 per cent of working women. Women born abroad represent 32.4 per cent of all those employed in domestic service, and Colombians account for 83 per cent of all foreign women so employed.

Unemployment indices vary according to period and type of employment. Table 19.9 indicates that agriculture and services had lower than average unemployment indices. A high proportion of Colombians work in these sectors, according to both the 1981 census and the Aliens Register. Table 19.10 shows the incidence of Colombians employed in crafts and factory work: more than 54 per cent of the Colombians described as non-agricultural workers are found in group 9. This includes the construction sector, where 63.2 per cent of the work-force in that group are employed. Of the men engaged in non-agricultural activities, 35.7 per cent are in construction. Few women are employed in crafts and factory work, but 52.5 per cent of those who are work in the tailoring and dress-making sub-group.

According to data from the Aliens Register, construction workers comprised 18.2 per cent of non-agricultural employment; another 52.3 per cent were listed merely as workers, so no further analysis is possible (7). The 1981 census also shows a fairly even spread of Columbian participation in jobs associated with industrial production. Only a few sectors stand out: footwear, smithing and iron-work, mechanics and fitters, electricians, welders and sheet metal workers.

The average wage of Colombians in Venezuela (8) is 1 920 bolivars, 2 267 for men and 1 488 for women. Wages for women in domestic service and for rural labourers are frequently supplemented by board and lodging, paid for by the employer, although there are bound to be substantial differences between the standard of accommodation and food for domestic workers in urban centres and rural labourers. This makes accurate evaluation of real wages difficult. The typical wages of Colombians in jobs where they are widely represented are as follows:

Table 19.9

UNEMPLOYMENT RATES IN VENEZUELA BY TYPE OF EMPLOYMENT
1961, 1971, 1978 and 1981

	1961	1971	1978	1981
Professional and technical	7.3	3.1	1.8	2.7
Management, public services	7.4	3.5	1.2	2.3
Office employees, etc.	12.2	3.6	4.2	5.4
Sales, etc.	10.2	4.0	2.3	2.6
Agriculture, livestock, fishery	5.0	1.9	1.4	1.9
Transport and communications	16.9	6.3	9.7	8.4
Miners, quarriers and related	18.5	5.5	3.9	5.5
Craftsmen, factory workers and related	21.4	8.9	5.7	8.5
Workers in services, etc.	6.9	4.2	2.9	3.9
National average	13.1	6.2	4.3	6.0

Source: 1961 and 1971 Population and Housing Censuses, OCEI, Household Survey, second semester 1978 and 1981. Unspecified occupations and those seeking work for the first time have been excluded. Table from Chi-Yi Chen, Economia Laboral, p. 118.

Table 19.10

COLOMBIANS EMPLOYED IN THE CRAFTS AND FACTORY WORK,
BY OCCUPATIONAL SUB-GROUP

	Absolute			Relative		
	Male	Female	Total	Male	Female	Total
Group 7	8 704	7 482	16 186	10.34	65.29	16.92
Group 8	30 047	1 414	31 461	35.68	12.34	32.89
Group 9	45 456	2 564	48 020	53.98	22.37	50.19
Total	84 207	11 460	95 667	100.00	100.00	100.00

Group 7: Mines and quarries, metal, wood and paper, textiles, food and beverages, tobacco, tailoring and dressmaking.

Group 8: Craftsmen: shoemaking, footwear, wood and iron. Mechanics and fitters, electricians, radio and television repairs; plumbers, solderers and welders; jewellers, potters, glaziers and related.

Group 9: Rubber and plastics, paper and cardboard, construction draughtsmen, machine operators and transport drivers.

Source: Eleventh National Population and Housing Census, 1981.

Domestic service (women)	1 000–1 500 bolivars
Agricultural labourers (men)	500–1 000 bolivars
Construction workers (men)	1 500–2 000 bolivars
Skilled workers in industry (a)	3 000–5 000 bolivars
Workers in tailoring and dressmaking, etc. (women)	1 000–1 500 bolivars

a)   Mechanics, fitters, and watchmakers. 3.2 per cent of Colombians are in this sub-group, and they make up 11.3 per cent of Colombian crafts and factory workers.

In 1980 the Central Co-ordination and Planning Office of the Presidency of the Republic (Cordiplan) defined a monthly shopping basket which "would enable a typical family of six to live in proper fashion" in the Caracas Metropolitan Area. The goods in the basket cost 3 541 bolivars a month (9). Table 19.11 shows the ranges of earnings for Colombians and for the general population in agriculture and non-agricultural work. Table 19.12 shows income distribution for the overall population, in three categories: basic minimum, poverty and other, using the definitions in Chi-Yi Chen (1982).

It can be assumed that illegal immigrants earn less than the averages shown, as they are among the least-skilled groups. In addition, their illegal position makes them more than usually dependent on their employers. That explains the acceptance of low wages and the total lack of social security cover or extra payments such as Christmas boxes, bonuses and holidays.

Decisive Factors in Migration Between Venezuela and Colombia

A number of reasons account for migration between Venezuela and Colombia. The shortage of agricultural manpower in Venezuela became more marked in the 1960s and 1970s with movement towards the towns creating a demand for rural labour and bringing flows of rural migration in a considerable variety of ways, depending on place of origin and type of work (permanent or seasonal). In addition, during the 1970s and especially after 1974 the volume of jobs expanded substantially, enabling Venezuela to bring the 1950s generation into the labour market and raise female participation from 22.6 per cent in 1971 to 26.5 per cent in 1981. At the same time, half a million foreigners entered the country: the labour force born abroad increased from 325 755 in 1971 to 632 702 in 1981. It should be mentioned that during this period Venezuela was atypical of South America.

The financial prosperity generated by tax revenue from oil earnings enabled Venezuela to hold its currency steady against the strong dollar. The strength and stability of the bolivar, combined with the expansion of employment, were the chief features that attracted foreign migrants during the 1970s. Successive devaluations of the bolivar began in February 1983, a process that has now stabilized the Venezuelan currency at some 30 per cent of its previous value against the dollar.

Table 19.11

EMPLOYMENT IN AGRICULTURAL AND NON-AGRICULTURAL ACTIVITIES, BY MONTHLY INCOME
TOTAL POPULATION OF VENEZUELA AND COLOMBIA, 1981

Total Venezuela

	Agricultural Absolute	Relative	Non-agricultural Absolute	Relative
Less than 300 bolivars	10 528	1.7	54 813	1.3
301–1 000	281 128	46.0	539 066	13.2
1 001–1 500	132 363	21.6	763 486	18.7
1 501–2 000	86 358	14.1	874 347	21.4
2 001–3 000	50 004	8.2	877 949	21.5
3 001–4 000	20 641	3.4	447 266	11.0
4 001–5 000	10 060	1.6	208 486	5.1
5 001 and over	16 929	2.8	280 042	6.9
Not stated	3 737	0.6	32 814	0.8
	611 748	100.0	4 078 269	100.0

Total Colombia

	Agricultural Absolute	Relative	Non-agricultural Absolute	Relative
Less than 500 bolivars	4 430	8.4	14 550	5.9
501–1 000	30 659	58.1	34 427	14.0
1 001–1 500	10 185	19.3	51 468	20.9
1 501–2 000	2 090	4.0	39 856	16.2
2 001–3 000	1 266	2.4	41 412	16.8
3 001–5 000	434	0.8	27 349	11.1
5 001–10 000	218	0.4	11 960	4.9
10 000 and over	116	0.2	3 102	1.3
Unsalaried	256	0.5	2 381	1.0
Not stated	3 141	5.9	20 080	8.1
	52 795	100.0	246 585	100.0

Sources: Total Venezuela, calculations by Chi-Yi Chen based on data from the sample survey of households. Colombians, personal calculations based on the special sections in the 1981 census.

Table 19.12

WORKERS CLASSIFIED BY INCOME LEVEL FOR AGRICULTURAL AND NON-AGRICULTURAL ACTIVITIES AND
OCCUPATIONAL CATEGORY, 1980-81
(Percentages)

Monthly income	Agricultural activities Workers and employees				Non-agricultural activities Employers and self-employed			
	1980	1981	1980	1981	1980	1981	1980	1981
Basic minimum (less than 1 501 bolivars)	89.9	85.6	64.0	60.2	42.0	37.7	33.6	31.9
Poverty (1 501-3 000 bolivars)	8.6	12.7	25.1	28.1	40.9	43.5	36.7	37.5
Other (3 001 bolivars and over)	1.5	1.7	10.9	11.7	17.0	18.8	29.7	30.6
Total (absolute terms)	231 066	233 315	3 238	317 438	2 637 285	2 668 363	8 725	877 558
Relative	100	100	100	100	100	100	100	100

Source: OCEI, Household Survey, second semester 1980 and first semester 1981 ("not stated" omitted). Taken from Chin-Yi Chen, Revista Sobre Relaciones Industriales y Laborales, p. 67, December 1982.

These factors have been decisive for Colombian immigrants. Although they found employment in comparatively unskilled sectors where wages were at poverty or basic minimum levels and living conditions were inferior to those they had enjoyed at home, the opportunity to send remittances in a strong currency increased the household budget and the possibility of saving. Again, according to the information available, the flow of Colombians is made up mainly of workers whose dependents stay in the care of relations at home. The strategy thus appears to be that part of the family emigrates and is prepared to live in straitened circumstances in order to save as much as possible and send remittances which are enhanced by the exchange rate differential. While these explanations are valid in the general sense, Colombian emigration to Venezuela is very diverse and the numerous components of the flow have complex and varied motives and integrate in the host country to varying degrees.

The expansion of the industrial sector in Venezuela in the 1970s and the comparative shortage of skilled manpower led to skilled workers and technicians being recruited from abroad. Although the overall participation rate of Colombians is not significant, it represents a considerable proportion of those born abroad, given the volume of Colombian emigration. Colombia developed its industry earlier than Venezuela so it has a pool of skilled manufacturing manpower. In addition, around 1967 Colombia began to develop its exports of manufactures, resulting in annual industrial GDP growth of about 6.5 per cent around 1970, together with a considerable increase in employment over the same period (8.4 per cent in 1972 and 7.6 per cent in 1973). But the need to adjust this process to conditions in the international market entailed a considerable reduction in real wages, which had fallen by 25.6 per cent by 1975 compared with 1970 (Bejarno, 1981). The emigration of technicians and skilled workers to Venezuela in the 1970s is linked directly to wage levels paid by Venezuelan industry. Real wages were advantageous, particularly for skilled workers, quite apart from the exchange rate differential. According to Gomez and Diaz (1983), the minimum shopping basket in Colombia would require between 1.38 and 2.5 times the industrial worker's wage. In Venezuela, the wages earned by Colombians working in skilled jobs would cover the cost of the Cordiplan shopping basket. In less-skilled employment wages are lower, meaning that migration may suit unmarried persons or those who come with as few dependants as possible.

The complexity of Colombian migration can be analysed only by detailed research into place of origin, previous occupations, the sequence of movement and occupation, and the extent of economic ties with the place of origin. Unfortunately, the migration survey conducted in Venezuela in 1981 does not provide this information. Some papers prepared in Colombia on the internal migration process and special studies on labour exporting regions, are helpful. The gradual dissolution of the traditional rural economy and the expansion of enterprise-type farming caused migration in Colombia to the towns or to expanding agricultural centres, where dependent employment was available within the country. It also encouraged migration to Venezuela, where substantial numbers of jobs were available in the farming and livestock sector. Other writers -- Gomez and Diaz, (1985b) and Urrea (1981) -- report a link between migration and family strategies to maintain family production units by sending a few members to work as wage-earners in order to keep up and strengthen the family holding through remittances. This situation may produce some permanent migration, with links with the family nucleus kept up at least temporarily, but it particularly generates temporary or seasonal migration when times are slack on the home plot.

Seasonal and harvesting jobs are poorly paid on the whole (in many cases not by the day, but by the quantity harvested) and working conditions are hard. The offsetting factor is being able to save as much as possible to keep the family for the rest of the year or allow small outlays to improve output on the family plot.

One point which deserves closer analysis is the role that women play. Although seasonal farm workers are usually identified as mainly responsible for the upkeep of the family production unit, observation of Colombians in domestic service in Caracas shows that their purpose is much the same. In many cases the women leave home at an early age to work in the towns, mainly in domestic service, in order to help the family group. It is common to find at least two stages in migration, the first move being towards a neighbouring town and the second to Venezuela; there too, a period in a town near the frontier is followed by a move to Caracas itself.

The attraction of the construction sector for men during the 1970s led to migration to towns within Venezuela. As construction is an unskilled area and a common starting point in urban work for migrants, the expansion of the construction sector in the 1970s probably drew many migrants who first entered the country to work in rural activities.

The decline in the value of Venezuela's currency after 1983 led to expectations that considerable numbers of Colombian migrants would return home. However, official migration balances with Colombia were negative after 1979 when the economy started to cool down and unemployment reached levels unknown in previous decades. A similar rise in unemployment in Colombia and phased devaluation of the Colombian peso did not make return an attractive option.

Unemployment in the industrial sector, together with the drive to improve education and train technicians and skilled workers in Venezuela, will no doubt mean fewer jobs being available in this sector for foreigners. In domestic service wages are higher than in Colombia, in spite of the devaluation of the bolivar. It seems unlikely that the supply of labour from locally born persons will increase in this sector. In addition, pay differentials between administrative and professional jobs and domestic service mean that this will continue to be the way for middle-class women to enter the labour market, leaving household duties to an employee. A shortage of rural manpower, both permanent and seasonal, will continue to attract farm workers from Colombia, though this will naturally depend on cyclical factors such as exchange rates, policy for farming and stockbreeding, and the resulting level of labour demand.

NOTES AND REFERENCES

1. The 1966 Immigration and Settlement Act defines immigrants in these terms: "Foreigners of clean record and good behaviour and steady employment as farmers, stockbreeders, craftsmen, technicians, mechanics, etc. ... with or without means of subsistence, who arrive in Venezuela or wish to move to Venezuela with the intention of settling in the country, founding a family and becoming a permanent part of the Venezuelan population".

2. Urban population: people living in centres with more than 2 500 inhabitants.

3. Earlier bilateral agreements include the 1942 pact on border arrangements, the 1951 demarcation treaty and the introduction, in 1952, of the border transit card.

4. "Legalisation" is the term used for the procedure regulating the status of people without proper papers.

5. These data are for all aliens on the Register, as nationalities are not specified.

6. Employment data in the Aliens Register are not broken down by nationality.

7. Although we have shown entries in the Aliens Register in line with the census classifications, the Register did not require specific occupational categories to be stated, so it is hard to give breakdowns.

8. The data on wages are taken from special sections in the 1981 census. The Aliens Register does not provide information on this point.

9. Cordiplan, Diasper, Informe Social No. 2, Caracas, p. 281, 1982.

BIBLIOGRAPHY

BEJARANO, Jesus Antonio
"Industrializacion y Politca Economica (1950-1976)", Colombia Hoy, Siglo XXI Editores, 1981.

BIDEGAIN, G., J. PAPAIL and A. PELLEGRINO
Los Inmigrantes en Venezuela (Primeros Resultados de la Encuesta de Migracion 1981), Caracas, IIES-UCAB, Working Document No. 11, 1984.

BIDEGAIN, G. and A. PELLEGRINO
Estimacion del Saldo Migratorio Externo en Venezuela (1971-1981), Caracas, IIES-UCAB, Working Document No. 13, 1985.

CARDONA, R. et al.
Migracion de Colombianos a Venezuela, Bogota, Corporacion Centro Regional de Poblacion, 1983.

CHEN, Chi-Yi
"Las Magnitudes del Desempleo y Subempleo en Venezuela", Revista Sobre Relaciones Industriales y Laborales, No. 10-11, January-December 1982.

Economia Laboral, Caracas, IIES-UCAB, 1984.

CHEN, Chi-Yi, J.I. URQUIJO and M. PICQUET
"Los Movimientos Migratorios Internacionales en Venezuela: Politicas y Realidades", Revista Sobre Relaciones Industriales y Laborales, No. 10-11, January-December 1982.

GOMEZ, A. and L.M. DIAZ
La Moderna Esclavitud: los Indocumentados en Venezuela, Bogota, FINES Oveja Negra, 1983.

Las Perspectivas de la Migracion Internacional en el Contexto de la Crisis Economica. La Experiencia Colombo-Venezolana, Bogota, mimeo, June 1985a.

El Impacto de la Crisis Economica Sobre las Migraciones Campesinas de Colombia a Venezuela, Bogota, mimeo, September 1985b.

MICHELENA, A. et al.
Inmigracion Ilegal y Matricula General de Extranjeros en Venezuela, Geneva, ILO, Working Document, August 1984.

PAPAIL, J.
Ensayo de Estimacion de la Inmigracion de Venezuela Durante el Periodo 1971-1981, Caracas, IIES-UCAB, Working Document No. 9, 1984.

PELLEGRINO, A.
 "Venezuela: Illegal Immigration from Colombia", International Migration Review, New York, Vol. 18, Fall 1984.

 Evolucion Reciente de La Inmigracion en Venezuela, Caracas, IIES-UCAB, Working Document No. 16, August 1985.

TORREALBA, R.
 El Trabajador Migrante en Situaction Irregular y su Legalizacion en Venezuela, Geneva, ILO, Working Document, February 1985.

URREA, F.
 "La Oferta de Trabajadores Campesinos en el Contexto de la Produccion y de la Reproduccion de la Fuerza de Trabajo: el Caso Colombiano", in Economia Campesina y Empleo, Santiago de Chile, PREALC, 1981.

VAN ROY, R.
 "Undocumented Migration to Venezuela", International Migration Review, New York, Vol. 18, Fall 1984.

Chapter 20

MEASURES TO ENCOURAGE RETURN MIGRATION AND REINTEGRATION
OF RETURNED MIGRANTS IN THEIR HOME COUNTRY

by

J. Condé

INTRODUCTION

Ever since the so-called OPEC oil crisis in 1973 industrialised OECD
Member countries have been living with a trade and financial crisis that has
caused nearly universal recession. One consequence has been a rise in structural unemployment, affecting primarily unskilled jobs held mainly by foreign
workers. This situation has obliged governments to take measures first to
check and then to halt migratory flows while allowing families to reunite
under certain conditions. An arsenal of laws and regulations concerning immigration sprang into being. Governments of OECD Member host countries began
reordering their immigration policies with the following three objectives in
mind: strict control of migratory flows and work permits;   integration of
immigrant communities wishing to settle in the country;   encouragement of
return by former immigrants and their families and their reintegration in
their home country.

The intention of this paper is to examine the third of these objectives
with special regard to: measures to encourage return migration; reasons and
motivation for return migration; measures to facilitate reintegration in the
home country; and return migration seen in relation to international migration as a whole.

Measures to Encourage Return Migration

An immigrant in possession of civil rights and not subject to legal
proceedings in his host country may, if he so wishes, leave for his home
country or any other country of his choosing. Although exit is not subject to
administrative formalities in most countries, restrictions are applied to
entry and residence. Until the late 1970s, most return migration was called
"natural", the migration cycle having been completed. Over recent years,
however, the governments of some European immigration countries have

instituted return migration policies. These are of three kinds: return facilities (aided return); systematic encouragement to return; means of pressure, or forcible measures.

While the reasons leading immigration countries to adopt such policies are understandable, international migration exceeds domestic considerations and extends into the field of international relations. In the policy-makers' and legislators' view, the return of immigrants to their home country frees jobs for unemployed nationals of the host country.

Deliberate government policy providing incentives for encouraging voluntary return can assume various forms. In France, the return aid policy adopted in 1983 falls under three main headings:

a) State aid for reintegration, consisting of payment of travel costs for the migrant, spouse and children, a flat-rate household removal grant, and a contribution to the migrant's reintegration effort; the aid ceiling is set at FF 20 000.

b) An aid contract under the unemployment insurance scheme, whereby an unemployed migrant collects two-thirds of the unemployment benefits that would have accrued to him (basic allowance plus expiry grant); this is a lump sum calculated on the basis of the migrant's last earnings;

c) Special assistance provided by the last employer, under the terms of a contract between the employer and the government or the National Immigration Office.

The total sum paid to a returning migrant varies from FF 70 000 to FF 200 000, although not every immigrant worker intending to return can claim amounts of this magnitude. Entitlement depends on certain conditions being met, for example, the migrant must have attained his or her civil majority (18 years), volunteer to return to his or her home country, not be entitled to unrestricted travel, to treatment as a French national, to permission to work by reason of his or her personal situation, nor to a renewal of his or her residence permit on the grounds of family reunion. He/she must also have been employed (legally, and as a permanent employee) by an enterprise that has subscribed to a contract with the government or the National Immigration Office to aid the reintegration of foreign workers in their home country. He/she must be involuntarily unemployed (as a result of a lay-off or notice under the terms of the contract between the employer and the government or the National Immigration Office) and have been out of work for less than six months at the time of application. He/she must also provide evidence of a personal plan for reintegration, duly approved by the appropriate services of the National Immigration Office. And, prior to the disbursement of aid, he/she must surrender work and residence permits.

As can be imagined, the number of migrants meeting all these conditions is limited. With the exception of some large firms, most enterprises have not signed contracts with the government or the National Immigration Office concerning reintegration of foreign workers in their home country. Most immigrant workers are illiterate and lack information about the provisions contained in the return aid packages. Many leave at their own expense because they are unaware of their rights. It is not within everyone's reach to draw

up a convincing personal project and provide evidence to support it. Moreover, even when approved by the National Immigration Office, the project may
not fit in with the social and economic realities (or the priorities) of the
home country.

In the Federal Republic of Germany, foreign workers have always been
considered as visiting guest workers (Gastarbeiter). If one studies the
length of stay of these guest workers, it is apparent that most of them are de
facto immigrants, as in other industrialised countries. Since 1960, however,
the official attitude of treating them as "guests" has meant that the government has adopted policies encouraging their repatriation.

Bilateral agreements were signed with countries in which the workers
were recruited (Italy, Turkey, Korea). Occupational training and a basic
course in management were provided to migrants volunteering to return. The
idea was to train semi-skilled workers needed by industry in the migrants'
home countries. Despite wide publicity given to these programmes, the results
were disappointing. On the one hand, due to the flourishing state of the
German economy, domestic industry reabsorbed the freshly trained workers. On
the other hand, they were discouraged from returning home by the lack of adequate administrative, financial and industrial structures in their home
countries.

While training was being given to prospective returning migrants, the
government also encouraged migrant workers to establish private companies in
their own countries. Promoters were provided with technical and financial
assistance. A special bank was created with half of the capital supplied by
the host country and half by the country of return in order to grant loans to
companies launched by guest workers. The country of return also granted
facilities in the form of tax exemption, exoneration from customs duties on
imported equipment and monetary compensation against high inflation.

Until 1983, German Government policy encouraged return mainly by giving
support to organisations founded through the joint, private initiative of
migrant workers. The watchword was: "Learn by doing and acting". To under-
line the voluntary character of repatriation, and unlike French practice,
until 1983 no cash grants were made, nor was any government body set up to
deal with these issues.

Non-governmental organisations, such as welfare institutions and religious societies, made themselves responsible for the migrant workers'
associations and federations. Private bodies managed assistance for planned
individual projects. Inter-government co-operation was limited to defining
and overseeing programmes, and to providing financial assistance for the
emigration countries.

This official trend was reinforced by the new policy (Konsolidierungs-
politik) adopted in 1980, which tended to stabilize the number of migrant
workers, halt fresh immigration and encourage return migration. It favoured
job creation and investment in the migrants' home countries. Simultaneously,
migrants intending to return were generously aided with their private future
projects.

When unemployment increased, the Bundestag, hoping to increase the pace
of repatriation, passed an Act designed to encourage voluntary return. Coming

into effect on 29th November 1983, it stipulated the benefits available to aliens willing to resettle in their home countries. Certain conditions had to be met by the workers concerned:

a) Only workers from Korea, Morocco, Portugal, Spain, Tunisia, Turkey and Yugoslavia were eligible;

b) They must have been unemployed after October 1983 as a result of the closure of an entire plant or essential parts of it, or as the consequence of bankruptcy;

c) Or they must have been on short-time work for at least six months at the date when their application was filed.

A fixed sum of DM 10 500 in aid, plus DM 1 500 per child, was granted to returning workers, provided that they left German territory immediately, accompanied by their family, i.e., spouse and all dependent children. A worker who did not leave immediately was penalised by a reduction in the fixed sum for each month spent in Germany. In addition to the cash grant, the worker was entitled to withdraw, before the due date, deposits eligible for State bonuses (building funds, savings plans, capital-forming life insurance contracts) without forfeiting the bonuses, and to obtain a refund of pension contributions. Prior to the 1983 Act, refunds of pension contributions had been subject to a waiting period of two years. The employers' share of pension contributions has never been refundable. The provisions of the Act lapsed in September 1984 and were not renewed. Since then, at both diplomatic and administrative levels, the German Government has maintained two-way contacts with the governments of emigration countries aimed at creating jobs for returning workers within the framework of those countries' development policies.

Belgium has also adopted measures (The Recovery Act of 22nd January 1985) concerning the voluntary repatriation of migrants. Reintegration grants are payable to foreign workers requiring a visa on the date the Act came into force. The conditions of entitlement are to have been in receipt of full-time unemployment benefits over a period of at least one year and to return to the country of origin accompanied by all dependents.

Grants vary according to the civil status of the beneficiary (single, in cohabitation, head of family), and equal 312 times the daily amount of unemployment benefits payable (after one year of eligibility) on the last day of receipt of such benefits, plus BF 50 000 for a spouse and BF 15 000 for each child aged under 18 living under the same roof as the applicant. Acceptance and payment of the grants cancel the work and residence permits of the beneficiary who, along with his family and other dependents, may not thereafter remain in Belgium for longer than three months. The provisions of the Act remain in force for three years and may be renewed by Royal Decree after Cabinet deliberation.

The Swedish example illustrates another approach to the repatriation of migrants. There is no provision for either direct or indirect incentives. Owing to the organisation of migrants into government-aided associations and the teaching of migrant children in their mother tongue, a cultural link between migrants and their home country is maintained. These factors ease the task of reintegrating returning migrants. Agreements have been signed with several manpower-providing countries concerning payment of retirement benefits to pensionable workers, and of unemployment benefits and family allowances to migrant workers and members of their families returning to their country of origin for good.

The other, very generous, conditions applicable to immigrants tend to act against their repatriation. The golden rule for both the government and the unions is "equal pay for equal work". As in other countries, foreign workers, and especially those newly arrived, occupy the most disagreeable, monotonous and dangerous jobs. But, in contrast with the other immigration countries, these workers, because they are less mobile than the Swedes, tend to rise quickly in the job hierarchy after a certain time. Comfortable working and housing conditions, political rights (automatic entitlement to vote in local or regional elections after three years' residence in Sweden), and ease of integration (possibility of acquiring Swedish nationality after five years' consecutive residence) all help reinforce the desire of immigrants to remain in the country.

Judging by the number of people taking advantage of repatriation assistance of any kind, measures to encourage return have had only a slight effect. The number of beneficiaries has been below government expectations. There are several explanations for this: social and economic conditions in home countries have barely improved and sometimes even deteriorated; children have not finished their schooling; the unemployed have hopes of finding work; and the existence of a "black" labour market.

Reasons and Motivation for Return Migration

While the main motive for emigrating is generally economic, reasons behind return are many, complex and sometimes seemingly contradictory. They appear to be associated with the various categories of migrants: those intending to take up permanent residence; workers who emigrate with a fixed target, e.g., to amass a capital sum x; those intending to emigrate for a fixed period; and those who leave their country without any firm idea of how long they will be away.

The reasons for return depend on attitudes at the time of departure. These may be grouped under the following headings:

-- Family motives, such as the children's schooling, a longing to see the family, and the need to look after elderly relations;

-- Retirement;

-- Difficulties encountered at work and insoluable problems of integration into the social fabric of the host country;

-- Sufficient money saved and objectives achieved;

-- Job possibilities in the home country;

-- Setting up one's own business;

-- Private reasons, such as homesickness, health problems, the death of a relation, inheritance, marriage, etc.;

-- A striking change for the better in the home country;

-- Loss of job in the host country;

-- Political, economic or social events in the host country (anti-foreign sentiment, racism, persecution, expulsion, etc.).

Although not exhaustive, this list indicates that motives are personal. Surveys and studies of motivation indicate that replies are not always precisely expressed and that the main reasons advanced often serve as an umbrella for numerous other reasons. Private and family pretexts conceal stated economic and social reasons relating to worsened job and living conditions.

Measures to Facilitate Reintegration in the Home Country

These measures may be adopted by the host country as well as by the country of origin. As already noted, incentive policies adopted by the host country include provisions for facilitating transfer of savings to the home country, association with individual projects and payment of travel costs.

The essential problem for reintegration of the returnee is that he faces tremendous social and economic difficulties. The factors responsible for outward migration remain and, in some cases, have grown worse, while such new problems as external debt may have arisen. The manpower-supplying countries, depending partly for balance of payments on the inflow of foreign exchange represented by currency transfers and remittances of their nationals living abroad, are disinclined to co-operate in major efforts designed to repatriate their citizens, unless special plans are made to compensate their economies.

Past experience has shown that countries of emigration are less than keen for their emigrants to return, especially those who are viewed as partial failures by the stay-at-home population. For all of these reasons, very few emigration countries have adopted coherent policies to encourage the return and reintegration of their nationals.

A description and review of the measures taken by the few countries which have done their best to attract returnees and help them find a place in society might provide a model for the numerous countries remiss in dealing with this issue.

Some governments accord priority to investing and creating jobs in areas particularly affected by emigration. By altering the economic and social situation in the departure zones, they attack the root causes of emigration. When the country concerned is equipped with centralised planning and administrative services, such a policy is easier to carry out. Job opportunities in the various regions can be publicised, tax and housing privileges granted and the establishment of small- and medium-sized agricultural, service or industrial undertakings encouraged in particular regions. The government can ensure that new industrial complexes are located in recognised priority areas. Promoters of the complexes may be granted loans on favourable terms and in order to encourage returning migrant workers to set up their own small businesses in priorty areas, they may be offered special incentives, ranging from tax breaks to duty-free imports of whatever products may be needed for their businesses. When the new production complexes are launched, the government may give priority to returning migrants. When a job description list is prepared, migrants with appropriate job profiles, either returned or still living abroad, may be sought.

Another type of encouragement to return, perhaps the most widely practised, is to grant emigrant workers permission to open foreign currency accounts in a bank in their home country. The money is kept in the currency denomination in which it is deposited, bears interest, and may be withdrawn by the depositor as foreign currency. Another method is to set a special exchange rate, always higher than the official rate, for transfer by emigrant workers of foreign currency to a bank in their home country. Special bonds affording privileges in addition to interest to those who make fixed-term deposits in foreign currency is another type of encouragement.

Banks from the emigration country are in some cases allowed to establish themselves in the host countries in order to funnel deposits and savings. These banks may be appointed as official intermediaries between the governments of emigration and host countries to act as a channel for repatriation assistance, individual benefits (the various allowances to which returnees are entitled), bilateral and multilateral aid for return and reintegration. Individual projects, planned in association with migrants as an incentive to return, are submitted to the banks for the purposes of financing.

Sometimes an official agency in the home country provides emigrants with information on available openings there. The reception services of the agency take charge of returning migrants, direct them to appropriate jobs or projects, settle them in the zones where they will be living and help them with the necessary formalities. The agency also has the task of informing local communities to integrate the migrants in cases where a certain reluctance to do so, or even hostility towards the returning workers, exists.

Some countries undertake action on behalf of the children of emigrants. Just as host countries attempt to fit children into their education systems, the emigration countries try to reintegrate these children into their own school systems. School-age children suffer a double handicap: when abroad, they often lag behind local children of their own age for cultural and linguistic reasons; when they return home, they have to cope with a different system, with the result that they become even more backward. Certain countries try to remedy this backwardness by providing lessons to newly returned children in the tongue of the host country, while at the same time offering them classes in the vernacular, the aim being to assimilate them completely into the local school system and eventually put them on the same footing as non-emigrant children.

It is difficult to gauge the effectiveness of measures designed to improve social readaptation and reintegration. The relations (extended family) or the local community in the home country generally assume responsibility for returning children. A study of countries where return has been high over a long period shows that government action has rarely been undertaken in this particular direction. The same holds true where the reintegration of young adults into the working environment is concerned. Since young non-emigrants are especially hard hit by unemployment, it would be unjust for governments to privilege one cateory over another.

The very mitigated success of the above-described measures is explained by the motives, nearly always of a private or family nature, that make a person decide to emigrate. During the 1960s, governments were involved in the hiring of workers under contract. Subsequently, however, migration became a spontaneous, individual affair in which governments played no part at all. In consequence, they apparently do not not feel that repatriation, whether forced or voluntary, concerns them, whence the lack of consistent, long-term policies for reintegrating emigrants. The way that a returning migrant behaves helps or hinders his reintegration more than the attitde of the community to which he returns. Workers' associations in the host country can play a useful role in this connection by helping the migrant preserve his culture and maintain a link with his home country. Ease of reintegration depends on the period spent abroad by the migrant; the longer the absence, the harder reintegration becomes.

Policy designed to encourage the reintegration of returnees and make best use of their potential should take account of the professional skills they have acquired, their working habits and knowledge of production techniques, their political consciousness and union experience, and also give thought to the productive investment of their transfers and savings.

Return Migration in Relation to International Migration

As the counterpart of emigration, return migration follows the same classification: permanent, temporary, illegal migration and refugee flows. Causes and effects may vary in accordance with the migratory status of the permanently returning migrant. Similarly, it may be assumed that a close connection exists between the various types of migration and the inclination or urge to return.

Some host countries have already adopted aid policies for repatriation and reintegration. Others have signed special agreements to promote business undertakings by providing finance for projects that generate employment. These examples ought to be followed by every country dependent on migrant labour. The need for a new strategy, as defined by OECD (1978) has lost none of its urgency. Of the five policy targets mentioned, four refer to the immigration countries:

a) Countries concerned by specific migratory flows should in future act in concert when required to take important decisions on migration policies, taking into account the long-term needs and social costs of both home and host countries;

b) Governments of immigration countries should increase efforts to evaluate the structural consequences of the use of migrant workers and better integrate migration policies with manpower and employment policies;

330

c) The future co-operation between countries of emigration and immigration should aim at creating an institutional framework for a new strategy of international and economic adjustment, based on a harmonization of objectives rather than traditional patterns of development aid;

d) In this new strategy, the co-operation of immigration countries in the industrial and technological development of emigration countries as an alternative or complement to migration is increasingly important.

The fourth policy target deserves special emphasis. It is highly desirable that migration should form an integral part of all bilateral and multilateral agreements on co-operation. As for the emigration countries, one of the targets identified in the same OECD document remains applicable today:

-- Governments of emigration countries must define their policy options more clearly and effectively include in their development plans both the desirable level of employment and the tolerable volume of emigration.

Emigration countries should, moreover, strive to correct regional imbalances, which are a source of both internal and international migration. Migration has hitherto acted as a safety valve (relieving population pressure, unemployment, underemployment and scarcity of arable land) for these countries. The global recession has changed the situation in industrialised countries -- they now protect their domestic labour markets and forbid immigration. The same recession has hit developing countries even harder, aggravating their previous difficulties. Internal migration, particularly of urban dwellers, is on the rise in many of these countries. As internal migration is the only alternative to international migration, policies for redeploying the domestic population are urgently required. Such policies must be related and subordinated to the general objectives of society. Many other policies strongly affect the way settlement occurs.

There is no fixed correlation between economic indicators and the measurement of population distribution. Such are the complexity and variety of situations prevailing in developing countries that it is impossible to propose a model of population distribution. Flexibility is a must, and planning should respect the peculiar features of each country. There is no way of deciding the optimum size of a city, since the notion of size has little meaning when divorced from the city's make-up, function and place in the urban hierarchy.

The balance between town and country can be a hazy concept -- it is sometimes defined in terms of population distribution and at others in terms of income and social well-being. Because there is a close relation between the two criteria, governments should tackle the problem of urban-rural equilibrium in terms of complementary aspects. Policies for reducing inequality between town and country require government action that fixes quantitative, qualitative and normative targets for the intra- and interregional redeployment of the population.

Governments have only limited means -- be they financial, technical or skilled human resources -- at their disposal. For these means to be sufficient, not only political will but also the participation of all those involved in redeployment are necessary at every level of discussion, decision and execution. Evaluation of a country's available resources is an often-neglected priority. Targets must be tailored to fit resources. External aid should be viewed as a supporting factor only. Return migration needs to be considered as part of internal migration policy; of policy for geographical redeployment of the population.

BIBLIOGRAPHY

CONDE, Julien
International South-North Migration -- Evolution up to 1981 of the Laws and Regulations Concerning Immigration in OECD Member Countries, forthcoming, to appear in "Development Centre Studies".

ICM
Unpublished contributions to the International Committee for Migration's symposium on Migrant Readaptation and Reintegration -- Social and Economic Aspects of Voluntary Return Migration, Geneva, 9-13th December 1985.

KUBAT, Daniel, ed.
The Politics of Return. International Return Migrations in Europe, Centro Studi Emigrazione, Rome, Centre for Migration Studies, New York, 1984.

OECD
The Migratory Chain, Paris, OECD, 1978.

TREBOUS, Madeleine
Migration and Development -- The Case of Algeria, Paris, OECD Development Centre, 1970.

Part III

GENERAL AND OVERVIEWS

Chapter 21

SOME CONSEQUENCES OF THIRD WORLD MIGRATION TO CANADA

by

Anthony H. Richmond
Lawrence Lam, Fernando Mata and Lloyd Wong (1)

In this chapter the term "Third World" refers to countries in Africa (excluding the Republic of South Africa), Asia (including the Middle East), Central America, the Caribbean, South America and Oceania. Not all these countries are in the low-income category, although most warrant description as "developing". The Asian region includes Hong Kong, together with middle- and high-income oil-exporting countries such as the United Arab Emirates. "Migration" refers to the movement of persons approved for admission to Canada on a permanent basis (officially described as landed immigrants), together with those admitted on a short-term basis for temporary employment and those issued student authorisations.

After World War II, Canada pursued a positive immigration policy encouraging the permanent settlement of immigrants from many countries. Since 1974, there has also been extensive use of temporary employment visas which enable people to work for periods up to one year with the possibility of renewal in certain cases. Third World countries have become an increasingly important source of temporary and permanent workers. In the latter case, the immigration of a spouse and other dependents has also been encouraged. However, temporary workers have not been allowed to bring family or dependents. In addition, refugees have been accepted from various countries in Asia and Latin America. "Family reunion" has been a component of this movement.

Immigration Trends

Prior to 1962, regulations restricted immigration from Third World countries to Canada. Only token numbers were admitted from India, Pakistan and Sri Lanka, together with a small number of domestic workers from Caribbean countries. After 1968, selection for permanent settlement was on the basis of education, skills and qualifications deemed to be in demand in Canada. As the proportion of Third World immigrants increased, the movement assumed the character of a brain drain. There was also a significant movement of students from Third World countries, some of whom remained in Canada after completing their studies. Temporary employment visas were issued to the less skilled, mainly seasonal workers in agriculture and domestic workers in hospitals, institutions or private homes. The former were mainly males and the latter mainly females (Wong, 1984).

A study of trends in Third World immigration to Canada between 1961 and 1977 showed that the proportion of permanent immigrants from these countries increased from 8 per cent in the early 1960s to more than 50 per cent by the end of the 1970s (Lanphier, 1979). Demographic characteristics indicated a predominance of young adults whose intended occupations reflected their high levels of education. The study reviewed research which had been undertaken by government agencies and by academics concerning the economic and social integration of Third World immigrants and concluded that they experienced greater problems of adjustment than other immigrants, largely because of prejudice and discrimination in Canada against visible minorities.

About 65 000 immigrants entered Canada from Latin American countries between 1971 and 1980 and a further 22 000 during the period 1981 to 1984. Mata (1983, 1985) identified four major immigrant waves from Latin America. The first occurred after World War II and included many professionals from industrially advanced areas. Many had previous links with Europe, being first or second generation re-migrants. In 1973, an Andean wave from Ecuador and Colombia comprised skilled and unskilled manual workers, mainly temporary as well as illegal who were able to regularise their status in Canada at a later date. Then came the migration of Chilean intelligentsia following the military coup. Finally, there was a Central American wave following the Sandinista revolution in 1979. The proprotion of Latin Americans thus rose from less than 1 per cent of total landed immigrants in 1957 to 6.7 per cent in 1983. The largest single intake was in 1975 when more than 10 000 were admitted from the region (Mata, 1985:32).

Recent trends: 1978-85 (2)

Details of the flow of landed immigrants to Canada for the period 1978 to 1985 are shown in Table 21.1. Although traditional source countries such as Great Britain continue to be important, Third World countries constitute a growing proportion of all immigrants admitted for permanent residence. Hong Kong and India each sent an annual average 5 000 persons, as did the Caribbean region as a whole. It should be noted that many of those who were admitted for permanent residence were dependents in the family reunion class and not expected to enter the labour force on arrival. In fact, landed immigrants destined to the labour market were about 40 per cent of the total. The scale of the permanent (landed) immigrants movement in recent years (1974-85) is also shown in Figure 21.1 which includes the refugee component. Permanent immigration from all countries averaged 139 431 per annum during this period. The proportion from Third World countries rose from 36 per cent in 1971 to 69 per cent in 1985. In absolute numbers, 1974 was a peak year with over 107 000 persons coming from Third World countries, mainly in Asia, the Caribbean and Latin America. The most important source countries were Vietnam, Hong Kong, India, the Philippines, Jamaica and, recently, El Salvador. A declining proportion of these immigrants intended entering the labour force; in 1984 the figure was 45 per cent. The government restricted selected worker immigration in favour of dependents in the face of poor

Table 21.1

PERCENTAGE DISTRIBUTION OF IMMIGRANTS BY COUNTRY OF LAST PERMANENT RESIDENCE AND
BY YEAR OF LANDING, 1978-85

Country of last permanent residence	1978	1979	1980	1981	1982	1983	1984	1985	Total
Great Britain	13.7	11.5	12.7	16.4	13.6	6.4	5.8	5.3	11.2
Rest of Europe	21.2	17.8	16.0	19.5	24.5	20.8	17.9	17.1	19.3
South Africa	1.9	1.2	1.0	1.1	0.8	0.5	0.4	0.4	0.9
Rest of Africa	3.0	2.3	2.1	2.7	2.9	3.6	3.7	3.8	2.9
Hong Kong	5.5	5.3	4.4	5.0	5.4	7.5	8.7	8.8	6.1
Rest of Asia	22.3	39.8	45.6	32.9	29.0	33.9	38.8	37.0	35.4
Australia	0.9	0.7	0.6	0.6	0.5	0.4	0.4	0.4	0.6
Rest of Australasia and Oceania (a)	1.4	1.2	1.1	1.2	1.4	1.0	0.9	0.9	1.2
United States	11.5	8.6	6.9	8.2	7.7	8.3	7.8	7.9	8.3
Rest of North and Central America	1.1	0.7	0.6	0.8	1.4	4.1	4.6	6.0	2.1
Caribbean	9.6	5.7	5.1	6.7	7.2	8.1	6.4	7.3	6.8
South America	7.9	5.3	3.8	4.8	5.7	5.4	4.6	5.2	5.2
Total	100.0	100.0	100.0	100.0	100.0	100.0	100.0	100.0	100.0
Number	86 313	112 096	143 133	128 632	121 166	89 177	88 239	84 302	853 058

a)   Including 258 persons classified as "Not Stated".

Source: Immigration Statistics, Employment and Immigration Canada, Ottawa, Supply and Services Canada, 1986, (adapted).

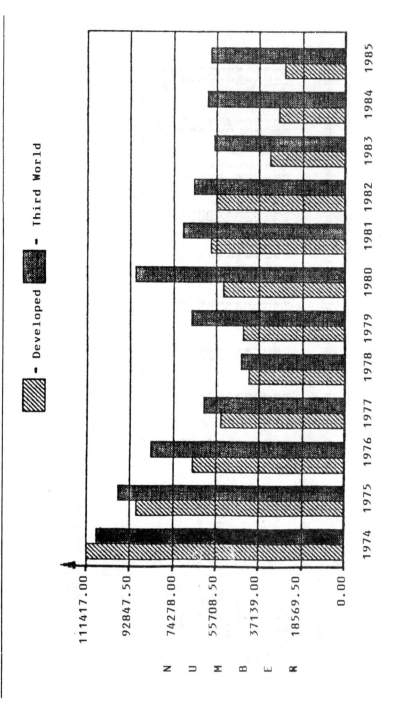

FIGURE 21.1: IMMIGRATION TO CANADA BY REGION, 1974-1985

- Developed   - Third World

economic conditions, although it has continued to issue temporary employment authorisations.

The refugee movement has been a significant component of permanent immigration, constituting more than 100 000 of the total between 1980 and 1984. Indochinese were the largest single component; 40 per cent of all "refugees and designated classes" admitted in 1980 but declining to 37.5 per cent in 1984. The number of refugees and designated classes in 1984 was 15 342 of whom 80 per cent were from Third World countries. Most of the refugees entering Canada were selected overseas by Canadian Government personnel. A small number, approximately 2 000 annually up to 1985, were admitted as internal refugee claimants. The internal refugee determination process in Canada has proved to be cumbersome with many delays before full refugee status is awarded. There has been some abuse of the system in which economically motivated migrants, who would not qualify for admission to Canada under the usual selection criteria, have entered as visitors and then attempted to remain in the country by claiming refugee status. By 1986, the numbers involved had become more than the system could handle. Consequently, the government adopted an "administrative clearance" procedure to remove the backlog, while tightening the scrutiny of new applications and restricting entry across the United States border.

Figure 21.2 gives a detailed breakdown of immigration to Canada in 1985 by regions of the world. Seventy per cent of landed immigrants were from Third World countries, of which the Asia and Pacific component was the largest.

The number of temporary employment authorisations increased from 63 320 in 1978 to 143 979 in 1984 when 39 per cent were issued to persons from the Third World. The percentage distribution by region is shown in Table 21.2, which indicates that Asia and the Caribbean were the main Third World regions involved. Specifically, domestic workers from the Philippines and the Caribbean, together with agricultural workers from the latter region were a large component of this temporary migration. On average, more than 123 000 short-term employment authorisations have been issued annually during the last decade, of which more than a third are renewed for more than one year. Lanphier (1981) and Wong (1984, 1987) examined trends in the issue of temporary employment authorisations, and discovered that although some of the increase can be attributed to their use by refugee claimants waiting adjudication, the evidence suggests a growing dependence by Canada on temporary workers to meet certain labour shortages, including those arising from seasonal employment demands and socially "undesirable" jobs such as fruit harvesting and domestic service. These shortages persist despite high unemployment because Canadians, able to take advantage of unemployment insurance or welfare assistance, are reluctant to accept unskilled jobs. Wong (1987) estimated that in 1984 Canada gained more than 58 000 person-years of employment from the use of temporary authorisations. Some short-term authorisations were issued to artists, scientists, teachers and entertainers, but the largest single recipient category was services, constituting almost a third of the person-years.

There is some re-migration and return movement to and from the Third World. Unfortunately, Canada does not maintain records of emigration so no reliable data are available on the scale of return migration. An analysis of 1981 census data compared with annual immigration figures for the decade 1971-81 allows estimates of settler loss to be calculated by the residual

FIGURE 21.2: IMMIGRATION TO CANADA BY WORLD AREA, 1985

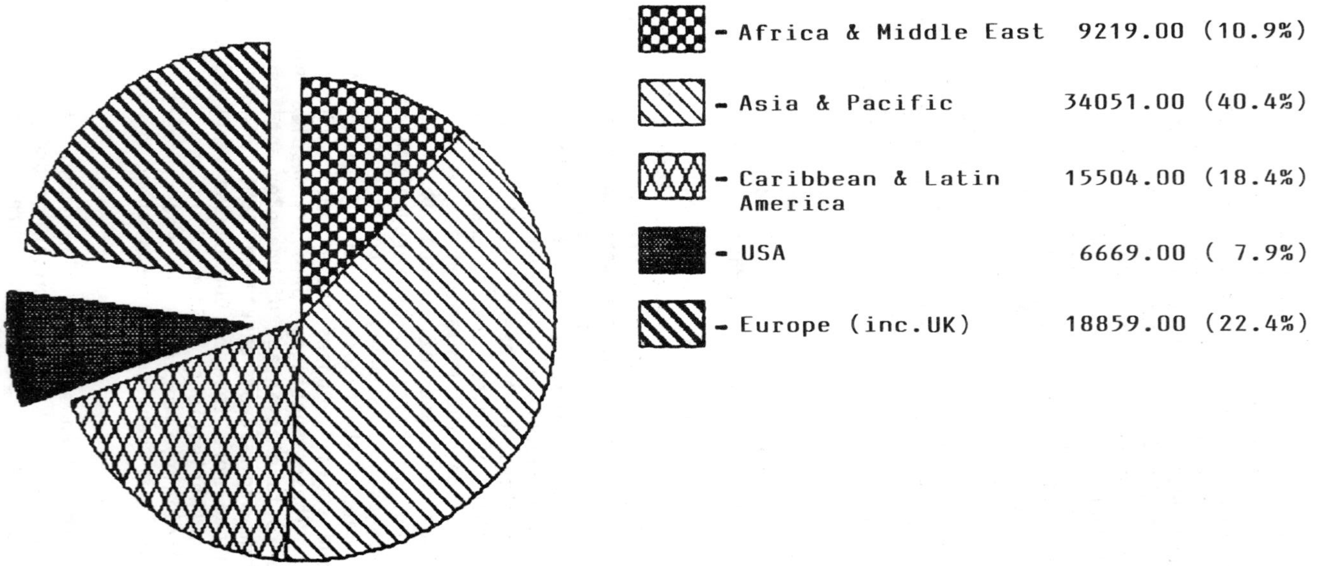

■ Africa & Middle East   9219.00 (10.9%)

■ Asia & Pacific   34051.00 (40.4%)

■ Caribbean & Latin   15504.00 (18.4%)
  America

■ USA   6669.00 (7.9%)

■ Europe (inc.UK)   18859.00 (22.4%)

TOTAL: 84302.00 (100%)

Table 21.2

PERCENTAGE DISTRIBUTION OF EMPLOYMENT AUTHORISATIONS BY COUNTRY OF LAST PERMANENT RESIDENCE, 1978-84

Country of last permanent residence	1978	1979	1980	1981	1982	1983	1984	Total
Great Britain	9.8	9.7	9.1	8.8	8.2	6.7	5.6	8.0
Rest of Europe	13.3	13.2	12.7	13.3	12.7	11.6	11.6	12.5
South Africa	0.3	0.2	0.2	0.2	0.1	0.1	0.1	0.2
Rest of Africa	1.6	1.8	1.8	1.3	1.9	2.1	2.2	1.9
Hong Kong	1.7	1.5	1.5	1.3	1.2	1.1	1.4	1.4
Rest of Asia	8.7	9.7	9.7	11.1	13.7	15.3	18.3	13.0
Australia	1.1	0.9	0.7	0.9	0.9	0.9	0.9	0.9
Rest of Australasia and Oceania (a)	0.5	0.7	0.7	0.8	0.6	0.5	0.6	0.6
United States	45.7	46.2	48.0	48.3	47.9	48.2	42.2	46.6
Rest of North and Central America	1.6	1.7	1.6	1.8	2.0	2.1	2.5	2.0
Caribbean	13.0	11.1	10.4	8.6	8.0	7.7	8.6	9.2
South America	2.7	3.4	3.5	2.9	2.8	3.6	6.0	3.7
Total	100.0	100.0	100.0	100.0	100.0	100.0	100.0	100.0
Number	63 320	94 420	108 871	126 583	125 901	130 717	143 979	793 791

a) Including 113 persons classified as "Not Stated".

Source: Immigration Statistics, Employment and Immigration Canada, Ottawa, Supply and Services Canada, 1986, (adapted).

341

method but, given the problem of census under-enumeration and inaccuracy in admission records, such estimates are not very reliable. Preliminary analysis suggests that return migration of Third World immigrants is less for persons admitted as landed immigrants. Nevertheless, overstaying has given rise to some illegal immigration although border controls make illegal entry unusual. The government estimated a maximum illegal resident population of 50 000 persons in 1983.

At the 1981 census, 16.1 per cent of the population of 24.3 million had been born outside Canada, 978 575 having come from Third World countries (see Figure 21.3). The number has since increased and now probably exceeds 1 million. The major source countries were China (including Hong Kong), Indochina (including Vietnam and Kampuchea), the Philippines, India, Pakistan, Jamaica, Trinidad and Chile, together with various East African and some Middle Eastern countries.

Canada has always welcomed immigrants with substantial capital to start a business and thereby create employment for Canadians. However, until recently Great Britain and the United States were the main source countries for such affluent migrants. Following a policy decision to encourage "Business Immigrants", the number of investors, self-employed persons and entrepreneurs almost doubled between 1979 and 1984 from 1 237 to 2 094. An increasing proportion came from Third World countries such as Hong Kong, the largest single source country in 1984 which supplied 31 per cent of the business class entrants. The latter category invested C$ 817 million in 1984 and were believed to have created more than 8 000 new jobs (Employment and Immigration, 1985).

Another category of temporary migration is students. The number of foreign student authorisations issued in 1978-84 is shown in Table 21.3. Between 50 000 and 100 000 student authorisations are issued annually, about half of which are renewals for second and subsequent years of study. Two-thirds of the students are from Third World countries. The largest single source is Hong Kong followed by Malaysia. A decline in the number issued in 1984 probably reflected an increase in fees charged by Canada. The majority of students were aged between 15 and 29 and about half enrolled for university studies. Foreign students (including those from the United States) make up about 5 per cent of all university enrolments in Canada.

Consequences of Third World Migration

The consequences of Third World migration for Canada are considered under three headings: (a) consequences for the immigrants, including economic adaptation and social integration; (b) consequences for Canada and (c) consequences for the sending countries.

Economic adaptation of immigrants

A report based on the 1971 census provided a demographic profile of all immigrants by ethnic origin and generation. It also examined the economic adaptation of immigrants in terms of labour force participation, unemployment rates, industrial and occupational distribution and income (Richmond and Kalbach, 1980). Generally speaking, post-war immigrants in Canada have

FIGURE 21.3: THIRD WORLD IMMIGRANTS IN CANADA , 1981

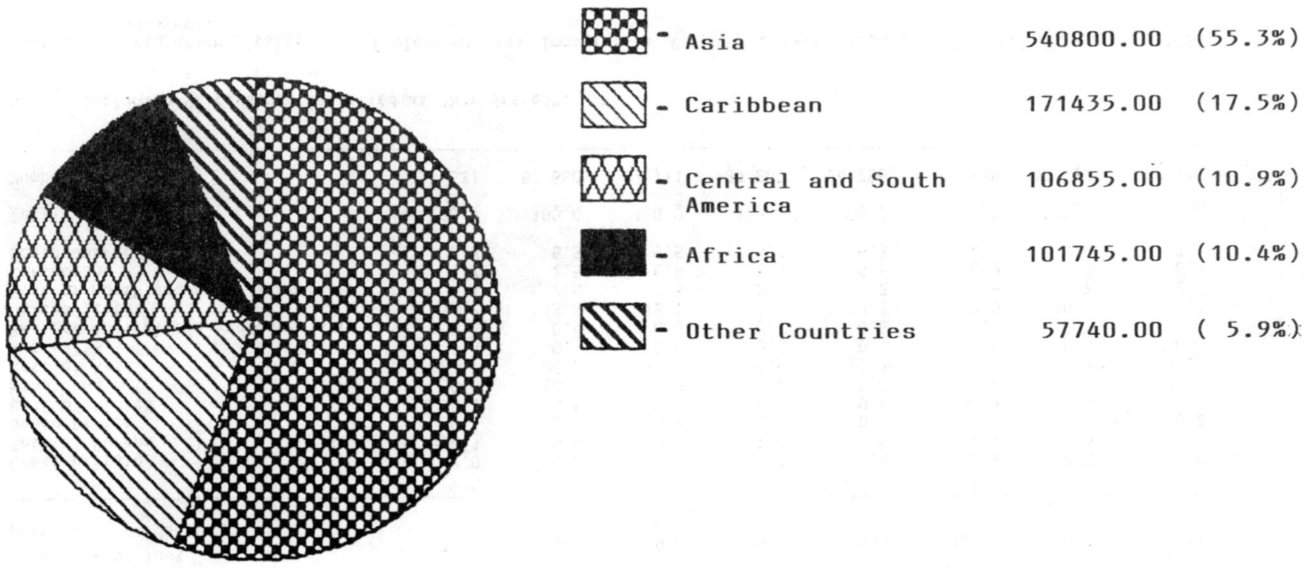

Asia	540800.00	(55.3%)
Caribbean	171435.00	(17.5%)
Central and South America	106855.00	(10.9%)
Africa	101745.00	(10.4%)
Other Countries	57740.00	(5.9%)

TOTAL: 978575.00 (100%)

Table 21.3

PERCENTAGE DISTRIBUTION OF STUDENT AUTHORISATIONS BY COUNTRY OF
LAST PERMANENT RESIDENCE, 1978-84

Country of last permanent residence	1978	1979	1980	1981	1982	1983	1984	Total
Great Britain	2.0	2.2	2.5	2.8	2.8	2.8	2.8	2.6
Rest of Europe	6.1	6.9	7.7	7.9	7.6	7.1	7.9	7.4
South Africa	0.2	0.3	0.2	0.1	0.2	0.1	0.2	0.2
Rest of Africa	9.1	9.5	8.3	8.3	9.9	10.7	10.8	9.6
Hong Kong	30.0	24.8	22.4	23.4	25.0	26.8	26.5	25.4
Rest of Asia	20.7	26.0	30.7	30.4	29.2	28.9	28.2	28.2
Australia	0.5	0.7	0.6	0.6	0.5	0.5	0.6	0.6
Rest of Australasia and Oceania (a)	0.5	0.6	0.6	0.7	0.6	0.6	0.7	0.6
United States	14.2	13.6	12.1	11.1	10.2	9.5	10.1	11.2
Rest of North and Central America	2.1	2.5	2.5	2.8	2.2	1.5	1.7	2.2
Caribbean	8.7	7.5	6.9	6.3	6.5	6.9	6.6	6.9
South America	5.8	5.5	5.5	5.7	5.3	4.7	4.0	5.1
Total	100.0	100.0	100.0	100.0	100.0	100.0	100.0	100.0
Number	51 521	57 680	67 771	84 809	94 786	95 378	86 167	538 112

a)   Including 92 persons classified as "Not Stated".

Source: Immigration Statistics, Employment and Immigration Canada, Ottawa, Supply and Services Canada, 1986,
(adapted).

344

benefited from their location in major metropolitan areas and have achieved an economic status, measured by occupation and income, superior to that of the Canadian-born.

The selective nature of Canadian immigration policy with its emphasis on education and qualifications has contributed to the higher status of immigrants. However, there are important exceptions. These include recently arrived immigrants, many of whom are from Third World countries who experienced rates of unemployment and income levels not commensurate with their educational qualifications. Employers and licensing bodies did not always recognise overseas qualifications and often insisted upon Canadian experience. Further comparative studies of immigrants in Canada and Australia, using 1971 census data, indicated that the adjustment problems of Third World immigrants were more serious than those of others, and emphasized the low earnings of women, who often faced the double disadvantage of being female and members of visible minorities (Richmond and Zubrzycki, 1984).

This conclusion corroborated Clodman and Richmond (1981) who reviewed available evidence on the incidence and cause of unemployment among immigrants and of Ornstein and Sharma (1983) who analysed a series of longitudinal surveys of immigrants in Canada, conducted between 1969 and 1978. Higher unemployment rates were experienced by immigrants from Third World countries and their incomes were below the average for other countries of origin. Women were particularly vulnerable in this respect. Richmond's review (1982) of various studies of the economic adaptation of refugees and other immigrants who had come to Canada in the 1970s confirmed that deterio- rating economic conditions were having deleterious effects on the economic situation of immigrants, and that recent Third World immigrants were the most adversely affected. Nevertheless, some members of visible minorities with longer periods of residence had successfully established small businesses and were not experiencing difficulties substantially greater than other small- scale entrepreneurs during a period of economic recession (Rhyne, 1983).

Age, sex, education and period of immigration were important determinants of the economic status of Third World immigrants in Canada, measured by total income in 1980 as reported in the 1981 census. Reflecting the selective nature of Canadian immigration policy, Asian immigrants on average had higher educational qualifications than Canadian-born, although the proportion with university degrees was lower among more recent arrivals due to the increasing proportion of family class migrants and refugees (Basavarajappa and Verma, 1985). Labour force participation rates were above average as were the proportions of employers and self-employed workers and professionals among longer-term Asian residents. More recent immigrants had lower occupational status and incomes. Before adjustment for age and education, the total incomes of Asian men and women exceeded that of Canadian-born, but standardised comparisons showed that the incomes of Asian-born males ranged from 89 per cent of equivalent Canadian males in the 1960-69 immigrant cohort to 70 per cent in the 1975-79 cohort. Asian women earned much less than men but standardized comparisons with Canadian-born women showed they were relatively better off than Asian men. Those in the earlier cohort earned 107 per cent of equivalent Canadian-born women and more recent arrivals earned 83 per cent. In common with other immigrants to Canada, part of the apparent advantage in terms of income related to the relative concentration of foreign-born in major metropolitan areas where unemployment is lower and average incomes higher than in other parts of the country.

Social integration

In addition to examining the economic dimension of immigrant adaptation, the 1971 Census Analytical Study (Richmond and Kalbach, 1980) also considered questions of family organisation, fertility, educational achievement, language and naturalisation. Immigrants from Asian countries (the largest Third World group) were above average in educational achievement, generally spoke at least one official language (English or French) and, like most other immigrants, had low fertility rates. Asians had a higher than average propensity to become naturalised Canadians.

Survey data collected in Toronto in 1970 were used to examine the family relationship and social integration of immigrants (Richmond and Goldlust, 1977). The number of Third World immigrants in the sample was small but evidence showed that other immigrants and native-born Canadians tended to exhibit significant degrees of prejudice and discrimination against blacks and Asians, and to maintain social distance from them. Subsequent studies by Sharma (1980; 1981a; 1981b) using survey data collected directly from immigrants, including those from Third World countries, confirmed problems of social adjustment experienced by recent immigrants. Men, women and children all faced problems of one kind or another that were sometimes aggravated by racism. While European immigrants indicated that language barriers were their greatest handicap, those from Third World countries tended to complain most about discrimination and the inadequacy of existing governmental and voluntary social agencies.

Third World immigrants: specific nationalities

Caribbean immigrants in the metropolitan Toronto area were studied by Ramcharan (1974; 1976; 1982). He examined the history of West Indian immigration to Canada, the economic status of immigrants in Toronto and the extent of perceived discrimination which, he concluded, was related directly to skin colour; dark complexioned blacks reporting more discrimination than light skinned blacks or Asians. He subsequently compared the experience of Caribbean immigrants with visible minorities from other countries and concluded that multicultural policies which encouraged pluralistic forms of integration tended, in the long run, to exacerbate adjustment problems. This led him to advocate "the dispersion of members of the racial minorities into the wider society", with a view to becoming part of the power structure and changing the institutions that presently support discrimination, prejudice and bigotry (Ramcharan, 1982:111).

Because they are French-speaking, Haitian immigrants are mainly found in Quebec, particularly in the Montreal area. In 1981 there were almost 27 000 Haitians in Canada. Although many were well-educated and had professional qualifications, they had difficulty finding suitable employment and generally faced prejudice and discrimination. Nevertheless, in 1971 their occupational distribution in Quebec, when compared with English-speaking West Indian immigrants, showed a higher proportion in teaching and nursing and fewer in administration, service occupations and manufacturing (Jean-Baptiste, 1979; Piche et al., 1983).

By 1981, the West Indian-born population of Canada numbered 211 120, including Guyanese. Women were in the majority (sex ration 0.83) and 71 per cent had arrived in the preceding decade. More than half of those aged 15 years and over had some post-secondary education compared with 36 per cent of the Canadian population. Labour force participation rates were high: 84 per cent for males and 72 per cent for females. Caribbean-born males were under-represented in managerial occupations but were above average in the professional and technical category. Almost one-third were working in manu-facturing compared with 19 per cent of the total male labour force. The occupation profiles of West Indian women was closer to that of the female labour force as a whole, but they were less likely to be in clerical and sales and more likely to be in manufacturing (15 per cent compared with 8 per cent).

Despite the high level of education, average total income levels for Caribbean males (including Guyanese) were only 91 per cent of the Canadian average, whereas all foreign-born males averaged 108 per cent. When controls for age, period of immigration and educational level were applied, Caribbean immigrant men consistently showed lower average incomes than equivalent Canadians or comparable immigrant groups. West Indian women earned less than men but did better, on the whole, when compared with other women, both immi-grant and Canadian-born. Incomes were approximately 11 per cent above the average for all women aged 15 years and over. However, more recently arrived West Indian women with post-secondary qualifications earned less than similar-ly qualified immigrant women from other countries (Statistics Canada, un-published tabulations).

Chinese immigrants can be divided between the "old" and the "new" migration from Hong Kong and elsewhere. Whereas the former were usually aged survivors of an earlier period when immigration from China was restricted and consisted mainly of unskilled workers who remained isolated in "Chinatown", recent immigrants are young, well-educated, English-speaking and enterpris-ing. They rarely remain within the residential confines of Chinatown (Con and Wickberg, 1982; Johnson, 1983; Lai, 1970). Chow (1983) considered the question of Chinese language classes attended by children who came to Canada very young, or who were born there and concluded that the extent of interest in Chinese language maintenance depended upon various aspects of family back-ground, including kinship networks.

Lam (1982, 1983) studied the adjustment problems facing Indochinese refugees from Vietnam, Laos and Kampuchea living in Montreal. In this mainly French-speaking environment, recently arrived immigrants were still recovering from the trauma of their often hazardous escape from war-torn countries. Many were afraid that the separatist movement in Quebec would force them to move yet again. They were experiencing serious difficulties in establishing them-selves in steady employment at a time of economic recession. Some were professionals or merchants who had lost their possessions and had little hope of regaining their prosperity. Nevertheless, they expressed satisfaction with their experiences in Canada and appeared to be resigned to their present fate. Their overwhelming preoccupation was with the fate of their relatives left behind and in trying to reunite their families. Their experience showed some of the typical psychological dimensions of refugee adjustment including a sense of loss and social dislocation. Significant effects on family relation-ships (particularly when husbands become economically and socially dependent on spouse or children), and consequent feelings of depression and various psychosomatic disorders have been reported (Chan and Lam, 1983).

Persons from South Asia (India, Pakistan, Bangladesh and Sri Lanka) and of similar ethnic origins from Kenya, Uganda, Trinidad and Fiji have formed an increasing proportion of the movement from Third World countries. The Sikh population has grown, particuarly in British Columbia, as has the Hindu and Muslim population from various parts of the world. The 1981 census reported 68 000 Sikhs, nearly 70 000 Hindus and over 98 000 persons of Islamic religion. A recent study of the South Asian population concluded a firm integration into Canadian life with selective retention of certain aspects of the varied cultural heritage through maintenance of close networks of family and friends together with the development of critical institutions such as temples, newspapers and business associations (Buchignani et al., 1985). As well as forming a significant proportion of Canada's visible minorities, these communities have also found themselves involved in controversial political issues arising from situations in their former countries. Fear of terrorism has been added to racial prejudice as a factor inhibiting their full integration into Canadian society.

Consequences for Canada

The demographic impact of Third World immigration to Canada has been significant. In the last twenty-five years gross immigration from these countries has been about 1.5 million. After allowing for re-migration and mortality an estimated 1.2 million people born in Third World countries are resident in Canada on a long-term or permanent basis and, possibly, an additional 0.25 million are temporary residents.

Despite the controversial nature of continued immigration at a time of economic crisis and high unemployment, Canada has clearly benefited economically from Third World migration, both temporary and permanent. In recent years entrepreneurs have brought substantial capital for investment. Immigrants and temporary workers have gravitated to the most prosperous regions of the country. They have undertaken jobs, both skilled and unskilled, that many Canadians would prefer not to do because they involve long hours, shift work, hard physical labour and rates of pay that are not competitive with other employment opportunities, or are only marginally above unemployment insurance benefit levels. Even professionally qualified immigrants have frequently found that they must accept employment that is not commensurate with their qualifications. Nevertheless, it must be recognised that there are costs involved for employers, government agencies and others. Transportation, language classes, initial welfare services and financial support for immigrants, together with funding of voluntary agencies that serve immigrants, must be set against the direct and indirect benefits of immigration to the country. A recent study of "programme delivery" for the Federal Government (Task Force on Programme Review, 1985) estimated the annual cost of various administrative services relating to immigration as approximately C$ 146 million. This included the cost of administering the selection procedures in Canada and overseas, handling refugee applications and assisting immigrants after arrival. It does not include indirect cost to provincial and municipal authorities for educational, health or welfare services.

The indirect social costs of immigration are harder to define. Infrastructures such as housing, schooling, multilingual communications and other services must be provided. A report of a Special Parliamentary

Committee on Visible Minorities in Canadian Society (Daudlin, 1984) made a total of 80 recommendations for government and private sector action in order to achieve "Equality Now" for immigrant and other ethnic minorities in Canada.

The political implications of migration to Canada from the Third World, particularly the growing number of refugees and others admitted for permanent residence, are substantial. The bilingual character of Canada (English and French being official languages) has already been modified by the post-war movement of European immigrants which has given Canada an increasingly poly-ethnic and multicultural character (Elliott, ed., 1983). Third World immi-gration further diversified the population, introduced more languages, religions and ethnic communities whose social and political integration must be facilitated. Naturalisation and citizenship requirements have been revised and the required period of residence reduced from five to three years. Never-theless, many immigrants do not become Canadian citizens, thereby excluding themselves from electoral rolls and full participation in the political process. In 1981, only 53 per cent of those who immigrated during the last decade had become naturalised Canadian citizens. The proportion of non-citizens was more than a third of all those from the Caribbean, Central and South America compared with about 20 per cent of all Asian immigrants (Statistics Canada, 1984). Global political conflicts and tensions influence internal political issues and external relations. The Economic Council of Canada has urged a review of Canada's trade relations and bilateral aid to Third World countries in the light of changing industrial strategies and world economic conditions. Recently, the Department of External Affairs issued a "Green Paper" dealing with Canada's international relations, in which ques-tions of competitiveness and security in the modern world were reviewed. It re-affirmed a commitment to assisting refugees, promoting human rights and recognised that foreign students brought short- and long-term benefits to Canada. The changing ethnic composition of the population as a consequence of Third World immigration is bound to influence Canada's relations with other countries in the future (Hockin and Simard, 1986).

Consequences for Sending Countries

In the absence of systematic research, any assessment of the impact of Third World migration to Canada on the sending countries must be largely speculative. The following ideas are put forward as hypotheses requiring further examination and testing, rather than as conclusions. Taken in iso-lation from other international movements of population, the demographic impact of migration to Canada on sending countries has been small. Relative to the huge populations and rapid rates of natural increase in many Third World countries, a million people moving to Canada has not made much impres-sion on the demographic crises facing Asia and Africa, where annual population growth by natural increase is in the order of 2 per cent per annum. However, taken in conjunction with movements to other developed countries such as the United States, Britain and Europe, international migration has provided some relief from demographic pressures, although it offers no long-term solution to the critical question of resource allocation and food supply.

The economic consequences for sending countries are a complex balance of costs and benefits, with many interaction effects. Net advantages or disadvantages would be extremely difficult to calculate. Given Canada's preference for educated and highly-qualified immigrants, permanent movement involves a substantial transfer of human capital from a developing to a developed country. If the per capita value of the education and training were estimated at a modest C$ 10 000, the total addition to Canada's stock of educational capital would be in the order of C$ 10 billion from Third World countries alone. Against this must be set remittances which the migrants send back to the former country. No official estimates are available on the amounts involved. However, a longitudinal survey of landed immigrants carried out by the Canadian Government between 1969-71 included questions concerning amounts remitted (3). The findings, as they apply to Third World immigrants, are reported in Table 21.4. In the first year, an average of 39.5 per cent of all immigrants (including Europeans and others) remitted funds. The proportion fell to 32 per cent in the second twelve-month period and 28 per cent in the third year. A similar trend was evident for immigrants from Third World countries although the actual proportions remitting were above average to all regions except Africa. The overall mean average value of remittances in the first year was C$ 173.59 although Asian immigrants remitted almost twice this amount. The average value of remittances fell to C$ 150.72 in the second but rose in the third year to C$ 540.50. As shown in Table 21.4, Asian immigrants, both men and women, remitted above-average amounts throughout their first three years in Canada. The gross amounts remitted (by sampled respondents from all countries) totalled C$ 2.67 million in the first year, C$ 2.36 million in the second and C$ 9 million in the third year. One-third of this was sent by immigrants originating from Third World countries.

Altogether, Third World immigrants in this sample remitted C$ 5 million in their first three years in Canada. Assuming that the sample was representative of all immigrants admitted to Canada in the years 1969 to 1971, the gross amount sent by these new arrivals from Third World countries would have been more than C$ 13 million annually. To this 1971 sum must be added the amounts sent by earlier arrivals. As shown in Figure 21.4, if it assumed that all employed immigrants (males and females) from Third World countries remitted an average of C$ 540 in 1971, the total funds sent back would have been in the order of C$ 155 million that year. A number of other highly-tentative assumptions must be made in order to arrive at an approximate figure for 1981. If remittances kept pace with inflation and the average per capita amount remained at the level reported by the sampled respondents in the longitudinal survey in their third year, the amount remitted to Third World countries in 1981 could have been in the order of C$ 1 billion although such an estimate is subject to a wide margin of error.

A more recent study reporting information on remittances was carried out in 1983-84 by the Institute of Environmental Studies, University of Toronto, in association with Employment and Immigration Canada, IDRC and the University of the West Indies, Institute of Social and Economic Research, Barbados. This study surveyed landed immigrants (family class) from the Eastern Caribbean to Canada. It was found that 46 per cent sent back money during their first few months in Canada, averaging C$ 72 per month (Whyte, 1984:2).

At the time of the longitudinal survey, remittances sent abroad to support dependent relatives were partially tax deductible in Canada. This provided an added incentive to remit funds and may even have given rise to some abuse. The tax benefit was subsequently removed which may have contributed to the decline in amounts remitted to former countries. Against

Table 21.4

CANADA: THIRD WORLD IMMIGRANTS, 1969-71 ARRIVALS
PERCENT REMITTING FUNDS TO FORMER COUNTRY
By year and sex

Region	First 12 months		Second 12 months		Third 12 months	
	Males	Females	Males	Females	Males	Females
Africa	29.1	34.9	29.5	20.6	24.8	11.1
Asia	55.7	59.6	48.7	44.2	45.3	36.0
Caribbean	47.0	47.8	39.2	35.8	33.4	30.9
Central & South America	43.0	35.7	38.3	27.0	35.6	24.3
Oceania	51.2	41.2	48.8	47.1	44.2	35.3

MEAN VALUE OF REMITTANCES PER PERSON (a)
By year and sex (Can. $)

Region	First 12 months		Second 12 months		Third 12 months	
	Males	Females	Males	Females	Males	Females
Africa	159.0	49.0	160.0	33.0	353.0	15.0
Asia	305.0	371.0	278.0	279.0	620.0	589.0
Caribbean	147.0	108.0	144.0	96.0	521.0	868.0
Central & South America	182.0	83.0	191.0	66.0	466.0	747.0
Oceania	240.0	194.0	217.0	271.0	426.0	184.0

a)   Includes those not remitting.

GROSS VALUE OF REMITTANCES BY SAMPLED RESPONDENTS
Males and females (Can. $)

Region	First 12 months	Second 12 Months	Third 12 Months
Africa	41 046.0	39 971.0	90 667.0
Asia	756 336.0	658 635.0	1 541 268.0
Caribbean	178 252.0	177 432.0	1 047 031.0
Central & South America	74 397.0	79 167.0	274 556.0
Oceania	12 949.0	13 447.0	21 424.0
All	1 062 980.0	968 652.0	2 974 946.0

Source: Employment and Immigration Canada, Longitudinal Survey, 1969-71.

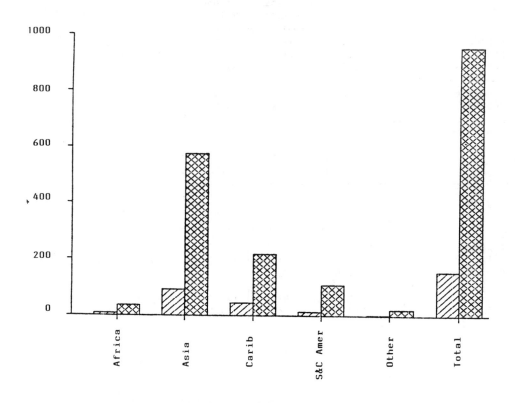

FIGURE 21.4: ESTIMATED GROSS ANNUAL REMITTANCES TO THE THIRD WORLD

Year 1971
Year 1981

this must be set the growing number of Third World immigrants in Canada since 1971, together with the number of temporary employment authorisations issued. The latter also gave rise to remittances and to funds saved and taken back to the former country at the end of a stay which may have been a few months or over a year. Little information is available concerning funds remitted by temporary workers, such as domestics from the Philippines. However, a study of farm workers from Barbados, Grenada and St. Vincent in the Caribbean showed that most sent some money back to their families while working in Canada and that the opportunity to save money for expenditure on return was a major incentive for undertaking such employment. Whyte (1984) estimated remittances varied from C\$ 50 to more than C\$ 600 per month with mean values of C\$ 102 (Grenada), C\$ 217 (Barbados) and C\$ 161 (St. Vincent) monthly for an average stay of four months. At the end of their stay, temporary workers brought back an average of C\$ 1 006 in cash and purchases.

The social and economic implications of these remittances for sending countries are important. The average GNP per head in many Third World countries, such as India, Pakistan and Bangladesh, was only US\$280 in 1982, according to the World Development Report, (World Bank, 1984). The Philippines averaged US\$820 and Jamaica US\$1 330. It is evident that the families of remitters received a very substantial boost to their income in local currency values. Further research is needed to determine whether these funds were used to improve subsistence, pay for education, improve housing, pay for travel, or to support elderly parents, wives or other dependents. The money would serve as a boost to the local economy and would provide governments and the private sector in the countries concerned with a valuable source of foreign currency. The example set would be a further inducement to migration, providing a role model for others and accelerating the chain migration effect.

Political and social effects

Refugees have been a significant element in migration to Canada from Third World countries. The initial crisis in Vietnam was followed by an orderly departure scheme which must have provided some relaxation of internal conflict as well as relief for the refugees themselves. Other source countries included El Salvador, Ethiopia, Guatamala, Iran, Iraq, Kampuchea and Laos. Others from Third World countries, such as Sikhs, have sought refugee status in Canada although their claims have not always been recognised. Sending countries no doubt benefited from the departure of potentially disturbing elements although, in some cases, nationalist or irredentist movements may have been able to obtain moral and financial support from refugees and other migrants overseas. The threat of terrorism, hijacking and counter-revolution has not been noticeably reduced as a result of international population movements. Overt and covert operations carried out by the superpowers in the Third World have exacerbated the refugee problem. Canada's role has been reactive rather than pro-active in this respect.

The social consequences of migration from the Third World to Canada can only be presumed. Return migration has occurred but has not been systematically studied. Students and temporary workers combine with returned migrants to provide a network of contacts and communication between Canada and the sending countries which is bound to influence their culture and social organisation. One area likely to be of importance concerns the status of women. Whether remaining in the former country, or part of the migration flow itself, women are likely to have achieved a greater degree of economic independence. Their role and status in the family is likely to change as a result of new responsibilities and exposure to different values and expectations. Religious observance, parent-child relations and authority structures in the family and community may be modified as a result of the migration experience.

CONCLUSION

The consequences of migration from Third World countries are far-reaching. They affect migrants themselves as well as the sending and receiving countries. Global communication systems, aided by satellites, combine with rapid transportation and economic inter-dependence to create a world in which state boundaries are no longer impermeable. The relatively homogeneous nation state is everywhere giving way to multicultural, polyethnic, plural societies between which there are multi-way flows of capital, income, people, goods, services and information. Countries of emigration and immigration can no longer be considered separate entities. There is a necessary symbiotic relation between sending and receiving societies, as well as between the increasing number where net gains and losses of population are small relative to the size of the international movement involved. Such movements have a potential for mutual advantage, but also generate conflicts and contradictions which threaten the stability of world order. As long as there are gross inequalities in the distribution of wealth, resources, and income between world regions, there will be net outward movements of economically motivated individuals and families from the Third World, as well as those who are victims of natural disasters, warfare, political persecution, civil strife, religious conflict, ethnic nationalism and international tensions generated by ideological differences and great power rivalries. The consequences of these population movements for both sending and receiving countries require much more research.

NOTES AND REFERENCES

1. The authors are indebted to Professors C. Michael Lanphier and Clifford Jansen for helpful comments on the first draft of this paper. We also wish to thank Employment and Immigration Canada for supplying 1985 admission data on landed immigrants prior to publication. Some sections of the paper are based on a chapter from Anthony H. Richmond, Immigration and Ethnic Conflict, London, Macmillan Press, 1987. The data have been updated for this article and extended to deal with the question of consequences for sending countries.

2. Tables 21.1-3 are based upon Immigration Statistics, 1984, a report published by Employment and Immigration Canada, Ottawa, 1986. The report noted that: "In the past, published statistics reflected only documents included in the year's historical data set. This has been revised to include all documents valid in a particular year. The total are revised on a regular basis to represent actual document count rather than previously published figures. Accordingly, some statistics in the historical tables will not match figures from earlier publications." (ibid., p. iii).

3. A sample of all household heads and other persons intending to enter the labour force and admitted for permanent residence was drawn. Questionnaires were completed at intervals of six months after arrival, twelve months, two years and after three years in Canada. For details of the sample design and methodology see Three Years in Canada, Ottawa, Information Canada, 1974. The data reported in this paper are hitherto unpublished and based on an analysis by Fernando Mata, using data tapes deposited at the Institute for Social Research, York University.

BIBLIOGRAPHY

BASAVARAJAPPA, K.G. and R.B.P. VERMA, "Asian Immigrants in Canada: Some Findings from the 1981 Census", International Migration, Vol. 23, No. 1, 1985.

BUCHIGNANI, Norman and D.M. INDRA with R. SRIVASTAVA
Continuous Journey: A Social History of South Asians in Canada, Toronto, McClelland and Stewart, 1985.

CIPS
Three Years in Canada: A Report of the Canadian Immigration and Population Study, Ottawa, Manpower and Immigration, 1974.

CHAN, Kwok and L. LAM
"Resettlement of Vietnamese-Chinese Refugees in Montreal: Some Socio-psychological Problems and Dilemmas", Canadian Ethnic Studies, Vol. 15, No. 1, 1983.

CHOW, Maria
Canadian Chinese Adolescents' Attitudes Towards Ethnic Language Maintenance, unpublished M.A. thesis, Toronto, York University, 1983.

CLODMAN, J. and A.H. RICHMOND, Immigration and Unemployment, Toronto, Institute for Behavioural Research, York University, 1981.

CON, Harry, E. WICKBERG et al.
From China to Canada: A History of the Chinese Communities, Toronto, McClelland and Stewart, 1982.

DAUDLIN, Bob
Participation of Visible Minorities in Canadian Society, Ottawa, House of Commons, 1984.

ELLIOTT, Jean L., ed.
Native Peoples: Minority Canadians, 1, Toronto, Prentice Hall, 1971.

Two Nations, Many Cultures: Ethnic Groups in Canada, 2nd edition, Toronto, Prentice Hall, 1983.

EMPLOYMENT AND IMMIGRATION CANADA
Business Immigrants, Ottawa, Employment and Immigration, 1985.

Immigration Statistics, 1984, Ottawa, Supply and Services Canada, 1986.

HOCKIN, T. and J-M. SIMARD
Independence and Internationalism, Ottawa, Supply and Services Canada, 1986.

JEAN-BAPTISTE, Jacqueline
Haitians in Canada, Ottawa, Supply and Services Canada, 1979.

JOHNSON, G.E.
"Chinese Canadians in the '70s: New Wine in New Bottles", in
J.L. Elliott, ed., Two Nations, Many Cultures: Ethnic Groups in
Canada, 2nd edition, Toronto, Prentice Hall, 1983.

LAI, Vivien
The Assimilation of Chinese Groups in Toronto, unpublished M.A. thesis,
Toronto, York University, 1970.

LAM, Lawrence
"Chinese-Canadian Families in Toronto", International Journal of the
Sociology of the Family, Vol. 12, No. 1, 1982.

Vietnamese-Chinese Refugees in Montreal, unpublished Ph.D. disser-
tation, Toronto, York University, 1983.

LANPHIER, Michael
A Study of Third World Immigrants, Ottawa, Economic Council of Canada,
1979.

"Canada's Response to Refugees", International Migration Review,
Vol. 17, No. 1, 1981.

"Refugee Resettlement Models in Action", International Migration
Review, Vol. 15, Nos. 1-2, 1983.

MANPOWER AND IMMIGRATION
Three Years in Canada, Ottawa, Canadian Immigration and Population
Study 3, 1974.

MATA, Fernando
"The Latin American Immigration to Canada, 1946-1981", paper presented
at the CALACS conference, Ottawa, Carleton University, 1983.

"Latin American Immigration to Canada: Some Reflections on the Immigration Statistics", Canadian Journal of Latin American and Caribbean
Studies, Vol. X, No. 20, 1985.

ORNSTEIN, M.D. and R.D. SHARMA, Adjustment and Economic Experience of
Immigrants in Canada: 1976 Longitudinal Survey of Immigrants, Report
to Employment and Immigration Canada, Toronto, Institute for
Behavioural Research, York University, 1983.

PICHE, V., S. LAROSE and M. LABELLE
L'Immigration Caraibéene au Canada et au Quebec: Aspects Statistiques,
Montreal, Centre de Recherches Caraibe, University of Montreal, 1983.

RAMCHARAN, Subhas
   The Adaptation of West Indians in Canada, Doctoral thesis, Toronto,
   York University, 1974.

   "Analysis of the Perception of Discrimination by West Indians in
   Toronto", Rikka, Vol. 3, No. 3, 1976.

   Racism: Nonwhites in Canada, Toronto, Butterworths, 1982.

RHYNE, Darla
   Visible Minority Business in Metropolitian Toronto, Toronto, Ontario
   Human Rights Commission, 1983.

RICHMOND, Anthony H.
   "Black and Asian Immigrants in Britain and Canada: Some Comparisons",
   New Community, Vol. 4, No. 4, 1975-76.

   "Migration, Ethnicity and Race Relations", Ethnic and Racial Studies,
   Vol. 1, No. 1, 1978.

   "Environmental Conservation: A New Racist Ideology?" in R.S. Bryce-
   Laporte, ed., Sourcebook on the New Immigration, New Jersey, Trans-
   action Books, 1981.

   "Immigrant Adaptation in a Post Industrial Society" in M.M. Kritz,
   C.B. Keely and S.M. Tomasi, eds., Global Trends in Migration: Theory
   and Research on International Population Movements, New York, Centre
   for Migration Studies, 1981.

   Comparative Studies in The Economic Adaptation of Immigrants in Canada,
   Toronto, Institute for Behavioural Research, York University, 1981.

   "Canadian Unemployment and the Threat to Multiculturalism", Journal of
   Canadian Studies, Vol. 17, No. 1, 1982.

   Immigration and Ethnic Conflict, London, Macmillan Press, 1987.

RICHMOND. A.H. and J. GOLDLUST, Family and Social Integration of Immigrants in
   Toronto, Toronto, Institute for Behavioural Research, York University,
   1977.

RICHMOND, A.H. and W.E. KALBACH
   Factors in the Adjustment of Immigrants and Their Descendants, Ottawa,
   Ministry of Supply and Services, 1980.

RICHMOND, A.H. and G.L. RAO
   "Recent Developments in Immigration to Canada and Australia: A Comparative Analysis", International Journal of Comparative Sociology, 17,
   1977.

RICHMOND, A.H. and F. RICHMOND, eds.
   Immigrants in Canada and Australia, Vol. 1 Demographic Aspects and
   Education; Vol. 2 Economic Adaptation; Vol. 3 Urban and Ecological
   Aspects, Toronto, Institute for Social Research, York University,
   1984-85.

RICHMOND, A.H. and R.B.P. VERMA
"Income Inequality in Canada: Ethnic and Generational Aspects", Canadian Studies in Population, 5, 1978.

RICHMOND, A.H. and J. ZUBRZYCKI
"Occupational Status in Canada and Australia: A Comparative Study of the Native and the Foreign Born", in R.F. Thomasson, ed., Comparative Social Research: An Annual Publication, Vol. 4, JAI Press, 1981.

Immigrants in Canada and Australia: Economic Adaptation, Toronto, Institute for Social Research, York University, 1984.

SHARMA, R.D.
Trends in the Demographic and Socio-economic Characteristics of Metropolitan Toronto, Toronto, Institute for Behavioural Research, York University, 1980.

A Multivariate Analysis of Difficulties Reported by Long Term Third World and non-Anglophone Immigrants, in Toronto Three Years or More, unpublished report, Toronto, Institute for Behavioural Research, York University, 1981a.

Perceived Difficulties of Foreign-born Population and Services of Agencies, unpublished report, Toronto, Institute for Behavioural Research, York University, 1981b.

STATISTICS CANADA
Canada's Immigrants, Cat. 99-936, Ottawa, Statistics Canada, 1984.

TASK FORCE ON PROGRAM REVIEW
Citizenship, Labour and Immigration, A Study Team report to the Task Force on Program Review, Ottawa, Supply and Services Canada, 1986.

WHYTE, Anne V.
The Experience of New Immigrants and Seasonal Farm Workers from the Eastern Caribbean to Canada, Final Report on Phase 1, Toronto, Institute for Environmental Studies, University of Toronto, 1984.

WONG, Lloyd
"Canada's Guestworkers: Some Comparisons of Temporary Workers in Europe and North America", International Migration Review, 18, 1984.

"Temporary Workers in Canada: Some Recent Trends", Working Document No. 8, presented at seminar organised jointly by OECD, ICM and CICRED, Paris, February 1987.

WORLD BANK
World Development Report, 1984, New York, Oxford University Press, 1984.

Chapter 22

OVERVIEW: ECONOMIC PERSPECTIVES

by

Charles W. Stahl

INTRODUCTION

For several reasons it is difficult to arrive at empirically meaningful generalisations regarding the impact of international migration on Third World development.

-- First, the economic characteristics of Third World countries vary greatly, viz. their population size, land area, size and quality of labour force, levels of unemployment and underemployment, capital and other resources, economic structures, export performance and so forth. Thus a migratory flow of a given volume and composition may be beneficial to one country, benign to another and detrimental to a third.

-- Second, the composition of migratory flows to and from Third World countries vary across time and space, often reflecting different stages in a process of structural transformation within the countries involved (Appleyard) (1). While two countries may experience the same volume of emigration/immigration, the composition of the flow can vary with differing developmental implications.

-- Third, poor countries vary in their ability to internalise developmental stimuli which are promoted by either immigration or emigration. The more integrated are the constituent parts of the economy and the more flexible its productive structure, the greater will be the developmental benefits deriving from any emigration/immigration-induced stimulus. For example, economies which are rigid, fragmented and compartmentalised will find that the potential benefits of remittances will be quickly dissipated through imports and price inflation.

-- Fourth, while one may identify a set of benefits and costs of emigration which accrue equally to several countries, these cannot be evaluated without specific knowledge of each country's national development objectives and the planning parameters pertinent to those objectives (Stahl, 1982).

-- Fifth, forms of migration can be very different in terms of both time and space, making the elaboration of a universal typology risky (Domenach and Picouet). Appleyard delineates five types of international migration, each with different economic impacts on sending or receiving countries, _viz._ permanent, refugee, contract labour, transient professional, illegal or undocumented and refugee.

This chapter is structured as follows. The first part contains two sections. The first is concerned with the output and employment consequences of labour emigration, the second focuses on major issues pertaining to the impact of remittances on poor, labour-sending countries. The second part addresses the developmental impact of immigration on poor countries. Three types of immigration will be considered: the return of citizen workers from abroad, the immigration of professional transient workers, and the influx of refugees.

Labour Emigration

The consequences of international migration for Third World countries should be evaluated within the context of specific countries and specific migratory situations. Within this specific context there are a number of potential impacts which researchers and policy-makers must consider when attempting to evaluate the developmental merits of international migration. One of the most important considerations is type of international migration, i.e., whether it is labour emigration (either temporary, permanent or clandestine), whether it is transient professional immigration, refugee immigration, or return migration. This section of the chapter is concerned only with labour emigration. Pertinent questions with respect to an evaluation of the impact of labour emigration are: how many workers emigrate relative to the size of the domestic labour force and how long do they stay; in the industrial context, the degree of difficulty encountered in replacing emigrant workers; in the rural context the effect of labour emigration on rural productivity and development; the pre-migration occupation of emigrants and whether they were employed or unemployed; occupation engaged in abroad relative to that pursued at home; in the case of temporary migration, whether skills were gained during the work experience abroad and whether those skills are employed upon return; the level of remittance inflow and its effect on investment, output and employment; and, the effect of emigration on savings, investment, population growth and hence long-run economic growth. The list is not exhaustive.

These numerous considerations can be combined into three major questions, the answers to which will determine the developmental impact of labour emigration. First, does emigration cause industry-specific labour shortages in the various sectors of the sending economy? Second, to what extent does emigration give rise to remittances; what determines their magnitude; what impact do they have on domestic output, employment and investment; what policies have been or might be pursued to facilitate their flow into the emigration countries and, more specifically, into productive investment; and, what is likely to happen in the future with regard to the direction and magnitude of remittances? Third, do emigrants acquire skills from abroad that are employed at home? The answers to each of these questions for any specific country will depend not only on the host of considerations noted above, but also on the type of migration.

Output and employment effects of labour emigration

The literature on emigration and employment appears to be sharply divided between those who argue that empirical evidence supports the hypothesis that emigration alleviates unemployment and those who argue that it refutes this hypothesis. One of the potential advantages of labour emigration is that it is an inexpensive and rapid method of alleviating unemployment. Indeed, a number of labour exporting countries view the emigration option as a safety valve to relieve social and economic pressures caused by unemployment (2). If emigrants were unemployed then their departure frees that portion of the GDP which they consumed for alternative uses. If emigrants were employed before emigrating a key consideration is the ease with which they can be replaced. If not easily replaced, the loss of labour will tend to be reflected in at least a short-run decline in GDP.

It is commonly believed that the existence of unemployment means that sectors losing labour through emigration can replace that labour from the ranks of the unemployed. But labour is highly differentiated on the basis of skill. If emigration leads to shortages in particular skill categories, then those firms affected will either have to bid that type of labour away from competitors, and in the process drive up wages, or replace lost workers with imperfect substitute labour. Concern has been expressed that it is the cream of the labour force which is skimmed off for export with the result that vacancies so created are filled by less competent and efficient workers (Finkle and McIntosh, 1982:181-182). Thus labour substitution can entail substantial training costs as attempts are made to upgrade the skills of replacement workers. Some types of labour obtain their skills through formal education. Replacement of this kind of worker may be difficult and costly (3). Output may recover as a result of the substitution of capital for labour, but this requires an initial investment expenditure which would not have been necessary had labour not emigrated. Moreover, capital-labour substitution in most cases saves unskilled labour, not skilled labour.

If we allow for different levels of skills amongst workers then we admit the possibility of complementary as well as substitutability amongst workers. Insofar as skilled and unskilled workers are complementary factors, a shortage of one will reduce the productivity and employment of the other. A further problem arises if emigration renders the education or training process difficult by removing those who impart skills. Such an outcome could impair the accumulation of skills over the long term. If emigration leads to labour shortages, then rising wages can squeeze profits and hence investment or it can lead to cost-push inflation, depending on the degree of competition in affected industries.

The brain drain/overflow. The potential impact of loss of skills in general has been emphasized. Of potentially greater negative impact is the loss through emigration of highly-skilled persons classified as PTKs -- the well-known "brain drain". The potentially adverse effects of such emigration can culminate in "... the perpetual postponement of major development efforts because of shortages of (PTK) manpower ... and the continuous dependence on expatriate manpower which has a high turnover" (Mundende).

The emigration of PTKs is usually long-term, and often permanent. It can have adverse developmental effects for several reasons (Stahl, 1982). First, the permanent loss of PTKs, who can be highly complementary to unskilled and semi-skilled labour, may generate short- and longer-term reductions in output and employment. Second, many such emigrants would have had savings higher than the national average. Presuming that they take their savings with them they will reduce the amount of investible funds per capita. If, as is likely, their savings rate exceeds the national average then their departure will reduce the national rate of savings with possible adverse consequences for longer-term development. Third, the departure of PTKs can also affect the rate of population growth. Usually, persons classified as PTK have smaller families than the national average. Thus their permanent departure will result in an increase in the rate of population growth. This, combined with a reduction in the national savings rate, does not auger well for future economic growth. Fourth, PTKs may also play an important role in the dissemination of skills and technical knowledge within the domestic labour force. Their departure may thus reduce the rate of human capital formation. Fifth, it may also be the case that the earning power of PTKs places them in a tax range where they pay an above-average level of taxes. Assuming that their consumption of public goods is no greater than average, their departure would thus lead to a long-run decline in the per capita provision of public goods. Finally, permanent migrants are less likely to remit a significant proportion of their earnings as do temporary migrants. Their financial requirements for a new home, etc., leaves little to send back to the country of origin (Mundende).

Most of these negative developmental consequences presume that the PTK was employed prior to emigration. This may not necessarily be the case. According to Logan, a second scenario is not only possible, but likely in the context of Africa: that the emigration country has a stagnant and deteriorating economy which cannot absorb additional PTKs. In such cases, by alleviating unemployment and contributing to foreign exchange earnings through remittances from abroad, emigration can be developmentally advantageous: the "brain drain" becomes essentially a "brain overflow" (4). Of course, such a scenario begs the question of the direction of causality: one of the principal reasons for stagnation and deterioration of the emigration country's economy could have been a continual loss of PTKs over time.

The general loss of human capital

The loss of PTKs through emigration is viewed by some as only part of the general loss of human capital to which labour emigration gives rise. In this view labour emigration is seen to represent a loss to society because of the considerable expense involved in rearing, educating and training a worker (Bohning, 1975). However, such a view is not wholly correct. While the current work-force does embody a great deal of human capital investment, the expenditures made to create this human capital were made in the past. They are historical or sunk costs and should, as d'Oliveira e Sousa shows, have no bearing on current decision-making regarding whether or not it is economically advantageous to engage in labour export. Thus if a society is availed of the opportunity to export labour, it should concern itself only with those socio-economic consequences which will flow from its decision. In what sense could one claim that society is materially worse off if it allows one of its un-employed workers to emigrate even if the worker embodied in the form of human capital a substantial amount of society's past resources? The emigration of such a worker cannot cause society to become materially worse off. What is true is that labour-importing countries gain substantially from the use of labour power for which they did not have to pay the (human) capital costs. However, their gain is not necessarily at the expense of the labour-sending country. This was essentially the reason why a group of government experts under the auspices of the United Nations could not reach agreement regarding schemes to compensate LDCs for their (alleged) losses through PTK emigration (d'Oliveira e Sousa).

When a country trains manpower specifically to fill the gaps in labour supply created by emigration, or when manpower training is undertaken specifi-cally for export purposes, then these training costs become part of the (human capital) costs of a policy of labour export. If and when this point is reached, it begins a new chapter in a country's labour export experience.

Some empirical evidence. Huguet's chapter shows that large-scale temporary emigration from Asian countries to the Middle East has not had a wholly beneficial effect on the sending economies because of resulting industry-specific labour shortages. However, these negative findings are counter-balanced by other studies which argue that dislocations in the labour market caused by emigration have been largely overrated (5). Several studies of international migration in the Arab World have been less than sanguine about the labour market impact of emigration. Martin (1983:10), claims that the emigration of Egyptian construction workers has led to a decline in worker productivity in that sector, as well as significant increases in wages. Internal migration by agricultural labour to fill vacated positions in con-struction has also led to rising wages within agriculture. According to Seccombe and Findlay, Jordan had to import labour to fill vacancies in both urban-based industries and in agriculture. Fergany (1982) argues that labour emigration from the Yemen Arab Republic has caused severe dislocations in the labour market and severely impaired development potential. According to Wilson (1979:39), several of the poorer Arab states have suffered a severe depletion of their managerial work-force through emigration to the richer Arab countries. At the height of Yugoslav migration to northern Europe, Begtic (1972:27) reasoned that the country could ill afford to continue to export workers without incurring severe economic dislocations.

Empirical evidence seems to suggest that the overall success or other-wise of out-migration in reducing unemployment is a combination of a direct positive contribution, i.e., the export of unemployment or the easy replace-ment of employed emigrants from the ranks of the unemployed, and a negative indirect contribution, the latter resulting from the departure of difficult-to-replace skilled workers with an ensuing reduction in output and an increase in unemployment amongst those workers who are complementary to the emigrant skilled workers. It might also be argued that the direct reduction in output following the emigration of skilled workers may, through inter-industry link-ages, cause further reductions in domestic employment. However, this pessimistic view of the consequences of labour export hinges upon the assumption that emigrating workers are impossible or very difficult to replace. Existing studies overwhelmingly support the view that international migration has been unfavourable in terms of its effects on the supplies of skilled labour, although there is reason to believe that the problem has been overstated. As has been pointed out by Abella (1984:495), inadequate labour market statistics (throughout Asia) make it exceedingly difficult to gauge the labour market consequences of emigration.

One important fact that most empirical studies fail to explicitly recognise is that emigration can make an indirect positive contribution to the relief of unemployment as a result of expenditure of remittance income on domestically-produced goods and services. This possibility is explored below.

The potential output and employment effects of labour emigration discussed above are also related to the form of migration. While permanent emigration will have both a short- and long-run impact on the labour force, labour market dislocations caused by temporary migration (both clandestine and legal) would be alleviated upon the return of the migrants. The immigration policies of the major countries of immigration favour the professional, technical and kindred occupational group (PTK). This can have decisively detrimental consequences for the longer-term development of sending countries. Clandestine migrants may be temporary or permanent (6). If permanent they are likely to be disproportionately drawn from occupational groupings other than PTK, the reason being that PTKs, because of their skills and education, can usually immigrate legally. The output and employment effects of permanent clandestine emigration should, therefore, be considerably less than for permanent PTK emigration.

The development consequences of remittances: major issues

According to Martin (1983:13), the magnitude and use of remittances provides the litmus test of benefits from labour emigration. Remittances from their nationals working abroad can provide a variety of benefits to emigration countries. First, remittances provide an important non-traditional source of foreign exchange which is often a scarce and a constraining factor on development. Second, abstracting from any direct negative consequences of labour export for indigenous industries, remittances should lead to an increase in real national income, savings and investment. Third, remittances should lead to an increase in the real income of a worker, his family and community.

The magnitude of remittances. Estimates of the magnitude of remittances from emigrant workers reported by the central banks of the sending countries are subject to a considerable margin of error because they record only those remittances reported by receiving banks that flow through formal banking channels. Remittances entering the sending country through informal financial channels are not counted by the central bank. Also, recipient banks within the formal financial sector may choose not to report their receipts of foreign exchange, using the funds instead for purposes which contravene regulations on the use of foreign exchange. Even so, over the last decade remittances have become a significant non-traditional source of foreign exchange for labour-exporting countries. For example, it has been estimated that the $7.9 billion remitted by Asian workers in 1981 to their home countries represented 2.3 per cent of their GNP (Abella, 1984:496). Officially measured remittances to Arab labour-exporting countries amounted to $8.4 billion in 1983, or 6 per cent of GNP (7). Remittances from the United States, mostly to Mexico and the Caribbean, amount to several billion dollars per year (North and Houston, 1976:81, Alba, 1984:5). The magnitude of remittances for all developed countries was estimated in 1984 to be $28 billion.

Such amounts represent substantial items in the balance of payments of labour-exporting countries. In Pakistan and Bangladesh, remittances amounted to 84 per cent and 98 per cent of merchandise exports in 1983, respectively. In the Philippines, Sri Lanka and Thailand, these figures were 19, 28 and 11 per cent, respectively (Stahl and Arnold, 1986). Remittances from Europe from the six major labour-exporting countries, viz. Algeria, Greece, Morocco, Tunisia, Turkey and Yugoslavia, accounted for more than 25 per cent of the value of their exports in 1976. In the same period, remittances received by the principal emigration countries of Asia and Africa, viz. Egypt, India, Jordan, Pakistan, Syria and the Yemen Arab Republic, constituted 33 per cent of their total exports (Ecevit and Zachariah, 1978:36). In 1983, official remittances constituted 67 per cent of the combined merchandise exports of the Arab labour-sending countries (8).

Determinants of remittances. The magnitude of remittances received by a labour-exporting country through official financial channels depends on a number of factors: (i) the number of its citizens abroad; (ii) their earnings; (iii) their savings rate; and (iv) the proportion of their savings they remit (9).

The number of citizens a country can place in employment abroad depends largely on unpredictable demand factors in the immigration countries and supply side marketing strategies. Several countries have developed effective marketing structures, e.g., the Philippines and, to a lesser extent, Thailand.

A number of studies in the Asian context indicate significant real earning differentials between home and abroad which result in a high rate of both savings and remittances (10). The proportion of savings which migrants remit through official channels depends on (a) the type of migration -- whether permanent, legal temporary or clandestine; (b) whether migrants are accompanied by dependents; (c) differentials between official and black market exchange rates at home; (d) restrictions on the use of foreign exchange within the sending country; (e) policies regarding the taxation of earnings abroad; and (f) rules governing the proportion of earnings that workers are required to remit.

Logic as well as empirical evidence suggests that permanent migrants will remit a smaller proportion of their earnings than those who plan to return. While the remittance contribution of clandestine temporary migrants should exceed that of permanent migrants, it is unlikely to be as beneficial as remittances from legal temporary migrants. This is because legal temporary migrants are more likely to use formal banking channels. Remittances transferred in this way may become a source of loanable funds, thus stimulating investment. However, because of fear of detection and deportation, clandestine migrants are more likely to use non-banking channels to transfer remittances. Not only does the banking system lose a valuable source of loanable funds, but the government loses control over the use to which the foreign exchange is put, which may or may not be a concern, depending on government policy regarding the use of foreign exchange. It is also to be anticipated that migrants accompanied by dependents will remit less dollars earned than would single migrants.

In a number of countries official exchange rates are substantially out of line with (black) market rates. Moreover, in many countries the central bank tightly controls the sale of foreign exchange in an attempt to influence the composition of imports. Again, both logic and evidence implies that this exercises a negative influence on propensity to remit through official channels. Choucri (1986:705-709) argues that by far the greatest proportion of remittances to Egypt and the Sudan circumvent normal banking channels, principally because of differences between official and black market rates of exchange and other foreign exchange controls. Migrants from Pakistan rely heavily on the "hundi" system which is, in effect, an international informal financial market. With respect to remittances to the Philippines, Stahl (1986:8-9) estimated a total of $1.5 billion in 1985, but the central bank reported only $955 million. It is probable that the difference (i.e., unrecorded remittances) was due to (a) money transferred through informal channels in order to take advantage of a higher exchange rate on the black market and (b) some recipient banks did not report their receipt of remittances to the central bank in order to avoid foreign exchange regulations. In general, empirical evidence from a number of remittance receiving countries indicates that transfers through informal channels do account for a signficicant proportion of the inflow of remittances to labour-exporting countries (11).

Finally, the magnitude of remittances can be influenced by regulations requiring emigrants abroad to remit a certain proportion of their earnings. Several Asian governments have attempted to increase remittances in this way (Shah and Arnold, 1986:74). For example, South Korea requires workers to remit 80 per cent of their earnings. The Philippines requires overseas contract workers to remit between 50 to 70 per cent of their earnings, depending on their occupation. Bangladesh requires that at least 25 per cent of earnings be remitted. Of course, in such cases there is often a significant discrepancy between legal requirements and actual behaviour.

The use of remittances (12). It is clear that remittances have become an important factor in the economies of a number of emigration countries. However, assessing the developmental impact which this international flow of funds has had on emigration countries is a difficult and complex task. A number of studies have attempted to address the issue by means of survey instruments designed to determine expenditure patterns of remittances. Unfortunately, comparability between studies is limited by significant differences in research design and, in some instances, poor questionnaire formulation, both of which appear to reflect a general lack of theoretical underpinning. No study has evaluated the expenditure patterns of a control group having average income levels equal to the remittance receiving households before migration. As a result, "it has been remarkably difficult to draw implications about the use of remittances and thus their socio-economic effects; this is primarily because the immediate use to which a specific amount of money is put is not necessarily the same as the use which remittances made possible or facilitated" (Standing, 1984:265).

Ignoring the methodological shortcomings of these studies, most have found that remittance receiving households typically increase their

368

expenditure on basic and luxury consumer goods, housing, land, debt repayment and education. Few households increase their expenditure on investment goods, i.e., undertake real capital formation. It is this latter finding which has formed the basis for the now widely-held belief that remittances contribute little to development.

It should not be an unexpected finding that a very small amount of remittance income is invested directly. Most migrants are workers (not risk-taking entrepreneurs) who feel a need to be cautious in their investments. Once they return, they do not have substantial resources to fall back on if they undertake an investment which proves to be a failure. Under the circumstances, it is naive to expect that overseas work experience will transform a poor peasant or a working class person into an industrial entrepreneur. More importantly, as will be discussed below, it is also naive to think that the developmental value of remittances is reduced because migrants do not directly invest their newly-acquired wealth in productive ways.

The development impact of remittances. The finding that only a very small proportion of remittance receivers (and returnees) direct their earnings into productive investments has lent strong support to the pessimistic view of labour emigration as an adjunct of development policy. However, this pervasive pessimistic view of the developmental role of remittances reflects inappropriate and partial theoretical analysis. To focus attention solely on the immediate use of remittance income is to ignore the considerable stimulus it provides to indigenous industries, as well as its contribution to the supply of loanable funds, i.e., investment capital.

Remittances are payment for exported labour services. As such, their expenditure generates a multiplier effect which leads to an increase in aggregate demand well in excess of the original value of the remittance inflow. Part of the initial increase in household income attributable to remittances will be lost to imports, just as part of the increase in aggregate demand to which the remittances give rise will be satisfied by imports. However, the expenditure of remittances will also be an important stimulus to local industry. One of the major obstacles to development is lack of effective demand, due to poverty which prevents firms from expanding operations. Of course, the extent to which local industries can respond to increased demand bears importantly upon the developmental benefit of remittances. It has often been argued that because of supply inelasticities remittance expenditures will lead not to output increases but to price increases. While there is some evidence that remittances have been associated with increased land prices (because of fixed supply), and in some instances increases in construction costs, no evidence has been provided to show that this has been manifest in general inflationary pressures. In short, it can be inferred from available evidence that remittances do stimulate output in indigenous industries.

As mentioned above, expenditure surveys of remittance receiving households indicate that a considerable portion of remittance income is spent on housing. In almost all countries the housing industry has the highest ratio of domestic to total inputs. That is, expenditure on construction usually generates a large multiplier effect, with its consequent impact on output and savings. We have also seen that large amounts of remittances are spent on the acquisition of assets. Such purchases do not result directly in an expansion of domestic output. However, sellers of those assets may use their newly-acquired funds to purchase domestically-produced goods and services, as well as add to their savings. These expenditures, too, will expand aggregate demand and aggregate supply. Savings out of the receipts for the sale of assets are also likely to find their way into investments via the financial system.

Remittances give rise to two sources of loanable funds: those arising directly from remittances and those arising indirectly through the process of output expansion. Although Choucri (1986) found that informal channels account for the majority of remittances from labour migrants to their families in Egypt, Sudan, and other Middle Eastern countries, several studies in Asia indicate that a very substantial proportion of remittances follow ordinary banking channels. This inflow of remittances into bank accounts in the sending country may serve as a "high-powered" monetary base from which banks may, collectively, expand their loan portfolio. A variety of constraints may limit the ability of the banking system to increase the money supply and credit on the basis of an increase in foreign exchange reserves. However, it is the purpose of banks and other financial intermediaries to collect small amounts of savings from a wide variety of sources and direct them to persons in need of funds for investment purposes. The empirical studies reviewed above generally indicate that there is a relatively high propensity to save out of remittances. Even if these savings are only short-term, collectively they constitute a huge supply of loanable funds which can be channeled into productive investment.

The common shortcoming of the empirical studies reviewed above is that they have not been formulated in a manner which would allow one to assess the impact of remittances on domestic output, employment and capital formation. While it would be relatively simple at the aggregate level to determine the impact of remittances on demand, from a policy perspective it would be much more interesting to disaggregate the impact of remittances in order to determine which industries and occupations are most affected by remittance expenditure. Several approaches are potentially rewarding in this regard. The easiest way to model the impact of remittances would be to first formulate a questionnaire and sample frame which would allow one to estimate the proportions of total remittance income spent on various kinds of goods. This information could then be fed into an input-output model of the economy. The results would indicate the industries most stimulated by remittance expenditures; not just those producing final goods and services, but also those producing intermediate inputs. Such an exercise has been undertaken by Habib (1985) for the economy of Bangladesh. He found that the expenditure of remittances had the potential of generating significant increases in output and employment. However, his model did not incorporate the household sector, and consequently underestimated the potential expansionary effects of remittance expenditure. By endogenising the household sector, the input-output model can also capture the second and further round effects of the impact of the intial expenditure of remittances. Thus the entire multiplier effect can be disaggregated. Given the availability of statistics on labour-output, capital-output and import-output ratios on an industry basis, this approach woud also provide an estimate of how much labour and investment demand would rise in each industry. Such information on the impact of remittance expenditures would be invaluable to planning authorities. Through simulation exercises, the economy-wide impact of varying levels of labour export on domestic output, employment and investment could be determined. Of course, the input-output model does have a number of well-known shortcomings.

A second approach to modelling the impact of remittances would be to construct a price endogenous computable general equilibrium model of the labour-exporting economy. Such a model would accomplish all that an input-output model would and, in addition, afford insights into the effect of remittances on prices and (depending on data availability) the distribution of income. Its incorporation of price adjustments in response to increases in expenditure is an improvement over the input-output model in that it allows for substitution in consumption and production due to changing prices. The only model of this type with which we are familiar was developed for the Egyptian economy by Choucri and Lahiri (1983). Theirs is a short-run ten-sector model which incorporates structural features of the Egyptian economy. The simulation exercises indicate that remittances can serve as a major stimulus to real output. Models such as these must be employed if we are to further our understanding of the broad effects of remittances. Partial analysis is no substitute for general equilibrium analysis in this area.

In sum, although the propensity of remittance recipients to undertake productive investment out of their new-found income is exceedingly low, this does not warrant the conclusion that the developmental value of remittances is negligible. Remittances spent on domestic goods and services can serve as a much-needed stimulus to indigenous industries and provide a potentially significant source of development capital. It is these broader macroeconomic benefits of remittances which seem to have been largely ignored in the literature and thus perhaps explains the pessimistic view of the developmental value of remittances.

There are however a number of reservations concerning the effects of remittances on sending countries, e.g., perceived costs which may detract from the benefits highlighted above. First, concern has been expressed that the expenditure patterns of remittance receiving households may create a demonstration effect whereby non-migrant households may be induced to increase their consumption of both domestic and imported goods. If such an effect is widespread, it can have a negative impact on the balance of payments, savings and investment, making the labour emigration country worse off in the long term. As we have seen, empirical evidence indicates that a significant proportion of remittance income is devoted to consumption, part of which is satisfied by imports. However, the author is not familiar with any studies which have attempted to evaluate the empirical validity of the demonstration effect hypothesis.

A second concern of scholars and policy-makers is that labour emigration and its consequent remittance inflow can augment income and wealth inequalities within labour-sending countries. Insofar as a reduction in inequalities is a development objective, such an impact of remittances may be viewed as a cost of labour emigration. However, there is neither a theoretical nor, to date, an empirical basis to support the proposition that remittances augment inequalities. Theoretically, it is not even certain that migrants gain unequivocally from emigration, let alone that non-migrants are made relatively worse off (Lundahl, 1985). Any conclusions based on theoretical reasoning are highly assumption-dependent. There is abundant empirical evidence to show that the inflow of remittances substantially increases the (money) income of receiving households. However, the expenditure of remittances and the consequent multiplier effect may change relative prices and hence the relative returns of productive factors in the economy. The end result, in terms of impact on income distribution, remains uncertain. In their simulation analysis of the Egyptian economy, Choucri and Lahiri (1983:14-15) found that an increase in remittances would slightly increase the share of wage income relative to profit income.

A third concern is that the expenditure of remittances may result in inflationary pressures. Many studies claim that the expenditure of remittances has increased prices, particularly in real estate and housing construction. In some cases it has been argued that this had fed through to increased demands for higher wages, with the inference being drawn that the result can be an inflationary spiral. Insofar as remittances are existing assets or non-traded goods whose supplies are relatively inelastic, then the prices of these items will rise, at least in the short run. However, such price rises may cause resources to be reallocated to the production of these goods in the longer term, mitigating or perhaps reversing price increases. Thus it is to be expected that the inflationary impact of a given percentage increase in aggregate demand induced by remittances will vary considerably between countries. With reference to traded goods, theoretically, prices should not rise, and may indeed decline, since remittances should improve balance of payments thus increasing the foreign exchange value of the domestic currency (assuming a free floating exchange rate). The study by Choucri and Lahiri (1983) simulated the effects on the Egyptian economy of a doubling of remittances. While their results are influenced by the assumptions underpinning their model, they found that the increase in remittances was not inflationary. With regard to the experience of Asian labour exporters, there is evidence that emigration and remittances have been associated with a rise in land prices and in some cases an increase in the cost of construction. However, it is impossible to judge on the basis of available information whether these price increases have contributed to general inflationary pressures.

A fourth concern relates to the uncertainty surrounding remittances as a source of export income. The argument here is that remittances "... fluctuate with short-term foreign labour demands and the savings and repatriation decisions of individual workers. Economic development is a long-term process, and development plans based on such a stream of remittances may be disrupted by recession in a labour-host nation, usually at a time when the labour-sending country most critically needs foreign exchange" (Martin and Richards, 1980:8). An inspection of remittance data from most labour-exporting countries, including the Asian labour exporters, indicates some annual fluctuations. However, the author is not familiar with any studies which have formally tested the hypothesis of remittance instability.

A fifth concern over the developmental impact of remittances relates to its effect on agricultural production. As pointed out by Stahl (1982), "... a portion of remittances may be consumed in the form of leisure time. Theoretically, if remittances are large enough and agricultural labouring is viewed as too arduous, remittances could wholly substitute for income from agricultural efforts". Martin and Richards (1980:8) also express concern over the potentially adverse impact of remittances on agricultural output. If agricultural production falls as a result of labour emigration then food may have to be imported to offset this lost output. An important empirical issue here is whether decline in agricultural output has been due to the loss of labour through emigration or the result of a reduced work effort on the part of those remaining behind. In an extensive literature review on the subject, Habib (1985:106-118) finds that very few studies report that emigration has had a favourable impact on the agricultural sector. In general, it appears to give rise to reduced output, rising labour costs, mechanisation, and idle land.

Finally, there is concern that "... emigration and associated remittances of foreign exchange have fostered complacency and have delayed the introduction of those economic policies which are desirable for longer term development" (Macmillen, 1982:265). Maybe, but it would be exceedingly difficult to empirically verify this hypothesis.

Policies to influence the magnitude and use of remittances. Empirical evidence suggests that a very substantial proportion of remittances is being channeled into labour-sending countries through unofficial channels, having unanticipated influences on exchange rates, interest rates and other monetary parameters. It also reduces the potential supply of loanable funds within the formal banking system. Moreover, policies designed to control the composition of imports by restricting uses of foreign exchange are frustrated. There are, however, a few policies which governments may pursue in an attempt to reduce the proportion of remittances flowing through informal channels. First, if the earnings of migrants remain in banks overseas they are of little use to the sending countries. If the principal reason for this is inadequately developed financial channels to transmit remittances, then the problem can be resolved by establishing either a correspondent bank or a branch bank of the sending countries' banks within the host country. For example, the Habib Bank of Pakistan has established branches throughout the Middle East which greatly facilitate the transfer of remittances of some 1.5 million Pakistanis working in the region. Often the problem is one of ignorance on the part of the overseas worker. A pre-departure orientation programme devoted to explaining how to use the international banking system to transfer remittances would be worthwhile. Indeed, several Asian labour-sending countries provide such a service for their migrants. If these measures fail, it may be possible to persuade the government of the host country to require employers to deposit the pay of their employees into branch banks or correspondent banks of the employee's country of origin.

Several European labour-sending countries allow overseas workers to establish foreign exchange accounts. In some instances they are paid interest on their accounts in foreign exchange; in other cases interest rate premiums are offered as an inducement to establish such accounts.

Another major reason why remittances circumvent formal banking channels is to avoid compulsory conversion at unsatisfactory official exchange rates and/or restrictions on the use of foreign exchange. To overcome this problem several sending countries have offered remittance recipients premium exchange rates, which is tantamount to offering them the black market rate of exchange. Of course, such a dual exchange rate system discriminates against those earning foreign exchange through traditional exports. Most economists prefer a solution that moves away from a fixed exchange rate to one determined by market forces, while removing restrictions on the use of foreign exchange.

While such policies may increase the magnitude of remittances being channeled through formal banking channels, they are likely to have only a marginal impact on the use to which remittances are put. The issue is to try and get remittance recipients and returnees to reduce or postpone their consumption of remittance income. An increase in the savings rate would have the dual benefit of increasing the amount of loanable funds in the banking system and reducing demand-pull price inflation for existing assets which remittance recipients seem so keen to buy, e.g., land and existing housing. It would also dampen any inflationary pressure which might exist for non-traded goods whose supplies are inelastic.

Future magnitude of remittances. The flow of remittances is obviously highly correlated with the international flow of labour. Thus the principal determinate of future remittance flows is future international labour migration. In the years of global economic expansion after World War II international labour migration was greatly encouraged by such host countries as Argentina, Britain, Canada, Malaysia, Nigeria, Singapore, South Africa, and those of Europe. In the early 1970s the major pole of attraction of international labour migration shifted to the wealthy oil exporting countries of the Middle East. The ambit of attraction was wide with millions of workers being drawn from the Arab world, South Asia, East Asia and Southeast Asia. However, with global recession after the mid-1970s, and the ensuing decade of slow and sometimes stagnating growth, countries of immigration, with the exception of the Middle East oil exporters, began to reassess the socio-economic benefits of labour immigration. That exercise led to the adoption of policies which attempted to restrict and reverse immigration. In Western Europe the emphasis was on stimulating return migration. In Africa, an expulsion of foreign workers occurred in Nigeria. In South Africa, growing unemployment amongst indigenous blacks led the mining industry to "internalise" its labour force, greatly reducing demand for foreign black mineworkers from neighbouring countries. In Singapore, despite continued rapid growth, a reappraisal of the desired future economic structure led to a substantial decline in demand for immigrant labour. In Latin America, contractions in the economies of Venezuela and Argentina dramatically reduced job opportunities previously available to immigrants. While these significant reductions in officially-sanctioned migration have been somewhat offset by an increase in clandestine migration, there is little doubt that both the growth and magnitude of international labour migration has declined.

In the late 1970s and early 1980s, declining demand for immigrant labour was more than offset by the historically unprecedented growth in demand for immigrant labour amongst the oil-exporting countries of the Middle East. However, this growth in demand has also collapsed due to falling oil prices, and with it demand for foreign labour. Evidence from the Philippines indicates that this process has particularly affected demand for construction workers. In 1983 some 249 000 Filipino construction workers found overseas employment, about 90 per cent of whom were placed in the Middle East. Two years later, the figure had declined by 40 per cent to 150 000. Middle East placements across all occupations declined by 57 000 or 17.6 per cent. A decline of this magnitude applying to all countries supplying labour to the oil-rich states would represent about 1 million jobs.

It has been argued in this chapter that because poor countries are so diverse with respect to economic structure and ability to internalise external stimuli, and because migratory flows are so varied in volume, composition and form, it is difficult to make generalisations concerning the development impact of labour emigration. Much of the literature is decidedly pessimistic about the developmental role of labour emigration in general and remittances in particular. It has been argued that this view is based largely on shaky theoretical foundations. However, criticism of these studies should not be misconstrued to be a general statement concerning the developmental merits of policies of labour export. Indeed, it is quite easy to envisage an emigration scenario which would be developmentally devastating. For example, the permanent emigration of a large number of PTKs with scarce skills who were previously employed in industries which employed unskilled and semi-skilled labour is likely to result in a substantial reduction in national output and employment, both directly and indirectly. Moreover, if their emigration was permanent its costs will not be offset to any great extent by an inflow of remittances.

The Developmental Impact of Immigration

Attention will now be focused on the development implications of three types of immigration: return, transient professional and refugee.

Return migration

The opportunity for workers to enhance their skills while working abroad and then return to employ those skills is an important perceived potential benefit of emigration. It is assumed that contemporary, mostly circular, labour migration can result in a net addition to the supplying economy's stock of human capital if either the amount of skill gained while in the host country is greater than what could have been gained if the migrant had remained at home, or if the kind of skill learned contributes more to the supplying economy's development than skills they would have learned had they remained home (Miracle and Berry, 1970:97-98).

To what extent do these expectations conform with reality? It appears that three criteria have to be met before return migrants can make a skill contribution to the sending country. First, migrants must learn skills while abroad. Second, those skills must be relevant to the needs of the sending country. Third, the returning migrants must use those skills upon return (Paine, 1974:132-133).

By far the largest proportion of current international migration is temporary (legal and clandestine). The majority of workers migrate to take up jobs which require the specific skills they already possess (Bohning, 1975:272). If emigrants are to obtain skills while abroad then they must be employed in positions which require a greater level of skill than they possess prior to emigration (13). However, typically temporary migrants are slotted into the secondary sector of the labour market in which jobs are low-skilled, (relatively) low-salaried, low-status and hence socially undesirable. In such positions it is unlikely that migrants will have the opportunity of learning the industrial discipline of working in large-scale industrial plants (Chaney, 1979:207). What developing countries lack most is experienced efficient supervisory and management staff. Yet in the context of Arab international migration, Halliday (1977:287) argues that it is indeed rare for migrant workers to become supervisors or foremen. Empirical evidence suggests that the opportunity of receiving high level occupational training is so infrequent as to be considered negligible (OECD, 1979:107). However, these findings are probably not unrelated to the type of migration observed. For example, Thomas-Hope and Nutter show that returning (long-term) migrants to Jamaica from the United Kingdom experienced significant skill acquisition and upward occupational mobility. They hypothesize that there are groups of migrants whose objective in migration is educational and occupational advancement not only for themselves, but also for their children.

One condition necessary for successful transfer of skills acquired abroad to the home country is that the migrant's occupation before and after migration should be closely related. The debate as to whether migrants learn new skills and whether such skills are appropriate becomes academic if the migrants prefer not to employ their acquired skills upon return. In view of the fact that the wage rate at home in the occupation pursued abroad is often five to ten times less, it is quite possible that the returning migrant will not take up work at home which uses skills acquired abroad. A number of studies have shown that returning workers prefer independent employment, and very often employment which does not use the skills they acquired abroad nor those they possessed before migration. Non-return to the work-force and a strong preference to establish small independent businesses, mainly in the tertiary sector, appears to be the dominant characteristic of return migrants throughout the world. Thomas-Hope and Nutter showed that long-stay Caribbean return migrants usually enter self-employment, chiefly in retail trade and transport. With regard to Asian countries of emigration, Smart (1984:23) has reported that 75 per cent of Filipino migrants see their futures back home in terms of starting businesses. The percentage of returnees interviewed in Pakistan planning to return to their former occupations was reported to be quite low (Ahmad, 1982:44). Another study on Pakistan reported that only 5 per cent of returnees expect to take a salaried job (Gilani, 1983:14). However, most of the information relates to intentions.

Another issue in skill acquisition is the question of the degree of match between previous skills and overseas job requirements. Smart, et al. (1983:11) found that almost 80 per cent of Filipino workers in the Middle East were employed in jobs which used the same skills which they used prior to emigration. Another study on Filipino migration reported an occupational continuity figure of almost 73 per cent, and a new skill acquisition rate of 13.6 per cent (Teodosio and Jimenez, 1983:133-34). For Bangladesh, Habib (1985:295) estimated that over 75 per cent of overseas migrants appeared to have a post-migration skill level no different from that possessed prior to migration. In his study of Thai overseas workers, Stahl (1986:22) found that almost 57 per cent pursued the same occupation abroad as they did at home.

Empirical evidence on skill gain by migrants is not very encouraging. Although there is scattered evidence of Asian emigrants acquiring skills abroad, it does not appear that this is the general outcome of Asian labour emigration (14). A few studies in the European context have also identified skill gains by migrants (15). This seemingly conflicting evidence might be partly resolved by realising that there are really two types of labour immigration, as so aptly pointed out by Portes (1981:281-285). One is directed into the primary labour market where workers have the same opportunities as their indigenous counterparts. Such immigrant workers have the opportunity for occupational and educational advancement. In contrast are those (usually temporary and clandestine) immigrants who are channeled into the secondary sector of the labour market. These immigrants learn few, if any, skills and work under unpleasant conditions and insecure tenure.

Transient professional immigration

The discussion above regarding the output and employment impact of labour emigration abstracted from the possibility that countries losing key workers through emigration could replace these workers by encouraging replacement immigration. Indeed, such a strategy may, in general, serve to widen bottlenecks caused by shortages of skilled labour. The movement of this type of worker from developed countries to LDCs or, for that matter, from LDC to LDC, has come to be termed transient professional immigration. According to Appleyard, transient professional workers "are characteristically highly-skilled or professional workers who are sent by their employers, or by governments under aid programmes, to work on assignments in overseas countries ...". They "are the conveyors of technology, and while their skills and experiences are directed primarily towards maximising returns for the investors, they are also instrumental in raising the general level of skills in the recipient country". As Salt and Findlay showed, this type of international migration seems set to increase relative to other forms of migration for two reasons. First, the task of economic development requires specialist skills and experience. Second, the increasing interdependence of the parts of the global economy requires the movement of highly-skilled technical and managerial workers to ensure that the constituent parts function harmoniously.

While this form of international migration is undoubtedly on the rise, there are severe difficulties concerning its measurement due to the way in which short-term and long-term emigration/immigration are defined in most countries. An exception is Australia emigration/immigration data. Employing this data, Price showed that Australian long-term emigration to LDCs has increased both relatively and absolutely between 1975 and 1985. Slightly over 80 per cent of such moves were for one to three years, while the composition of the flow was substantially PTK. It is most likely that the same trend would be revealed for other developed countries if data quality permitted.

Of importance is the impact of skill transfer upon development in LDCs. Clearly, this form of immigration can have immediate beneficial effects by alleviating labour shortages hampering overall economic expansion. But what of its longer-term developmental consequences? Salt and Findlay argued that there has been a weak level of skill transfer to the local population from professional transient immigrants and that a lack of social contact between immigrant PTKs and the local population further reduces the longer-term developmental advantages of this form of immigration. Although this form of international mobility is clearly growing rapidly, its longer-term developmental implications for LDCs are still uncertain.

The economic impact of refugee immigration

In the years immediately after World War II developed countries were the main destination of the world's displaced persons. However, in the last two decades, poor developing countries have experienced the greatest influx of refugees (Appleyard). Africa has been particularly affected by refugee movements. According to Adepoju, of the world's twelve countries with the highest ratio of refugees to local population, eight are in Africa. These countries are among the poorest in the world.

There appears to be a general consensus that the influx of refugees imposes an economic burden on poor countries whose resources must be stretched to provide for the newcomers. This is not altogether correct. First, the developmental impact of refugee influxes can vary considerably (Chambers, 1986:255). In some cases they impose an economic burden on the host population and also pose a security risk. In other circumstances refugees' labour, skills and trade contacts, as well as the international aid which their presence attracts, can be a positive stimulus to development. The outcome appears to depend heavily on policies and interventions. Second, the apparent losses of some groups may be offset by the gains of others. According to Chambers (1986:249-254), in rural areas experiencing an influx of refugees, those members of the host population who produce surpluses are likely to experience significant gains as a result of rising food prices and cheap and convenient refugee labour. In contrast, poorer members of the host population can be hidden losers. Rising food prices, falling wages, a reduced per capita supply of already inadequate public services and increased competition from refugees for common property resources all serve to seriously disadvantage the poor hosts without land.

The population of refugee camps comprise a disproportionate number of women, children and the physically disabled. Khasiani estimated that women account for 50 to 60 per cent of all refugees in Africa. She argues that these demographic facts have not been adequately taken into account in the design of programmes for the successful integration of refugees. In many cases the demographic characteristics of refugee camps are an outcome of the survival strategy of household-splitting whereby the able-bodied members of households leave their dependents behind in the camps while they are away attempting to find new places of settlement.

When refugee flows are generated by political or ethnic persecution then it is usually the most educated within a target population who feel most threatened. Thus many refugee streams contain a disproportionate percentage of PTKs. However, whether or not they have an opportunity to employ their skills in the host country depends on prevailing economic conditions and the employment situation in general, and the employment policies and practices of the host countries in particular, as well as their attitude towards refugee PTKs (Khasiani). In very poor countries experiencing a brain overflow, prospects for employment are bleak. According to Adepoju, in a number of African host countries this group is particularly affected by heavy rates of unemployment, with attendant social and psychological problems. On the positive side, however, the more skilled of the urban refugees can make a positive addition to the host country's human capital. Adepoju reported that refugees are filling places vacated by Sudanese emigrants to the Gulf countries, thereby alleviating critical manpower shortages.

It is not easy to make generalisations about the developmental impact of refugee influxes. Some groups in the host population gain; others definitely lose. What this points to is the need (unfortunately not widely enough recognised) to ensure that programmes aimed at refugee groups explicitly take into account the possible losses which the influx will have on the more vulnerable members of the host population.

SUMMARY AND CONCLUSIONS

We have learned that some poor countries permit labour emigration with the expectation that benefits will accrue in the form of skill acquisition by migrants, reduction of unemployment, and balance of payments relief. It is also hoped that by increasing savings and providing scarce foreign exchange, remittances would stimulate investment, the _sine qua non_ for economic development. However, a number of studies have cast doubt on the extent to which labour export has achieved these goals. It appears that the most significant discrepancy between anticipated benefits and actual outcome is in the area of skill formation. With the exception of a few positive findings, the majority of empirical studies indicate that returning migrants have not, to any significant extent, experienced skill formation. On the whole, the majority of emigrants work at jobs which require the skills they possessed at the time of their emigration. Of course, if newly-acquired skills are not employed upon return then any acquisition of skills makes little difference. In this regard, some studies have found that returnees are reluctant to rejoin the labour force as wage employees, preferring instead to use their accumulated savings to acquire small businesses in the service sector. Whether these attitudes persist is an issue requiring further study.

Other studies on the impact of labour emigration have provided evidence, albeit often anecdotal, that in some countries a few industries have complained of shortages in particular occupations as a result of labour emigration. Some writers claim that these shortages can result in a contraction of domestic economic activity and promote unemployment amongst those workers and other factors of production complementary to scarce skills lost through emigration. Thus, rather than alleviating unemployment, emigration may actually promote it. However, studies concerned with the negative employment consequences of labour emigration have ignored the positive contribution to domestic employment which expenditure of remittances can make. In the two studies which have attempted to model this impact, the potential contribution of remittances to domestic output and employment was shown to be considerable. Thus, any negative consequence due to the loss of workers through emigration may be more than offset by the positive stimulus to employment that the expenditure of remittances will provide. Another consideration with regard to the employment creation effects of labour emigration is that insofar as emigrants are unemployed then the country is saved the large cost of providing complementary inputs necessary to provide a job for that worker in the domestic economy.

Empirical studies on the use of remittances and returnee savings indicate that the greatest proportion are spent on basic necessities, some luxury consumer goods in the form of electrical appliances which are usually imported, debt repayment, housing, and education. Very little is used for real investment purposes. This finding has led many to conclude that the developmental value of remittances is negligible. We have seen that such a conclusion is not warranted, and actually reflects a lack of understanding of the complex economic processes set in motion by an inflow of remittances. The fact is that remittances can augment the supply of loanable funds as well as indirectly stimulate demand for those funds with a consequent increase in the level of real capital formation.

It seems relatively certain that labour emigration has provided substantially more benefits to some labour emigration countries than it has costs, particularly in labour-abundant countries of Asia. However, these findings do not imply that labour emigration stimulates development in all or even most poor countries. What the findings do imply is that if certain conditions exist, e.g., that a country's economic structure is relatively diverse, that it has an adequate supply of labour, and that there is a financial system capable of mopping up small amounts of savings from a wide variety of sources and channeling them to businesses willing and able to respond to rising demand for their output, then remittances should, as would any other external stimulus to the economy, promote economic growth. In the absence of these conditions neither remittances nor any other stimulus will be of much value to national development. In short, the failure of remittances to provide a positive stimulus to development in a number of labour-exporting countries may be due largely to the structural features of underdevelopment.

Remittances are developmentally advantageous to countries with sufficient productive flexibility to respond positively to their stimulus. This raises the question as to whether labour emigration can result in such a large-scale loss of labour or a depletion of critical skills that an economy loses its productive flexibility. There are a few countries which have experienced such large-scale emigration. Lesotho in southern Africa and the Yemen Arab Republic are cases in point. In effect, the cream of these countries' labour forces has been skimmed off by their wealthy neighbours. Left with a sparse and relatively low-skilled labour force, these economies have been unable to respond on a broad front to the remittance stimulus. Rather, consumption needs (other than house construction and some services) have been satisfied through imports. What these cases suggest is that there may be a level of labour emigration beyond which a country risks impairing the productive flexibility of its economy necessary to transform an external stimulus into a positive growth promoting force (Fergany, 1985). The larger, more diversified, and more developed an economy is, the greater will be the contribution of labour emigration to development. Conversely, the more rigid, inflexible and hence underdeveloped is a country's socio-economic system, the less labour emigration and remittance inflow will be of developmental advantage.

NOTES AND REFERENCES

1.   References without year of publication refer to chapters in the present
     volume.

2.   In their chapter on labour emigration policies in the Arab World,
     Seccombe and Lawless note that Jordan and Tunisia actively encourage
     labour emigration. A number of the labour-abundant countries in Asia
     also actively encourage labour emigration, viz. Pakistan, Sri Lanka,
     Bangladesh, Thailand, Indonesia and the Philippines (Stahl, 1986).

3.   Of course, there exists the possibility that skill losses through emi-
     gration may be counterbalanced by skill immigration from other
     countries. This issue will be taken up in the section on skill trans-
     fers through immigration.

4.   Mundende reviews the literature which makes the distinction between
     brain drain and overflow.

5.   In Sri Lanka, according to Fernando (1984:4), bottlenecks have emerged
     in development projects as a consequence of a shortage of skilled
     workers. In 1980, a number of industries in the Philippines, especial-
     ly oil refineries, claimed to have experienced skill shortages (Palmer,
     1981:80). Wilson (1979:39) quotes the concern of a Pakistani official
     that "... we are losing our skilled engineers, our best construction
     managers, our most energetic and imaginative men to the Middle East".
     Three years later Ahmad (1982:17) reported that in Pakistan serious
     shortages still existed for masons and carpenters and, to a lesser
     degree, for welders and plumbers, plus noteworthy shortages of elec-
     tricians, steel fixers and painters. In general, Pakistan estimates
     that 83 per cent of its migrants are production workers and blames the
     loss for declining workmanship in new building construction and in
     textile products (Palmer, 1981:80). Ahmad (1982:46) also refers to the
     low skill standards now prevalent in Pakistan which has resulted in
     delays in the construction sector, inadequate maintenance of equipment
     and rising costs. Gilani, et al. (1981:Part II:39) opine that the
     decline in productivity in Pakistan occurred not because of the un-
     availability of replacement workers but because of a fall in quality
     resulting from skilled jobs vacated by departing emigrants having to be
     filled by hastily-trained formerly unskilled workers. They also
     expressed concern that the predominance of production and related
     workers in the emigration stream may create bottlenecks for the non-
     agricultural sector in Pakistan (p. 50). Sarmad (1985:22-23) reviews
     the findings of a report by the Manpower Division which estimated man-
     power requirements for Pakistan's Fifth Five-Year Plan (1978-83). The
     report claims that for the large majority of occupational groups
     experiencing emigration, anticipated shortages were only marginal.
     Those occupational groups with the greatest anticipated shortages were

in the "production workers" category, specifically machine tool setters and operators, plumbers and welders. These were also the occupations experiencing the greatest level of emigration.

Jayme (1979:85, 88-93) cautioned that it was unlikely that the Philippines could long sustain the heavy drain on professional, technical and other skilled workers without incurring some costs. In Bangladesh, Siddiqui (1986:247) suggests that overseas employment may have caused dislocation in the production process due to the loss of skilled labour, but that this could have been minimised by proper management practices.

On a more positive note, a study on Thai emigration argues that the country has not reached the point of serious shortages of skilled let alone unskilled labour (Roongshivin, 1982:26). For the Philippines, Tan (1983) found little evidence that labour emigration had caused any dislocations. Despite the fact that large numbers of Filipino construction and transport workers were recruited for overseas work, Tan reported that high rates of unemployment still prevailed in these sectors. A similar note is present in a study by Addleton (1984:586-587), who maintains that the relative abundance of labour in Pakistan made it possible for the labour market to respond relatively easily to the migration of large numbers of unskilled workers, although he recognises the possibility of bottlenecks occurring in the supply of some categories of skilled production workers. Perwaiz (1979-22) condemns the unqualified complaint of labour shortage in Pakistan made by the Planning Commission as conveying the "erroneous impression of a general labour shortage". For Bangladesh, Ali, et al. (1981:159-171) assess the effects of labour migration on the manning of production and service establishments. They conclude that Bangladesh is unlikely to lose anything substantial on account of the migration of unskilled and semi-skilled workers as the time and cost involved in training replacements is small. Siddiqui (1983:37) reports that there was a surplus of doctors and engineers in Bangladesh despite emigration within these occupational categories. For India, Weiner (1982:5) claims that emigration has reduced unemployment in the states of Kerala, Karnataka, Goa, Maharashtra and Gujarat, as well as in the Punjab. This is particularly true for the educated unemployed. While there is evidence of shortages of skilled workers in the construction sector in the state of Kerala, "emigration from India has not produced the kind of loss of human resources experienced by some of the Mediterranean countries" (Weiner, p. 5). Smart (1984:17) makes the more general observation that labour markets of the Asian labour exporting countries have met through formal and informal training, and with "relative ease", both foreign and domestic demand for manpower. This was particularly easy with regard to service workers who, because of their low level of skill, presented few replacement problems.

6. Lohrmann provides an excellent overview of facts and issues pertaining to the growing phenomenon of clandestine migration.

7. The countries are Algeria, Egypt, Jordan, Morocco, Sudan, Syria, Tunisia, Yemen Arab Republic and Yemen PDR. The figures were calculated from Table 1 and Table 14 of World Development Report, 1985 (World Bank, 1985:174, 200).

8.   Calculated from Tables 9 and 14 of <u>World Development Report, 1985</u> (World Bank, 1985:190, 200).

9.   Quibria (1986:90) reports that empirical studies indicate that the first two of these factors account for over 90 per cent of variations in the inflow of remittances.

10. See Smart, <u>et al.</u> (1986) and Go, <u>et al.</u> (1983) for the Philippines; Stahl (1986) for Thailand; Korale (1986) for Sri Lanka; and Arnold and Shah (1986) for Korea; Mahmud and Osmani (1980) for Bangladesh; and Gilani, <u>et al.</u> (1981) for Pakistan.

11. Russell (1986:682-684) reviews the findings of several studies which had as one of their concerns the extent to which remittances were transferred through informal channels and the extent to which this was a reflection of differential exchange rates.

12. This and the following section draws upon and extends the findings and arguments contained in Stahl and Arnold (1986).

13. Thomas-Hope and Nutter show that temporary contract workers from Caribbean countries do not usually upgrade their skills as a result of their work experience abroad.

14. A study of Pakistani migrants revealed that while some 25 per cent of returnees claimed to have learned new skills, only 7 per cent thought that these skills were of any use to them once they returned home (Gilani, 1983:18). A study from India found that the "skill component" of overseas employment was only 24 per cent, indicating that the skill acquisition rate is not very encouraging (Mathew and Nair, 1978:1149). Smart <u>et al.</u> (1986:30) reported that new skills were acquired by just over 24 per cent of Filipino workers going to the Middle East, but that the skills could have been acquired just as easily within the Philippines. Stahl (1986:22) compared the pre-migration skills of Thai overseas workers with those necessary to perform their overseas job. He found "probable skill acquisition" in the case of almost 37 per cent of migrant workers. Using a similar approach, Habib (1985:295) found that less than one per cent of Bangladeshi migrants took up occupations abroad which required a higher degree of skill than they possessed before departure. In another Thai study, Roongshivin (1982:18) claimed that the Middle Eastern countries normally use state of the art technologies in almost every area of industrial activity, and that Thai workers, who have been engaged extensively in these activities should have acquired new skills.

15. See Millar (1976:166) for Turkish migrants to West Germany, [cited in Finkle and McIntosh (1982:141-142)]. Penninx (1982:790) again for Turkish migrants in Germany. Adler (1980:91, 100) for Algerians in France. For evidence to the contrary, regarding migrants in Germany, see Salt (1973:769).

BIBLIOGRAPHY

ABELLA, Manolo I.
"Labour Migration from South and South-East Asia: Some Policy Issues", International Labour Review, Vol. 123, No. 4, 1984.

ADDLETON, Jonathan
"The Impact of International Migration on Economic Development in Pakistan", Asian Survey, Vol. 24, No. 5, 1984.

ADLER, Stephen
"Swallow's Children: Emigration and Development in Algeria", World Employment Programme Working Paper No. WEP2-26/WP46, Geneva, ILO, 1980.

AHMAD, Mansoor
"Emigration of Scarce Skills in Pakistan", International Migration for Employment Working Paper No. 5, Geneva, ILO, 1982.

ALBA, Francisco
"Economic Impact of International Migration on Sending Countries, with Special Emphasis on Employment and Remittances", paper presented at the Workshop on the Consequences of International Migration, 16th-19th July, Canberra, Australia, IUSSP Committee on the Economic and Social Aspects of International Migration, 1984.

ALI, Syed Ashraf, et al.
Labor Migration from Bangladesh to the Middle East, World Bank Staff Working Paper No. 454, Washington, D.C., The World Bank, 1981.

ARNOLD, Fred and Nasra M. SHAH
Asian Labor Migration: Pipeline to the Middle East, Boulder, Colorado, Westview Press, 1986.

BEGTIC, Mustafa
"Yugoslav Nationals Temporarily Working Abroad", Yugoslav Survey, Vol. 13, No. 1, 1972.

BOHNING, W. Roger
"Some Thoughts on Emigration from the Mediterranean Basin", International Labour Review, 111, 1975.

CHAMBERS, Robert
"Hidden Losers? The Impact of Rural Refugees and Refugee Programs on Poorer Hosts", International Migration Review, Vol. 20, No. 2, 1986.

CHANEY, Elsa M.
"The World Economy and Contemporary Migration", International Migration Review, Vol. 13, No. 2, 1979.

CHOUCRI, Nazli
"The Hidden Economy: A New View of Remittances in the Arab World",
World Development, Vol. 14, No. 6, 1986.

CHOUCRI, N. and S. LAHIRI
Short-Run Energy-Economy Interactions in Egypt, Cambridge, Mass., Technology Adaptation Program, Massachusetts Institute of Technology, 1983.

ECEVIT, Zafar and K.C. ZACHARIA
"International Labor Migration", Finance and Development, Vol. 15,
No. 4, 1978.

FERGANY, Nader
"The Impact of Emigration on National Development in the Arab Region:
The Case of the Yemen Arab Republic", International Migration Review,
Vol. 16, No. 4, 1982.

"The Future of International Migration: Views from the Developing
World", paper presented at the IUSSP Workshop on the Determinants of
International Migration, 22nd-26th April, Bellagio, Italy, IUSSP Committee on the Economic and Social Aspects of International Migration,
1985.

FERNANDO, Dallas F.S.
"Economic Impact of International Migration on Sending Countries, with
Special Emphasis on Employment and Remittances: The Case of Sri Lanka
with Special Reference to Migration to the Middle East", paper prepared
for the IUSSP Workshop on the Consequences of International Migration,
16th-19th July, Canberra, Australia, IUSSP Committee on the Economic
and Social Aspects of International Migration, 1984.

FINKLE, Jason L. and C. Alison McINTOSH
The Consequences of International Migration for Sending Countries of
the Third World, report prepared for the Bureau of Program and Policy
Coordination, USAID, by the Centre for Population Planning, University
of Michigan, 1982.

GILANI, Ijaz S.
"Overseas Pakistanis: An Overview about the Volume of Migration and
its Socio-Economic Impact on the Home Communities", paper presented at
the East-West Population Institute Conference on Asian Labor Migration
to the Middle East, 19th-23rd September, Honolulu, Hawaii, East-West
Centre, 1983.

GILANI, Ijaz, M. Fahim KHAN and Munawar IQBAL
"Labour Migration from Pakistan to the Middle East and Its Impact on
the Domestic Economy", Research Report No. 127, Islamabad, Pakistan
Institute of Development Economics, 1981.

GO, Stella, Leticia POSTRADO and Pilar RAMOS-JIMENEZ
The Effects of International Contract Labor, Manila, De La Salle University, Integrated Research Unit, 1983.

HABIB, Ahsanul
Economic Consequences of International Migration for Sending Countries: Review of Evidence from Bangladesh, Ph.D. Thesis, University of Newcastle, Australia, 1985.

HABIB, Ahsanul, Peeratheep ROONGSHIVIN and Charles W. STAHL
"Remittances as a Source of Loanable Funds: the Case of Thailand", Seminar Paper, East-West Population Institute, Honolulu, 1985.

HALLIDAY, Fred
"Migration and the Labour Force in the Oil Producing States of Middle East", Development and Change, Vol. 8, No. 3, 1977.

HARRIS, Nigel
"The New Untouchables", research project outline, NH/20, London, University College, 1979.

JAYME, Rebecca B.
"Implications of Labor Emigration from the Philippines", Master's Thesis, Department of Economics, University of the Philippines, 1979.

KING, Russell
"Return Migration: A Review of Some Case Studies from Southern Europe", Mediterranean Studies, Vol. 1, No. 2, 1979.

KORALE, Raja B.M.
"Migration for Employment in the Middle East: Its Demographic and Socio-economic Effects on Sri Lanka", in Fred Arnold and Nasra M. Shah, eds., Asian Labor Migration: Pipeline to the Middle East, Boulder, Colorado, Westview Press, 1986.

LUNDAHL, Mats
"International Migration, Remittances and Real Incomes: Effects on the Source Country", Scandinavian Journal of Economics, Vol. 87, No. 4, 1985.

MACMILLEN, M.J.
"The Economic Effects of International Migration: A Survey", Journal of Common Market Studies, Vol. 20, No. 3, 1982.

MAHMUD, Wahiduddin and Siddiqur OSMANI
"Impact of Emigrant Workers' Remittances on the Bangladesh Economy", Bangladesh Development Studies, Vol. 8, No. 3, 1980.

MARTIN, Philip L.
"The Economic Effects of Temporary Worker Emigration", paper presented at the East-West Population Institute Conference on Asian Labor Migration to the Middle East, 19th-23rd September, Honolulu, Hawaii, East-West Centre, 1983.

MARTIN, P.L. and A. RICHARDS
"International Migration of Labor: Boon or Bane?", Monthly Labor Review, Vol. 103, 1980.

MATHEW, E.T. and P.R. Gopinathan NAIR
"Socio-Economic Characteristics of Emigrants and Emigrants' Households
-- A Case Study of Two Villages in Kerala", Economic and Political
Weekly, Vol. 13, No. 28, 1978.

MILLER, Duncan
"Exportation of Labour" in Nermin Abadan-Unat, ed., Turkish Workers in
Europe: 1960-1975, Leiden, E.J. Brill, 1976.

MIRACLE, Marvin P. and Sara S. BERRY
"Migrant Labour and Economic Development", Oxford Economic Papers,
Vol. 22, No. 1, 1970.

NORTH, David S. and Marion F. HOUSTON
The Characteristics and Role of Illegal Aliens in the United States
Labor Market: An Exploratory Study, Washington, D.C., Linton, 1976.

OECD
"Economic Consequences of Migration from North Africa to France",
Development Digest, Vol. 17, No. 4, 1979.

QUIBRIA, M.G.
"Migrant Workers and Remittances: Issues for Asian Developing
Countries", Asian Development Review, Vol. 4, No. 1, 1986.

PAINE, Suzanne
Exporting Workers: The Turkish Case, Cambridge, Cambridge University
Press, 1974.

PALMER, Jay D.
"They are Like Shadows: A Mass Exodus of Asian Labor", Time,
16th November 1981.

PENNINX, Rinus
"A Critical Review of Theory and Practice: The Case of Turkey", International Migration Review, Vol. 16, No. 4, 1982.

PERWAIZ, Shahid
"Home Remittances", Pakistan Economist, 19, September 1979.

PORTES, A.
"Modes of Structural Incorporation and Present Theories of Labor Immi-
gration" in M.M. Kritz, C.B. Keeley and S.M. Tomasi, eds., Global
Trends in Migration: Theory and Research on International Population
Movements, New York, Centre for Migration Studies, 1981.

ROONGSHIVIN, Peerathep
"Some Aspects of Socio-Economic Impacts of Thailand's Emigration to the
Middle East", working paper, ASEAN/Australian Population Project,
Institutional Development and Exchange of Personnel, Bangkok, 1982.

RUSSELL, Sharon S.
"Remittances from Intenational Migration: A Review in Perspective",
World Development, Vol. 14, No. 6, 1986.

SALT, John
"Job-Finding in a United Europe", <u>Geographical Magazine,</u> Vol. 45, No. 11, 1973.

SARMAD, Khwaja
"Pakistani Migration to the Middle East Countries", Studies in Population, Labour Force and Migration Project, Report No. 9, Islamabad, Pakistan, Pakistan Institute of Development Economics, 1985.

SHAH, Nasra M. and Fred ARNOLD
"Government Policies and Programs Regulating Labor Migration", in Fred Arnold and Nasra M. Shah, eds., <u>Asian Labor Migration: Pipeline to the Middle East,</u> Boulder, Colorado, Westview Press, 1986.

SIDDIQUI, A.M.A.H.
"Economic and Non-Economic Impact of Migration from Bangladesh: An Overview", paper presented to the East-West Population Institute Conference on Asian Labor Migration to the Middle East, 19th-23rd September, Honolulu, Hawaii, East-West Centre, 1983.

"The Economic and Non-economic Impact of Labour Migration from Bangladesh", in Fred Arnold and Nasra Shah, eds., <u>Asian Labor Migration: Pipeline to the Middle East,</u> Boulder, Colorado, Westview Press, 1986.

SINGHANETRA-RENARD, Anchalee
"Going Abroad: Thai Labor Movement to the Middle East from the Village Standpoint", paper presented at the East-West Population Institute Conference on Asian Labor Migration to the Middle East, 19th-23rd September, Honolulu, Hawaii, East-West Centre, 1983.

SMART, John E.
"Economic Impact of International Migration on Sending Countries, with Special Emphasis on Employment and Remittances", paper presented at the IUSSP Workshop on the Consequences of International Migration, 16th-19th July, Canberra, Australia, IUSSP Committee on the Economic and Social Aspects of International Migration, 1984.

SMART, John E., Virginia A. TEODOSIO and Carol J. JIMENEZ
"Skills and Earnings: Issues in the Developmental Impact on the Philippines of Labor Export", in Fred Arnold and Nasra Shah, eds., <u>Asian Labor Migration: Pipeline to the Middle East,</u> Boulder, Colorado, Westview Press, 1986.

STAHL, Charles W.
"Labor Migration and Economic Development", <u>International Migration Review,</u> Vol. 16, No. 4, 1982.

<u>International Labor Migration: A Study of the ASEAN Countries,</u> New York, Centre for Migration Studies, 1986.

STAHL, Charles W. and Fred ARNOLD
"Overseas Workers' Remittances in Asian Development", <u>International Migration Review,</u> Vol. 19, No. 3, 1986.

STAHL, Charles W. and Ahsanul HABIB
"Emigration and Development in South and Southeast Asia", in D. Papademitrios, ed., Emigration and Development: The Unsettled Relationship, Westport, Conn., Greenwood Press, forthcoming.

STANDING, Guy
"Income Transfers and Remittances", in R.E. Bilsborrow, A.S. Oberai and G. Standing, eds., Migration Surveys in Low Income Countries: Guidelines for Survey and Questionnaire Design, London, Croom Helm, 1984.

TAN, Edita
"Adjustment of the Labour Market to the Foreign Outflow of Skilled Labour: The Case of Construction Workers", mimeo., Bangkok, ILO-ARPLA, 1983.

TEODOSIO, Virginia A. and Carolina J. JIMENEZ
"Socio-Economic Consequences of Contract Labor Migration in the Philippines", Manila, Institute of Labor and Manpower Studies, Ministry of Labor and Employment, 1983.

WEINER, Myron
"International Migration and Development: Indians in the Persian Gulf", Population and Development Review, Vol. 8, No. 1, 1982.

WILSON, Paul
"The Middle East Boom Starts to Tail Off", Far Eastern Economic Review, Vol. 104, No. 19, 1979.

Chapter 23

OVERVIEW: SOCIOLOGICAL AND RELATED ISSUES

by

Maurice D. Van Arsdol, Jr. (1)

INTRODUCTION

Current international migration systems have been classified in terms of migration policies by the United Nations Population Division (1985a, 1985b): (i) traditional receivers -- the United States, Canada, Australia, New Zealand, and Israel -- whose policies now admit diminishing numbers of migrants to become citizens; (ii) European labour importers, whose policies once favoured temporary worker immigration but whose migration streams are now diminished; (iii) Arab labour importers whose intakes have also diminished; (iv) refugee-receiving countries in Asia and Africa. Each of these migration systems involves impacts on the Third World.

International migration is part of a global social system of "flows" of communications, capital, resources, goods and services which have development consequences for both sending and receiving countries, including social and economic conditions, population stocks, and population flows (Hoffman-Nowotny, 1981; McCarthy and Ronfeld, 1983).

CICRED has been concerned with international migration since its 1974 Buenos Aires migration seminar (Tapinos, 1974). The current project, however, emphasizes the role of internationalisation of capital and transnational corporations in establishing new migration streams, the formation of new modes of migration and the revival of old ones, the establishment of new migration policies and the appearance of new impacts. Some of the topics -- shifting migration policies, the opening and closing of temporary migration streams, clandestine migration, transient migration, permanent migration, refugees and return migration -- cover newly-identified or rediscovered phenomena associated with the world system.

The contributors to this volume indicate that some forms of migration have been defined as social problems in a number of nations and by the international community. Social movements have been described as including (i) agitation of actions to obtain recognition, (ii) legitimation or official acknowledgment of the problem; (iii) bureaucratisation and reactions and

(iv) re-emergence of social movements (Spector and Kitsuse, 1973). Refugees, clandestine migrants and asylum seekers, for example, are sometimes defined by private, government, and international agencies as posing problems after their migration becomes public knowledge (Ford Foundation, 1983). Solutions include demographic settling in the host country, repatriation or resettlement in a third country. Further responses include research, redefining migrant categories and the establishment of programmatic agencies.

Since the work of Ravenstein (1885, 1889), demographers have given more attention to economic than to social determinants and consequences of migration. This may reflect the perceived interests in MDCs, which often attract immigrants from their former colonies. Nevertheless, non-economic determinants and consequences of migration are playing more important roles in current migration systems.

Social impacts of migration appear to be less understood than economic impacts. The impacts of migration for sending countries may be less understood than those for receivers. Social impacts of migration for Third World sending countries are perhaps understood least of all. The transmission of technology from migration receivers to LDC senders may lead to some economic gain for LDC senders, but almost always at the cost of changes in population, culture, family; and religious, educational, and economic systems. Social consequences of migration for LDCs are further complicated by the entry of clandestine migrants, transients and refugees into migration systems which may have been driven initially by economic development. Migration is normally activated by economic and technological growth, but social, moral and political factors (sometimes translated by governments into migration policies) are now recognised as proximate determinants of migration. Appleyard, for example, indicates that it was not until after World War II that most LDCs obtained control of their own migration policies. Questions relating to these and other issues are addressed in the papers.

Views of Migration

Theoretical issues. Population flows between nations have been interpreted as responsive to economic factors, population and area size and distance; and as including migrant stocks with characteristics between those at origin and destination (Lee, 1966). Chains of individuals known to each other have been described as co-migrants who propel persons into migration streams (McDonald and McDonald, 1964). Impacts of migration have also been outlined at the global, national, local and social psychological level. Geographers have described how migration, migrants and migrant adjustment reflects and contributes to national development (Zilensky, 1971).

The work of scholars of international migration has been problem, rather than theory driven. Explanations usually emphasize tangible determinants of migration, including economic differentials and time-cost distance. Explanations are typically derived from destination vantage points in MDCs and are not tailored to the economic and political needs of LDCs. Concerns with non-economic impacts include effects on population structure, and social affects at areas of destination and origin.

Two chapters in the volume fit the theoretical rubric. Domenach and Picouet outline elements of a typology of the possibility of reversible migration which could be useful in describing return migration. Types based on degree of reversibility include: (i) one-way flows of all kinds; (ii) reversible flows following long stays; (iii) flows with renewed reversibility; (iv) sporadic flows and instability marked by variable stays and (v) flows of itinerants. The authors do not relate their types to social or economic impacts, but these could be tested.

Federici considers migration to and from Italy within an historical framework from the time when Italy was an LDC. She argues that historical changes in the intensity of flows from Italy to other countries result from differential population pressures between areas of origin and destination, and are mediated by demographic inertia, climate, geography, cultural affinity, and judicial-political functions. Currently important is Italy's attraction as a migration destination for foreigners who take jobs shunned by Italians. The analysis suggests that as development occurs, emigration impacts change.

Measurement. In 1985 the co-ordinator of the current CICRED migration project proposed a "methodological investigation premised on the proposition that migration flows are in a state of constant transformation linked to the evolution of economic structures in both sending and receiving countries" (Appleyard, 1985).

Policies. Descriptions of reported migration policies, as well as current migration systems, are now available from the Population Inquiry Monitoring Reports (United Nations, 1980a, 1980b, 1982a, 1982b, 1985a, 1985b). Migration is now more severely scrutinised and controlled by the important receivers outside of the refugee system (Van Arsdol and Gorwaney, 1985). More of these countries are perceiving migration as significant and are implementing policies to curb it. A few countries are beginning to exert more control over emigration. Migration policies affect the flow of "legal" immigrants and emigrants, and sometimes push migrants into clandestine channels.

Seccombe and Lawless provide examples of policy formation and implementation for Arab countries which are potential labour sources. These policies are described as "prohibition" (Algeria, Oman, and the People's Demographic Country of Yemen); "restrictive regulation" (Egypt and Syria); laissez faire (Lebanon, the Yeman Arab Republic and Morocco); "positive encouragement" (Egypt after 1973, Jordan and Tunisia); and "participating in bilateral and multilateral arrangement" (Tunisia and France in 1973, Libya and Tunisia in 1971, Libya and Morocco in 1975). Data used by Seccombe and Lawless may also be useful in validating emigration policy data derived from the United Nations Population Inquiry Monitoring Reports.

Types of Migration

Temporary migration. One chapter describes "traditional" short-term movements from less to more developed areas. Huguet shows that increases in technology and capital in the Middle East led to increases in Asian labour migration after the mid-1970s. Meanwhile, Pacific migration is to traditional receivers on the rim, to other Pacific Islands or out from the Philippines. Huguet describes social impacts of migration including impacts of family relations, children's education, status of women, risks of fraud from labour agents, and re-entry problems that include finding suitable employment and social impacts of remittances.

Clandestine migration. Recent concerns with clandestine migration may in part reflect more control of border activity and the tightening of migration policies. Clandestine migration has been described as accounting for sizeable population movements (United Nations, 1985a). Increasing economic and technological disparities between nations generate both regular and clandestine migration.

Lohrman summarises pattens of irregular migration for Third World countries. He indicates that: (i) African migration is largely irregular, sometimes regulated by mass expulsion and proceeds towards perceived economic opportunity; (ii) irregular Asian migration follows opportunity and is mostly temporary; and (iii) irregular migration dominates international moves in Latin America. LDCs of origin are described as facing problems of mass return, hosting deportees and conflict with host countries.

Pellegrino summarised legal aspects and characteristics of clandestine migrants, including employment, and factors determining such migration. Most undocumented immigration to Venezuela from Colombia is seasonal and migrants stay in the border region. During the 1970s, this migration increased due to the expansion of the Venezuelan industrial sector. Urban migrants are described as primarily women who gain employment as domestics.

Transient migration. Transient migrants often overlap at areas of origin or destination. Price deals with the Australian case of highly-qualified workers from MDCs to IDCs, and associated flows of young LDC workers and students to MDCs for educational or work-qualifying experience. Australia's international links, Price argues, provide positive employment opportunities for MDC residents while contributing to the education and training of LDC migrants. Price indicates that circular migration of MDC persons and their LDC affiliates is part of the development process.

Salt and Findlay describe transient emigration of highly-skilled manpower from MDCs as "brain exchange" of professional transients involving personnel of transnational corporations with headquarters in MDCs. A circulation of highly-skilled immigrants between MDCs, LDCs and socialist economies is considered necessary to meet transnational corporate objectives. Corporate arrangements are described as leading to moves at certain career points and to a blending of business travel and longer migration, lubricated by recruitment, placement and relocation assistance. Using data from United States corporations, they describe the inter-country movement of United States and other nationals to facilitate large development projects which absorb local labour, transfer little technology, and develop MDC institutions, attitudes and values.

Permanant migration. Considerations of permanent migration are limited to brain drain or "reverse transfer of technology" from LDCs to MDCs. The papers illustrate a number of social impacts.

Mundende indicates that brain drain impacts are described by nationalists as human capital losses resulting in increased inequality; by internationalists as providing for relief through brain overflow and by humanists as expressing basic rights but inhibiting development. Possible solutions are described as preventive (a more supportive local atmosphere) or restrictive (tightening immigration and emigration policies).

Sousa argues that increased international concern in the 1960s and 1970s with the brain drain reflected the "technological gap between (MDC) and (LDC) countries" and that brain drain costs for LDCs can be partially recouped by compensation, income transfers and voluntary contributions from benefitting MDCs. Bilateral and multilateral arrangements are seen as necessary to trigger offsetting cost payments which, in turn, require the measuring and setting of economic values. The latter activity is described as floundering because of disagreements between MDCs and LDCs over whether to use historic or present discounted values in estimating human capital values.

Refugees. The movement of refugees typically results from global conflicts which have local impacts (Zolbery, Suhrke and Aguayo, 1981). Consideration of refugee impacts are confined to two papers on Africa and one on Asia.

Adepoju argues that economic, ecological, political and conflict problems activate most African refugee movements. Impacts may be mitigated by kinship ties. Competition with national populations is a growing urban problem which strains the resources of the poorest countries. Khasiani argues that refugees strain economic and environmental resources and that inadequate programmes for refugees "marginalise" refugee women and professionals and lead to manpower loss of professionals.

Cox traces the recent Australian response to refugee problems. He emphasizes that the "whites only" policy changed in the 1970s; and that Australia will not be a major future destination for LDC refugees. Of particular importance is his observation that refugees in Australia may tune the country more effectively into the needs of the refugee-sending countries.

Return migration. The papers regarding return migration consider impacts of economic problems at destination upon return, role shifts associated with migration, policies influencing return, who returns, and how returnees may impact ideology. They suggest that returnees can play an important role in changing social and economic life at areas of origin.

Perez-Itriago and Guendelman examine how return migrants adjust to and influence their communities of origin. The authors examined the experience of women returnees for two towns in Mexico and found that working couples establish co-operative roles in the United States and then revert to parallel roles on return. Non-working women in the United States became more dependant and regained their dominant household positions on return. The authors maintain that women's remittances are marginal, but these women are strong role models for other women and in the face of new values may experience role conflict.

395

Condé was concerned with European countries. He describes incitement policies, reasons for returning, facilitating policies in the country of origin, and return migration in the global context. Condé indicates that the impact of incitement policies in receiving countries is small; reasons for returning are individual. Few countries of origin have measures to facilitate return of their inhabitants. Condé argues that emigration countries should inhibit regional disequilibria which are causes of internal and international migration.

Thomas-Hope and Nutter provide a case study of return migration to Kingston, Jamaica leading to higher levels of living and upward occupational mobility in the Caribbean. They identify two main return migrant groups: (i) short-stay migrants -- primarily oriented towards capital accumulation, including vendors, contract workers, itinerant migrants, international business commuters; (ii) long-stay migrants -- also oriented towards capital accumulation, including settlers, long-term migrants returning after retirement or on a regular basis, and dependents, particularly children oriented towards education. Returnees in Kingston thus support an ideology favouring migration and tend to gain professional and managerial positions.

CONCLUSIONS

The chapters which cover sociological aspects of international migration on the Third World raise several important issues. The first concerns social impacts of the relationship between internationalisation of capital to new migration patterns in developing countries. Recent movements of capital from MDCs to LDCs, for example, have provided new manufacturing jobs in LDCs at the expense of jobs in MDCs, and are associated with the creation of more managerial jobs and more low-paying service sector jobs in MDCs. The world system is dominated by a few MDCs and by transnational corporations, whose interests do not necessarily coincide (Walton, 1986). Determining how international movements of capital by transnational corporations affect migration policies, patterns and impacts, will be an important future endeavour of social scientists.

A second question concerns how new migration patterns are to be classified, described, accounted for and incorporated into explanations of migration-related phenomena. CICRED's concern with migration is based on the perception that migration is a social problem. Effective solutions to such problems are best obtained when there is appropriate theoretical guidance. Pryor (1981) has suggested that one way to proceed is to study regions where theories can be developed and tested in a programmed way.

A third question concerns methods of analysing migration. It has been suggested that there is a need for a world international migration survey (Tabbarah, 1984a, 1984b). A world migration survey would hopefully include data compilations on consequences of migration for migrants as well as non-migrants in both sending and receiving LDCs and MDCs. Crucial to such compilations would be further elaborations of emigration and immigration policy data now being collected by the United Nations (1985a, 1985b). Beyond direct measurement of migration, demographers may profitably use data describing global flows. A number of such data sets are available from economic, political and social reports of international agencies. Others are available in the files of academic institutions (Azar, 1982).

NOTES AND REFERENCES

1.   The assistance of Mrs. Nina Barnes, Ms. Amentha Dymally, Ms. Rebecca Gronvold, Ms. Jael Mongeau, and Mr. Greg Mohr is gratefully acknowledged.

BIBLIOGRAPHY

APPLEYARD, R.
Joint Meeting on The Impact of International Migration on Third World Development, 5th-7th June 1984, Geneva, Switzerland, Report of General Co-ordinator, Paris, CICRED and ICM, 1985.

AZAR, E.
Conflict and Peace Data Bank (COPDAB, 1948-1978: Daily Events Records, International and Domestic Files CICPSR 7767), E. Azar, University of Carolina at Chapel Hill, University Consortium for Political and Source Research, P.O. Box 1248, Ann Arbor, Michigan, 48106, Second ICPSR Edition, 1982.

BIRKS, J. and C. SINCLAIR
"Demographic Settling Amongst Migrant Workers", IUSSP International Population Conference, Manila, 1981, Vol. 2, Liege, 1981.

FORD FOUNDATION
Refugees and Migrants: Problems and Program Responses, New York, 1983.

HOFFMAN-NOWOTNY, H.
"A Sociological Approach Towards a General Theory of Migration", in M. Kritz, C. Keeley and S. Tomasi, eds., Global Trends in Migration: Theory and Research on International Population Movements, Staten Island, Centre for Migration Studies, 1981.

LEE, E.
"A Theory of Migration", Demography, Vol. 3, No. 1, 1966.

McCARTHY, K. and D. RONFELD
"Immigration as an Intrusive Global Flow: A New Perspective", in M. Kritz, ed., U.S. Immigration and Refugee Policy: Global and Domestic Issues, Lexington, Lexington Books, D.C. Heath and Company, 1983.

McDONALD, J. and D. McDONALD
"Chain Migration, Ethnic Neighborhood Formation and Social Networks", The Milbank Memorial Fund Quarterly, Vol. XLII, No. 1, January 1964.

PRYOR, R.
"Integrating International and Internal Migration Theories", in M. Kritz, C. Keeley and S. Tomasi, eds., Global Trends in Migration: Theory and Research on International Population Movements, New York, Centre for Migration Studies, 1981.

RAVENSTEIN, E.
"The Laws of Migration", Journal of the Royal Statistical Society, Vol. XLV III, Part 2, June 1885.

"The Laws of Migration", Journal of the Royal Statistical Society, Vol. III, June 1889.

SPECTOR, M. and J. KITSUSE
"Social Problems: A Reformulation", Social Problems, Vol. 21, 1973.

TABBARAH, R.
"Future Prospects of International Migration", International Social Sciences Review, Fall, 1984a.

"Economic and Social Implications of International Migration", Organiser's Statement, 7th World Congress of IEA, Madrid, 5th-9th September 1984b.

TAPINOS, G., ed.
International Migration: Proceedings of a Seminar on Demographic Research in Relation to International Migration, Buenos Aires, Argentina, 5th-11th March 1974, CICRED, 1974.

UNITED NATIONS
World Population Trends and Policies, 1979 Monitoring Report Vol. I, Population Trends, ST/ESA/SER.A/70, New York, 1980a.

World Population Trends and Policies, 1979 Monitoring Report Vol. I, Population Policies, ST/ESA/SER.A/70/Add. 1, New York, 1980b.

International Migration, Policies and Programmes: A World Survey, ST/ESA/SER.A/80, New York, 1982a.

World Population Trends and Policies, 1981 Monitoring Report, Vol. II, Population Policies, ST/ESA/SER.A/79, New York, 1982b.

World Population Trends and Policies, 1981 Monitoring Report, Vol. II, Population Policies, ST/ESA/SER.A/79/Add. 1, New York, 1982c.

World Population Trends, Population and Development Interrelations and Population Policies, 1983 Monitoring Report, Vol. I, Population Trends, ST/ESA/SER.A/93, New York, 1985a.

World Population Trends, Population and Development Interrelations and Population Policies, 1983 Monitoring Report, Vol. II, Population Policies, ST/ESA/SER.A/93/Add. 1, New York, 1985b.

VAN ARSDOL, Jr., M. and N. GORWANEY
"International Migration, Social Integration and Global Conflict", International Union for the Scientific Study of Population, International Population Conference, Florence, 5th-12th June 1985, Liege, 1985.

WALTON, J.
Sociology and Critical Inquiry, Chicago, The Dorsey Press, 1986.

ZILENSKI, W.
"The Hypothesis of the Mobility Transition", The Geographical Review, Vol. LXI, No. 2, 1971.

ZOLBERG, A., A. SUHRKE and S. AGUAYO
"International Factors in the Formation of Refugee Movements", International Migration Review, Vol. XX, No. 2, Summer 1986.

THE CONTRIBUTORS

Reginald Appleyard
Professor and Director
Centre for Migration and Development Studies
University of Western Australia
Nedlands
Western Australia

Hervé Domenach
Chargé de recherches en démographie
ORSTOM, Paris
France

Michel R. Picouet
Vice-Président de la Commission scientifique des sciences sociales
Chargé de la démographie
ORSTOM, Paris
France

Nora Federici
Professor Emeritus
Department of Demographic Sciences
University of Rome
Italy

Chantal Blayo
Responsable, Unité de recherche "Conjoncture démographique 1", INED
Chargée de cours, Institute d'études démographiques
Université de Bordeaux 1
France

I.J. Seccombe
Centre for Middle Eastern and Islamic Studies
University of Durham
United Kingdom

R.I. Lawless
Centre for Middle Eastern and Islamic Studies
University of Durham
United Kingdom

Jerrold W. Huguet
Population Affairs Officer
Population Division
ESCAP, Bangkok
Thailand

Allan M. Findlay
Department of Geography
University of Glasgow
Scotland

Reinhard Lohrmann
Intergovernmental Committee for Migration
Geneva
Switzerland

Charles A. Price
Professorial Fellow
Department of Demography
Australian National University, Canberra
Australia

John Salt
Senior Lecturer
Department of Geography
University College, London
United Kingdom

D. Chongo Mundende
Department of Geography
Michigan State University
Michigan
U.S.A.

Mr. J. d'Oliveira e Sousa
Economic Affairs Officer of the Technology Division
United Nations Conference on Trade and Development (UNCTAD)
Geneva
Switzerland

Chen Chin Long
Associate Professor of International Economy
College of Economics
Jinan University
China

Aderanti Adepoju
Professor and Head
Research and Advisory Services Unit
University of Lagos
Nigeria

Shanyisa Khasiani
Lecturer
Population Studies and Research Institute
University of Nairobi
Kenya

David Cox
Department of Social Studies
The University of Melbourne
Victoria
Australia

Auristela Perez-Itriago
School of Public Health
University of California
Berkeley, California
U.S.A.

Sylvia Guendelman
School of Public Health
University of California
Berkeley, California
U.S.A.

Elizabeth M. Thomas-Hope
Department of Geography
University of Liverpool
Liverpool
United Kingdom

Richard D. Nutter
Department of Geography
University of Liverpool
Liverpool
United Kingdom

Adela Pellegrino
Universidad Catolica Andres Bello
Urb Montalban
Caracas
Venezuela

Julien Condé
Administrateur Principal
Service recherche-démographie -- migrations
Centre de Développement
OCDE, Paris
France

Anthony H. Richmond
Professor of Sociology
York University
Ontario
Canada

Lawrence Lam
Department of Sociology
York University
Toronto
Canada

Ferdando Mata
Department of Sociology
York University
Toronto
Canada

Charles W. Stahl
Senior Lecturer
Department of Economics
University of Newcastle
New South Wales
Australia

Maurice D. Van Arsdol, Jr.
Professor of Sociology
Director, Population Research Laboratory
University of Southern California
U.S.A.

WHERE TO OBTAIN OECD PUBLICATIONS
OÙ OBTENIR LES PUBLICATIONS DE L'OCDE

ARGENTINA - ARGENTINE
Carlos Hirsch S.R.L.,
Florida 165, 4º Piso,
(Galeria Guemes) 1333 Buenos Aires
Tel. 33.1787.2391 y 30.7122

AUSTRALIA - AUSTRALIE
D.A. Book (Aust.) Pty. Ltd.
11-13 Station Street (P.O. Box 163)
Mitcham, Vic. 3132   Tel. (03) 873 4411

AUSTRIA - AUTRICHE
OECD Publications and Information Centre,
4 Simrockstrasse,
5300 Bonn (Germany)   Tel. (0228) 21.60.45
Gerold & Co., Graben 31, Wien 1 Tel. 52.22.35

BELGIUM - BELGIQUE
Jean de Lannoy,
Avenue du Roi 202
B-1060 Bruxelles   Tel. (02) 538.51.69

CANADA
Renouf Publishing Company Ltd
1294 Algoma Road, Ottawa, Ont. K1B 3W8
Tel: (613) 741-4333
Stores:
61 rue Sparks St., Ottawa, Ont. K1P 5R1
Tel: (613) 238-8985
211 rue Yonge St., Toronto, Ont. M5B 1M4
Tel: (416) 363-3171
Federal Publications Inc.,
301-303 King St. W.,
Toronto, Ont. M5V 1J5   Tel. (416)581-1552
Les Éditions la Liberté inc.,
3020 Chemin Sainte-Foy,
Sainte-Foy, P.Q. G1X 3V6, Tel. (418)658-3763

DENMARK - DANEMARK
Munksgaard Export and Subscription Service
35, Nørre Søgade, DK-1370 København K
Tel. +45.1.12.85.70

FINLAND - FINLANDE
Akateeminen Kirjakauppa,
Keskuskatu 1, 00100 Helsinki 10   Tel. 0.12141

FRANCE
OCDE/OECD
Mail Orders/Commandes par correspondance :
2, rue André-Pascal,
75775 Paris Cedex 16   Tel. (1) 45.24.82.00
Bookshop/Librairie : 33, rue Octave-Feuillet
75016 Paris
Tel. (1) 45.24.81.67 or/ou (1) 45.24.81.81
Librairie de l'Université,
12a, rue Nazareth,
13602 Aix-en-Provence   Tel. 42.26.18.08

GERMANY - ALLEMAGNE
OECD Publications and Information Centre,
4 Simrockstrasse,
5300 Bonn   Tel. (0228) 21.60.45

GREECE - GRÈCE
Librairie Kauffmann,
28, rue du Stade, 105 64 Athens Tel. 322.21.60

HONG KONG
Government Information Services,
Publications (Sales) Office,
Information Services Department
No. 1, Battery Path, Central

ICELAND - ISLANDE
Snæbjörn Jónsson & Co., h.f.,
Hafnarstræti 4 & 9,
P.O.B. 1131 – Reykjavik
Tel. 13133/14281/11936

INDIA - INDE
Oxford Book and Stationery Co.,
Scindia House, New Delhi 110001
Tel. 331.5896/5308
17 Park St., Calcutta 700016   Tel. 240832

INDONESIA - INDONÉSIE
Pdii-Lipi, P.O. Box 3065/JKT.Jakarta
Tel. 583467

IRELAND - IRLANDE
TDC Publishers - Library Suppliers,
12 North Frederick Street, Dublin 1
Tel. 744835-749677

ITALY - ITALIE
Libreria Commissionaria Sansoni,
Via Benedetto Fortini 120/10,
Casella Post. 552
50125 Firenze   Tel. 055/645415
Via Bartolini 29, 20155 Milano   Tel. 365083
La diffusione delle pubblicazioni OCSE viene
assicurata dalle principali librerie ed anche da :
Editrice e Libreria Herder,
Piazza Montecitorio 120, 00186 Roma
Tel. 6794628
Libreria Hœpli,
Via Hœpli 5, 20121 Milano   Tel. 865446
Libreria Scientifica
Dott. Lucio de Biasio "Aeiou"
Via Meravigli 16, 20123 Milano   Tel. 807679

JAPAN - JAPON
OECD Publications and Information Centre,
Landic Akasaka Bldg., 2-3-4 Akasaka,
Minato-ku, Tokyo 107   Tel. 586.2016

KOREA - CORÉE
Kyobo Book Centre Co. Ltd.
P.O.Box: Kwang Hwa Moon 1658,
Seoul   Tel. (REP) 730.78.91

LEBANON - LIBAN
Documenta Scientifica/Redico,
Edison Building, Bliss St.,
P.O.B. 5641, Beirut   Tel. 354429-344425

MALAYSIA/SINGAPORE -
MALAISIE/SINGAPOUR
University of Malaya Co-operative Bookshop
Ltd.,
7 Lrg 51A/227A, Petaling Jaya
Malaysia   Tel. 7565000/7565425
Information Publications Pte Ltd
Pei-Fu Industrial Building,
24 New Industrial Road No. 02-06
Singapore 1953   Tel. 2831786, 2831798

NETHERLANDS - PAYS-BAS
SDU Uitgeverij
Christoffel Plantijnstraat 2
Postbus 20014
2500 EA's-Gravenhage   Tel. 070-789911
Voor bestellingen: Tel. 070-789880

NEW ZEALAND - NOUVELLE-ZÉLANDE
Government Printing Office Bookshops:
Auckland: Retail, Bookshop, 25 Rutland Stseet,
Mail Orders, 85 Beach Road
Private Bag C.P.O.
Hamilton: Retail: Ward Street,
Mail Orders, P.O. Box 857
Wellington: Retail, Mulgrave Street, (Head
Office)
Cubacade World Trade Centre,
Mail Orders, Private Bag
Christchurch: Retail, 159 Hereford Street,
Mail Orders, Private Bag
Dunedin: Retail, Princes Street,
Mail Orders, P.O. Box 1104

NORWAY - NORVÈGE
Narvesen Info Center – NIC,
Bertrand Narvesens vei 2,
P.O.B. 6125 Etterstad, 0602 Oslo 6
Tel. (02) 67.83.10, (02) 68.40.20

PAKISTAN
Mirza Book Agency
65 Shahrah Quaid-E-Azam, Lahore 3 Tel. 66839

PHILIPPINES
I.J. Sagun Enterprises, Inc.
P.O. Box 4322 CPO Manila
Tel. 695-1946, 922-9495

PORTUGAL
Livraria Portugal, Rua do Carmo 70-74,
1117 Lisboa Codex   Tel. 360582/3

SINGAPORE/MALAYSIA -
SINGAPOUR/MALAISIE
See "Malaysia/Singapor". Voir
« Malaisie/Singapour »

SPAIN - ESPAGNE
Mundi-Prensa Libros, S.A.,
Castelló 37, Apartado 1223, Madrid-28001
Tel. 431.33.99
Libreria Bosch, Ronda Universidad 11,
Barcelona 7   Tel. 317.53.08/317.53.58

SWEDEN - SUÈDE
AB CE Fritzes Kungl. Hovbokhandel,
Box 16356, S 103 27 STH,
Regeringsgatan 12,
DS Stockholm   Tel. (08) 23.89.00
Subscription Agency/Abonnements:
Wennergren-Williams AB,
Box 30004, S104 25 Stockholm Tel. (08)54.12.00

SWITZERLAND - SUISSE
OECD Publications and Information Centre,
4 Simrockstrasse,
5300 Bonn (Germany)   Tel. (0228) 21.60.45
Librairie Payot,
6 rue Grenus, 1211 Genève 11
Tel. (022) 31.89.50
Maditec S.A.
Ch. des Palettes 4
1020 – Renens/Lausanne   Tel. (021) 635.08.65
United Nations Bookshop/Librairie des Nations-
Unies
Palais des Nations, 1211 – Geneva 10
Tel. 022-34-60-11 (ext. 48 72)

TAIWAN - FORMOSE
Good Faith Worldwide Int'l Co., Ltd.
9th floor, No. 118, Sec.2, Chung Hsiao E. Road
Taipei   Tel. 391.7396/391.7397

THAILAND - THAILANDE
Suksit Siam Co., Ltd., 1715 Rama IV Rd.,
Samyam Bangkok 5   Tel. 2511630
INDEX Book Promotion & Service Ltd.
59/6 Soi Lang Suan, Ploenchit Road
Patjumamwan, Bangkok 10500
Tel. 250-1919, 252-1066

TURKEY - TURQUIE
Kültur Yayinlari Is-Türk Ltd. Sti.
Atatürk Bulvari No: 191/Kat. 21
Kavaklidere/Ankara   Tel. 25.07.60
Dolmabahce Cad. No: 29
Besiktas/Istanbul   Tel. 160.71.88

UNITED KINGDOM - ROYAUME-UNI
H.M. Stationery Office,
Postal orders only: (01)873-8483
P.O.B. 276, London SW8 5DT
Telephone orders: (01) 873-9090, or
Personal callers:
49 High Holborn, London WC1V 6HB
Branches at: Belfast, Birmingham,
Bristol, Edinburgh, Manchester

UNITED STATES - ÉTATS-UNIS
OECD Publications and Information Centre,
2001 L Street, N.W., Suite 700,
Washington, D.C. 20036 - 4095
Tel. (202) 785.6323

VENEZUELA
Libreria del Este,
Avda F. Miranda 52, Aptdo. 60337,
Edificio Galipan, Caracas 106
Tel. 951.17.05/951.23.07/951.12.97

YUGOSLAVIA - YOUGOSLAVIE
Jugoslovenska Knjiga, Knez Mihajlova 2,
P.O.B. 36, Beograd   Tel. 621.992

Orders and inquiries from countries where
Distributors have not yet been appointed should be
sent to:
OECD, Publications Service, 2, rue André-Pascal,
75775 PARIS CEDEX 16.

Les commandes provenant de pays où l'OCDE n'a
pas encore désigné de distributeur doivent être
adressées à :
OCDE, Service des Publications. 2, rue André-
Pascal, 75775 PARIS CEDEX 16.

72380